Common Law and Civil Law Perspectives on Tort Law

Common Law and Civil Law Perspectives on Tort Law

MAURO BUSSANI, ANTHONY J. SEBOK, &
MARTA INFANTINO

OXFORD
UNIVERSITY PRESS

OXFORD
UNIVERSITY PRESS

Oxford University Press is a department of the University of Oxford. It furthers the University's objective of excellence in research, scholarship, and education by publishing worldwide. Oxford is a registered trade mark of Oxford University Press in the UK and certain other countries.

Published in the United States of America by Oxford University Press
198 Madison Avenue, New York, NY 10016, United States of America.

Library of Congress Cataloging-in-Publication Data
Names: Bussani, Mauro, author. | Sebok, Anthony James, 1963– author. | Infantino, Marta, author.
Title: Common law and civil law perspectives on tort law / Mauro Bussani, Anthony J. Sebok, & Marta Infantino.
Description: New York, NY : Oxford University Press, [2022?] |
Includes bibliographical references and index.
Identifiers: LCCN 2021045030 (print) | LCCN 2021045031 (ebook) | ISBN 9780195368383 (hardback) |
ISBN 9780199365975 (epub) | ISBN 9780199365968 (updf) | ISBN 9780199365982 (online)
Subjects: LCSH: Torts.
Classification: LCC K923 .B873 2022 (print) | LCC K923 (ebook) |
DDC 346.03—dc23/eng/20211006
LC record available at https://lccn.loc.gov/2021045030
LC ebook record available at https://lccn.loc.gov/2021045031

DOI: 10.1093/oso/9780195368383.001.0001

Note to Readers

This publication is designed to provide accurate and authoritative information in regard to the subject matter covered. It is based upon sources believed to be accurate and reliable and is intended to be current as of the time it was written. It is sold with the understanding that the publisher is not engaged in rendering legal, accounting, or other professional services. If legal advice or other expert assistance is required, the services of a competent professional person should be sought. Also, to confirm that the information has not been affected or changed by recent developments, traditional legal research techniques should be used, including checking primary sources where appropriate.

(Based on the Declaration of Principles jointly adopted by a Committee of the American Bar Association and a Committee of Publishers and Associations.)

Contents

Foreword

The purpose of this book is to provide scholars, lawyers, and law students with a comparative overview of the law of civil liability, hopefully paving the way to future discussions and debates. At the outset, however, we wish to highlight some features and multiple important limitations on the scope of the project.

First, our analysis may provide useful insights into the tort law of many Western and non-Western jurisdictions. Yet, the comparison carried out in this book covers only—besides some cursory reference to other legal systems—five outstanding legal systems of the common law and civil law traditions we were more familiar with, that is to say, England, the United States, France, Germany, and Italy.

Second, the comparison is of civil liability for injuries arising outside of contract and in order to compensate the plaintiff for a wrongful loss. This category is denoted in English is as "tort law," in French "*responsabilité civile*," in German "*Deliktsrecht*," and in Italy "*responsabilità civile*." The contrast is not only to contract, but also to other private law remedies that may be triggered by a wrongful loss, such as restitution or unjust enrichment.

Third, the analysis focuses on a selected number of foundational issues that lie at the core of tort law: the structure and context of tort law architectures (Chapter I); notion and role of negligence and the continuum between fault and strict liability (Chapter II); the rules on recovery for personal injuries (in medical malpractice: Chapter III); for non-economic losses (claimed by primary and secondary victims: Chapters IV and V); and for pure economic losses (Chapter VI); the scope and techniques for assessing the causal relationship between the defendant's tortious activity and the plaintiff's harm (Chapter VII); commonalities and differences across products liability regimes (Chapter VIII). The selection keeps out of focus a number of areas and situations that are, or will likely be covered by tort law, such as traffic accidents liability, environmental harm, climate change liability, mass torts, liability for violations of civil and human rights, liability for emerging technologies and artificial intelligence, as well as current and future litigation stemming from the use of opiod drugs and the COVID-19 pandemic. The reason underlying our choice is twofold. On the one hand, we were severely limited by space constraints; on the other hand, the fields we selected are the ones we deemed as both the most settled and the most valuable in the view of an analytical, not cursory comparison.

A brief word about method is also in order. This is an analytic study, not a treatise. Each chapter is divided into a study of certain "patterns of questions," and the analysis delves into the relevant law and arguments used by judges and academics in their respective systems. We hope that we have picked points of comparison and contrast that reveal something beyond the rules and technicalities related to the individual field of tort liability, giving the reader the flavor of the kind of language, narratives, and cultures that dominate the tort law process in each legal system.

Since the book is in English, for non-English speaking countries we made reference as much as possible to treatises, manuals, and articles written in English. As to statutory sources, an English translation of the French, German, and Italian statutory materials quoted in the book can be found in Ken Oliphant and Barbara C Steininger (eds), *European Tort Law. Basic Texts* (2nd edn, Jan Sramek Verlag 2018).

The authors jointly conceived the overall architecture and the inner content of the book. The authors also jointly wrote this foreword and Chapter One. Mauro Bussani wrote Chapters Two and Six. Marta Infantino wrote Chapter Seven. Marta Infantino and Mauro Bussani wrote Chapter Four. Anthony Sebok wrote Chapters Three and Five. Marta Infantino and Anthony Sebok wrote Chapter Eight.

List of Abbreviations

A	Atlantic Reporter
ABA	American Bar Association
ABGB	*Allgemeines bürgerliches Gesetzbuch*
AC	Law Reports, Appeal Cases (England)
AcP	*Archiv für die civilistische Praxis*
AI	artificial intelligence
AJCL	American Journal of Comparative Law
Ala	Alabama
Alb LR	Albany Law Review
ALI	American Law Institute
All Eng Rep	All England Law Reports
Am Bar Found Res J	American Bar Foundation Research Journal
Am Bus LJ	American Business Law Journal
Am J Juris	American Journal of Jurisprudence
Am Rep	American Reporter
Am U LR	American University Law Review
App	*Corte di appello*
App Div	Appellate Division
Arch giur circol sin	*Archivio giuridico della circolazione e dei sinistri stradali*
Ariz	Arizona
Ariz LR	Arizona Law Review
Ark	Arkansas
art	article
arts	articles
BGB	*Bürgerliches Gesetzbuch*
BGBl	*Bundesgesetzblatt*
BGH	*Bundesgerichtshof*
BGHZ	*Entscheidungen des Bundesgerichtshofs in Zivilsachen*
BIICL	British Institute of International and Comparative Law
BJS	Bureau of Justice Statistics
BLR	Building Law Reports
BP	British Petroleum
Bracton LJ	Bracton Law Journal
Brook J Corp Fin & Com L	Brooklyn Journal of Corporate, Financial & Commercial Law

Brook LR	Brooklyn Law Review
Buffalo LR	Buffalo Law Review
Bull civ	*Bulletin des arrêts de la chambre civile*
Bull crim	*Bulletin des arrêts de la chambre criminelle*
BU LR	Boston University Law Review
BVerfG	*Bundesverfassungsgericht*
BW	*Burgerlijk Wetboek*
CA	*Cour d'appel*
Cal	California
Cal Ct App	California Court of Appeals
Cal LR	California Law Review
Cal Rptr	California Reporter
Cambridge LJ	Cambridge Law Journal
Camp	Campbell's Reports
Campbell LR	Campbell Law Review
Can Bar R	Canadian Bar Review
Can JL&Jur	Canadian Journal of Law and Jurisprudence
Cardozo LR	Cardozo Law Review
Cass	*Corte di cassazione*
Cass civ	*Cour de cassation, chambre civile*
Cass com	*Cour de cassation, chambre commerciale*
Cass crim	*Cour de cassation, chambre criminelle*
Cass req	*Cour de cassation, chambre des requêtes*
Cass soc	*Cour de cassation, chambre sociale*
CC	Civil Code
cf	compare
ch	chapter
Ch	Law Reports, Chancery Division
Chi-Kent LR	Chicago-Kent Law Review
Cir	Circuit
CJEU	Court of Justice of the European Union
CLJCiv	*Colección Legislativa de España. Jurisprudencia Civil*
CLR	Commonwealth Law Reports
Cmnd	Command
cmt	comment
co	company
Col	Colorado
Col LR	Colorado Law Review
Colo App	Colorado Court of Appeals
Colum LR	Columbia Law Review
comm	*commentaire*
Conn	Connecticut
Cornell Int'l LJ	Cornell International Law Journal

Cornell LR	Cornell Law Review
CP	Common Pleas
Cr App R	Criminal Appeal Reports
CRCI	*Commissions Régionales de Conciliation et d'Indemnisation des accidents médicaux*
CUP	Cambridge University Press
Current Leg Probls	Current Legal Problems
D	*Dalloz*
Danno resp	*Danno e responsabilità*
DC	District of Columbia
DC Cir	District of Colombia Circuit
D chr	*Dalloz chronique*
DDC	District of District of Columbia
Del	Delaware
DePaul LR	DePaul Law Review
DES	diethylstilbestrol
DH	*Dalloz hebdomadaire*
Dir fam pers	*Diritto di famiglia e delle persone*
DLR	Dominion Law Reports
DMd	District of Maryland
DNJ	District of New Jersey
DP	*Dalloz Pratique*
Drexel LR	Drexel Law Review
DSC	District of South Carolina
EB & E	Ellis, Blackburn and Ellis' Queen's Bench Reports
EC	European Community
ECHR	European Convention for the Protection of Human Rights and Fundamental Freedoms
ECJ	European Court of Justice
ECR	European Court Reports
ed	editor
ED La	Eastern District of Louisiana
edn	edition
eds	editors
EE	Edward Elgar
EEC	European Economic Community
eg	*exemplii gratia*
EGTL	European Group on Tort Law
Emory LJ	Emory Law Journal
Eng Rep	English Report
ERPL	European Review of Private Law
ESI	*Edizioni Scientifiche Italiane*

esp	especially
&	*et* (and)
etc	*et coetera*
EU	European Union
Eur J Health L	European Journal of Health Law
EWCA Civ	England and Wales Court of Appeal (Civil Division)
EWHC	England and Wales High Court of Justice
F	Federal Reporter
Fed Reg	Federal Register
ff	following
Fla	Florida
Fla 5th DCA	Florida Fifth District Court of Appeal
fn	footnotes
Fordham	Fordham Law Review
Fordham Urb LJ	Fordham Urban Law Journal
Foro it	*Foro italiano*
Foro pad	*Foro padano*
F Supp	Federal Supplement
Ga	Georgia
Ga LR	Georgia Law Review
Gaz Pal	*Gazette du Palais*
GCCF	Gulf Coast Claims Facility
GDP	Gross Domestic Product
Geo LJ	Georgetown Law Journal
Geo Wash LR	Georgetown Washington Law Review
Giur it	*Giurisprudenza italiana*
Giust civ	*Giustizia civile*
Giust civ mass	*Massimario della giustizia civile*
GmbH	*Gesellschaft mit beschränkter Haftung*
GRERCA	*Groupe de recherche européen sur la responsabilité civile et l'assurance*
Harv LR	Harvard Law Review
Hastings Int'l & Comp LR	Hastings International & Comparative Law Review
HL	House of Lords
HR	*Hoge Raad*
ibid	*ibidem*
Id	Idaho
i.e.	*id est*
IIED	intentional infliction of emotional distress
ill	illustration
Ill	Illinois
Ill App Ct	Illinois Appellate Court

Ill U LR	Illinois University Law Review
Ind	Indiana
Ind Ct App	Indiana Court of Appeals
Ind LR	Indiana Law Review
IR	*informations rapides*
JCP	*Juris-Classeur périodique*
JETL	Journal of European Tort Law
J Health Care L&Pol'y	Journal of Health Care Law and Policy
J Leg Stud	Journal of Legal Studies
J Tort L	Journal of Tort Law
J Trib	*Journal des Tribunaux*
Jur	*Jurisprudence*
JUR	*Sentencias y autos de la Audiencia Nacional, Tribunales Superiores de Justicia, Audiencias Provinciales y Juzgados Aranzadi*
JZ	*JuristenZeitung*
Kan	Kansas
Kan LR	Kansas Law Review
KB	King's Bench
Ky	Kentucky
Ky LJ	Kentucky Law Journal
KG	*Kammergericht* (Germany)
L	*Loi*
La	Louisiana
La Ct App	Louisiana Court of Appeal
La LR	Louisiana Law Review
Law Com	Law Commission
Leb	*Recueil des arrêts du Conseil d'Etat*
LEd	Lawyers' Edition
Leg Stud	Legal Studies
Leg Theory	Legal Theory
L&Cont Probls	Law and Contemporary Problems
L&Phil	Law and Philosophy
L&Soc'y R	Law and Society Review
LG	*Landesgericht* (Germany)
LGDJ	*Librairie générale de droit et de jurisprudence*
Lloyd's Rep	Lloyd's Law Reports
L, Med & Health Care	Law, Medicine and Health Care
Loy LA LR	Loyola Los Angeles Law Review
Loy LR	Loyola Law Review
LQR	Law Quarterly Review
LR	Law Reports (England)

Ltd	Limited
Man & G	Manning and Granger's Common Pleas Reports
Mass Cass pen	*Massimario della Cassazione penale*
Md	Maryland
MD Fla	Middle District of Florida
Md LR	Maryland Law Review
MDR	*Monatsschrift für Deutsches Recht*
Med L	Medicine and Law
M & W	Meeson and Welsby's Exchequer Reports
Mich	Michigan
Mich LR	Michigan Law Review
Mich St LR	Michigan State Law Review
Minn	Minnesota
Misc	Miscellaneous Reports
Miss	Mississipi
Miss C LR	Mississippi College Law Review
Miss LJ	Mississippi Law Journal
Mo	Missouri
Mo Ct App	Missouri Court of Appeals
Mod LR	Modern Law Review
Mo LR	Missouri Law Review
Mont	Montana
n	note
NATO	North Atlantic Treaty Organization
NC	North Carolina
NCSC	National Center for State Courts (US)
ND Ct App	Court of Appeals of North Dakota
ND Ill	Northern District of Illinois
NE	North Eastern Reporter
Neb	Nebraska
Nev	Nevada
NGCC	*Nuova giurisprudenza civile commentata*
NH	New Hampshire
NHS	National Health Service
NIED	negligent infliction of emotional distress
NJ	New Jersey
NJB	*Nederlands Juristenblad*
NJ Ch	New Jersey Court of Chancery
NJW	*Neue Juristische Wochenschrift*
NJW-RR	*NJW-Rechtsprechungs-Report*
NLJ	New Law Journal
NM	New Mexico

NM Ct App	New Mexico Court of Appeals
no	number
Not giur lav	*Notiziario di giurisprudenza del lavoro*
Nuova riv dir comm	*Nuova rivista di diritto commerciale*
NY	New York
NY App Div	New York Supreme Court, Appellate Division
NYS	New York Supplement
NYU J	Int'l L&Pol New York University Journal of International Law & Politics
NYU LR	New York University Law Review
NW	North Western Reporter
Nw U LR	Northwestern University Law Review
NZV	*Neue Zeitschrift für Verkehrsrecht*
OGH	*Oberster Gerichtshof*
Ohio State LJ	Ohio State Law Journal
OLG	*Oberlandesgericht*
ONIAM	*Office National d'Indemnisation des Accidents Médicaux*
OPA	Oil Pollution Act
Or	Oregon
Osaka U LR	Osaka University Law Review
OUP	Oxford University Press
Ox J Leg Stud	Oxford Journal of Legal Studies
P	Pacific Reporter
Pa	Pennsylvania
para	paragraph
PEH	Physical and Emotional Harm
Penn State LR	Penn State Law Review
Pepp LR	Pepperdine Law Review
PIQR	Personal Injuries and Quantums Reports
PRL	Patient's Rights Law (France)
PWQ	person without qualities
QB	Queen's Bench
QBD	Queen's Bench Division
Quinnipiac LR	Quinnipiac Law Review
RabelsZ	*Rabels Zeitschrift für ausländisches und internationales Privatrecht*
Rass dir farm	*Rassegna di diritto farmaceutico e della salute*
RAJ	*Real Academia de Jurisprudencia y Legislación*
Rb	*Rechtbank*
Rec D	*Recueil Dalloz*
Rep	*Repertorio*
Resp civ ass	*Responsabilité civile et Assurances*

Resp civ prev	*Responsabilità civile e previdenza*
Rev Als Lorr	*Revue juridique d'Alsace et de Lorraine*
Rev crit jur belge	*Revue critique de jurisprudence belge*
Rev jur Ouest	*Revue Juridique de l'Ouest*
RG	*Reichsgericht*
RGZ	*Entscheidungen des Reichsgerichts in Zivilsachen*
RI	Rhode Island
RIDC	*Revue internationale de droit comparé*
Riv dir comm	*Rivista di diritto commerciale e del diritto generale delle obbligazioni*
Riv dir sport	*Rivista di diritto dello sport*
Riv giur amb	*Rivista giuridica dell'ambiente*
Riv giur circ trasp	*Rivista giuridica della circolazione e dei trasporti*
Riv pen	*Rivista penale*
RJ	*Repertorio de Jurisprudencia Aranzadi*
RTD civ	*Revue trimestrielle de droit civil*
s	section
S	Sirey
San Diego LR	San Diego Law Review
SAP	*Sentencia de la Audiencia Provincial* (Spain)
SCt	Supreme Court Reporter
SDNY	Southern District of New York
SE	South Eastern Reporter
Seton Hall LR	Seton Hall Law Review
SKL	*skadeståndslagen*
SMU LR	Southern Methodist Law Review
So	Southern Reporter
So Cal LR	Southern California Law Review
somm	*sommaire*
SpA	*Società per azioni*
Stanford LR	Stanford Law Review
St Louis U LJ	SaintLouis University Law Journal
STS	*sentencia del Tribunal Supremo*
Sup Ct	Supreme Court
SW	South Western Reporter
SZ	*Entscheidungen des österreichischen Obersten Gerichtshofes in Zivilsachen*
Tenn	Tennessee
Tenn LR	Tennessee Law Review
Tex	Texas
Tex Int'l LJ	Texas International Law Journal
Tex LR	Texas Law Review

Theo Inq L	Theoretical Inquiries in Law
TLR	Times Law Reports
transl	translator
Trib	Tribunal
Tulane Civ L Forum	Tulane Civil Law Forum
Tulane LR	Tulane Law Review
UCC	Uniform Commercial Code
UC Davis LR	University of California Davis Law Review
U Chi LR	University of Chicago Law Review
U Cin LR	University of Cincinnati Law Review
UCLA LR	University of California Los Angeles Law Review
U Ill L Forum	University of Illinois Law Forum
U Ill LR	University of Illinois Law Review
UK	United Kingdom
UKHL	United Kingdom House of Lords
U Miami Int'l & Comp LR	University of Miami International and Comparative Law Review
U Pa LR	University of Pennsylvania Law Review
U Pitt LR	University of Pittsburgh Law Review
U Rich LR	University of Richmond Law Review
US	United States Supreme Court
USC	United States Code Service
USD	United States dollars
v	*versus*
Va	Virginia
Va LR	Virginia Law Review
Vand LR	Vanderbilt Law Review
VCF	September 11 Victims Compensation Fund
VersR	*Versicherungs Recht*
vol	volume
vols	volumes
Vt	Vermont
Wake Forest LR	Wake Forest Law Review
Wash	Washington
Washburn LJ	Washburn Law Journal
Wis	Wisconsin
Wis LR	Wisconsin Law Review
WLR	Weekly Law Reports
WM	*Zeitschrift für Wirtschafts- und Bankrecht, Wertpapiermitteilungen*
Wm Mitchell LR	Mitchell Hamline Law Review
W Va	West Virginia

Wyo	Wyoming
Yale LJ	Yale Law Journal
ZR	*Revisionsverfahren in Zivilsachen*

List of Cases

AUSTRIA

CANADA

ENGLAND

EUROPEAN UNION

FRANCE

GERMANY

ITALY

NETHERLANDS

SPAIN

UNITED STATES

I

The Place of Tort Law

1. Tort Law Systems in Context

Tort law is commonly understood as the branch of private law whose set of rules, institutions, and procedures aims to shift the costs of accidents from the victim to a different subject. This set of rules is defined by statutory texts, judicial precedents, and/or scholarly writings, and is ultimately applied by courts to the disputes brought before them.

But tort law does not live in legislatures, law firms, courts, and law books only. It also lives "in the shadow" of the official system of adjudication. It lives in the offices of insurance companies, which provide coverage for damages caused by the insured or third parties. It lives in people's notions about injury and risk; responsibility and justice; determining people's conduct in day-to-day activities; and, once a harm occurred, their litigation/non-litigation choices. Tort law lives in the language and images associated with law in mass-generated popular culture—newspapers, television, movies, novels—as well as in public debates about what values should be protected and promoted, at what cost, and at the expense of whom. From this perspective, tort law can be seen as a "set of cultural responses to the broader challenges of addressing risk and assignments of responsibility, compensation, valuation, and obligation related to injury that may be shared with or addressed by a range of other social institutions."[1]

[1] David M Engel & Michael McCann, "Introduction," in David M Engel & Michael McCann (eds), *Fault Lines: Tort Law as a Cultural Practice* (Stanford University Press 2009) 7; see also Mauro

Common Law and Civil Law Perspectives on Tort Law. Mauro Bussani, Anthony J. Sebok, & Marta Infantino,
Oxford University Press. © Mauro Bussani, Anthony J. Sebok, & Marta Infantino 2022.
DOI: 10.1093/oso/9780195368383.003.0001

Each tort law system is therefore enmeshed in its own context that consists of its social, political, and legal culture. A better understanding of these contexts is essential to appreciate the features of any legal system, and makes it more useful to compare them with the others. For our purposes, there are two important strands that are worth mentioning, since they have deeply affected the development of liability law in the jurisdictions surveyed: social history and legal culture (section 2, respectively, *a* and *b*). The varied impact that social historical developments and legal culture have had on tort laws will allow us to grasp the commonalities and differences in the ideas and architectures that underpin civil liability in the systems under review (sections 3–8).

2. Legacies and Projections

a. On the impact of social history on current tort law developments, three brief remarks are in order. First, all the legal systems examined are the by-product of a long history made up of gradual developments and revolutionary moments. Such a history stretches from Roman law to canon law to nation-states and modern democracies. But while in modern Western Europe the law was embraced by the emerging bureaucracy as a tool of the new nation-state (what Weber called the phenomenon of "formal rationality"[2]), the revolution and evolutions in the United States were often accompanied by an egalitarian impulse that envisioned law as a tool for the expression of political rights in defense of liberty, and sometimes against the state.[3]

Bussani & Marta Infantino, "Tort Law and Legal Cultures," 63 AJCL 77–108 (2015). With specific regard to the American context, see Anne Bloom, David M Engel, & Michael McCann (eds), *Injury and Injustice. The Cultural Politics of Harm and Redress* (CUP 2018); Kenneth Abraham, *The Liability Century: Insurance and Tort Law from the Progressive Era to 9/11* (Harvard University Press 2008); Marshall S Shapo, *An Injury Law Constitution* (OUP 2012); Marshall S Shapo, *Tort Law and Culture* (Carolina Academic Press 2003); on European tort law culture(s), see Ken Oliphant, "Cultures of Tort Law in Europe" (2012) 3 JETL 147.

[2] In Weber's view, "formal rationality" was absent in the English common law. For a thorough review of Weber's account of European law, its origins, and its limits, see James Q Whitman, "The World Historical Significance of European Legal History: An Interim Report," in Heikki Pihlajamäki, Markus D Dubber, & Mark Godfrey (eds), *The Oxford Handbook of European Legal History* (OUP 2018) 3, 8–10.

[3] See, for all, Harold J Berman, *Law and Revolution I. The Formation of the Western Legal Tradition* (Harvard University Press 1985).

Second, while the United States, the United Kingdom, and the major economies of Europe experienced industrialization at almost the same time (roughly the period spanning the end of the eighteenth and the nineteenth centuries), the details of this evolution as well as the differences across the Atlantic are well known and manifested themselves in significant differences in the environment in which tort law operated in the twentieth century. The United Kingdom and Europe, on the one hand, developed strong labor movements which gained significant political power, notwithstanding the tragic turn taken by Germany and Italy during the middle of the century.[4] The United States, on the other hand, has always had a relatively weaker labor movement, and this movement weakened tremendously in the last part of the twentieth century to the point where it is unclear whether labor, as an interest, plays much of a role in the expansion and articulation of legal rights.[5]

Third, and finally (and perhaps as a combination or a reflection of the previous two points), there is a palpable difference between the "New World" cultures of the former British colonies and the "Old World" of England and Europe in the appreciation and valorization of the individual and individualism as a moral template. Since this point seems to be the beginning assumption of countless popular sociological studies on both sides of this divide, it may be so obvious as to be banal. Yet we believe that it is worth reminding the reader that there may be a relationship between the widespread culture of individualism and the patterns of litigation proneness followed by societies marked by the ideology of individualism, as the case of the United States clearly shows.[6]

b. There are multiple dimensions upon which one can measure the differences and similarities of legal cultures. The most pronounced divide in popular culture seems to be, again, between the United States and the rest of the systems that are the subject of this book.

[4] Bruno Aguilera-Barchet, "The Law of the Welfare State," in Pihlajamäki, Dubber, & Godfrey (eds) (n 2) 1000; Christine Sypnovich, "The Left and the Wrongs: Marxism, Law and Torts," in Michael Lobban & Julia Moses (eds), *The Impact of Ideas on Legal Development* (CUP 2012) 150.

[5] Lawrence M Friedman, *A History of American Law* (2nd edn, Simon & Schuster 1985) 554–565, 681–684. Ironically, to the extent that unions exercised power in the development of private law in the United States, it was primarily to suppress it, through the substitution of tort law by workman's compensation. See John Fabian Witt, *The Accidental Republic: Crippled Workingmen, Destitute Widows, and The Remaking of American Law* (Harvard University Press 2006).

[6] See David Nelken, *Comparing Legal Cultures* (Routledge 2017); Carol J Greenhouse, Barbara Yngvesson, & David M Engel, *Law and Community in Three American Towns* (Cornell University Press 1994) 2–4; Mary Ann Glendon, *Rights Talk: The Impoverishment of Political Discourse* (Free Press 1991); but see also Alan MacFarlane, *The Origins of English Individualism: The Family, Property and Social Transition* (Blackwell 1978).

This divide mainly manifests itself in two ways, only one of which will be of direct interest to us. In the Western world, the United States is seen both internally and by observers as unique in its harsh criminal law, especially in its continued embrace of capital punishment,[7] and in its excessive reliance on litigation, especially in the area of tort law (although often domestic critics of the American "litigation crisis" fail to distinguish between tort litigation and other forms of civil litigation.)[8] Describing what he calls "the American way of law," Kagan has coined the term "adversarial legalism" to capture the peculiar way of settling conflicts and pursue political ends that sets the United States apart from most European countries.[9]

Do Americans in fact litigate more often today than in the past?

Turning first to the question of litigation and adversarial legalism more generally, the available data on the costs of the tort system, although often criticized as unverifiable, documents an absolute rise in tort costs as percentage of GDP in the United States between 1950 and 2006 (from 0.62% to 1.87% with 2006 at an all-time high of 2.24% in 2003).[10] According to the same source, in 2016 the ratio of tort costs as to GDP reached 2.3%.[11] Tort costs as percentage of GDP in the United States are considerably higher as

[7] Lawrence M Friedman, *Crime and Punishment in American History* (Basic Books 1994).

[8] For example, tort litigation has always comprised a very small portion of the civil caseload in the state courts in the United States. According to the National Center for State Courts ("NCSC"), tort filings are currently approximately 4% of all civil cases filed in the state courts. See National Center for State Courts, *Court Statistics Project. State Court Caseload Digest. 2018 Data* (National Center for State Courts 2020) 10, at https://www.courtstatistics.org/__data/assets/pdf_file/0014/40820/2018-Digest.pdf. While it is true that tort cases comprise a larger share of the federal caseload (United States Courts, *Federal Court Management Statistics. United States District Courts—National Judicial Caseload Profile*, March 2020, at https://www.uscourts.gov/sites/default/files/data_tables/fcms_na_distprofile0331.2020.pdf), it should be recalled that the vast majority of tort suits are filed in *state* courts, not *federal* courts. Most important, however, is that in recent years the relative share of the caseload comprised by tort in federal courts has been shrinking: the Bureau of Justice Statistics (BJS) reports that, after reaching a peak of 3,600 trials in 1985, the number of tort cases concluded by bench or jury trial before federal courts has declined by nearly 80% in 2003 (BJS, *Publications (Civil Cases)*, at http://www.bjs.gov/index.cfm?ty=tp&tid=451). Meanwhile, contract suit filings continue to dominate state and federal civil case filings, and are growing as a share of the caseload relative to tort.

[9] Robert A Kagan, *Adversarial Legalism. The American Way of Law* (2nd edn, Harvard University Press 2019).

[10] Towers Perrin, *2007 Update on US Tort Cost Trends* (2007) at prisonlegalnews.org/media/publications/towers_perrin_report_subj_tort_cost_trends_2007.pdf, 5. For criticism of this source, see Jay M Feinman, *Un-Making Law: The Conservative Campaign to Roll Back the Common Law* (Beacon Press 2005) 71.

[11] US Chamber's Institute for Legal Reform, *Costs and Compensation of the US Tort System* (October 2018) at instituteforlegalreform.com/uploads/sites/1/Tort_costs_paper_FINAL_WEB.pdf, 22.

compared to various European nations, even though such costs are going up everywhere.[12]

However, we must be careful about what the growth in tort costs means. There is no reason to infer that Americans are more hot-headed and touchy today than in the past; only that more Americans are able to claim, since (i) the apparatus for claiming is more fully developed (providing, for instance, more lawyers) and (ii) there is more access to the courts as social discrimination against minorities and women declined. Also, the growth in tort costs may not reflect a change in the willingness to blame, but merely an increase in the number of accidents. Finally, the growth in tort costs may not reflect an increase in the willingness to blame or the number of accidents, but a relatively "richer" valuation of the cost of accidents—for example, as the law developed in the 1960s, the same accident (wrongful death) could produce multiple sources of injury, including pain and suffering awards that had heretofore not been recognized.[13]

Turning now to litigation rates, we can see that there is some truth to the claim that the United States is a highly litigious society, although it is not uniquely litigious. Based on data from the fundamental 1998 study by Wollschläger on civil litigation rates (comprising "general civil," "family," "labour," and "debt collection" cases), Germany appears to be the most litigious society in the survey, with 123.2 cases filed per 1,000 inhabitants. The United States ranks substantially lower with 74.5 cases, followed by England and Wales with 64.4 cases. Of the countries covered in this book, France lies at the bottom, with 40.3 cases.[14]

However, there are many complicating factors that make a simple conclusion from this and similar statistics hard to make.[15] The difficulty in

[12] US Chamber's Institute for Legal Reform, *International Comparisons of Litigation Costs. Canada, Europe, Japan, and the United States* (June 2013) at instituteforlegalreform.com/uploads/sites/1/ILR_NERA_Study_International_Liability_Costs-update.pdf, 2.

[13] On this point, see Chapter V, section 3.1.

[14] See Christian Wollschläger, "Exploring Global Landscapes of Litigation Rates," in Jürgen Brand & Dieter Strempel (eds), *Soziologie des Rechts: Festschrift fur Erhard Blankenburg zum 60. Geburtstag* (Nomos 1998) 577–588. Wollschläger's survey has been called by one of America's leading empirical legal scholars "the most comprehensive effort to compile cross-national data on litigation rates" (Herbert M Kritzer, "Lawyer Fees and Lawyer Behavior in Litigation: What Does the Empirical Literature Really Say?" (2002) 80 Tex LR 1943, 1981). In particular, Wollschläger's results about Germany resonate with Blankenburg's insights about Germany as overly litigious insofar as "the German court system, being very cost efficient, attracts masses of petty claims" (Erhard Blankenburg, "The Infrastructure for Avoiding Civil Litigation: Comparing Cultures of Legal Behavior in the Netherlands and West Germany" (1994) 28 L&Soc'y R 789).

[15] On the role played by social security systems in shaping national tort law scenarios, see Chapter III, sections 1 and 2.1.

collecting reliable civil litigation rates cannot be understated. Not all nations collect litigation rates, or if they do, not all make them available to the public. For example, while the United States Justice Department's Bureau of Justice Statistics (BJS) has sponsored periodic surveys examining tort trials in state courts, not only are federal suits not counted, but the BJS only surveys a significant portion, but not all, of the states.[16] European national governments, despite their history of centralization, have an even less comprehensive approach to compiling litigation-related statistics. But even where statistics have been compiled of, for example, lawsuits filed (as opposed to tried) throughout a country, there is still a problem of transnational comparison, given the differences between the organization of the different national court systems and differences between the procedural and substantive laws.[17] Moreover, much depends on the actual type of data one is relying on. For instance, a recent survey of the Council of Europe on the number of incoming first instance "civil and commercial" litigious cases per one hundred inhabitants seems to contradict Wollschläger's result about the litigiousness of Germany and England. According to the survey, Germany has the quite low rate of 1.5, surpassed by the United Kingdom (1.8), France (2.2), and Italy (2.6).[18] But it may also be possible that the notion of "civil and commercial" cases adopted by the Council of Europe is only partially overlapping with the notion of "civil litigation" embraced by Wollschläger. Further, data might be aggregated and packed in a way that in fact hide relevant similarities and differences between and within countries. For instance, while investigating patterns of litigating behavior in "common civil disputes" on the basis of thousands of interviews of randomly selected individuals for the 2011 edition of the World Justice Project's "Rule of Law Index®," the interviewers discovered that the aggregated data obscured the significance that, in some countries as opposed to others, personal income played on litigation patterns. In particular, interviewers found out that, while the approach to litigation by low- and high-income individuals in continental Europe was the same, only high-income people were willing to sue in the United States and

[16] See Bureau of Justice Statistics, *Publications (Civil Cases)* at https://www.bjs.gov/index.cfm?ty=tp&tid=451.

[17] Koen von Aeken, "Civil Court Litigation and Alternative Dispute Resolution," in David S Clark (ed), *Comparative Law and Society* (EE 2012) 216, 226–232.

[18] Council of Europe, *European Judicial Systems. CEPEJ Evaluation Report. Part 1–2020 Evaluation Cycle* (Council of Europe 2020) at https://rm.coe.int/evaluation-report-part-1-english/16809fc058, 112. According to the same study, the highest values in Europe were those of Belgium and Romania, respectively with 6.7 and 6.4 new incoming cases per 100 inhabitants.

in the United Kingdom. Low-income people in these countries acted very differently than high-income ones: the absolute majority relinquished their claims and only a few had ever filed a lawsuit.[19]

This takes us to some other features of the legal culture that bear on litigation patterns, such as lawyers' role in the justice system and the nature of the legal process. Among the factors that may feed into the environment of adversarial legalism which defines the United States, is the presence of an "entrepreneurial" torts bar. To a degree unknown on the continent and only partially known in England, American lawyers who do tort litigation are divided into two somewhat permanent "camps" of defense-oriented lawyers (who are typically retained on a repeat basis by insurers and either charge by the hour or receive an annual or monthly retainer); and plaintiff-oriented lawyers, who typically work for a "contingent" fee. The contingent fee, which is an American innovation dating back to the early twentieth century, is a particular kind of conditional fee agreement. It allows a party to a lawsuit to make a "bet" with the lawyer handling the lawsuit: if the lawsuit fails (eg, there is no recovery at all), the lawyer is paid nothing. If the lawsuit succeeds (if there is any sort of recovery, including a settlement), the lawyer receives a portion of the recovery, typically between 25% and 40% of it.[20]

The contingent fee is perhaps the most important procedural feature that characterizes the entrepreneurial aspect of American tort law,[21] yet others bear note. The United States is unique among the jurisdictions that are studied in this book in that it rejects the "loser-pays" rule whereby the loser of a tort suit pays the costs of the winning side. There is nothing logically incompatible between the contingent fee and the loser-pay rule; in fact, many European countries have recently (albeit cautiously) adopted modified forms of the contingent fee without abandoning the loser-pay system.[22]

[19] Juan-Carlos Botero, Angela M Pinzon-Rondon, & Christine S Pratt, "How, When and Why Do Governance, Justice and Rule of Law Indicators Fail Public Policy Decision" (2016) 8 Hague J Rule of Law 51, 64–65.

[20] See American Bar Association, *Model Rules of Professional Conduct*, Rule 1.5(c) (2020). On the role of the contingent fee in the United States legal system, see Herbert M Kritzer, *Risks, Reputations, and Rewards. Contingency Fee Legal Practice in the United States* (Stanford University Press 2004).

[21] It should be noted that the contingent fee can be used by American lawyers in any matter except in the representation of a defendant in a criminal matter or in a divorce. See American Bar Association (ABA), *Model Rules of Professional Conduct*, Rule 1.5(d) (2020).

[22] This is for instance the case in England, Germany, and Italy: see Mathias Reimann, "General Report," in Mathias Reimann (ed), *Cost and Fee Allocation in Civil Procedure* (Springer 2012) 3, 45; Ulrich Magnus, "Why Is US Tort Law so Different?" (2010) 1 JETL 102, 112–113.

It should further be stressed that while public legal aid schemes are well-rooted in Europe, legal aid is largely unavailable in the United States for tort litigation.[23]

Another important aspect of the legal culture that must be noted is the difference both in terms of civil procedure and the role of the court in tort suits. Here the difference really is between the civilian and common law systems. Civilian civil procedure is said to be "inquisitorial" where common law civil procedure would be "adversarial."[24] Civilian judges take control of the development of evidence, whereas common law judges leave the collection of evidence to the two opposing counsel. The upshot of this different division of labor is that the rules of discovery, especially in the United States, are more liberal, in that parties may demand that their opponent produce all "relevant" evidence even if the requesting party does not know exactly what the defendant possesses. The consequences of the liberal discovery rules in the United States cannot be overstated.[25] To begin with, it means that a lawyer can, with a relatively small investment of resources, begin a process against a well-funded opponent in which the opponent bears the cost of producing evidence which the plaintiff's lawyer will then use. Of course, the temptation for parties to resist handing over relevant evidence (or to "overlook" a piece of evidence) may be great. To meet this risk, parties will often try to involve American judges into the discovery process, but, if the American discovery process ultimately requires judicial involvement, one might wonder how different it really is from the continental "inquisitorial" process. Of course, one major difference is that in the American process the judge may be used as a weapon by either side, either to push for even more evidence, or to produce the impression on the judge's part that the other side is noncooperative (this suggesting that the latter's case is weak). Still more importantly, the American tort process retains its exceptionalism insofar as it is the only one where decisions are made by the judge and the jury, whose presence affects not only the size of the awards, but also American lawyers' litigation choices,

[23] Reimann (n 22) 36–37; Magnus (n 22) 114.

[24] Mirjan R Damaška, *The Faces of Justice and State Authority: A Comparative Approach to the Legal Process* (Yale University Press 1986); Mirjan R Damaška, *Evaluation of Evidence. Pre-Modern and Modern Approaches* (CUP 2018).

[25] The normative implications of these consequences, on the other hand, are fiercely debated. Compare John H Langbein, "The German Advantage in Civil Procedure" (1985) 52 U Chi LR 823 and Samuel Gross, "The American Advantage: The Value of Inefficient Litigation" (1987) 85 Mich LR 734.

cultures, strategies, and style, which are bound to reach judges as well as laymen.[26]

3. The Idea of Civil Liability

A separate dimension of comparison which we want to ensure is given a full hearing is between the ideas of liability that define or underpin each tort system. This is typically seen as the heartland of legal scholarship, where law professors, courts, and members of the bar attempt to identify the architectonic principles which define, with greater and lesser degrees of specificity, the internal logic and norms of the tort system.

While the chapters that follow will actively compare many specific liability rules of national tort systems, modern comparative tort law is replete with broad generalizations about the conceptual and structural qualities of these systems, especially on a relative scale.[27] We do not reject the utility of these rough generalizations, as long as they are viewed as tools, not as scientific facts. Where we differ with some other authors is not in the utility of these tools, but of the specific terms used. Often national tort systems are compared along a single spectrum that measures the relative generality or specificity of the rules of liability of the system. On this spectrum, France is at one extreme, since the articles that establish both negligence and strict liability are drafted in the broadest language compared with other civilian systems. The general consensus seems to be that England (and maybe the United States) are at the other end of the extreme, where the common law creates a structure of specific and denominated headings for every element of a tort action, which Ferdinand Stone described as "pigeonhole systems of nominate torts."[28]

[26] See Valerie P Hans, *Business on Trial: The Civil Jury and Corporate Responsibility* (Yale University Press 2000); Michael D Green, "The Impact of the Civil Jury on American Tort Law" (2011) 38 Pepp LR 337; Magnus (n 22) 111.

[27] Cf for instance Gerhard Wagner, "Comparative Tort Law," in Matthias Reimann & Reinhard Zimmermann (eds), *Oxford Handbook of Comparative Law* (2nd edn, OUP 2019) 994–1030; Thomas Kadner Graziano, *Comparative Tort Law: Cases, Materials and Exercises* (Routledge 2018); Cees van Dam, *European Tort Law* (2nd edn, OUP 2013); Walter van Gerven, Pierre Larouche, & Jeremy Lever, *Cases, Materials and Text on National, Supranational and International Tort Law* (Hart 2000); Christian von Bar, *The Common European Law of Torts* (2 vols, OUP 1998–2000); Frederick H Lawson & Basil S Markesinis, *Tortious Liability for Unintentional Harm in the Common Law and the Civil Law* (2 vols, CUP 1982). See also the "Tort and Insurance Law Series" published by the European Centre of Tort and Insurance Law formerly with Springer and now with de Gruyter at ectil.org.

[28] Ferdinand F Stone, "Touchstones of Tort Liability" (1950) 2 Stan LR 259, 272.

We believe that the national tort systems can be analyzed on multiple axes. The first axis is the degree to which a legal system explicitly divides the grounds of liability along different culpable mental states. One could imagine systems that had no negligence law and were all strict liability and liability for intentional torts (such as New Zealand) or systems that were all negligence law and had no form of strict liability or liability for intentional torts. Along this spectrum, there is very little difference across the European jurisdictions and between civil and common law systems. All systems have a mixture of negligence and strict liability, with some local variation as to which injuries are handled under each form of liability, and the common law jurisdictions have in addition a form of liability for intentional wrongdoing, which, it turns out, is statutorily established in Germany and functionally reproduced in France and Italy because of the effect of intent on causation and damages.[29]

The next axis upon which one can deploy the various legal system is really along a bipolar choice. It is between systems of liability that require the plaintiff to identify those who owe to him or her an obligation to comply with the rules of conduct imposed by the system, and those systems that do not. England and, arguably, the United States until the Third Restatement, have what Goldberg and Zipursky call the "proper-plaintiff" rule[30]—that is, that a defendant who causes harm to a person as a result of unreasonable or otherwise wrongful conduct is not necessarily obliged to redress that harm unless the victim of the injury can demonstrate that, in addition to causing the harm, the defendant owed a duty of care to the plaintiff or was under some other legal obligation to the same plaintiff. In this context, all the civilian systems adopt the identical position—especially in claims for redress due to carelessness, they reject the need for an independent duty analysis by the court, and especially the need for the plaintiff to bear that particular burden of proof.

The third axis is the one that we identified as the conventional one, upon which most comparative treatises focus—the method by which what is sorted out are the interests of the victim that are worthy of protection within the tort system. Here, as already mentioned, France seems to occupy one side of the spectrum, with its very general article 1240 (former 1382) of the

[29] See James Gordley, "The Architecture of the Common and Civil Law of Torts: An Historical Survey," in Mauro Bussani & Anthony J Sebok (eds), *Comparative Tort Law. Global Perspectives* (2nd edn, EE 2021) 160–185; see also Chapter II, sections 11–12 and Chapter VII, section 4.2.

[30] John C Goldberg & Benjamin C Zipursky, *Recognizing Wrongs* (Harvard University Press 2020)202 ("each tort has a proper-plaintiff requirement built into its substantive elements").

Civil Code.[31] Only slightly more restrictive than its French counterpart is the Italian general clause of delict, article 2043 of the Italian Civil Code. By contrast, Germany adopts a more cautioned approach, providing multiple headings of protected interests under § 823 I BGB. England and the United States have conventionally been seen to fall at the other end of the spectrum—England especially, with its "pigeonhole" approach to duty.

Having deployed these three highly stylized analytic generalizations, we want to note that they are useful only if one then looks at the rules, conventions, and features of the legal process of a given jurisdiction to see how the general concepts mentioned before actually "play out" in the real world of tort litigation. For example, as we will see in the next section, there are many doctrines that limit the application of the famously broad French rule for the identification of interests to be defended by tort law, such as *non-cumul* and low damages, so that in the end the protection of the individual against negligent injury in France does not look too different from Italy and Germany's, although the differences between all three of these civilian codes and the common law rules in England and the United States are still significant and worth a careful scrutiny.

4. France: The General Claim

Among the five systems within the scope of this study, France stands out as the most liberal in its conceptual scope and structure. Article 1240 (former article 1382) of the *Code Civil* sets out a ground for liability under the general heading of "*faute*," which permits liability whenever "any act whatever of man, which causes damage to another, obliges the one by whose fault it occurred, to compensate it." The French approach to negligence liability

[31] The law no 2016-131 reforming the law of obligations in the Civil Code changed the numeration of the chapter on tort, but left the content of the provisions untouched. A comprehensive reform of tort law is now under way. In March 2017 a draft reform of French tort law was published by the French Ministry of Justice (justice.gouv.fr/publication/Projet_de_reforme_de_la_responsabilite_civile_13032017.pdf); in July 2020, the Law Commission of the French Senate released a "Rapport d'information," where it was suggested to drop some of the Projet's most controversial proposals and to adopt a law on the Projet's least controversial elements (Jacques Bigot & André Reichardt (au nom de la commission des lois), *Rapport d'information n° 663* (2019–2020), July 22, 2020, at senat.fr/rap/r19-663/r19-6631.pdf). Following the Law Commission's suggestions, a legislative bill was drafted and is currently pending before the Parliament: Sénat, *Proposition de loi n° 678*, at senat.fr/leg/ppl19-678.html. For a commentary on the 2017 draft, see GRERCA, *La réforme du droit de la responsabilité en France et en Belgique: Regards croisés et aspects de droit comparé* (Bruylant 2020); Jean-Sébastien Borghetti & Simon Whittaker (eds), *French Civil Liability in Comparative Perspective* (Hart 2019).

stands in sharp contrast to the German and common law approach in that it does not rely on a concept of objective wrongfulness or duty of care. Any unreasonable act relative to a risk of injury to anyone else's person, property, or immaterial interest can generate a claim for compensation. Further, the broad French concept of *faute* does not apparently rule out intent, insofar as both negligent and intentional conduct qualify as *fautif*.

Moreover, article 1242 I (former article 1384 I) of the Civil Code states that "one is liable not only for the harm which one causes by one's own action, but also for that which is caused by the action of persons for whom one is responsible, or of things which one has in one's keeping." The *Cour de cassation* has developed this article to include strict liability for persons who were in control of a thing that injured others (*le gardien de la chose*) and strict liability for persons for the acts of people under their supervision.[32]

The French approach can be seen as solving the problem of when liability attaches in tort by generating overlapping spheres of liability, which are then reduced in scope by court decisions that reflect judicial and academic judgments about the relative competencies of each mode of liability. For example, read literally, it would seem that article 1242 sweeps so broadly that the area covered by negligence law in France would be reduced to a small, almost irrelevant margin (Ripert noted that, taking of article 1384 [current article 1242] and its attribution of strict liability of the *gardiens* seriously, "[i]t would [...] be necessary to imagine a collision between two persons practicing nudism before article 1382 [current article 1240] would apply"[33]). However, this is where a careful reading of the entirety of the French liability system, especially with an eye toward using terms transnationally in a consistent fashion, becomes important. As we will note in the chapters that follow, the French tort rules, although extremely liberal in their conceptual framework, are limited by collateral or associated rules which might set up constraints unknown to other systems. For example, in principle under French law a claimant injured by a party with whom he or she has a contract must lodge a contractual suit, and significant consequences may follow from this choice (the so-called rule of "*non-cumul*," imposing on plaintiffs tied to a contract with the harmdoer to sue the latter in contract only).[34] Even when a

[32] See, respectively, Cass civ (Plenary) 13 February 1930, DP 1930.1.57 (*arrêt Jand'heur*), and Cass civ (Plenary) 29 March 1991, D 1991, 324 (*arrêt Blieck*).

[33] Georges Ripert, "Note à l'affaire Jand'heur," D 1930.1.59, translated by Brice Dickson, *Introduction to French Law* (Pitman 1994) 161. But see also Chapter II, section 11.2.

[34] Jonas Knetsch, *Tort Law in France* (Wolters Kluwer 2021) 38–39. See also Chapter VI, section 5.1.

tort law action is available, and despite the fact that duty of care or protected interests provide no aid to the defendant, it is through doctrines such as causation and damages that French courts often develop justifications for non-liability, or limitations to liability.[35] Furthermore, it is worth noting that the generosity of French courts while establishing liability seems to be countered by their well-known tendency to award "symbolic" damages for pain and suffering (*dommage moral*), especially when personality rights are at stake.[36]

5. Italy: Openness with Caveats

Italian tort law is often described as hybrid, insofar it would stand in a middle way between the French and the German models. Tort law rules in the 1942 Civil Code (which replaced the heavily French-inspired first Italian Civil Code of 1865) are indeed a mixture of French and German influences, as well as of original domestic developments.

Article 2043 of the 1942 Code provides that "any intentional or negligent act that causes a wrongful injury to another obliges the person who has committed the act to pay damages." The clause is clearly in line with article 1240 of the French Civil Code, but for German-inspired qualification that the injury should be a "wrongful" one. The Code, however, does not provide any guidance as to what might amount to a wrongful harm. After some hesitations, courts and scholars now read the requirement in a manner that is not substantially different from the notion of "damage" under (article 1151 of the 1865 Italian Civil Code, and current) article 1240 of the French Civil Code.[37]

Italy's originality also emerges in the field of strict liability. The 1942 Code reproduces the different headings of custodial and vicarious liability that were already provided by the 1865 code (and, in France, by—at that time—articles 1384 and 1385 of the *Code civil*). Even though Italy has never developed a principle of liability for things comparable to that existing in France,[38] the drafters of the 1942 Code introduced a new—and, at that time,

[35] See Chapter VI, section 5.1.

[36] Suzanne Carval, *La responsabilité civile dans sa fonction de peine privée* (LGDJ 1995) 32.

[37] Marta Infantino, "Diffusing Tort Law Softly: Insights into the European Travels of Italian Tort Law" (2015) 6 JETL 260, 261–265 (2015); Michele Graziadei, "Liability for Fault in Italian Law: The Development of Legal Doctrine from 1865 to the End of the Twentieth Century," in Nils Jansen (ed), *The Development and Making of Legal Doctrine* (CUP 2010) 126, 127–134.

[38] Francesco D Busnelli & Giovanni Comandé, "Italy," in Bernhard A Koch & Helmut Koziol (eds), *Unification of Tort Law: Strict Liability* (Kluwer 2002) 207, 211–212, 218.

quite innovative—strict liability rule upon whoever carries out a "dangerous activity" (article 2050),[39] as well as a presumption of liability on drivers of vehicles not guided by rails (article 2054).

Italy has always rejected the French principle of *non-cumul*, admitting instead plaintiffs to bring simultaneously causes of action both in contract and in tort,[40] and has broadened the size of compensation for non-economic loss through the innovation carried on by the notion of "*danno biologico*."[41] Moreover, since the 1990s, Italian courts have transplanted and applied in many sectors the German idea of "contracts with protective effects towards third parties," thus expanding the scope of protection of contractual actions.[42]

That being said, within the Italian legal framework, it is up to the traditional requirements of liability (fault, causation, and damage) to determine whether there is liability and what is recoverable. When Italian courts screen out a claim, they rarely do it by relying on the idea of (lack of) wrongfulness. The limiting factors for the recovery continue to rest upon causation, certainty of damage, and the occasional need to show that the defendant's conduct crossed the threshold of blameworthiness required for liability.[43]

6. Germany: The Formal Pyramid

Driven by skepticism toward the general clause of former article 1382 of the French Civil Code, which seemed to grant extensive powers to the judiciary—and by the fascination for Roman law texts "which had been accepted in Germany for centuries, and expressed the German *Volksgeist*"[44]—the drafters of the German Civil Code of 1896 (*Bürgerliches Gesetzbuch*—BGB) opted for a basic rule that, though not casuistic, clearly delimits the scope of liability. Section 823 I BGB provides for liability in the case of unlawful infringement of a list of specific legally protected interests—namely life, body,

[39] The Italian choice has been followed, for instance, by Poland and Portugal: see art 435 of the Polish Civil Code of 1964 and art 493(2) of the Portuguese Civil Code of 1967.

[40] Mauro Bussani, *L'illecito civile* (ESI 2020) 74–81.

[41] The notion of "*danno biologico*" refers to a way of assessing the non-economic consequences of personal injuries on the basis of pre-fixed schemes translating into monetary terms the victim's percentage of temporary or permanent disability. On this point, see Francesco D Busnelli & Giovanni Comandé, "Italy," in WH Horton Rogers (ed), *Damages for Non-Pecuniary Loss* (Kluwer 2001) 135, 146, as well as Chapter IV, section 6.

[42] See, for instance, Cass 4 March 2004, no 4400, in Giust civ, 2005, I, 2115 (medical liability) and Cass 10 January 2003, no 157, in Foro it, 2003, I, 78 (state liability).

[43] See Chapter VI, section 5.3.

[44] Gordley (n 29) 182.

health, freedom and property, and any other comparable "right," readily understood by German judges and scholars as meaning "absolute right" (i.e., a right protected against the world at large). The narrow scope of the general clause for liability is however extended by further provisions. According to § 823 II BGB, liability may be established in cases where the defendant breached a statute which was intended to protect persons such as the plaintiff against the risk of harm. Even more general is the phrasing of § 826 BGB, which grants protection against damage that is incurred contrary to *boni mores*, if the latter is the result of the intentional behavior of the defendant. Parallel to the main tort law rules just mentioned, the German Civil Code abounds with specific torts, such as § 824 BGB on untrue statements, § 825 BGB on sexual assault, and § 839a on the liability of court-appointed experts. Vicarious liability for employees and minors is provided for in §§ 831 and 832 BGB, while the only form of strict liability established by the Code applies to keepers of non-domestic animals (§§ 833–834 BGB).[45] Despite the lack of "proper-plaintiff" rules, the choice for a system of nominate causes of action, the hostility toward the recovery of pure economic losses in negligence claims,[46] and the refusal of adopting general instances of strict liability,[47] show a close resemblance with the common law approach.

German tort law maintains nevertheless its own distinctive traits. The point is not only that, through the twentieth century, German courts have worked to open up the interpretation of tort law provisions, adding new "absolute" rights to the list drawn by § 823 I BGB, broadening the meaning of "infringement of a statute intended for the protection of others" under § 823 II BGB, and lowering the threshold of intentional conduct under § 826 BGB to cover also gross negligence.[48] A distinctive innovation lies in fact that, since the adoption of the BGB, German courts have expanded the sphere of contractual liability beyond the limits marked by the code, extending the scope of contractual duties before the conclusion and after the termination or the performance of the contract itself, and stretching their range to include

[45] German law recognizes other forms of strict liability, which are not covered by the Code but established by special statutes, such as the 1952 Road Traffic Act (*Straßenverkehrsgesetz*), the 1961 Medicinal Products Act (*Arzneimittelgesetz*), the 1978 Liability Act (*Haftpflichtgesetz*), the 1989 Product Liability Act (*Produkthaftungsgesetz*), the 1990 Environmental Liability Act (*Umwelthaftungsgesetz*).

[46] See Chapter VI, section 5.2.

[47] Reinhard Zimmermann, *The Law of Obligations: Roman Foundations of the Civilian Tradition* (OUP 1996) 1034–1035

[48] See Chapter VI, section 5.2.

a duty of care in favor of beneficiaries who are not party to the contract.[49] Many cases that in other countries are treated as falling solely under tort law rules are seen and considered actionable by Germans under contract law.

7. England: Between Pigeonholes and General Clause

Dozens of causes of action, designed in detail by the cumulative works of thousands of judicial architects, have historically compartmentalized the English law of tort. Most of these torts, such as trespass and nuisance, were originally conceived of in defense of the plaintiff's life, limb, and property. A few others, mostly based on the defendant's malicious intent, developed to protect the plaintiff's personality rights and pure economic losses. Some torts have more recently been created or inferred by legislation, such as, for instance, the tort of harassment and the tort of breach of the 1950 European Convention for the Protection of Human Rights and Fundamental Freedoms (ECHR).[50] Besides the application of the principle of "*respondeat superior*" for employees' wrongful acts, very few causes of action recognize that a defendant might be liable without fault, strict liability remaining an anomaly.[51]

Looking at the English scenario, the by-far most important tort nowadays is the tort of negligence. The tort is based on a limited set of requirements: a duty of care and the negligent breach of such a duty, damage, causation, and lack of remoteness. In May 1932 the House of Lords famously established that manufacturers of consumers' goods, despite lack of privity, owe a duty to ultimate consumers to ensure that goods put into circulation are free from defects that they should have foreseen might cause physical injury or damage

[49] These developments have to a large extent been included in the BGB through the comprehensive reform of the law of obligations carried out by the 2002 Act on the Modernization of the Law of Obligations (*Gesetz zur Modernisierung des Schuldrechts*, in BGBl, 29 November 2001, I, Nr 61, 3138, effective as from 1st January 2002). See now § 241 I BGB (on the principle of *culpa in contrahendo*) and § 311 III BGB (on the "contract with protective effects for third parties").

[50] See, respectively, the Protection from Harassment Act 1997 and the Human Rights Act 1998. It is worth reminding that, while the United Kingdom withdrew from the European Union on 31 January 2020, it is still a member of the Council of Europe, which enacted the ECHR. EU-derived legislation in force in the United Kingdom before the withdrawal is still applicable in England: see legislation.gov.uk/eu-legislation-and-uk-law.

[51] In *Rylands v Fletcher* [1868] LR 3 HL 330, the House of Lords held the owner of a reservoir liable without fault for the damages caused by the escaped water. However, in the more recent case *Cambridge Water Co Ltd v Eastern Counties Leather* [1994] 2 AC 264, the court held that *Rylands* did not stand for a general principle of strict liability but a more limited one of liability in nuisance. See also Chapter II, section 11.2. On the development of English product liability, see Chapter VIII, sections 3.1 and 4.

to property.[52] In particular, one of the five judges, Lord Atkin, addressed the question of how to formulate a general conception of relations giving rise of a duty of care and notoriously elaborated what has become known as the neighbor principle:

> The liability for negligence, whether you style it such or treat it as in other systems as a species of 'culpa,' is no doubt based upon a general public sentiment of moral wrongdoing for which the offender must pay. But acts or omissions which any moral code would censure cannot in a practical world be treated so as to give a right to every person injured by them to demand relief. In this way rules of law arise which limit the range of complaints and the extent of their remedy. The rule that you are to love your neighbour becomes in law, you must not injure your neighbour: and the lawyer's question, Who is my neighbour? receives a restricted reply. You must take reasonable care to avoid acts or omissions which you can reasonably foresee would be likely to injure your neighbour. Who, then, in law, is my neighbour? The answer seems to be—persons who are so closely and directly affected by my act that I ought reasonably to have them in contemplation as being so affected when I am directing my mind to the acts or omissions which are called in question.[53]

This statement remains controversial, especially insofar as Lord Atkin made no reference to the distinction between physical harm (whether to person or to property) and pure economic loss. Nevertheless, "in its decisive rejection of the traditional, narrow formulation of duty situations [the opinion] marks the starting point for the analysis of the modern tort."[54]

Since then, the tort of negligence has experienced a staggering expansion, becoming a sort of general clause covering all forms of negligent behavior in the realm of protection from physical harm (bodily injury or damage to property). Yet, notwithstanding such an expansion, English courts have maintained—especially in borderline areas of non-economic and purely economic losses—an instinctive fear of wide liability. They have thus resorted to a number of control devices to confine what would otherwise be an overly extensive legal liability. While some courts have achieved this by reference to

[52] *Donoghue v Stevenson* [1932] AC 562 (HL). Strictly speaking, *Donoghue v Stevenson* is a Scottish case; yet English law and Scots law are identical on the subject. See also Chapter VIII, section 7.1.
[53] *Donoghue v. Stevenson* [1932] AC 562 at 580 (per Lord Atkin).
[54] Simon Deakin & Zoe Adams, *Markesinis and Deakin's Tort Law* (8th edn, OUP 2019) 87.

causation, it is "above all the concept of *duty of care* which they have used to shape the tort of negligence."[55]

8. United States: Experimenting within Constraints

The set of torts refined by the English common law historically provided the building blocks for the autonomous development of United States tort law. The latter is usually depicted as largely common law and primarily state law. Most of its groundings can be found in a "common core" of common law that can be on the whole regarded as roughly similar in all the states.

In the American common law too, the historical development of tort law has produced an English-style judicial proliferation of rights to recover damages under specific actions, each containing its own specific requirements, or elements. The long gallery of causes of action is mainly directed at protecting bodily integrity, the personal sphere, and possessory interests, but also exceptionally covers contractual interests and emotional well-being.[56] Almost all the torts require a specific subjective element, from negligence to intention to cause harm, although the range of strict liability causes of action under American common law is definitely broader than the English one.[57] As in England, other torts have been added by statute.[58] As in England (and actually before England), the tort of negligence has become the hallmark of United States tort law, experiencing in the twentieth century a veritable expansion through the judicial multiplication of common law duties of care. While American law has retained a English-like fear of "liability in an indeterminate amount for an indeterminate time to an indeterminate class,"[59] most notably in the field of recovery of pure economic losses, American courts have also explored and charted many "regions of the common law that are as yet *terra incognita* in the English system."[60]

[55] Ibid.

[56] Goldberg & Zipursky (n 30) 27–43.

[57] Besides vicarious liability, United States tort law provides forms of strict liability for defective products (in case of manufacturing defects or inadequate instructions/warnings), injuries caused by animals, nuisances, and abnormally dangerous activities. See, for instance, the rules contained in Chapter 4 ("Strict Liability") in the Restatement (Third) of Torts—Liability for Physical and Emotional Harm (PEH) (2010) (§ 20 Abnormally Dangerous Activities, § 21 Intrusion by Livestock or Other Animals, § 22 Wild Animals, and § 23 Abnormally Dangerous Animals) and in the Restatement (Third) of Torts—Product Liability (1998); see also Chapter VIII, sections 2–6.

[58] See, for instance, the statutory wrongful death and survival actions: Chapter VI, section 5.5.

[59] *Ultramares Corporation v Touche*, 255 NY 170 (NY 1931), at 179 (per Cardozo CJ).

[60] Percy H Winfield, "Restatement of the Law of Torts: Volume IV" (1940) 18 NYU LR 66, 67—the quote, as we will see across the remaining chapters of this book, holds true today as well.

The reasons of the marked American experimentalism in tort are manifold, and largely related to contextual and structural features of tort lawmaking and legal process. Besides what we mentioned above in this chapter, at section 3, American federalism implies that, despite its shared foundation, tort law is constantly shaped at the state level by courts, which always had, and still have, the power to define the elements of the existing torts and to find out new ones. Yet, internal divergence is kept under control by many drivers of uniformity across state laws—from the alignment of law schools and legal scholarship in teaching and debating the fundamentals of tort law with little interest to the law applied in the different states, to the nationwide influence of the defense- and plaintiff-bar, to the harmonizing role played by the American Law Institute's work through the publication of its Restatements of the Law of Torts. Further, in spite of minor state variations, the tort law process in the United States has largely developed out of, and has contributed to the development of, specific procedural features, such as the adversarial system, the presence of the jury, the availability of collective actions, the practice of contingent fees (some of which, somewhat ironically, were originally transplanted from England and then flourished in the United States, while largely falling into disuse in their homeland[61]). While many of these features—first and foremost the jury—makes American tort law quite exceptional among the systems herein studied, the creative forces that propel American tort law developments have made it an unavoidable reference point, either positive or negative, for tort laws elsewhere.[62]

[61] Magnus (n 22) 120. The case of the jury is particularly illustrative of this historical trajectory: while omnipresent at the dawn of the common law, the jury has nowadays survived in England only in cases of fraud, malicious prosecution, and false imprisonment (see s 69 of the Supreme Court Act 1981). Until 2013 there was a presumption in favor of trial by jury also in defamation cases, which was however abolished by s 11 of the Defamation Act of 2013.

[62] Magnus (n 22) 119–120.

II

Negligence (and Strict Liability)

1. Introduction

As the reader knows, there is a long-standing quarrel on whether liability was historically based on fault or simply on damage and causation.[1] According to the latter view, in the process of allocation of responsibility, "primitive" legal cultures disregarded the subjective, individual, "moral" aspects of conduct, which by contrast underlie the very idea of liability in modern societies.[2] Others emphasize the historical inaccuracy and oversimplifying analysis underpinning this "evolutionary" scheme and its all-too-linear narration that

[1] Cf John H Wigmore, "Responsibility for Tortious Acts: Its History" (1894) 7 Harv LR 315–337, 383–404, 441–463; James B Ames, "Law and Morals" (1908) 22 Harv LR 97; Oliver W Holmes, *The Common Law* (Little Brown 1923) 66, 111; Reinhard Zimmermann, *The Law of Obligations: Roman Foundations of the Civilian Tradition* (OUP 1996) 907–1142; David J Ibbetson, "The Tort of Negligence in the Common Law in the Nineteenth and Twentieth Century," in Eltjo JH Schrage (ed), *Negligence: The Comparative Legal History of the Law of Torts* (Duncker & Humblot 2001) 229–271; John Bell & David J Ibbetson (eds), *Comparative Studies in the Development of the Law of Torts in Europe* (6 vols, CUP 2010).

[2] Eg, Rudolf von Jhering, *Das Schuldmoment in römischen Privatrecht* (E Roth 1867) 8–9, 20; Roscue Pound, *The Spirit of the Common Law* (Beacon Press 1963—original edn 1921) 5, 140–141. See also John G Fleming, *The Law of Torts* (8th edn, The Law Book Co Ltd 1992) 327; André Tunc, "Introduction - Torts," in *International Encyclopedia of Comparative Law* (Mohr 1972), vol 11, ch 1, 63, 75.

Common Law and Civil Law Perspectives on Tort Law. Mauro Bussani, Anthony J. Sebok, & Marta Infantino, Oxford University Press.
DOI: 10.1093/oso/9780195368383.003.0002

neglects the manifold turns, variations, and refinements history and geography produced in the different forms of tort liability.[3]

This is not the place to survey in detail the contents of the debate. Yet, the fact remains that, in the aftermath of World War II, "[a]s votes started to matter [...] [i]ndifference to the weak and the needy was something that few politicians could afford to display."[4] Especially in societies where social welfare has become a common value and a distinctive political goal, increasing attention has been paid to the need of shifting accident losses by widely distributing their cost.[5] This attitude certainly pervaded the development of continental tort laws, where the expansion of liability (for omissions and) without fault have been seen also as pursuing the overall goal of social solidarity, a pillar of the so-called social market economy.[6] Such a creed

[3] See for instance Stephen G Gilles, "Inevitable Accident in Classical English Tort Law" (1994) 43 Emory LJ 575, 576; Robert L Rabin, "The Historical Development of the Fault Principle: A Reinterpretation" (1981) 15 Ga LR 925, 959–961. See also Yvonne Salmon, "Technological Change and the Development of Liability for Fault in Italy," in Miquel Martín-Casals (ed), *The Development of Liability in Relation to Technological Change* (OUP 2010) 89, 114–117; Jed H Shugerman, "A Watershed Moment: Reversals of Tort Theory in the Nineteenth Century" (2008) 2 J Tort L 1, 36; John M Kleeberg, "'From Strict Liability to Workers' Compensation: The Prussian Railroad Law, the German Liability Act and the Introduction of Bismarck's Accident Insurance in Germany, 1838–1884" (2003) 36 NYU J Int'l L&Pol 53–132; Andrea Cazzetta, *Responsabilità aquiliana e frammentazione del diritto comune civilistico (1865–1914)* (Giuffrè 1991) 427–447.

[4] Simon Deakin & Zoe Adams, *Markesinis and Deakin's Tort Law* (8th edn, OUP 2019) 45. See also Fleming (n 2) 327: "Public opinion became—because it could afford to be—more social minded."

[5] See John CP Goldberg, "Twentieth Century Tort Theory" (2003) 91 Geo LJ 513–584, at 524: "By empowering plaintiffs to commence suits that would be litigated for the most part under the objective reasonableness standard, the common law of tort had come to delegate power to judges and juries to legislate on matters of social policy. [...] Tort suits thus ceased to be "cases and controversies" adjudicated under law and became instead occasions for judges and juries to regulate behavior on a forward-looking basis. In sum, tort had transformed itself from private to "public" law, whereby it functioned to achieve collective, not corrective, justice." See also Gregory C Keating, "Is Tort Law 'Private'?," in Paul B Miller & John Oberdiek (eds), *Civil Wrongs and Justice in Private Law* (OUP 2020) 351–372; John Bell & David Ibbetson, *European Legal Development. The Case of Tort* (CUP 2012) 59–66, 161–162, 173–175; Robert L Rabin, "Some Thoughts on the Ideology of Enterprise Liability Theory" (1996) 55 Md LR 1190, 1193; Leon Green, "Tort Law Public Law in Disguise. Part I" (1959) 38 Tex LR 1–13; Leon Green, "Tort Law Public Law in Disguise. Part II" (1960) 38 Tex LR 257–269.

[6] Christian von Bar, *The Common European Law of Torts* (II, OUP 2000) 346. The pressure upon tort law remedies obviously decreases whenever automatic compensation for all or part of the loss, such as medical expenses and loss of earnings, is provided by social security schemes or similar official programs. Indeed, in many countries, accident victims' medical expenses are paid by the appropriate general health insurance agency (and that agency may then have a subrogation claim against the wrongdoer). For a general discussion, see Daniel Jutras, "Alternative Compensation Schemes from a Comparative Perspective," in Mauro Bussani & Anthony J Sebok (eds), *Comparative Tort Law. Global Perspectives* (2nd edn, EE 2021) 140–158; Thierry Vansweevelt & Britt Weyts (eds), *Compensation Funds in Comparative Perspective* (Intersentia 2020); GRERCA, *La socialisation de la réparation: fonds d'indemnisation et assurances* (Bruylant 2015); Anthony J Sebok, "What's Law Got to Do with It? Designing Compensation Schemes in the Shadow of the Tort System" (2013) 53 DePaul LR 501–525; Willem H van Boom & Michael Faure (eds), *Shifts in Compensation between Private and Public Systems* (Springer 2007); Ulrich Magnus (ed), *The Impact of Social Security Law on Tort Law* (Springer 2003).

has not been shared by the common law jurisdictions so far. In the latter jurisdictions, strict liability for breach of contract promotes the freedom of commercial actors to do business through contract, but is not supposed to restrain their freedom to cause harm to those outside the contract. Yet, even there, besides ever-lasting debates vividly discussing the possible expansion of the scope of strict liability (as to, eg, enterprise liability[7]), the role of negligence has undergone a significant transformation, from that of watchdog of physical injuries, to a legal container filled with explicit policy considerations, which are open to absorb, albeit only slowly and incrementally, the need of protection for interests different from property, life, and limb.[8]

2. From Absolute Liability to Negligence

In all legal systems reviewed in this book there is a widespread awareness that the various situations where liability is possible end up as arrayed along a single, broad scale. Along this graduated scale the role of the defendant's conduct is assessed as a factor that can, or cannot at all, affect the imposition of liability, moving from cases in which the proof of actual intent is required toward those cases involving so-called absolute liability.[9]

The latter, as a form of liability resting on a merely factual test of causation, is extremely rare.[10] Tort law literature refers to it when liability is imposed in respect of technical risks that are *a priori* deemed susceptible of causing catastrophic harm.[11] The most common example is drawn from the international liability regimes for damages arising from the exploitation of nuclear

[7] See George L Priest, "The Invention of Enterprise Liability: A Critical History of the Intellectual Foundations of Modern Tort Law" (1985) 14 J Leg Stud 461–527; Rabin (n 3) 925–961; see also Gregory C Keating, "The Theory of Enterprise Liability and Common Law Strict Liability" (2001) 54 Vand LR 1285, 1290.

[8] For a similar account, with regard to the United States legal framework, see Gary T Schwartz, "The Character of Early American Tort Law" (1989) 36 UCLA LR 641–718; Gary T Schwartz, "The Beginning and the Possible End of the Rise of Modern American Tort Law" (1992) 26 Ga LR 601, esp 699–700.

[9] See the survey of the debate in von Bar (n 6) 202–210, 336–398.

[10] Franz Werro, Vernon V Palmer, & Anne-Catherine Hahn, "Synthesis and Survey of the Cases and Results," in Franz Werro & Vernon V Palmer (eds), *The Boundaries of Strict Liability in European Tort Law* (Carolina Academic Press 2004) 387, 456–457.

[11] Ibid; Stephen R Perry, "Risk, Harm, and Responsibility," in David G Owen (ed), *Philosophical Foundations of Tort Law* (OUP 1997) 321, 340–341; European Group on Tort Law (EGTL), *Principles of European Tort Law* (Springer 2005) 102–103.

energy.[12] Yet, under these regimes too the absoluteness of liability is tempered by many limiting factors.[13]

Outside the small coverage of absolute liability, there is a long list of activities that entail high risks of harm, which frequently materialize (with or without "catastrophic" consequences), and sometimes despite all possible precautions. The use of criteria such as those grounded on the foreseeability, or avoidability of the specific harm, appears ill-suited to a tort law scrutiny of these activities. Thus, whenever the latter are to be put on their way to liability, the most common reaction of the legal systems is to make this liability rest not on negligence, but on the so-called strict liability.[14] In principle, under a rule of strict liability a defendant can avoid liability only if she proves that the accident was caused by a third person, by the victim herself, or by an "act of God." However, reliance on the expression "strict liability" and its equivalent in other languages is in some ways unfortunate. Some tort actions that are today taken to fall within the category of strict liability share important features of negligence law, which has generated a good deal of terminological

[12] See the 1960 Paris Convention on Third Party Liability in the Field of Nuclear Energy, and the 1963 Vienna Convention on Civil Liability for Nuclear Damage. The former was adopted under the auspices of Nuclear Energy Agency and covers sixteen European countries, while the latter was promoted by the International Atomic Energy Agency, and has been ratified by forty-three states from all the world's regions (see, respectively, oecd-nea.org/jcms/pl_31798/paris-convention-latest-status-of-ratifications-or-accession and legacy.iaea.org/Publications/Documents/Conventions/liability_status.pdf). Even with regard to nuclear accidents, however, nuclear operators' liability does not extend to all possible risks. First of all, under art 3(a) of the Paris Convention and art I (1) (k) of the Vienna Convention, the nuclear operator is not liable neither for pure economic losses, nor for damage to the nuclear installation itself, on-site property, and means of transport of the nuclear material. Secondly, the operator is not liable for damage caused by a nuclear incident due to an act of armed conflict, hostilities, civil war, insurrection, or grave natural disaster of an exceptional character (art 9 Paris Convention, and art IV (3) (a) Vienna Convention). Thirdly, both the conventions set a cap for liability (art 7 Paris Convention, and art V Vienna Convention). Fourthly, art 6 (c) (ii) of the Paris Convention states that "the operator shall incur no liability outside this Convention for damage caused by a nuclear incident." Fifthly, the Vienna Convention refers to the "law of the competent court" in respect of the possibility to relieve the operator from the obligation to pay compensation for damage suffered by a person who has caused or contributed to causing such damage through gross negligence or an intentional act or omission (art IV (2) Vienna Convention). Sixthly, and notwithstanding the fact that proving damage, especially with regard to long-term personal injury, might be particularly hard (Philippe J Sands, *Chernobyl: Law and Communication* (CUP 1993) 22–30), the plaintiff bears the burden of alleging that the damage was caused by the nuclear incident (see art 3 (a) Paris Convention, and art II.1 Vienna Convention).

[13] See the previous footnote. One should also be aware that it is possible to provide compensation for accident victims through a system that entirely abandons tort concepts, as was done in New Zealand. See Peter Cane, "Searching for United States Tort Law in the Antipodes" (2011) Pepp LR 257–282; Stephen MD Todd, "Privatization of Accident Compensation: Policy and Politics in New Zealand" (2000) 39 Washburn LJ 404–495; Richard Mahoney, "New Zealand's Accident Compensation Scheme: A Reassessment" (1992) 40 AJCL 159–211; Craig Brown, "Deterrence in Tort and No-Fault: The New Zealand Experience" (1985) 73 Cal LR 976–1002.

[14] See Fleming (n 2) 328–333.

confusion.[15] To skirt possible confusions, some attempts have been made to replace "strict liability" with phrases such as liability "without fault" or "without personal misconduct."[16] Nominal refinements, however, do not solve problems. In any legal systems, there are so many crossovers, common elements, and mere shiftings of nuance between the various liability models that it appears impossible to force them all unto the same representation.

3. Outline of the Chapter

In a book whose main ambition is to pave the way to future in-depth discussions, there are three issues that deserve the spotlight in this chapter. All of them are worth noting because, in a comparative law perspective, they highlight not a divergent stream between national jurisdictions, but a common trend dictated by the similarities of cultural approaches, which overcome technical differences—be they stemming from legislative provisions, judicial rules, or theoretical views.

The issues to be discussed have to do with the way tort liability is usually approached. To our purposes we shall equate the phrase "negligence liability" to the continental meaning of *responsabilité pour faute*, *responsabilità per colpa*, *Verschuldenshaftung*, and "strict liability" to the continental meaning of *responsabilité de plein droit*, *responsabilità oggettiva*, and *Gefährdungshaftung*. All these notions differ, of course,[17] but these differences may sometimes be more apparent than actually influential on the judicial solutions, and other times even though considerable, these differences are irrelevant to the perspective pursued in the following pages. On this assumption, we will first (sections 4 to 5) briefly address the traditional and still widespread (especially in, but not exclusive to, civil law jurisdictions[18]) understanding of the

[15] John CP Goldberg, Leslie C Kendrick, Anthony J Sebok, & Benjamin C Zipursky, *Tort Law: Responsibilities and Redress* (5th edn, Wolters Kluwer 2021) 869–871.

[16] For the latter phrase, see, eg, Christian von Bar, "Non-Contractual Liability Arising Out of Damage Caused to Another" (Sellier 2009) 7–10.

[17] For a comparative analysis, see James Gordley, Hao Jiang, & Arthur T von Mehren, *An Introduction to the Comparative Study of Private Law* (2nd edn, CUP 2020) 459–464; James Gordley, *Foundations of Private Law. Property, Tort, Contract, Unjust Enrichment* (OUP 2006), 159, 196–204; Walter van Gerven, Jeremy Lever, & Pierre Larouche, *Cases, Materials and Text on National, Supranational and International Tort Law* (Hart 2000) 44–74; Christian von Bar, *The Common European Law of Torts* (I, OUP 1998) 6–8, 20–39, 281–282, 297–305; Pierre Catala & J Anthony Weir, "Delict and Torts: A Study in Parallel. Part I" (1963) 37 Tulane LR 574, 589–598.

[18] Common lawyers show greater awareness of the problems herein addressed. For a critique of the "conceptual structure of negligence," see Jane Stapleton, "Controlling the Future of the Common Law by Restatement," in M Stuart Madden (ed), *Exploring Tort Law* (CUP 2005) 262, 268–272; Tony Weir,

elements of the tort cause of action. This is the tendency to represent each of the elements as a separate and independent variable with a distinctive role of its own in establishing the facts and bearing upon the solution.[19] We call this the "modular" approach.

Secondly (sections 6 to 10), we will challenge the normative view according to which, under a rule of fault liability, a person's behavior should conform to the standard of care expected of the so-called reasonable person, a fictitious individual traditionally endowed with conventional knowledge, average musculature, normal reactions, commonplace skills, and ordinary intelligence and memory. We will refer to this view as the "person without qualities" (PWQ) rule.

A Casebook on Tort (10th edn, Sweet & Maxwell 2004) 6–18. Fleming (n 2) 103 criticizes the great "number of artificial concepts, like 'duty of care' and 'remoteness of damage'" invented by judges to allocate liability within the framework of the cause of action for negligence. See also Jerome Frank, *Law and the Modern Mind* (Peter Smith 1970, repr 1963, original edn 1930) 30, who notes that negligence is but one of many words of common usage which have "the vaguest meaning" but are nevertheless used as though they "had a precise and clear definition," so as to create "an appearance of continuity, uniformity and definiteness which does not in fact exist"; along the same lines, Jane Stapleton, "Evaluating Goldberg and Zipursky's Civil Recourse Theory" (2006) 75 Fordham LR 1529, 1559–1562; John CP Goldberg & Benjamin C Zipursky, "Accidents of the Great Society," 64 Md LR 364, 367–370, 381–384, 386–395 (2005); John A Jolowicz, "Procedural Questions," in *International Encyclopedia of Comparative Law* (Mohr 1972), vol XI, ch 13, 34.

[19] See, eg, Peter Cane & James Goudkamp, *Atiyah's Accidents, Compensation and the Law* (9th edn, CUP 2018) 40–41; Grégoire Maitre, *La responsabilité civile à l'épreuve de l'analyse économique du droit* (LGDJ 2005) 82–85; Fleming (n 2) 106–124; André Tunc, *La responsabilité civile* (2nd edn, Economica 1981) 109–112; K Larenz, *Lehrbuch des Schuldrechts* (I, 14th edn, Beck 1987) 289 ff; Jean Limpens, Robert M Kruithof, & Anne Meinertzhagen, "Liability for One's Own Act," in *International Encyclopedia of Comparative Law* (Mohr 1983), vol XI, ch II, 13–15; Edward Green, "The Reasonable Man: Legal Fiction or Psychosocial Reality?" (1968) 2 L&Soc'y R 241–257; Noël Dejean de la Batie, *Appréciation in abstracto et appréciation in concreto en droit civil français* (LGDJ 1965); Erwin Deutsch, *Fahrlässigkeit und erforderliche Sorgfalt: Eine privatrechtliche Untersuchung* (Heymann 1963) 326–327, 329–331, 348–349; Fleming James Jr, "The Qualities of the Reasonable Man in Negligence Cases" (1951) 16 Mo LR 1–26. Among older works see Carlo Fadda, *Il buon padre di famiglia nella teoria della colpa* (Tipografia della Regia Università 1901); William W Buckland, "Diligens paterfamilias," in *Studi in onore di Pietro Bonfante* (II, Fratelli Treves 1930) 85–108. Anton Menger, *Das Bürgerliche Recht und die besitzlosen Volksklassen. Eine Kritik des Entwurfs eines bürgerlichen Gesetzbuches für das deutsche Reich* (H Laupp 1890) 191–198; Alfred Légal, *De la négligence et de l'imprudence comme source de la responsabilité civile délictuelle* (Louve 1922) 70, 115; Alan P Herbert, *Uncommon Law* (Metheum 1935) 2–6, all criticized the paradigm of the "reasonable man/bonus paterfamilias," without identifying an alternative model with any degree of precision.

For the observation that, both in the common law and in the civil law tradition, the "reasonable man/bonus paterfamilias" is traditionally embodied by an idealized and stereotypical white, adult, middle-class, and healthy man, see Guido Calabresi, *Ideals, Beliefs, Attitudes, and the Law: Private Law Perspectives on a Public Law Problem* (Syracuse University Press 1985) 22–25; Mauro Bussani, *La colpa soggettiva. Modelli di valutazione della condotta nella responsabilità extracontrattuale* (Cedam 1991); Caroline A Forell & Donna M Matthews, *A Law of Her Own: The Reasonable Woman as a Measure of Man* (NYU Press 2000) esp 3–7; Mayo Moran, *Rethinking the Reasonable Person. An Egalitarian Reconstruction of the Objective Standard* (OUP 2003) esp 131–163; Martha Chamallas & Jennifer B Wriggins, *The Measure of Injury: Race, Gender, and Tort Law* (NYU Press 2010), 89–117.

The third issue (sections 11 to 12) concerns the operative solutions through which the frontier between fault and strict liability are actually shaped. We will start with the fault-stretching judicial trends, and then survey the tools exploited by courts to reduce the scope of strict liability rules, reserving the scrutiny of other forms of strict liability to Chapters III and VIII, on medical malpractice and products liability, respectively.

4. The Elements of the Cause of Action: The Modular Approach

In a comparative perspective, the usual elements of a tort cause of action can be listed as follows: harm, fault, or the other factor (be it a status, a condition, or an activity) triggering the application of a strict liability rule, causation, abstract recoverability of the damage—the latter depending on the finding of a further quality of either the conduct or the damage, that is, the *illicéité*, the *Rechtswidrigkeit*, the *ingiustizia*, or the breach of a duty of care.

The aforementioned list does not necessarily mirror the order in which the various jurisdictions take on the liability issue, but a common and long-standing tradition[20] presents and analyzes each of these elements as completely separate and independent from one another.[21] This attitude—which will be referred to as the "modular" approach—does not simply shape the description of negligence liability; it also determines the way one thinks of, and actually solves, tort law cases. Following this approach, the nature of the infringed interest should have no bearing on either the determination of the standard of conduct expected of the defendant, or the ascertainment of the causal link. Similarly, the measure of damages shall be determined only by the casual connection between the defendant's activity and its consequences, while fault is to be simply assessed by comparing the difference between the defendant's conduct and that of the so-called reasonable person.

[20] For some caveats, see above, n 18.

[21] See, eg, in the older literature, Auguste Sourdat, *Traité général de la responsabilité* (I, 2nd edn, LGDJ 1872) 417–419, 458; Emanuele Gianturco, *Sistema di diritto civile italiano* (I, 2nd edn, Pierro 1894) 227; Gian Petro Chironi, *Colpa extracontrattuale* (I, 2nd edn, Fratelli Bocca 1903) 48–68, 76–80; René Savatier, *Traité de la responsabilité civile* (I, 2nd edn, LGDJ 1951) 5. More recently, Hermann Lange & Gottfried Schiemann, *Schadensersatz* (3rd edn, Mohr 2003) 9; Geneviève Viney, Patrice Jourdain, & Suzanne Carval, *Les conditions de la responsabilité* (4th edn, LGDJ 2013) 238–239; Maximilian Fuchs, *Deliktsrecht* (4th edn, Springer 2013) 10; Mauro Bussani, *L'illecito civile* (ESI 2020) 161–167.

In other words, under the modular view the establishment or denial of liability is nothing else than the result of a series of analytical assessments, each of which would remain constant and indifferent upon examination of the other components of the cause of action.

Now, no one doubts of the operational destiny of tort law and of the centrality of the role of legal actors in dealing with notions that are necessarily broadly worded. But the elements of a cause of action are factors that cannot be treated as strangers among themselves. The core and the limits of each one of these elements can be understood only through the lenses of the others—and of the other factors that may affect the assessment of the case at issue.[22] It is only by adopting such a perspective that one can understand why the plaintiff may have successfully proven breach of duty, causation, fault, and damage, and yet the defendant escapes liability.[23] It is in the same light that one can explain why the defendant has to pay damages in cases in which, although one or more elements of the cause of action cannot be established, an appreciation of actual circumstances (eg, the relevance of the duty breached by the defendant, or her intentional behavior) compels judges to find for the plaintiff.[24] Every rigid definition that does not come to terms with this interconnection between the elements of the cause of action is therefore doomed to fail, under both the descriptive and the normative point of view.

A good example in this respect—because challenging the self-reassuring approaches widely accepted by legal actors in other jurisdictions—comes from the use of the notion of "duty of care" in the United States experience.[25]

[22] On this point, see, among many others, George L Priest, "The Current Insurance Crisis and Modern Tort Law" (1987) 96 Yale LJ 1521, 1535–1539; Geneviève Viney, *Le déclin de la responsabilité civile* (LGDJ 1967); Bussani (n 21) esp 161–167. From a comparative law perspective, eg, Bill W Dufwa, "Insurance in a European Tort Law Perspective," in Mauro Bussani (ed), *European Tort Law. Eastern and Western Perspectives* (Stämpfli 2007) 133, 144–145; Gert Brüggemeier, *Common Principles of Tort Law* (BIICL 2004) 270–274; Jane Stapleton, "Tort Insurance and Ideology" (1995) 58 Mod LR 819, 824–832 (1995); Basil S Markesinis, "La perversion des notions de responsabilité civile délictuelle par la pratique de l'assurance" (1983) 35 RIDC 301–317; Albert A Ehrenzweig, "Assurance Oblige. A Comparative Study" (1950) 15 L & Cont Probls 445–454.

[23] See further indications (and caveats) in Mauro Bussani & Vernon V Palmer, "The Liability Regimes of Europe – Their Façades and Interiors," in Mauro Bussani & Vernon V Palmer (eds), *Pure Economic Loss in Europe* (CUP 2003) 120, 139–158.

[24] Marta Infantino & Eleni Zervogianni, "Summary and Survey of the Results," in Marta Infantino & Eleni Zervogianni (eds), *Causation in European Tort Law* (CUP 2017) 587, 662–666; Goldberg, Kendrick, Sebok, & Zipursky (n 15) 392–396; see also Glanville Williams, "The Risk Principle" (1961) 77 LQR 179, 201; Jeremiah Smith, "Legal Cause in Actions of Torts" (1912) 26 Harv LR 223, 231.

[25] Among may other possible examples, one can think of the usual representation that continental lawyers make of the role of damages as aiming to reinstate the plaintiff in the status quo ante (Lange & Schiemann (n 21) 9–10; von Bar (n 6) 156–162). As is well known, in common law jurisdictions intentional torts might entail an award of punitive damages. This is so in England (eg, *Rookes v Barnard* [1964] AC 1125–1129 (HL)), and in the United States, where, in the words of the Restatement Third of Torts—PEH, "[w]hile a showing of negligence generally suffices for compensatory damages, the

5. American Duty

Under negligence rules, courts must determine the level of due care as a legal standard in order to see whether the injurer was negligent or not. This is true everywhere, and yet, from a comparative point of view, one should be aware that in the United States the issue is defined in a peculiar way.

The American experience is exceptional, also in the common law world, in the sense that, if the issue in dispute is described as a question of fact, be it concerning breach of the duty of care or scope of liability, that issue will be for a jury.[26] This means that the decision on that point, at least in principle, will be protected from appellate review (leaving aside certain especially high hurdles available to the parties on appeal), and it will not provide per se any

standard for awarding punitive damages commonly refers to the defendant's reckless conduct—or reckless indifference to risk, or reckless disregard for risk" (Restatement Third of Torts—PEH, Section 2, cmt b). By contrast, the notion is essentially rejected in continental tort law jurisdictions and the EU institutions have taken a negative approach toward them (see Regulation (EC) no 864/2007 of the European Parliament and of the Council on the law applicable to non-contractual obligations (Rome II), 11 July 2007, whereas 32). Yet, the defendant's ill-will does sometimes lead the courts to revive civil punishment—even though on a selective and situational basis, and through devices that do not correspond to the punitive damages (label and) technicalities. For instance, in Germany, in case of grave violations of personal dignity by the press, it is maintained that it would be useless to impose only compensatory damages on journals who invent scandalous interviews with real people to improve circulation: the sums awarded would be considered trifling. Accordingly, the German BGH decided that "the notion of prevention demands that resultant profits be taken into account in calculating the quantum of damages" (BGH 15 November 1994, NJW 1995, 861). Since the first half of the nineteenth century, French courts have employed the partly punitive, partly coercive concept of *astreinte* (which has then made its way into statutory law: see now Articles L131-1 and ff of the *Code des procédures civiles d'exécution*), according to which a judgement debtor may be sanctioned with a fine for each day of noncompliance with a court order. The level of the fine, depending on all the circumstances of the case and especially on the gravity and obstinacy of the defendant's refusal to perform, may be fixed (by the Court) and collected (by the obligee) in an amount exceeding the plaintiff's actual damage. Many provisions allow an Italian judge to order the defendant to pay a specified total sum or a per diem sum as a penalty for failure to comply promptly with judicial orders in the field of trademark infringements (see now art 124, Law no 30 of 2005), anti-consumer behavior (art 140, Law no 206 of 2005), wrongful dismissal (art 18, Law no 300 of 1970), and specific performance (art 614bis, Code of Civil Procedure); in cases of defamation and intentional injury to property, courts awarding damages to the plaintiff should also charge the defendant with the payment of an additional fine to the state as a form of punishment which would deter further misbehavior (arts 3–11, Legislative Decree no 7 of 2016). Further, Italy, as other European countries, implemented the Directive 2004/48/EC of the European Parliament and of the Council of 29 April 2004 on the enforcement of intellectual property rights, allowing the victim of an infringement of an intellectual property right to sue its author for (what a common lawyer would dub) disgorgement of profits: see Ewoud Hondius & André Janssen, "Disgorgement of Profits: Gain-Based Remedies Throughout the World," in Martin Schauer & Bea Verschraegen (eds), *General Reports of the XIXth Congress of the International Academy of Comparative Law* (Springer 2017) 115, 123–125.

[26] Juries have disappeared from common law trials in civil matters everywhere else: see John G Fleming, *The Law of Torts* (8th edn, The Law Book Co 1992) 308–313. See also Chapter I, section 8; and Chapter VII, section 3.

precedent in the future. But establishing duty is a matter of law for the court, and whatever factual features potentially allowing for a relaxation of the no-duty rule also become a matter of law for the court and not the jury. In other terms, the modular approach expresses itself through the airtight isolation of a single component of the cause of action: the duty, and the decision on it, in turn, controls over all the other elements.

Such a division of labor is well illustrated by the comments to the (much debated[27]) section 7 on "duty" in the Restatement Third of Torts—Liability for Physical and Emotional Harm (PEH). In personal injuries cases, there usually exists a duty to exercise reasonable care to avoid causing physical harm. Yet, when reasons of principle or policy dictate that liability should not be imposed, courts might

> use the rubric of duty to apply general categorical rules withholding liability. For example, a number of modern cases involve efforts to impose liability on social hosts for serving alcohol to their guests. A jury might plausibly find the social host negligent in providing alcohol to a guest who will depart in an automobile. Nevertheless, imposing liability is potentially problematic because of its impact on a substantial slice of social relations. Courts appropriately address whether such liability should be permitted as a matter of duty.[28]

Following a restraining perspective, the doctrine of duty, in spite of judicial inconsistencies and scholarly disagreements about its role and content,[29] enables courts (especially appellate courts) to elaborate firm no-duty rules of wide precedential influence, thereby controlling the scope of the tort of

[27] On the terms of such a debate, see John CP Goldberg & Benjamin C Zipursky, "Shielding Duty: How Attending to Assumption of Risk, Attractive Nuisance, and Other 'Quaint' Doctrines Can Improve Decisionmaking in Negligence Cases" (2006) 79 So Cal LR 329–361; John CP Goldberg & Benjamin C Zipursky, "The Restatement (Third) and the Place of Duty in Negligence Law" (2001) 54 Vand LR 657–750 (criticizing the drafters of the Restatement Third PEH for their refusal to treat duty as a matter of substantive obligation and the limited role they assigned to the duty element); for some responses to such criticism, cp W Jonathan Cardi & Michael D Green, "Duty Wars" (2008) 81 So Cal LR 671–733; Dilan A Esper & Gregory C Keating, "Putting 'Duty' in Its Place: A Reply to Professors Goldberg and Zipursky" (2008) 41 Loy LA LR 1225–1293; Dilan A Esper & Gregory C Keating, "Abusing 'Duty'" (2006) 79 So Cal LR 265–328.

[28] Restatement Third of Torts—PEH, Section 7, cmt a; see also Stapleton, "Controlling the Future" (n 18) 262; Mark P Gergen, "The Jury's Role in Deciding Normative Issues in the American Common Law" (1999) 68 Fordham LR 407, 430.

[29] For an account of both, see W Jonathan Cardi, "The Hidden Legacy of Palsgraf: Modern Duty Law in Microcosm" (2011) 91 BU LR 1873–1913; Alani Golanski, "A New Look at Duty in Tort Law: Rehabilitating Foreseeability and Related Themes" (2011) 75 Alb LR 227–278.

negligence. In its turn, the use of no-duty rules, garnished with fact-sensitive exceptions, may then be exploited by appellate courts also to regulate "unorthodox" first instance rulings. In sum, folding (most of) the ingredients of the cause of action in the "duty" mixer, and thus preserving the issue from the jury, appears to be the most effective way American courts can disallow recovery and control any undesired expansion of liability.[30] But even more important, from our perspective, is to highlight how this very attitude denies, in and of itself, any actual role one would think proper to the modular approach.

6. The Standard of Care—or the "Person without Quality" Rule

The very acknowledgment that a close relationship exists between the elements of the cause of action should suggest that, in America as elsewhere, no theory of liability can be taken seriously if it views each of these elements as autonomous and independent. Nor can one expect that the very core of the negligence cause of action, the notion of fault, might be exclusively approached in isolation, in the abstract, rudimentary terms afforded by the reasonable person/person without quality standard. The following explains why.

The "person without qualities" (PWQ) rule is widely used to measure, under the circumstances, the deviation of a person's behavior from the expected standard. The rule finds its way across all jurisdictions. To speak modern history, the rule has been rooted in common law since *Vaughan v Menlove*,[31] where C. J. Tindal observed:

> instead [...] of saying that the liability for negligence should be co-extensive with the judgment of each individual, which would be as variable as the length of the foot of each individual, we ought rather to adhere to the rule

[30] Among others, see Peter W Huber, *The Legal Revolution and Its Consequences* (Basic Books 1988); Walter K Olsen, *The Litigation Explosion. What Happened when America Unleashed the Lawsuit* (Truman Talley 1991); see also (although in much less critical terms), Kenneth S Abraham, *The Liability Century: Insurance and Tort Law from the Progressive Era To 9/11* (Harvard University Press 2008) esp 1–13.

[31] [1837] 132 Eng Rep 490 (CP).

> which requires in all cases a regard to caution such as a man of ordinary prudence would observe.[32]

But the rule is also enshrined in many civil codes, such as the German BGB, where § 276 II reads: "a person acts negligently if he fails to exercise reasonable care." Along the same lines one can find article 1176 of the Italian Civil Code, article 1903(6) of the Spanish Civil Code, and scores of civilian authorities.[33]

There is little effort, however, to qualify the stereotype. Is he or she, Caucasian, adult, healthy, not too old (nor pregnant)? Is the benchmark grounded on what (the judge—or the jury—think) the majority or the average member of the society would or should do? No more clear-cut solution can be found when one takes the approach suggesting that whether a person's conduct is negligent depends on whether the aggregate risks (expected losses or costs) created by the conduct are greater than its overall utility (in terms of expected social gains or benefits).[34] What seems certain is this: (a) that following any of the above approaches the judge should compare the defendant's conduct with a general model whose features could be defined in abstract terms. But if one asks, "In what terms?," the answer is (b) that civil and common law rules all call on the judge to ignore the characteristics peculiar to the individual on trial.[35] What should be taken into account are only the "external" characteristics of the wrongdoer, together with the time and place in which she caused the fact under dispute to occur.

We have now to highlight the merits of this model, but also to show how it falls short of the reality it aims to describe and create.

[32] Id at 494. Further references in W Page Keeton et al (eds), *Prosser and Keaton on the Law of Torts* (5th edn, West 1984) 173–175. See also Restatement Third of Torts—PEH, Section 3: "A person acts negligently if the person does not exercise reasonable care under all the circumstances."

[33] See Bénédict Winiger, Ernst Karner, & Ken Oliphant (eds), *Digest of European Tort Law. Essential Cases on Misconduct* (de Gruyter 2018) 21–105; Bussani (n 19) 1–6.

[34] See, eg, Fleming (n 2) 114–19; Keeton et al (n 32) 170–173 and fn 46; Cane & Goudcamp (n 19) 39–44; Patrick J Kelley, Teaching Torts: "The Carroll Towing Company Case and the Teaching of Tort Law" (2001) 45 St Louis U LJ 731, 732–35 & fns 4–5. Cf van Gerven, Lever, & Larouche (n 17) 305 and fn 107; and, for a critical appraisal, Robert L Rabin, "The Legacy of Five Landmarks in Tort Law," in Madden (n 18) 52, 74–75; Richard W Wright, "Justice and Reasonable Care in Negligence Law" (2002) 47 Am J Juris 143, 150–58, 167–194; Richard W Wright, "Hand, Posner, and the Myth of the 'Hand Formula'" (2003) 4 Theo Inq L 145–274.

[35] This principle appears to only recognize one exception, namely that those whose overall capacity is incompatible with adopting the operational standards required of the person of ordinary diligence, are wholly or partly exempt from liability. This applies particularly to young children and the mentally infirm. But on this "exception," see below, n 43, and accompanying text.

7. The Judge's Perspective

The commonly accepted model is startling in its simplicity,[36] for at least in appearance its application is quick and transparent. Judges' discretion about the interpretation of the factual circumstances comes along with the responsibility of seeking to limit the distortions which would be produced by an "excessive" attention (paid by themselves or by the juries) to the unstable and variable individual features of the defendant. From this perspective, the possible implications of a judge's proximity to the facts, and their peculiarities, need to be counterbalanced. Thus, the judge may stress his impartiality by obliterating or concealing any degree of respect she might pay to the wrongdoer's subjective peculiarities, showing loyalty to the accepted rule instead.

The neglect for the subjective profiles of tort is understandable in view of the limits and constraints of decision-making. A decision venturing too far from the importance averagely attributed to the wrongdoer's aptitudes and/or ineptitudes could unlikely survive the scrutiny of the court of appeal, whose judges usually are facts-remote and may be less inclined to approve of departures from the standard. Further restrictions to decision-making come from the opportunity of channeling juries' assessments (in the United States),[37] or from the need to ground judicial conclusions on precedents vested with authority within the circle of one's peers that ensure that the decision will encounter their favor (a concern shared by all courts, regardless of location).[38]

Within this framework, reliance on the measure of care of the man endowed with standard qualities is a device which may help uniformize the appearance of judicial solutions. The advantages of this parameter include a simpler search for the applicable rule and the possibility of portraying the judge (and her judgment) in a more socially acceptable and less individualistic light. The use of the paradigm, in other words, not only increases the predictability of judgments, but also contributes to earning them the approval of both one's peers and laymen.

[36] The remark can be read in Nicholas Kasirer, "The infans as bon père de famille: 'Objectively Wrongful Conduct' in the Civil Law Tradition" (1992) 40 AJCL 343, 370.

[37] Restatement Third of Torts—PEH, Section 3, cmt f ("As far as instructing the jury is concerned, pattern jury instructions frequently explain the negligence standard in terms of the reasonably prudent person").

[38] Mauro Bussani & Vernon V Palmer, "The Recoverability of Pure Economic Loss in Europe within the Perspective of a European codification," in Bussani & Palmer (n 23) 537, 544–546.

8. The Rationale Underlying the PWQ Rule

The premises underlying the PWQ rule rest on shaky grounds, yet at the policy level, several functions traditionally attributed to "objective" fault end up being frustrated in the adjudication of liability, if that notion is applied to persons whose characteristics are, so to speak, "weaker" or "stronger," when compared to those of the average/majority[39] member of society. At the practical level, we will see that case law ends up contradicting any aspiration to apply an immutable objective standard to the above subjects.

Let us first take on the policy argument, starting with the "stronger" wrongdoers. When applied to the conduct of subjects endowed with a physical and/or intellectual potential higher than the average person, the shortcomings inherent in applying a common standard, that is, the PWQ rule, are easy to understand. Should defendants endowed with special skills that could have enabled them to foresee and/or prevent the occurrence of the harm, be exempt from liability? Whenever the availability to the wrongdoer of specific information, a privileged cultural background, professional expertise, or any outstanding physical attributes are established, the question should become whether those features would have made it possible for the particular individual to adopt levels of care which cannot be expected of the reasonable person—and the answer should be considered decisive in establishing or denying liability upon the specific individual on trial. In the words of the Restatement Third of Torts—PEH, Section 12,

> [i]f an actor has skills or knowledge that exceed those possessed by most others, these skills or knowledge are circumstances to be taken into account in determining whether the actor has behaved as a reasonably careful person.[40]

[39] On the distinction between average, reasonable, and rational standard of care, see Goldberg (n 5) 523; Rabin (n 3) 931; Gregory C Keating, "Reasonableness and Rationality in Negligence Theory" (1996) 48 Stan L Rev 311–384.

[40] Section 12; see also Restatement Second of Torts, Section 289, cmt m: The standard of the reasonable man requires only a minimum of attention, perception, memory, knowledge, intelligence, and judgment in order to recognize the existence of the risk. If the actor has in fact more than the minimum of these qualities, he is required to exercise the superior qualities that he has in a manner reasonable under the circumstances. The standard becomes, in other words, that of a reasonable man with such superior attributes.

No less debatable are the results shepherded by the traditional rule as to those persons who are weaker than the average, that is, minors, the elderly, and those who suffer from a physical or psychological disability. For a start, applying the objective standard to these people is hardly reconcilable with the general principle of substantial equality before the law.[41] From this principle one should derive interpretive criteria which, when applied to the law of tort, could guarantee an equal respect and the protection of the fundamental rights of minors, the elderly, or the diversely able.[42] More particularly, to impose upon these persons the PWQ rule means to compel them to exercise a harsh choice between inactivity and the exposure to a higher risk of (and possible higher insurance costs for) liability than that faced by "ordinary" people for the same actions. The rule, in other words, would be, "stay put or pay."[43] Further, as far as omissions are concerned, it is quite evident that any right to abstain/duty to intervene materialize very differently as regards "weaker" subjects and average, healthy adults. It is common knowledge—even for those who frame omissions into a broader notion of liability, based on ideas of mutual solidarity[44]—that the duty to take a reasonable action arises from a pre-assessment of a situation, carried out by the legal system in terms of the greater utility of an active behavior, compared to that of a passive one, in any given situation. It follows that the parameter commonly employed to assess whether a behavior is socially advantageous, or to determine the cost of an individual effort of self-activation, is hardly compatible with a standardized obligation to intervene, with which a child or disabled person could be burdened. For these persons, obeying that command not only entails greater

[41] On the equality of treatment issue, usually approached with exclusive regard to the victims of the wrong, and on the limits of this perspective, see Avihay Dorfman, "Reasonable Care: Equality as Objectivity" (2012) 31 L&Phil 369–407; John G Fleming, *The American Tort Process* (Clarendon Press 1988) 26–31, 169–174, 265–266.

[42] On the reasons for which many European jurisdictions (among them, France, and, to a lesser extent, Germany and Italy) treat childhood and long-lasting mental impairments as unaffecting the assessment of fault, see Werro & Palmer (n 10) 389; Miquel Martín-Casals (ed), *Children in Tort Law. Part I: Children as Tortfeasors* (Springer 2006) 427–428. A similar solution is adopted in many common law jurisdictions: see Werro & Palmer (n 10) 97–98; Goldberg, Kendrick, Sebok, & Zipursky (n 15) 189–193. For some remarks questioning the actual applications of these rules (and their abstract rationale), see Mauro Bussani, "Responsabilité des sujets atteints de troubles mentaux en Italie et en common law," Gaz Pal 1997, no 45–46, 11–13.

[43] For similar considerations, see Kasirer (n 37) 369–371; Calabresi (n 19) 25–44; James (n 19) 1, 17–26.

[44] This is a typical continental view. Cfr Gert Brüggemeier, "Gesellschaftliche Schadensverteilung und Deliktsrecht" (1982) 182 AcP 385–452; Guido Alpa, *Il problema dell'atipicità dell'illecito* (ESI 1979) 127–176; Paul Appleton, "L'abstension fautive en matière délictuelle civile et pénale" (1912) RTD civ 593, 606–607. But see also, in the common law scenario, Warren F Schwartz, "Objective and Subjective Standards of Negligence: Defining the Reasonable Person to Induce Optimal Care and Optimal Populations of Injurers and Victims" (1989) 78 Geo LJ 241–279.

energy expenditure than for the average person, but often results in an inefficient outcome, and in an increased risk of harm to third parties, following the imperfect completion of that activity.[45]

9. Variable Standards

The above normative arguments do not stand alone. If strong policy reasons align with the idea that the adjudication of liability process should be open to include any fragile or "better" features of the tortfeasor, judicial solutions, in their turn, show acute awareness of the need to introduce some degree of flexibility into the fault parameter. Although its shape and configuration varies, this ductility can be reconducted to three broad categories.

First (a), it goes without saying that many assessments of the standard of conduct merely look at the factual link between the occurrence of the harm and its author, thereby disregarding any possible subjective feature of the harmdoer. Thus, the threshold of the required standard of care may be remarkably raised without its metric be altered. This is often the case when the person who caused the damage (and whose conduct is to be evaluated) is not the same person who will be finally held to compensate the victim (an example comes from the fault of infants, lunatics, and employees, when it entails guardian's, supervisor's, or employer's liability[46]). But this may also be the case when the damage is the result of the failure to obey specific and detailed rules prescribing or forbidding that particular conduct—an example is given by the English fault-based car accidents liability.[47]

Secondly (b), there is a majority of situations where fault is established by comparing the defendant's conduct with the objective, abstractly conceptualized behavior expected of the reasonable person under the circumstances. This model—the PWQ rule—is usually applied whenever the interest

[45] See, on similar lines, Bussani (n 21) 513–518; Dejean de la Batie (n 19) 149–152.

[46] On the "objective" assessment of fault with regard to employees, see the cases quoted by Gyula Eörsi, "Private and Governmental Liability for the Torts of Employees and Organs," in *International Encyclopedia of Comparative Law* (Mohr 1972), vol XI, ch 4, 60–61; as to children and persons affected by long-lasting mental impairments, see Martín-Casals (n 43) 427–428; Werro & Palmer (n 10) 389; Franz Werro, "L'homme raisonnable a perdu sa pipe," in Peter Gauch & Pascal Pichonnaz (eds), *Figures Juridiques/Rechtsfiguren: Mélanges Dissociés pour Pierre Tercier* (Schulthess 2003) 109–120; Goldberg, Kendrick, Sebok, & Zipursky (n 15) 189–193.

[47] See below, n 73, and accompanying text.

pursued by the wrongdoer through her activity is not worthy of particular protection when compared to the victim's infringed interest.[48]

Thirdly (c), there are patterns of assessment pursuant to which greater attention is paid to a personal or subjective notion of defendant's fault. This type of assessment recurs frequently, for example, when (all the liability conditions being established) the use of an objective paradigm to evaluate the defendant's conduct would lead to outcomes considered unacceptable.

On the latter patterns, often left out of mainstream narrations, a few examples will help clarify. Let us start with some instances related to wrongdoers whose special skills stem from their knowledge relevant to the case at stake. An art gallery owner, who publicly voiced his doubts as to the authenticity of two paintings, thus frustrating the paintings' owner's hopes of profiting from the sale, was held to be negligent—upon the painter's acknowledgment of his paternity of the paintings—when it emerged that the dealer had acted as an exclusive art merchant for that painter for a very long time and had previously examined and familiarized himself with the vast majority of that painter's work.[49] Another example can be the case of a surgeon who, in operating on a woman who had injured herself in a fall during a walk in the suburbs, omitted to give her a tetanus shot, thus causing the woman's death within a few days. At that time the accepted view in the medical profession was that tetanus shots were seldom absolutely necessary (and, therefore, according to a widespread basic rule, the surgeon would have escaped liability).

[48] To name but a few, see the cases and references quoted by Henri Mazeaud, "La 'faute objective' et la responsabilité sans faute,'" in D chr 1985, 14; Jean Deliyannis, *La notion d'acte illicite: considéré en sa qualité d'élément de la faute délictuelle* (LGDJ 1952) 34; Boris Starck, *Essai d'une théorie générale de la responsabilité civile considérée en sa double fonction de garantie et de peine privée* (Rodstein 1947) 201, 440–442; for the common law experiences, Goldberg, Kendrick, Sebok, & Zipursky (n 15) 187–193; Keeton et al (n 33) 171–173, 357; Leon Green, "The Duty Problem in Negligence Cases" (1928) 28 Colum LR 1029, fn 33; (1929) 29 Colum LR 255–257, 277–279.

[49] Trib Rome 21 January 1989, Temi Romana 1989, 85. Among many other examples—on which see Bussani (n 19) 230–254—we may recall the case of a scientist who injected his rabbits with a toxic new substance. When animals started to die in the area, due to the spreading of the microbes, the scientist was found liable for damages, not because of his risky activities, but because he had previously carried out similar experiments, and "having long studied and researched in the past, should have been able to imagine the damaging effect which the microbes might produce": Trib Dreux 24 September 1954, D 1954, 690 (our translation); affirmed by CA Paris 25 January 1956, D 1956, 184. Along the same lines, the sophisticated antiques expert who, intending to buy a gift for his spouse, acquired off-market a stolen object without realizing its illicit provenance, was found negligent: not only was he "a mature professional," but also had such deep knowledge of that particular kind of goods, that he should have immediately guessed the suspicious origin of the thing (CA Paris 15 February 1961, D 1961, Somm 43). Similarly, liability was established upon an expert technician who, skilled in operating a tractor, nevertheless negligently allowed a young employee to step onto the mud-guard of the vehicle, which caused the vehicle to roll over and the youth to die as a consequence: Cass 7 January 2002, no 89, Giust civ 2003, I, 524.

Nevertheless, what seemed decisive to the court was that the defendant was a doctor who had long studied the properties of the vaccine and had become a strong supporter of the beneficial effects of the injection, so much so that he would encourage his collaborators always to administer it. Besides, on that particular occasion the defendant could fully appreciate that resorting to the serum was indispensable, given his knowledge of where the fall had taken place and of the risk of tetanus infections that could derive from the type of soil which was found in that area.[50]

The informational advantage which qualifies the tortfeasor's conduct is not always or necessarily of a professional nature. A good example is that of a cyclist riding on a country road, who collided against a young horse who suddenly appeared from a side path. The cyclist was found liable: since he would ride his bike daily along that route, he was aware of the vicinity of a farm and knew that the animal was free-roaming in the area without any apparent supervision.[51] The same outcome was reached in the case of a driver who, signaling with his hand out of car window, invited the driver of the car behind to overtake him, notwithstanding that the road would soon come to a very dangerous turn, which was not otherwise signposted or visible. The careless behavior of the first driver was culpable, for he was a commercial agent who knew the route and was aware of its dangers, having taken it at least one hundred times per year.[52] The standard of the reasonable person can be cast out

[50] CA Paris 10 February 1954, D 1954, 257. From the same perspective, the doctor who, facing a rare and anomalous post-operative complication, fails to take suitable measures to avoid the damage, is found negligent, if it turns out that he was one of the country's top specialists in that type of operation and had often (some 600 to 800 times) previously been successful in adopting precautions of a special nature, which had avoided the same unpleasant consequences lamented by the victim in that case: *Valentine v Kaiser Foundation Hospitals*, 194 Cal App 2d, 282, 15 Cal Rptr 26 (Cal 1961). For similar cases, see, in Germany, BGH 10 February 1987, BGHZ 100, 51 (an orthopedic surgeon); in the United States, *McClarin v Grenzfelder*, 147 Mo App 478; 126 SW 817 (Mo 1910) (a specialist in the treatment of hernia); *Lewis v Read*, 80 NJ Super 148, 193 A 2d 255 (NJ 1963) (an obstetrician).

[51] *Holland v Bartch*, 120 Ind 46, 22 NE 83 (Ind 1889); for similar cases, in France, Trib Arras 27 July 1938, DH 1938, 572; Trib Rouen 28 November 1956, in D 1957, 62; Cass civ 6 February 1957, Bull civ 1957 II, 117, 72; Cass civ 20 October 1961, Bull civ 1961 II, 683, 476; Cass civ 8 April 1970, Bull civ 1970 II, 113, 89. In assessing the degree of fault of a Parisian pedestrian, it can matter that he "knew the crossroads between du Havre street and Haussman avenue to be particularly dangerous" ("qu'il connaissait et savait particulièrement dangereux le carrefour de la rue du Havre et du boulevard Haussmann"): Trib Amiens, 16 March 1939, DH 1939, 348.

[52] *Shirley Cloah & Dress Co v Arnold*, 92 Ga App 885, 90 SE 2d 622 (Ga 1956); see also *Thelen v Spilman*, 251 Minn 89, 86 NW 2d 700 (Minn 1957); *Armstead v Holbert*, 146 WVa 582, 122 SE 2d 43 (WVa 1961), and the cases cited in Mauro Bussani, "Problemi dell'illecito: superiorità soggettive e giudizio sulla colpa," in Paolo Cendon (ed), *La responsabilità extracontrattuale* (Giuffrè 1994) 81, 93–96; Fleming (n 44) 5–17. See also Cass (criminal division) 4 December 2001, Riv pen 2002, 476: in the case of a truck driver who, seeing another vehicle coming onto its lane in the opposite direction, steered abruptly and collided with a van, causing the death of its seven passengers, the Italian Supreme Court held that the driver's fault consisted in being able to imagine the potential

of the judicial picture also when it is found that it is the wrongdoer's physical and psychological skills would have enabled her—in the circumstances of the case and differently from any other "average person"—to foresee and avoid the loss-causing event.[53] Thus, an experienced skier, who was especially skilled in alpine skiing and was therefore capable of veering abruptly and performing movements technically unthinkable for any average skier, was held liable for not avoiding the crash with another skier.[54]

Sometimes it is the sheer muscular force that is emphasized. Thus, the English Court of Appeal held liable a young man who, being fully aware of his physical superiority, engaged an older man (who had provoked him) in a fight, and hit the older man with such force that his skull was fractured.[55] In another case, an amateur boxer who, in the course of training, improvised a short noncompetitive match with a colleague, but then repeatedly hit his comparatively smaller opponent, was held liable for his opponent's death, which ensued a few hours later. The court argued that the more experienced contender must have been aware of his vastly superior muscular strength when compared with the beginner victim, given also the latter's age and inexperience, and that the amateur nature of the match was known to the senior boxer.[56]

Turning now our attention to "weaker" wrongdoers, the chief embarrassment to the PWQ rule occurs in its inconsistent adoption where the plaintiff is "weaker" than the defendant, and where the harm is caused by both the

consequences of an accident on the road, made slippery by the rain, for not only was he a professional, but he also "was well-acquainted with that route, for he would take it several times a day for work."

[53] For example, a man who, climbing over the fence of a riding ground, provoked a reaction from the enclosed young horses and suffered damage upon their bolting, was found negligent and held to a higher standard of care than the ordinary man, for, having formerly trained as a jockey, he could have promptly guessed how the young horses would have reacted to his action (Cass civ 15 March 1956, D 1956, 445). Similarly, a woman who slipped and fell while visiting a cave site (in this case, the Italian Grotte di Castellana), was found at fault, notwithstanding darkness and the absence of a banister, and held to a higher standard than the "average woman," for it was established that she was a caving expert who had visited several sites before but had not, on that particular occasion, worn suitable shoes to explore that type of path (Cass 14 January 2000, no 366, Foro it 2001, I, 205). In the United States this pattern has recurred in the context of the imposition of heightened duty on professional truck drivers. See *Dakter v Cavallino*, 866 NW 2d 656 (Wis 2015) and *Cervelli v Graves*, 661 P 2d 1032 (Wyo 1983).

[54] Cass 6 May 1986, no 3031, Giur It, I, 1, 1527; for a similar judgment involving one expert skier (as the plaintiff) and a ski instructor with expert knowledge (as the defendant), see *La Vine v Clear Creek Skiing Corp*, 557 F2d 730 (10th Cir 1977).

[55] *Murphy v Culhane* [1977] QB 94 (CA).

[56] App Milan 14 October 1960, Riv dir sport 1961, 196, affirmed by Cass (criminal division) 22 November 1961, in Resp civ prev 1962, 507.

defendant's and the victim's conduct. The apportionment of liability depends then not only on each party's causal contribution to the damage, but also on the comparative value attributed to each party's interest in behaving as they did. Here what deserves attention is a widespread doctrine driven by policy concerns for the freedom of action of physically disadvantaged people. This doctrine makes it possible that liability be established upon the sole defendant, even when (a) the latter's conduct can be seen as plainly aligned with that of the reasonable person under the circumstances, and (b) the harm is the factual and direct consequence of the victim's action.[57]

This line of cases regards those who are permanently physically disabled, put at a disadvantage by their age, or affected by temporary and yet deeply enfeebling conditions, who fall victim of personal injuries in the course of activities in which their own biological baggage plays a decisive role. In assessing both the defendant's fault and the plaintiff's comparative negligence (including the latter's possibility of a prompt reaction in the circumstances in which she finds herself), the traditional metric has undergone significant qualifications.[58] Therefore, judges have dismissed any allegation of negligence on the part of a victim when she, while directly contributing to the causation of the harm, was found physically challenged by blindness, deafness, or a lame leg, or had recently undergone surgery, or had been involved in a road accident moments before,[59] or when the old person's clumsiness, due to physical feebleness, contributed to cause his injuries in getting off a train,[60] a bus,[61] a streetcar,[62] or a cab.[63]

[57] On the need to revise the official tenet—in the sense that the degree of care expected of the person who is physically impaired, is to be the same expected of the average person, should she find herself in the same conditions of disability—see Kasirer (n 37) 369–341; John G Fleming, *An Introduction to the Law of Torts* (Clarendon Press 1969) 32; James (n 19) 17–26; along the same lines (though with more general regard to the entire category of weak persons) see also Calabresi (n 19) 25–44. See also the results collected by Miquel Martín-Casals, Piotr Machnikowski, & Richard W Wright (eds), *Standards of Care* (Intersentia forthcoming 2022).

[58] See Avihay Dorfman, "Negligence and Accommodation" (2016) 22 Leg Theory 77, 90 (all the Unites States cases cited by treatise writers for the "canonical" claim that "physical disadvantage warrants a watered-down standard of care are cases of contributory or comparative negligence").

[59] In France, see Cass civ 4 January 1964, in Bull civ 1964, II, 17, 13; Trib Epinal, 11 July 1925, Gaz Pal 1925, 2, 629 (deafblind woman); Cass civ 17 November 1941, S 1942, 1, 13 (person who lacked one leg); Trib Rouen, 24 June 1954, D 1954, 739 (disability in the legs); Trib Paris, 21 July 1930, Gaz Pal 1930, 2, 435 (disability in the legs); in Germany, BGH 22 September 1981, VI ZR 144/79 (disability in the pelvis); OLG Hamburg, 25 June 1953, VersR 1964, 1273 (blind person).

[60] *Watts v Spokane P&SR Co*, 88 Or 192, 171 P 901 (Or 1918).

[61] *Shanahan v St. Louis Transit Co*, 109 Mo App 229, 83 SW 783 (Mo Ct App 1904).

[62] *Poak v Pacific Electric R Co*, 177 Cal 190, 170 P 159 (Cal 1918).

[63] *Borus v Yellow Cab Co*, 52 Ill App 3d 194 (Ill App Ct 1977); *Loring v Yellow Cab Co*, 33 Ill App 3d 154 (Ill App Ct 1975).

Needless to say, the lowering of the threshold of carefulness required from the disadvantaged person eventually corresponds to a hardening of the standard of care to be met by the reasonable defendant. But it is equally true that the application of an objective standard of care to the weaker victims would inevitably favor adults in good health. This is because to allocate to the weaker person a portion of the responsibility for an event which she could not possibly have avoided, means to reduce the burden of liability that would otherwise be charged on the other wrongdoing party by a significant amount. The logic underlying the opposite conclusion, instead, is enhanced as soon as one realizes that infirmity, youth, or old age most of the times are easily recognizable, so that often, when these conditions materialize in an individual, his or her conduct is easily foreseeable to the reasonable person.[64]

This is not only the case for those who are physically disabled and contribute to the causation of the harm to themselves, but also of those defendants who, due to the onset of an unforeseeable illness or a lack of mental lucidity when the event occurred, does not in principle qualify as negligent. However, in order to result in an exemption from liability, the so-called agony of the moment[65] must have overcome the person at the time in which she caused the loss. By contrast, no exemption from liability will be granted, again on the basis of a subjective inquiry, whenever the defendant was or should have been aware that the onset of that illness was possible.[66]

[64] Cfr Schwartz (n 45) 241; this point is accurately made in HLA Hart & Tony (Anthony) M Honoré, *Causation in the Law* (2nd edn, Clarendon Press 1985) 153–158. Of course, the wrongdoer cannot appreciate the physical and psychological characteristics of the victim whenever she cannot have enough information regarding the victim of the wrong to evaluate the latter's peculiar conditions.

[65] The phrase is by Fleming (n 2) 258. In Italy, cf Cass (criminal division) 7 December 1979, Mass Cass pen 1980, 1420; Cass (criminal division) 26 January 1979, Mass Cass pen 1980, 1266; Cass (criminal division) 26 May 1969, Riv giur circ trasp 1970, 400; in France, Cass crim 6 March 1956, Bull crim 1956, 222, 402; in Germany, BGH 20 October 1987, NJW 1988, 909; in common law jurisdictions, *Waugh v James K Allen* [1964] 2 Lloyd's Rep 1; *Roberts v Ramsbottom* [1980] 1 All ER 7; *Wingate v United States Services Auto Ass'n*, 480 So 2d 665 (Fla 5th DCA 1985); for further American case law, see Restatement Third of Torts—PEH, Section 11, Reporter's Notes to cmt d. On this topic see also Tunc (n 19) 111; Deutsch (n 19) 329–331, 348.

[66] Case law shows that a wrongdoer incurs liability when the judge finds that the person delayed avoidance of an object hindering his route because he was driving a vehicle "in a state of extreme exhaustion, after working for three days and three nights in a row without rest" (Trib Corr Seine 2 May 1955, JCP 1955, II, 8916); liability was established upon the driver who did not properly react to the symptoms of the onset of an epileptic crisis when the same symptoms had clearly been experienced by the same driver a few kilometers ahead of the accident site (Trib Avignon 23 December 1949, D 950, 153; Cass (criminal division) 16 January 1978, Arch giur circol sin 1978, 207; see also Cass civ 18 December 1964, D 1965, 191); liability was also established upon the driver who had neglected to seek medical attention regarding some frequent convulsions which he experienced immediately prior to the accident, thus being seized with a spasmic attack while behind the wheel (Trib Colmar 10 December 1953, Rev Als Lorr 1954, 155; similarly, Cass (criminal division) 13 January 1981, Arch giur circol sin 1982, 50). For further references, Bussani (n 53) 81, 91–93.

In all these cases, leaving aside any reference to the PWQ rule, the judgment focuses on what could have been expected in that particular situation from "that" individual.

10. Veils and Needs

Many other examples and their rationales could be presented and discussed.[67] What is worth stressing once more, however, is that the few hints we made at the inner dynamics of the "standard of care" element allow us to understand how judicial evaluations taking into account the tortfeasor's individual features (that are relevant to the case at stake) pursue the same goals that are targeted, in ordinary cases, by the traditional rule. The two judicial standards coexist as alternatives: the judge may choose between them in assessing how the parties' subjective peculiarities help, or not, to establish the relative weight of the conflicting interests of the parties and in deciding which interest deserves to prevail. Underneath the thick veil made up of monolithic notions and formulas, this is the way the standard of care operates at the service of the dynamics of negligence law.

11. Between Strict Liability and Negligence: A Transparent Curtain

The same articulated legal framework can be found outside the negligence compound.

"Strict liability" is a phrase whose prima facie meaning falls often short of providing an accurate basis for description and prescription.[68] Many factors may affect the purity and immutability that in a black and white dimension would be assigned to that locution. Sometimes negligence liability embodies features that mirror those pertaining to stricter forms of liability (section 11.1)

[67] See the cases cited by Bussani (n 19) 159–254 and Winiger, Karner, Oliphant (n 34) 763–871, 946–1020, 1062–1082. For an argument that negligence liability should be based entirely on an actor's failure of "one's individual agency at meeting one's [individual] competency" (as the defendant in *Vaughan* wanted), see Ori J Herstein, "Nobody's Perfect: Moral Responsibility in Negligence" (2019) 32 Can JL&Jur 109, 119.

[68] This is particularly so in common law jurisdictions, in which some form of intent is a requirement for many strict liability torts, such as trespass and battery. See also above, in this chapter, section 2 as well as below, section 11.2 and n 93.

and other times strict liability disputes can be permeated by elements that makes it depending on that kind of subjective assessments that should in principle be stranger to the solution of the case at stake (section 11.2).

11.1. The Stretching of Fault

In any national system, fault liability frequently oversteps strict liability frontiers. This mainly happens through one or both of the following legal instruments:[69] imposing duties of care that go beyond what is technically possibly or economically reasonable (a), and altering the balance stricken by the ordinary distribution of the burden of proof to the benefit of the plaintiff (b).

(a) Courts use several techniques to stretch standard of care. One is to increase the required level of knowledge and ability.

In assessing the deviation of the defendant's conduct from the standard of care required under the circumstances, judges usually apply the objective test, typically referring to the benchmark of the reasonable person, whose features may be adjusted according to the nature and risk of the defendant's activity.[70] In many cases, however, the rules applied by the courts may lie far away from any reasonable standard evaluation. Courts can equip on their own the reasonable person with excellent knowledge and abilities and shape it like the ideal person. Examples can be drawn from the cases we referred to above,[71] where negligent liability is established upon the sole defendant, even if it is the victim, a "weaker-than-average" person, who caused (or contributed to cause) her own harm. Another series of examples comes in particular from English and Scots law, where liability for road traffic accidents is formally based on the law of negligence, and in practice

[69] Cf, in general, Cees van Dam, *European Tort Law* (2nd edn, CUP 2013) 297–307; Werro & Palmer (n 10) 7; Brüggemeier (n 22) 57; Pierre Widmer, "Comparative Report on Fault as a Basis of Liability and Criterion of Imputation (Attribution)," in Id (ed), *Unification of Tort Law: Fault* (Kluwer 2005) 331, 356–359; Peter Cane, "Fault and Strict Liability for Harm in Tort Law," in William Swadling & Gareth Jones (eds), *The Search For Principle: Essays in Honour of Lord Goff of Chieveley* (OUP 1999) 171, 172; Josef Esser, *Grundlagen und Entwicklung der Gefährdungshaftung* (Beck 1941) 30. See also Anthony Gray, *The Evolution from Strict Liability to Fault in the Law of Torts* (Hart 2021); Alan Calnan, "The Fault(s) in Negligence Law" (2007) 25 Quinnipiac LR 695–750 (2007); Frederick H Lawson & Basil S Markesinis, *Tortious Liability for Unintentional Harm in the Common Law and the Civil Law* (I, CUP 1982) 144–146.

[70] On this, see also van Dam (n 69) 264–264.

[71] See above, section 9 in this chapter.

it is hardly less strict than under the strict liability statutes that exist in continental legal systems.[72]

Further examples are given by the transnational judicial departing from the basic rule according to which the victim's voluntary act break the chain of causation between the defendant's fault and the injury.[73] The rule, indeed, is not applied where courts verify that the defendant neglected a duty that is expressly, or impliedly, imposed upon her to protect the safety of others. As a result, once again, the standard of care with which the defendant's conduct is usually compared turns out to be significantly increased. In fact, judges found for the plaintiff when the defendant, driving over the speed limit on a city street, hit a policeman who, due to the unbearable pain, took out his gun and committed suicide before the ambulance arrived.[74] Liability is also established when a person, as a result of driving negligently, induces a passenger of his car to jump out of the moving vehicle,[75] when an employee commits suicide two years after he became permanently disabled as a result of exposure to poisonous gas that his employer negligently allowed to escape in the work area,[76] or when prison guards' failure to accurately supervise a prisoner with well-known suicidal tendencies provides him with the actual opportunity to kill himself.[77]

[72] Jan Smits, *Advanced Introduction to Private Law* (EE 2017) 42–43. Even if courts rarely admit it, compulsory liability insurance affects the balance between plaintiff and defendant, since the issue is no longer whether the defendant "deserves" to be made liable for the victim's loss, but rather whether the case is such that the victim should bear the loss instead of the defendant's insurer, which ultimately spreads it over all insurance policyholders (van Gerven, Lever, & Larouche (n 17) 593–594).

[73] Restatement Third of Torts—Apportionment of Liability, Section 7; Williams (n 24) 202, fn 56; Marcel Planiol, Georges Ripert, & Jean Boulanger, *Traité pratique de droit civil français* (II, LGDJ 1957) 787; Pietro Trimarchi, *Causalità e danno* (Giuffrè 1967) 129.

[74] Cass 7 February 1996, no 969, Foro it 1996, I, 2482.

[75] *Jones v Boyce* [1816] 170 Eng Rep 540; Restatement of Torts, 2d, Section 444, ill 1; *Twomley v Central Park, N&E River R Co*, 69 NY 158, 25 Am Rep 162 (NY 1877).

[76] Cass (labor division) 23 February 2000, no 2037, Giust civ mass 2000, 442. The solution is the same when an employee commits suicide six years after a workplace accident due to the employer's fault: *Corr v IBC Vehicles* [2006] EWCA Civ 331.

[77] *Commissioners of Police for the Metropolis v Reeves* [1999] UKHL 35; [2000] 1 AC 360; [1999] 3 All ER 897. See also the cases quoted in the Restatement Third of Torts—Apportionment of Liability, Section 1, cmt c, Reporter's Notes, and in the Restatement Third of Torts—PEH, Section 33, cmt e-f, Reporter's Notes.

Along the same lines, but with regard to the rule according to which the negligent defendant should be exempted from liability when the harm is brought about by the subsequent intentional act of a third party (on which see von Bar (n 6) 482; Hart & Honoré (n 64) 198; Paolo Cendon, *Il dolo nella responsabilità extracontrattuale* (Giappichelli 1976) 133, fn 4; Hart & Honoré (n 64) 47), courts frequently do not apply the rule when the negligent defendant is found to owe a duty of protection to the victim against the danger of the third party's intentional act. Needless to say, compliance with this duty entails a standard of care, whose discharge may be very hard to prove. Thus, the defendant may be held liable when he is a painter and decorator who forgets to close the door of the house where he was working, thus allowing a thief to enter and steal the silverware of his client: *Stansbie v Troman* [1948] 2 KB 48. Policemen may be held liable if they allow a witness involved in a trial

(b) Without apparently altering or stretching the standard of care, the position of the victim can be improved by shifting the burden of proof, a technique that under different legal skies can go under the refined labels of prima facie or res ipsa loquitur rules. The use of all these devices allows the plaintiff to limit her evidentiary effort to the proof of damage, thereby putting upon the defendant the charge of providing the judge (and the jury, if the case may be) with all the pieces of evidence necessary to escape liability.

On the so-called prima facie rule, it will suffice to recall here *Byrne v. Boadle*,[78] in which a flour barrel rolled out of an upstairs window and struck the plaintiff. In this case, the court stated:

> [H]ere the evidence before the court was [...] that the plaintiff and his wife were passing along the Scotland Road, in Liverpool, and when they were [close] against the defendant's warehouse, the whole of which was in his occupation, used by him as a flour dealer, there came down suddenly upon the man a barrel of flour, and thus the accident occurred to the plaintiff of which he complained. This is one of those cases in which [...] a presumption of negligence by defendant is raised, and it was for him, who had all

against a gangster to be murdered by an anonymous person (*Schuster v City of New York*, 145 NE 534 (NY 1958)); a psychiatric hospital may be held liable if as a result of the careless supervision of their patients, one of them murders another patient (Cass 16 June 2005, no 12965, Giust civ 2006, 72; Restatement Second of Torts, Section 302, ill 20). Similarly, a school may be held liable if a student is molested by a school employee (*Kansas State Bank & Trust Co v Specialized Transp Servs*, 819 P 2d 587 (Kan 1991)), or if the student is allowed to leave the school premises before the end of the school day and he is attacked by an unknown assailant (Cass 4 February 2005, no 2272, in Foro it Rep 2005, Responsabilità civile, no 339; Cass 30 March 1999, no 3074, Danno resp 1999, 916). A county may be held liable if its department of social service ignores the numerous calls warning about the insanity of woman, thus allowing her to throw her grandchild into a container of boiling water (*Scott v County of Los Angeles*, 32 Cal Rptr 2d 643 (Cal Ct App 1994)); the result is the same for a city, whose emergency telephone operator fails to give priority to a caller, wishing to report a murder attempt, allowing the murder to take place (*Hutcherson v City of Phoenix*, 961 P 2d 449 (Ariz 1998)). Furthermore, the financial advisor who counsels a client to trust a bank, may be held liable if the bank misappropriates the client's money (*De la Bère v Pearson Ltd* [1908] 1 KB 280); the owner of a night club may be held liable if he hires a bouncer who is notorious for involvements in fights, and the bouncer subsequently awaits a client in the parking lot and knocks him down (*Medina v Graham's Cowboys*, 113 NM 471 (NM Ct App 1992); similarly *Mattis v Pollock* [2003] EWCA 887); prison guards may be held liable if they allow some prisoners to escape, during which the prisoners destroy a yacht (*Dorset Yacht Co v Home Office* [1970] 2 All ER 294); a psychiatrist may be held liable if, upon discovering that his patient intends to kill his girlfriend, he fails to warn the woman of this danger, resulting in her murder (*Tarasoff v Regents of the University of California*, 17 Cal 3d 358 (Cal 1976)).

[78] [1863] 159 Eng Rep 299 (CE); for modern applications of *Byrne v Boadle* in United States tort law, see *Larson v St Francis Hotel*, 83 Cal App 2d 210, 188 P 2d 513 (Cal Ct App 1947); *Cox v Northwest Airlines*, 379 F 2d 893 (7th Cir 1967).

> the means of evidence and knowledge within his reach, to meet it. It having been shown that the defendant had the entire possession and exclusive use of this warehouse, it would be presumed that the accident arose from his want of care, unless he gave some explanation of the cause by which it was produced, which explanation the plaintiff could not be expected to give, not having the same means of knowledge.

This case, as well as the early res ipsa jurisprudence on common carriers' liability,[79] represents a delicate attempt by judges to cut out an "intermediate zone" between the two extremes of (i) a negligence standard that might leave plaintiffs without relief for legitimate harms where they lacked affirmative evidence, and (ii) an unsought strict liability standard that might saddle businesses with over-burdensome litigation costs.[80] Another example (outside the flourishing ground of medical malpractice, to be dealt with in Chapter III) is that of a driver colliding with the back of the car in front of her. Courts everywhere will generally presume that he acted negligently and will charge the defendant with the onus of rebutting this presumption[81]—as is well-known, the presumption mimics insurances' routinized standards of liability assessments trying to strike a compromise between accuracy and simplicity in the management of compensation claims.[82]

What has to be further noted is that not only courts, but also legislators, can enact rules of negligence liability that incorporate such proof-reversal techniques. Examples of this sort can be drawn from Italian and German legal systems. Italian law, for example, provides for a series of *presumptions of fault*, imposing liability on the guardians of persons lacking legal capacity (arts 2047–2048 Civil Code), on enterprises running activities that are to be considered particularly dangerous (art 2050 Civil Code), on drivers (art 2054 Civil Code), and on owners of collapsing buildings (art

[79] See Goldberg, Kendrick, Sebok, & Zipursky (n 15) 161, 166.

[80] G Gregg Webb, "The Law of Falling Objects: Byrne v. Boadle and the Birth of Res Ipsa Loquitur" (2007) 59 Stan LR 1065, 1105–1006; see also Alex Stein, "The Domain of Torts" (2017) 117 Colum LR 535, 542–543, 579.

[81] Comparative references in van Dam (n 69) 304.

[82] Ina Ebert, "Tort Law and Insurance," in Bussani & Sebok (n 6) 133–139; Richard Lewis, "Insurance and the Tort System" (2005) 25 Leg Stud 85, 88. On the "res ipsa loquitur" principle in the United States, see the Restatement Third of Torts—PEH, Section17:

> The fact-finder may infer that the defendant has been negligent when the accident causing the plaintiff's harm is a type of accident that ordinarily happens as a result of the negligence of a class of actors of which the defendant is the relevant member.

2053 Civil Code). These presumptions can be rebutted by the (very hard to give) proof of having adopted reasonable precautionary measures. German liability of persons having to supervise minors is a negligence liability with a reversed burden of proof (§ 832 BGB), as it is employers' vicarious liability (§ 831 BGB). German law (§§ 836–838 BGB) also adopts presumptions of fault in the context of damage caused by collapsing buildings or man-made structures. The person usually liable will be the owner, but liability may also be imposed upon the mere possessor (§ 836 I BGB), the former possessor (§ 836 II BGB), the builder or constructor (§ 837 BGB). Further, § 833 (sentence 2) BGB establishes a rebuttable presumption of fault against the keeper of "domestic or useful animals."

11.2. Strict Liability Reduced

On the reverse scale, strict liability may in turn be permeated by fault-based arguments, thereby lightening the defendant's burden of proof to avoid compensation. Here are a few illustrations.

In France, liability for things causing damage is usually presented as strict upon the keeper, inasmuch as the plaintiff can always get recovery unless the defendant proves that the harm is due to the victim's negligence only, to an act of a third party, or to an act of God. In the causation of harm, however, the thing must play an "active role," in the sense it must show an "abnormal behavior." The keeper is not liable when the thing is found to have remained "inactive," that is, when it has played a role "purement passif." Thus a slippery floor has been held to be "abnormal," that is to say, "active."[83] Where the floor is not too slippery, its role might be deemed "normal" and hence "purely passive."[84] In the same vein, the installer of a trampoline was held not liable for the accident of the person who jumped on it, insofar as the trampoline was not defective, and therefore did play no active role in the accident,[85] while a different ruling has been adopted when a child fell through a glass door, because judges concluded from the very fact that the glass shattered that the door had been the active instrument of the child's harm.[86] Upon consideration that all these cases deeply depend on factual assessments, which

[83] Cass civ 24 January 1985, Bull civ 1985 II, 21, 14.
[84] Cass civ 29 May 1996, Bull civ 1996 I, 227, 157.
[85] See eg Cass civ 8 June 1994, Bull civ 1994 II, 152, 88.
[86] Cass civ 29 April 1998, Bull civ 1998 II, 142, 83.

are hidden to the reader from the traditionally short-styled French rulings,[87] and that they are remote from a persuasive rationalization, it is of no surprise that there is quite a widespread agreement on that French "negligence and gardien liability are barely, if at all, distinguishable from each other."[88]

Needless to say, the common law traditional reluctance to expand the strict liability realm offers further examples.

A case in point is represented by developments of the English rule of strict liability for unnatural uses of land. In the 1866 case *Rylands v. Fletcher*,[89] water in a reservoir leaked into the tunnels of neighboring mines, making them unusable. The House of Lords held the owner of the reservoir strictly liable to his neighbor mine owner, relying on premodern absolute liability: one who uses his land "unnaturally" is liable for harm to his neighbor regardless of fault. Yet, in what is the most recent leading precedent, *Cambridge Water Co v. Eastern Counties Leather*,[90] the House of Lords decided that liability under the *Rylands v. Fletcher* rule required foreseeability of the harm, thereby establishing the exemption from liability for the defendant who was unable to foresee that substances flowing from his land were leaking into plaintiff's property.[91]

Another example of how subjective elements may permeate domains apparently insensitive to their influence comes from American law. Therein, the common assumption is that that trespass is a strict liability tort. While the description is accurate, trespass might also accurately be described as an intentional tort. As is well known, trespass

87 The French *Cour de cassation* has now reformed the style of its own decisions, in order to provide more detailed reasons for the holdings: see Cour de cassation, "Guide des nouvelles règles relatives à la structure et à la rédaction des arrêts," June 2019, at courdecassation.fr/institution_1/reforme_cour_7109/reformes_mouvement_8181/reforme_mode_redaction_arrets_9223/.

88 von Bar (n 6) 349. See also Werro & Palmer (n 10) 419–421; van Gerven, Lever, & Larouche (n 17) 544.

89 [1866] LR 3 HL 330.

90 [1994] 1 All ER 53.

91 *Cambridge Water Co v Eastern Counties Leather* [1994] 1 All ER 53. The case was about a leather manufacturer who, for many years, had been using a chemical solvent in its tanning process. Until 1976, when the tannery changed its manufacturing process, part of this solvent regularly seeped through the floor into the soil and the underground strata from which the plaintiffs, a water company, extracted water. It was only in 1983 that the plaintiffs discovered the solvent. The level of pollution being too high, the water company moved its pumping station upstream and, for the cost thus incurred, claimed compensation from the leather manufacturer. The House of Lords found for the defendant, under the argument that, as an element of causation, foreseeability of the type of harm suffered by the plaintiff is as much a prerequisite of liability under the *Rylands v Fletcher* rule as it is in the law of negligence, and that this condition was not met in the case. A sharp critique of the judgment can be read in Tony Weir, "The Polluter Must Pay – Regardless," Cambridge LJ 17–20 (1993).

> requires that one person acts so as to cause a certain kind of interference with a property possessor's rights of exclusive possession and control. Implicit in this formulation is the idea that the defendant's interfering act must have been intentionally undertaken.[92]

These two aspects of the tort of trespass appear self-contradictory. On the one hand, there is no need that the defendant intended to do harm to the plaintiff, or to invade property that she knows to be owned or possessed by someone else. On the other hand, the defendant's act itself must have been intentional. Thus, for an action in trespass to succeed, it is necessary to show that (a) the plaintiff owns or possesses a swath of land, and that (b) the defendant intentionally "invades" the swath in question.[93] The point then is that what the fact-finder has to ascertain is whether the defendant's state of mind is amenable to a voluntary/intentional act with respect to that piece of land.[94] In these situations, no trespass equals no intention, and vice versa.

A further example is given by the cases where both parties to a tort suit respond under the same strict liability rule. In these situations, no matter how strict liability may be defined, the fault principle generally comes in. This is

[92] Goldberg, Kendrick, Sebok, & Zipursky (n 15) 889–890. See also the Restatement Third of Torts—Intentional Torts to Persons, for accounts of the debate on whether, under the tort of battery, it is sufficient that the defendant intends a bodily contact that turns out to be either harmful or offensive ("single intent") or whether battery should require intent to cause a bodily contact that the defendant intends to cause either harm or offense ("dual intent").

[93] The invasion might be made by the defendant walking on the plaintiff's land, driving across it, throwing things onto it, digging it up, flooding it, building on it, etc: Goldberg, Kendrick, Sebok, & Zipursky (n 15) 890.

[94] To further illustrate, if the defendant unintentionally loses control of his car and crashes it into a building, she does not commit a trespass, because she had no intention to enter in contact with the building in question (although she may be liable for negligence). See Goldberg, Kendrick, Sebok, & Zipursky (n 15) 890.

On the ambiguous wording United States courts usually adopt (quite often hinging on reasonableness standards and activity level factors) in establishing or denying strict liability for abnormally dangerous activities under the circumstances set forth by the Restatement Second of Torts, Section 520 (now also enshrined in Section 20 of the Restatement Third of Torts—PEH), see Peter M Gerhart, "The Death of Strict Liability" (2008) 56 Buffalo LR 245–313.

In England, defamation is often cited as an example of strict liability at common law. The defendant may be found liable for a defamatory statement albeit he neither intended to defame the plaintiff nor was negligent in so doing. However, (a) there must be a deliberate intent to publish and the risk of publication is thus found to rest with the publisher, (b) the apparent strictness of the rule in defamation is mitigated by the provision (enshrined in s 3 of the Defamation Act 2013) of a statutory defense of honest opinion. See, from a comparative perspective, Vincent R Johnson, "Comparative Defamation Law: England and the United States" (2016) 24 U Miami Int'l & Comp LR 1, 27–29; van Gerven, Lever, & Larouche (n 17) 569; van Dam (n 69) 114–116. For the American debate on the same point, see Keith N Hylton, *Tort Law: A Modern Perspective* (CUP 2016) 301–333; John CP Goldberg & Benjamin C Zipursky, "The Strict Liability in Fault and the Fault in Strict Liability" (2016) 85 Fordham LR 743, 751–752.

illustrated by the collision of a car and a motorbike in jurisdictions in which the use of both cars and motorbikes is subject to strict liability.[95] In these jurisdictions, the very implication of a car and a motorbike in an accident creates a presumption of responsibility. This prima facie responsibility can generally be rebutted or at least reduced, for example, by showing that different operational risks are attached to the vehicles involved, or, more importantly, by proving that the other driver was at fault.[96]

12. A Liability Spectrum

We have cursorily surveyed how different techniques may produce a complex amalgam of the two forms of liability, thus making a binary classification scheme too simplistic.[97] To be sure, whatever way judges reshape standard doctrines, they present the outcomes as ad hoc moldings of either fault or strict liability ordinary rules, rather than as a reasonable shift to the other regime. This is probably due, on the one hand, to judges' preference for seeing themselves as a legal body whose task is "developing the law on an incremental basis rather than through abrupt changes,"[98] and, on the other hand, because of the awareness that "this gradualism allows them to do justice between the parties without giving the impression that new law is being made."[99] But the point still is that a better theoretical approach should consist in recognizing that these variations and combinations fit within a continuum of liability standards, ranging from the strictest to the most subjective ones, with a fair number of intermediate positions in between.[100] This would also help explain why, as judges and legislators continue to experiment along the liability spectrum, one may single out fewer pure or classical structures and many more forms of liability to be presented and discussed as mixed and hybrid.[101]

[95] See the survey by Werro & Palmer (n 10) 400–409, covering Austrian, Danish, Dutch, French, German, Greek, Italian, Portuguese, and Spanish law.

[96] Werro & Palmer (n 10) 408–409. See also Franz Werro & Erdem Büyüksagis, "The bounds between negligence and strict liability," in Bussani & Sebok (n 6) 186–213.

[97] Cane (n 69) 172.

[98] Werro & Palmer (n 10) 13.

[99] Ibid.

[100] Izhak Englard, *The Philosophy of Tort Law* (Dartmouth 1993) 21; Vernon V Palmer, "In Quest of a Strict Liability Standard Under the Code" (1982) 56 Tulane LR 1317; similarly, Ernst von Caemmerer, *Reform der Gefährdungshaftung* (de Gruyter 1971) 13.

[101] Werro & Palmer (n 10) 7.

III
Recovery for Physical Harm: The Case of Medical Malpractice

1. Introduction

In all the jurisdictions studied in this book, medical malpractice is one of the paradigm examples of liability for personal injury. The basis of a defendant's liability to the plaintiff is clear, given that typically the defendant, a physician, has more or less actively committed herself to the plaintiff, a patient, and the content of that commitment may involve great risk and often an imbalance of information. One might think, then, that the duty of care issue, which is often so difficult to ascertain in common law jurisdictions, and which is viewed as an unnecessary hurdle in civilian jurisdictions, would be an easy question in cases of medical malpractice.

As a practical matter, in every system and in almost all circumstances, courts take it for granted that an obligation runs between victim and medical provider,[1] but that does not mean that it is not worth focusing on medical malpractice precisely for that reason. We think, in fact, the contrary. Given that all the systems studied in this book provide a roughly identical answer to the question of when and to whom the obligation of care is owed in the context of medical malpractice, we can compare how the different

[1] The torts of "wrongful life" and "wrongful birth" are exceptions to the rule, and are discussed in this chapter, section 3.1.1.

Common Law and Civil Law Perspectives on Tort Law. Mauro Bussani, Anthony J. Sebok, & Marta Infantino,
Oxford University Press. © Mauro Bussani, Anthony J. Sebok, & Marta Infantino 2022.
DOI: 10.1093/oso/9780195368383.003.0003

theoretical commitments of the various systems handle identical tasks. As this chapter illustrates, beneath relatively similar outcomes lay deep theoretical disagreements about the foundation of liability (whether it should be based on tort or contract) as well as pragmatic adjustments in the rules of causation and the burden of proof.

2. Preliminary Matters

2.1. The Role of the State

A major feature of medical malpractice liability in contemporary Europe is the massive role that the state plays in the delivery of medical care. While private medical services still exist in England, since 1948 the National Health Service (NHS) has taken over about 89% of care.[2] In France, 77% of all healthcare spending is provided by the public health insurance system,[3] 86% of medical providers work in the public sector, and 65% of hospital capacity is in public institutions.[4] Germany is a mixed system where the public share of total health expenditure is around 75%,[5] but registered physicians in the private practice have a "monopoly" on outpatient care and public hospitals represent only a third of all capacity.[6] In Italy, around 80% of all healthcare spending is provided by the public health insurance system, and health care is mainly delivered by public providers.[7] The United States, of course, is a different story: public funds cover about 50% of all healthcare expenditures, and, except for a handful of municipal health systems and the federal

[2] See Jonathan Cylus, Erica Richardson, Lisa Findley, Marcus Longley, Ciaran O'Neill, & David Steel, "United Kingdom—Health System Review" (2015) 17 Health Systems in Transition 1, 55, according to which "approximately 11% of the population of the United Kingdom has private medical insurance of some kind."

[3] Karine Chevreul, Karen Berg Brigham, Isabelle Durand-Zaleski, & Cristina Hernández-Quevedo, "France—Health System Review" (2015) 17 Health Systems in Transition 1, 59.

[4] Florence G'sell-Macrez, "Medical Malpractice and Compensation in France: Part I: The French Rules of Medical Liability since the Patients' Rights Law of March 4, 2002" (2011) 86 Chi-Kent LR 1093, 1093.

[5] Reinhard Busse & Miriam Blümel, "Germany—Health System Review" (2014) 16 Health Systems in Transition 1, 110–111.

[6] Franz M Petry, "Medical Liability in Germany," in Bernhard A Koch (ed), *Medical Liability in Europe: A Comparison of Selected Jurisdictions* (deGruyter 2011) 233–237.

[7] Francesca Ferré, Antonio G de Belvis, Luca Valerio, Silvia Longhi, Agnese Lazzari, Giovanni Fattore, Walter Ricciardi, & Anna Maresso, "Italy—Health System Review" (2014) 17 Health Systems in Transition 1, 41–42.

Veterans Administration, almost all medical care is provided by private medical providers, although some of them may be charitable institutions.[8]

Especially in common law jurisdictions, the rise of state-funded medical care clearly had the potential to affect the legal landscape of medical malpractice, and the traditional principle of sovereign immunity was designed precisely to insulate the state from liability.[9] The truth, however—as we will see in this chapter—is that the expansion of public health services did not inhibit the growth of tort liability for medical malpractice either in the United States or in England.

2.2. The Choice between Contract and Tort

Another significant difference among the systems compared in this book is the initial basis for the ground of liability for injuries flowing from medical malpractice. In the United States, a medical malpractice action is a civil action for damages resulting from the negligence of a physician in treating a patient. Although originally a contract action, negligence in the field of medicine received recognition as a separate tort since the early nineteenth century.[10] As one American court put it, "it is the nature of the duty breached that should determine whether the action is in tort or in contract. [...] On principle then, we consider a malpractice action as tortious in nature whether the duty grows out of a contractual relation or has no origin in contract."[11]

[8] Public health insurance (including Medicare and Medicaid) provides 48% of funds used for health care, and private insurance (including self-insurance) provides 52% of funds used for health care. Thomas Rice, Pauline Rosenau, Lynn Y Unruh, Andrew J Barnes, Richard B Saltman, & Ewout van Ginneken, "United States of America—Health System Review" (2013) 15 Health Systems in Transition 1, 91.

[9] While state immunity has historically been (and still partially is) broadly conceived in common law jurisdictions, civil law jurisdictions have traditionally restricted state immunity to the so-called acta jure imperii, that is to say, acts that are expressions of discretionary political decisions (typically covering fields such as foreign policy, military affairs and legislation): Ken Oliphant, "The Liability of Public Authorities in Comparative Perspective," in Ken Oliphant (ed), *The Liability of Public Authorities in Comparative Perspective* (Intersentia 2016) 849, 850–854; Gyula Eörsi, "Private and Governmental Liability for the Torts of Employees and Organs," in *International Encyclopedia of Comparative Law*, vol 11, ch 4 (Mohr Siebeck 1976) 120–125; see also Giacinto della Cananea & Roberto Caranta (eds), *Tort Liability of Public Authorities in European Laws* (OUP 2021).

[10] Kenneth A De Ville, *Medical Malpractice in Nineteenth-Century America: Origins and Legacy* (NYU Press 1990) 171–173. Some would argue that the contract terminology in American law was nothing more than a "legal fiction." Theodore Silver, "One Hundred Years of Harmful Error: The Historical Jurisprudence of Medical Malpractice" (1992) Wis LR 1193, 1198, fn 20 (noting that many courts referred to the physician's obligation as "arising from a contract implied by law").

[11] *Kozan v Comstock*, 270 F2d 839, 844–845 (5th Cir 1959). This is mirrored in the other major branch of professional malpractice in the United States, involving lawyers. Legal malpractice (and the duty owed to a client) does not depend on the existence of a contract.

In the United States today, medical malpractice tort claims are based on the physician-patient relationship created by express or implied agreement between the parties.[12] A patient may rely on the doctor to use reasonable skill and learning and to exercise his best judgment.[13] Correlatively, unless specifically stated in a written contract between the medical provider and the patient, American courts do not hold that a physician guarantees the success of her efforts.[14] But the presence of a contract is of limited importance, since a medical provider is almost never permitted to limit her tort liability to her patient by contract, for various reasons, the most prominent being that such limitations are typically found to violate public policy.[15] The few cases where courts have upheld waivers have typically involved experimental treatments, the risks of which the patient was fully informed.[16] The qualification of the claim does not matter in determining the period of limitations applicable to medical malpractice actions, which are almost everywhere governed by statutory rules especially devoted to physicians' liability.[17]

In England, the situation is much the same, except even more so. As was noted in the 1925 case of *R v Bateman*, if someone holds themselves out to possess special expertise and skill and accepts the responsibility to undertake treatment of a patient, "he owes a duty to the patient [...] No contractual relation is necessary."[18] The duty extends beyond a duty not to injure the patient's interest in health, but to the interest "in a cure or palliation of his condition" since a special relationship was created by the physician's indication of a

[12] Sharon M Glenn, "Liability in the Absence of a Traditional Physician-Patient Relationship: What Every 'On Call' Doctor Should Know" (1993) 28 Wake Forest LR 747, 753.

[13] See Maxwell J Mehlman, "Fiduciary Contracting: Limitations on Bargaining between Patients and Health Care Providers" (1990) 51 U Pitt LR 365.

[14] This is not to say that a doctor may not be held contractually liable for failing to produce a specific result if she chooses to make such a promise. See *Safian v Aetna Life Ins*, 24 NYS2d 92 (App Div 1940).

[15] The leading case for this proposition is *Tunkl v Regents of University of California*, 383 P2d 441 (Cal 1963); see also *Emory University v Porubiansky*, 248 Ga 391 (Ga 1981) and *Leidy v Deseret Enterprises, Inc*, 252 Pa Super 162 (Pa 1977).

[16] See, eg, *Colton v New York Hospital*, 414 NYS2d 866 (NY Sup Ct 1979). This tendency, allowing tort to trump contract, has been criticized by various academics. See Richard A Epstein, "Contractual Principle versus Legislative Fixes: Coming to Closure on the Unending Travails of Medical Malpractice" (2005) 54 DePaul LR 503; Richard A Epstein, "Medical Malpractice, Imperfect Information, and the Contractual Foundation for Medical Services" (1986) 49 L&Cont Probs 201; Richard A Epstein, "Medical Malpractice: The Case for Contract" (1976) 1 Am Bar Found Res J 87; see also Clark C Havighurst, "Private Reform of Tort-Law Dogma: Market Opportunities and Legal Obstacles" (1986) 49 L&Cont Probs 143; and Glen O Robinson, "Rethinking the Allocation of Medical Malpractice Risks between Patients and Providers" (1986) 49 L&Cont Probs 173.

[17] John CP Goldberg, Leslie C Kendrick, Anthony J Sebok, & Benjamin C Zipursky, *Tort Law: Responsibilities and Redress* (5th edn, Wolters Kluwer 2021) 215.

[18] *R v Bateman* [1925] 19 Cr App R 8 (CA) 12–13. An early case of malpractice liability independent of contract is *Pippin v Sheppard* [1822] 147 Eng Rep 517.

willingness to cure.[19] As noted earlier, and on the one hand, the rise of the NHS reinforced the dominant role of tort, since under the English law of contract—which requires an exchange of consideration between contracting parties—the NHS cannot be sued in contract by those who fall under its care.[20] On the other hand, for those private health service plaintiffs who do actually have contracts with their healthcare providers, contract is an option. "In theory a private patient has two claims," but other than as a matter of pleading there is "no practical difference" between them, since in England the breach of an implied term (such as the obligation to exercise reasonable care in the performance of a service) must be proven by the plaintiff.[21]

On the continent, contract plays an important role in liability for medical malpractice. The foundation of this difference is that civilian contracts for medical care do not require the exchange of consideration but only an agreement between the parties. In Germany, therefore, an agreement to treat by a healthcare provider is a private law contract regardless of whether the patient (or anyone else, for that matter) pays for the services received.[22] In France, the law of contract governed the medical treatment relationship, without any need of consideration, until a reform in 2002 created new pathways for recovery (as we will see in more detail later in this chapter).[23] Until 2017, in Italy, the doctrine of *responsabilità da contatto sociale* (liability stemming from a social contact) based medical treatment contracts between parties on the social interaction that occurred between them, with the result that a patient might sue in contract a doctor who is an employee of a hospital even

[19] Marc S Stauch, *The Law of Medical Negligence in England and Germany: A Comparative Analysis* (Hart 2008) 14.

[20] Stauch (n 19) 10.

[21] WV Horton Rogers, "Medical Liability in England," in Koch (ed) (n 6) 165, at 187. There is no difference as to the limitation period either, since s 11 of the 1980 Limitation Act provides that a three-year period of limitation applies "to any action for damages for negligence, nuisance or breach of duty (whether the duty exists by virtue of a contract or of provision made by or under a statute or independently of any contract or any such provision)." See also Ken Oliphant & Vanessa Wilcox, "England," in Israel Gilead & Bjarte Askeland (eds), *Prescription in Tort Law. Analytical and Comparative Perspectives* (Intersentia 2020) 243, 252–253; Richard Goldberg, "Causation and Defences," in Andrew Grubb, Judith Laing, & Jean McHale (eds), *Principles of Medical Law* (3rd edn, OUP 2010) 325, 366–368.

[22] Stauch (n 19) 11. Since the reform carried out by the Patient's Rights Act (Act of 26 February 2013, BGBl I, 277), the rule is codified in §§ 630a–630h BGB. Where a patient cannot consent to treatment, either because she is unconscious or temporarily incompetent, a contract is considered to be formed under the doctrine of *Geschäftsfuhrung ohne Auftrag* (presumed permission). See Stauch (n 19) 11, as well as new § 630d (1): "If consent to a measure which cannot be delayed cannot be acquired in good time, it may be implemented without consent if this is in line with the implicit will of the patient."

[23] Simon Taylor, "The Development of Medical Liability and Accident Compensation in France," in Ewoud Hondius (ed), *The Development of Medical Liability* (CUP 2010) 70, 71.

though the patient only agreed to be admitted to the hospital and had no contractual relationship with the doctor.[24] Even the hospital's contractual liability did not need to be based on an explicit agreement with the patient: "the mere admission of the patient [...] generates a contract."[25] In 2017 a statutory reform established that doctors are subject to tort liability, but reaffirmed the principle that public and private institutions providing health care are liable in contract, no matter whether they entered into a contract with the patient or not.[26]

With the exception of France, both tort and contract provide parallel paths to redress in the civilian systems. France differs from its peers in one important respect: it adopts the unique approach of *non-cumul*, which may privilege contract over tort (this shall be discussed in greater detail). Although other differences may exist, in civilian systems there is very little practical difference in the definition of breach in tort and contract in the medical malpractice context. Almost every civilian system distinguishes between an obligation to use reasonable care and skill (*Diensvertrag* in Germany, *obligation de moyens* in France, *obbligazione di mezzi* in Italy) and an obligation to achieve a specific result (*Werkvertrag* in Germany, *obligation de résultat* in France, *obbligazione di risultato* in Italy). In most cases, medical services are treated under the former category, which means that, in principle, plaintiff must prove a defendant's fault, thereby making the test of breach of contract look very much like negligence.[27]

Given the similarities of the basis for responsibility in claims for medical injury in civilian systems, the choice between tort and contract is determined by other factors, including specific advantages that might be secured for the plaintiff by choosing one form of action over another as well as larger forces of legal culture. For example, while it could be said that contract was the "primary" source of legal obligations owed to a patient in Germany, until recently there were advantages to using tort in certain cases.[28] Originally, German

[24] Alessandro P Scarso & Massimo Foglia, "Medical Liability in Italy," in Koch (ed) (n 6) 329, at 345.

[25] Ibid at 342.

[26] Art 7 of the Law no 24 of 2017. See also Miquel Martín-Casals, "The Borderlines of Tort Law. Comparative Report," in Miquel Martín-Casals (ed), *The Borderlines of Tort Law* (Intersentia 2019) 711, 805. In order to bring an action against the doctor or the healthcare institution, the plaintiff should preliminarily either resort to mediation (according to art 5(1 bis) of the legislative decree no 28 of 2010) or carry out a "preliminary technical expertise for the settlement of the dispute" under art 696 bis of the Italian Civil Procedure Code (according to art 8 of the law no 24 of 2017).

[27] Dieter Giesen, *International Medical Malpractice Law* (Mohr Siebeck 1988) 13.

[28] Colm Peter McGrath, *The Development of Medical Liability in Germany. 1800–1945* (Vittorio Klostermann 2019) 139–162; Stauch (n 19) 11.

contract law excluded compensation for non-pecuniary loss.[29] Therefore, a claim against a physician in malpractice brought under the old BGB § 611 for breach of contract would compensate only for pecuniary losses, such as the cost of the procedure; out-of-pocket expenses associated with the medical error, and loss of wages; but not pain and suffering or bereavement damages to the family. In 2002, BGB § 253 was revised to allow for pain and suffering damages in contract and tort in case of an injury to the plaintiff's body or health,[30] thus removing the most important benefit of pursuing a remedy in tort for this kind of cases. Further, since vicarious liability standards set by the BGB are strict in contract (§§ 278 and 280 BGB) and fault-based in tort (§ 831 BGB), it has been noted that after 2002 the plaintiff's position became more advantageous under contract law rules than under tort law ones.[31] In 2013, a new subsection (§§ 630a to 630h) devoted to the "treatment contract" (*Behandlungsvertrag*) was inserted in the German Civil Code, cementing contract law as the primary legal basis for bringing medical liability actions.[32] Nevertheless, the reform has not modified the plaintiff's right to pursue concurrent claims in tort and contract, choosing the remedy which appears to her the most advantageous[33]—a practice that German courts have allowed since at least 1916.[34]

In Italy there may be other advantages for claiming liability in contract: the statute of limitations for contract claims is ten years, compared to five years for torts claims; once the patient proves that she suffered harm under a medical contract, the burden of proof in contract falls on the healthcare provider to disprove the breach of contract, whereas the tort plaintiff has the burden of proving that her harm is due to the practitioner's negligence.[35] It was because

[29] McGrath (n 28) 162–164; Giesen (n 27) 34. Arguably, under an outdated reading of art 2059 of the Italian Civil Code, the same could be said for Italian law as well. Recent developments have made the strict exclusion of non-pecuniary damages under art 2059 CC a non-issue. See Chapter I, section 5 and Chapter IV, section 6.

[30] Ulrich Magnus, "Germany," in Gilead & Askeland (eds) (n 21) 339, 345–346; Stauch (n 19) 11. The reform also harmonized the limitation periods applying to contract- and tort-based claims for damages based on injuries to life, body, health, or liberty. Current § 199(2) BGB sets a uniform limitation period of thirty years, applying to both types of actions.

[31] Paula Giliker, *Vicarious Liability in Tort: A Comparative Perspective* (CUP 2012) 45. But on these provisions, see also section 2.3 in this chapter.

[32] Cf Colm McGrath, "Medical Liability," in Basil S Markesinis, John Bell, & André Janssen, *Markesinis's German Law of Torts* (5th edn, Bloomsbury 2019) 136, 137–138; Marc S Stauch, "The 2013 German Patient's Rights Act—Codifying Medical Malpractice Compensation" (2015) 6 JETL 85.

[33] McGrath (n 32) 137–138; Gerald Spindler & Oliver Rieckserer, *Tort Law in Germany* (Kluwer 2011) 37; Lena Schneider, *Neue Behandlungsmethoden im Arzthaftungsrecht* (Springer 2010) 63–64.

[34] RG 13 October 1916, RGZ 88, 433.

[35] Giovanni Comandé & Elena Occhipinti, "Italy," in Gilead & Askeland (eds) (n 21) 413, 415–417; Scarso & Foglia (n 24) 343–344. It should be noted that courts in Italy have developed a

of these advantages that courts, since the end of the eighties and until the 2017 reform, framed the liability of both doctors and hospitals as contractual. Yet, as already indicated, the 2017 statute established that liability claims against doctors should be pursued as tort actions, while hospitals are liable in contract. The new system channels patients toward suing healthcare institutions under contract law rather than doctors under tort law, as in the former case plaintiffs can benefit (from hospitals' deeper pockets, as well as) from the more lenient ten years' limitation period and the more benevolent rules on the burden of proving evidence under contract law as opposed to tort law.[36]

In France the situation is somewhat different. Actions against private providers of medical care were until 2002 based on a contractual obligation owed by the defendant to use reasonable care or skill (*obligations de moyen*) based on (former) article 1147 (now article 1231-1) of the Civil Code.[37] The emergence of contract to remedy injuries resulting from medical malpractice came relatively late to France, through the *Mercier* case in 1936.[38] Prior to this, medical malpractice liability of public medical providers was based on tort, because the prevailing view was that there was no contract between the patient and the hospital. Private medical providers' liability (and most medicine was privately provided in the early twentieth century[39]) was governed by former articles 1382 and 1383 of the Civil Code (now articles 1240 and 1241), but under a set of judicial doctrines that were quite favorable to the defendant. First, since the *Cour de cassation* refused to make judgments about "medical science," it was almost impossible for plaintiffs to prove fault by relying upon evidence drawn from medical theories or methods.[40] Second, even when evaluating an error which did not require a judgment about medicine, the court remained somewhat deferential to the medical profession, stating that under former articles 1382 and 1383, liability would be established only if a "*faute lourde*" (a grave or obvious mistake) was found in the defendant's conduct.[41]

burden-shifting rule in tort in certain cases, thus easing the burden of tort plaintiffs in medical malpractice. Scarso & Foglia (n 24) 337.

[36] Martín-Casals (n 26) 805.
[37] Taylor (n 23) 71.
[38] Cass civ 20 May 1936, *Mercier*, D 1936.I.88.
[39] Taylor (n 23) 86.
[40] Taylor (n 23) 79.
[41] Taylor (n 23) 79–80.

After *Mercier*, medical malpractice in France focused on the contractual liability of the health provider. Even though the *Cour de cassation* preserved the requirement of fault after *Mercier*, in its new contract-based malpractice law, that fault became increasingly easy to prove as the twentieth century progressed.[42] The only exceptions were cases in which it was not possible to conceive of a contractual basis for the victim's claim, such as in cases of emergency care performed on a comatose person.[43] Up until 2002, the contractual or tortious nature of the claim was a point of primary importance in France, because of the already-mentioned principle of *non-cumul des responsabilités*: liability for medical malpractice in delict was impossible if the plaintiff had a contract with the medical provider.[44] Under the alternative approach of concurrent or alternative liability, which is the standard rule in Europe,[45] an aggrieved patient can sue in either contract or tort, and in some systems both (although of course they could only collect their damages once).[46] In France, by contrast, patients were limited to contract (or, in the exceptional cases just mentioned, in tort) only.[47] Third parties, such as families members who were claiming for *préjudice d'affection* (a subheading of pain and suffering), had to sue in tort since they had no conceivable contractual relationship with the defendant.[48]

After 2002, however, the *non-cumul* rule has greatly lost its significance in this field. The Patient's Rights Law of 4 March 2002 ("PRL," also known as "*Loi Kouchner*"), which resulted in substantial amendments to the "*Code de la santé publique*" (the "Public Health Code"), changed the landscape, reforming and expanding French medical malpractice law, at least in four respects.

First, the reform created a hybrid basis for medical liability, establishing "a 'legal regime' that is neither contractual nor tortious."[49] This rendered

[42] See Jean Penneau, *Faute et erreur en matière de responsabilité médicale* (LGDJ 1973).
[43] Jean-René Binet, *Droit médical* (Lextenso 2010) 118–120.
[44] Giesen (n 27) 36.
[45] Martín-Casals (n 26) 787–793. Very few European countries follow the French principle of *non-cumul*: one example is Hungary, whose § 6:145 of the 2014 Civil Code provides that where there is a contractual relationship between the plaintiff and the defendant, parallel damage claims in extra-contractual liability are excluded. See Ádám Fuglinszky, "Some Structural Questions on the Relationship between Contractual and Extracontractual Liability in the New Hungarian Civil Code," in Attila Menyhárd & Emőd Veress (eds), *New Civil Codes in Hungary and Romania* (Springer 2017) 107, 111–116.
[46] Giesen (n 27) 34.
[47] Giesen (n 27) 36.
[48] Cass civ 1 April 1968, D 1968.653.
[49] Yvonne Lambert-Faivre & Stéphanie Porchy-Simon, *Droit du dommage corporel. Systèmes d'indemnisation* (7th edn, Dalloz 2012) 674; G'sell-Macrez (n 4) 1097.

irrelevant the doctrine of *non-cumul*, and unified claims for redress under a single basis of liability that is fault-based, except for a handful of pockets of strict liability, with a single statute of limitations (ten years).[50] Strict liability rules only apply in cases of hospital-related infections[51] and of damages caused by a defective product.[52]

Second, although the PRL preserves the procedural divide between suits against private and public medical providers (private defendants appear in the ordinary courts and public defendants in the administrative courts), the rules of liability controlling each are now uniform.[53]

Third, the PRL established a new alternative dispute resolution system (that does not bar the victim's right to bring her claim to the court, but is meant) to encourage early settlement and to reduce litigation against private and public health providers.[54] The law, in particular, created "regional commissions of conciliation and compensation for medical accidents" ("Commissions Régionales de Conciliation et d'Indemnisation des accidents médicaux"—CRCI). The CRCIs are designed to facilitate the amicable settlement of disputes by seeking a conciliation agreement between the victim and the insurer of the health professional or the public medical provider.[55] A patient may bring a claim to a CRCI if she believes that she has suffered an injury caused by the fault of a private or public medical provider, or for which the latter may be held strictly liable. The CRCI reviews the claim and determines whether the injury was caused by the provider's negligence or was such as to entail the latter's strict liability. If the committee concludes that the injury entails the liability of the provider, the latter's insurer[56] must make

[50] Jean-Sébastien Borghetti, "France," in Gilead & Askeland (eds) (n 21) 309, 310–313; Susan Carval & Ruth Sefton-Green, "Medical Liability in France," in Koch (ed) (n 6) 207, 210; Taylor (n 23) 73. In 2008 France unified the statute of limitation for contract and tort law actions in general. The new limitation period, whether for a contract-based claims or for actions based on tort, is now five years (art 2224 *Code Civil*), which raises up until ten years as far as actions on liability for corporal damage are concerned (art 2226 *Code Civil*).

[51] According to art R6111-6, *Code de la santé publique*, hospital-related infections are "the infections associated to the care received in a health institution."

[52] See art L1142-1, *Code de la santé publique* and G'sell-Macrez (n 4) 1107–08. In the case of damages caused by defective medical products, patient associations might bring a collective action against the producer and/or the supplier: see art L1143-2, *Code de la santé publique* (as modified in 2016). See also L1142-28, *Code de la santé publique*, which sets a ten years' limitation period for any liability action brought against any healthcare provider—no matter whether natural or legal person, or of private or public nature.

[53] Carval & Sefton-Green (n 50) 213; Lambert-Faivre & Porchy-Simon (n 49) 658–659.

[54] See G'sell-Macrez (n 4) 1118.

[55] G'sell-Macrez (n 4) 1119.

[56] Art L1142-14, *Code de la santé publique*.

an offer of compensation.[57] If the victim accepts the offer the claim is settled; if she rejects the offer, she may sue the defendant in court.[58] If the provider or its insurer refuses to make the offer, the *Office National d'Indemnisation des Accidents Médicaux* (ONIAM) may elect to step into the shoes of the provider and make an offer.[59] The victim then has the option to accept the offer from the ONIAM, which, in case of acceptance, is subrogated in the victim's claim. If the victim rejects the offer from ONIAM, then she may bring her claim before the courts.[60]

Fourth, the PRL created a national compensation fund for a specific kind of serious injuries as defined under the PRL itself. A serious injury is defined as permanent partial disability of at least 24%;[61] as a temporary incapacity of at least six consecutive months or six non-consecutive months in a period of twelve months; or, in exceptional cases, as the inability to carry on business, or as particularly serious disturbances in the conditions of existence.[62] When a patient suffers a serious injury of the above kind (aside from some residual cases[63]), which is due to a medical hazard—that is, an accidental risk inherent to the medical procedure and which occurred without any fault of the practitioner arising from acts of prevention, diagnosis, or treatment,[64] or to a hospital-acquired infection (regardless of whether they were caused by negligence of the hospital), the victim has the right to obtain redress from the ONIAM.[65] When the above-mentioned circumstances are met, the victim may either initiate a claim in court against the ONIAM[66] or start a procedure

[57] Ibid; see also Kenneth Watson & Rob Kottenhagen, "'Patients' Rights, Medical Error and Harmonisation of Compensation Mechanisms in Europe" (2018) 25 Eur J Health L 1, 19.

[58] If then the court agrees that the designated party should be responsible, and that the insurer's offer was inadequate, it can also add a penalty up to 15% of the compensation due—the penalty is to be paid to the ONIAM: art L1142-14, *alinéa* 9, *Code de la santé publique*.

[59] See art L1142-15 *Code de la santé publique*, as well as Watson & Kottenhagen (n 57) 19.

[60] G'sell-Macrez (n 4) 1119–1120.

[61] See art D1142-1 *Code de la santé publique*. Annex XI-2 of the Code lists the most common injuries that may result from medical malpractices and determines the percentage of disability that can be placed on each of them.

[62] Art D1142-1 *Code de la santé publique*.

[63] For instance, the PRL incorporated an existing public compensation scheme for injuries caused by the transfusion of HIV-infected blood and extended it to include blood infected with Hepatitis C in 2008: Lambert-Faivre & Porchy-Simon (n 49) 738–739; Geneviève Helleringer, "Medical Malpractice and Compensation in France, Part II: Compensation Based on National Solidarity" (2011) 86 Chi-Kent LR 1125, at 1127.

[64] These are the so-called *aléas thérapeutiques*: Conseil d'État 9 April 1993, *Bianchi*, Leb 127. See Helleringer (n 63) 1126.

[65] See art L1142-1, *Code de la santé publique*, and Law 2002–1577 *relative à la responsabilité civile médicale*; generally, Lambert-Faivre & Porchy-Simon (n 49) 736–738; Helleringer (n 63); Carval & Sefton-Green (n 50) 214. Such a right, of course, does not bar the victim from bringing her claim to the court or to the CRCI, provided that she proves all the elements of a tort.

[66] Helleringer (n 63) 1133.

before the CRCI. If the Commission reaches the conclusion that there was a medical hazard, a hospital-acquired infection, or any other grounds prompting compensation by the fund, it informs ONIAM, indicating nature and scope of the losses.[67] ONIAM shall then make an offer to the victim, who can accept it or not. If she does not, she may sue the ONIAM in court.[68]

Although many note that the availability of no-fault public compensation for medical hazards and hospital-related infections, only in case of "serious injury" limits the scope of these provisions of the law to a relatively small number of victims,[69] and the PRL remains the European most important effort to experiment with some form of alternative dispute resolution in the field of medical injuries other than the initiatives taken in the seventies by Sweden[70] and the other Scandinavian countries which followed the Swedish example.[71] The justification for this system of publicly funded no-fault compensation under the PRL is indicated by the term used to describe it: "national solidarity." The repair of the victim of medical misadventure is a matter of state concern since the loss is randomly inflicted.

2.3. Direct and Vicarious Liability

Direct liability for medical malpractice is often about holding natural persons, whether physicians, nurses, or others, responsible for the injuries they have caused. Legal persons, such as partnerships, private corporations, charitable institutions, and public entities can be held directly responsible for

[67] Art L1142-17-1, *Code de la santé publique.*

[68] Art L1142-18, *Code de la santé publique.*

[69] Lambert-Faivre & Porchy-Simon (n 49) 732; Taylor (n 23) 94. Taylor estimates that medical accidents resulting in more than 24% permanent partial incapacity represent less than 4% of all medical accidents.

[70] See Vibe Ulfbeck, Matte Hartlev, & Mårten Schultz, 'Malpractice in Scandinavia' (2012) 87 Chi-Kent LR 111–129; Bernhard A Koch, "Medical Liability in Europe: Comparative Analysis," in Koch (ed) (n 6) 611, 651.

[71] Schemes for the coverage of medical accidents were enacted in Finland in 1987 (Martti Mikkonen, "Compensation in the Finnish Health Care Sector," in Jos Dute, Michael G Faure, & Helmut Koziol (eds), *No-Fault Compensation in the Health Care Sector* (Springer 2004) 186–191), in Norway in 1988 (Rolf G. Jørstad, "The Norwegian System of Compensation to Patients" (2002) 21 Med L 681–686), in Denmark in 1992 (Martin Erichsen, "The Danish Patient Insurance System" (2001) 20 Med L 355–369). Following the French example, on 31 March 2010 Belgium enacted the "*Loi relative à l'indemnisation des dommages résultant de soins de santé*" establishing a two-track system under which the patient has a choice whether to bring a claim before the courts, or to apply to the newly established Medical Accidents Fund for compensation. See Thierry Vansweevelt, Steven Lierman, & Wannes Buelens, "No-Fault Law on Medical Accidents in Belgium: An Evaluation after Six Years" (2019) 10 JETL 257–285.

harms they have caused but typically they are held vicariously liable for the injuries brough about by their employees or agents.

In the United States, hospitals and other institutions are vicariously liable for the torts of their employees to the same extent as any other employer. The test of whether an employee was acting within the scope of her employment when the accident occurred can vary from state to state, but the variations are not very great.[72] It is also not that difficult to identify who is an employee of a hospital or another medical institution: nurses, paramedics, and medical trainees receiving a salary from the institution are employees.[73] The more difficult questions arise when the tort is committed by a physician or another medical professional who is not employed by the hospital. Here, the trend has been away from a legal regime which protected hospitals under numerous doctrines to one which is increasingly open to holding hospitals responsible for the torts of non-employees. At the beginning of the twentieth century many hospitals were protected by the doctrines of charitable and governmental immunity, which meant that charitable and public hospitals could not be sued at all, or under very limited circumstances. In addition, until the middle of the twentieth century, private hospitals were protected by a doctrine, embraced in many states, which held that, since corporations could not practice medicine, they could not be sued for medical malpractice, either.[74] Once these archaic doctrines were overcome, patients seeking to sue hospitals for the errors of their physicians were still faced with the barrier that in most cases their treating physicians were independent contractors and not employees of the hospitals.[75]

Although it is still good law, courts have found various exceptions to the rule that, since doctors are independent contractors, hospitals cannot be vicariously liable for their torts. First, courts began to apply the principles of apparent or ostensible agency to hold hospitals responsible for the negligence of physicians who, although they were independent contractors in fact, were in positions where patients might assume they were agents of the hospital.[76] Second, some courts began to apply the doctrine of non-delegable

[72] See generally Dan B Dobbs, Paul T Hayden, & Ellen M Bublick, *Torts and Compensation, Personal Accountability and Social Responsibility for Injury* (8th edn, West 2017) 685–688; Dan B Dobbs, *The Law of Torts* (West 2000) 907 and *passim*.

[73] See, eg, *Register v Wilmington Medical Center, Inc*, 377 A2d 8 (Del 1977).

[74] See, eg, *Bernardi v Community Hosp Ass'n*, 443 P2d 708 (Colo 1968) and *Bing v Thunig*, 143 NE2d 3, 8 (NY 1957).

[75] See *Oehler v Humana Inc*, 105 Nev 348 (Nev 1997).

[76] See, eg, *Gilbert v Sycamore Mun Hosp*, 622 NE2d 788 (Ill 1993); *Clark v Southview Hosp & Family Health Ctr*, 628 NE2d 46 (Ohio 1994).

duty to certain medical activities, thus forcing the hospital to be vicariously responsible for certain specialists, such as emergency room physicians and radiologists, whose work was deemed an inherent function of the hospital.[77]

Natural persons too could be held vicariously liable for the medical malpractice of others. American law once held that a surgeon who was an independent contractor was nonetheless vicariously liable for the torts of *everyone* in the operating room, including the employees of the hospital, as long as they were under his immediate control.[78] This rule is in decline, in part because the trend has been to attribute responsibility for medical errors to institutions and not persons.[79] The logical extension of this trend is to make hospitals and other institutions directly liable for injuries. This theory of corporate negligence is not based on vicarious liability but on the duty of the hospital itself to carefully select, train, review or supervise personnel, or to provide sufficient resources (equipment, etc.) to the personnel.[80]

In England, the dominance of the NHS in the provision of medical services limits the practical significance of vicarious liability. The NHS is responsible for the malpractice of its staff, and although the individual staff members are also personally liable for their acts, suit against them is only a "theoretical possibility" because they can, and usually do, get the state to take responsibility for their liability under a scheme established by the NHS and known as "NHS Indemnity."[81] NHS Indemnity does not automatically cover most general practitioners under contract with the NHS or private medical clinics and these must carry their own insurance.[82] But if the independent contractor chooses to place itself under NHS Indemnity (and most do), then the liability will run vicariously to the NHS.[83] This has led one commentator

[77] See *Jackson v Power*, 743 P2d 1376 (Alaska 1987).

[78] See, eg, *Harris v Miller*, 335 NC 379 (NC 1994).

[79] See Clark C Havighurst, "Making Health Plans Accountable for the Quality of Care," 31 Ga LR 587, 595 (1997).

[80] Theories of direct liability could extend to managed care organizations (that is, organizations providing health coverage to insureds under dedicated insurance plans) when they make staffing decision that affect the delivery of medical care by physicians. See, eg, *Darling v Charleston Community Memorial Hospital*, 211 NE2d 253 (Ill 1965); and *Jones v Chicago HMO Ltd of Illinois*, 730 NE2d 1119, 1137 (Ill 2000) (theory of "institutional negligence"). True enterprise liability for hospitals, however, is still only a speculative idea encouraged by legal academics. See Havighurst (n 79) 603–604.

[81] National Health Service, *Health Service Guidelines (96)48. NHS Indemnity: Arrangements for Handling Clinical Negligence Claims against NHS Staff*, 1996. See resolution.nhs.uk/wp-content/uploads/2018/10/NHS-Indemnity.pdf, as well as Horton Rogers (n 21) 184.

[82] Horton Rogers (n 21) 169–170. One decision seems to suggest that, where the NHS has contracted with a private medical provider to provide medical services in toto, it will not be vicariously liable for the private contractor's errors: *A v Ministry of Defence* [2004] EWCA Civ 641, [2005] QB 183.

[83] Horton Rogers (n 21) 185.

to suggest that, although the recent trend has been to loosen the NHS monopoly on medical treatment by allowing it to contract with independent contractors, liability is, for the most part, borne by the NHS, either directly or through some sort of indemnity scheme.[84]

In Germany, vicarious liability for the errors of subordinates and others further down the "vertical" division of labor (such as nurses) can be handled under § 831 BGB or § 278 BGB.[85] The former imposes a tort law duty of reasonable care in the selection and supervision of those "employed" by the principal (whose fault is presumed), while the latter imposes vicarious liability upon the principal for contractual liabilities of the principal's agents.[86] Differences between the vicarious liability rules in tort and contract may have an impact on plaintiff's choices. Yet, in evaluating the two regimes, one has to keep in mind that, since liability under § 831 is presumed, with the burden of proof on the defendant to rebut, liability under § 831 is often as easy for the plaintiff to establish as liability under § 278.[87] Further, the significance of the distance between the two sets of rules is lessened in practice by the circumstance that German case law allows plaintiffs to choose whether to pursue their claims through tortious or contractual actions.[88]

In the extra-contractual domain, besides being vicariously liable for its employees under § 831 BGB, a hospital might also be directly liable under § 823 I for the conduct of doctors causing harm to the plaintiff's health.[89] Generally, claims of vicarious liability under § 831 are most likely to succeed against institutions for failure to properly train and schedule staff, rather than against individual physicians, who may claim that the responsibility for managing support staff lay entirely with the hospital.[90]

Under German contract law, depending on how the patient was injured and with whom the patient had had a contact, she can make a claim under §§ 276–280 BGB against the hospital, the doctor, or both. It is important to remind that, like elsewhere in the continent, in Germany contracts can exist

[84] Horton Rogers (n 21) 186.

[85] As noted above, pain and suffering damages were not awarded in contract until 2002. See above, section 2.2 in this chapter.

[86] Markesinis, Bell, & Janssen McGrath (n 32) 117–119.

[87] See Paula Giliker, *Vicarious Liability in Tort: A Comparative Perspective* (CUP 2010) 45–46; Petry (n 6) 247.

[88] See above, n 33.

[89] Marc S Stauch, "Medical Malpractice and Compensation in Germany" (2011) 86 Chi-Kent LR 1139, 1145 (2011).

[90] There could be cases, such as where a senior physician supervises a junior physician, or where the physician requests specialized nursing procedures in an operation, where § 831 may apply against these individuals. See Petry (n 6) 252–253.

between a patient and her medical provider even if the patient is under no obligation to pay for the services she receives; the contract is a product of the mutual intention shared by the parties that medical treatment be provided.

Where a patient suffers an injury in the hospital, she typically would have been admitted under a *totaler Krankenhausvertrag*, or "total hospital" contract, under which the hospital would be liable under § 278 for all the errors committed by its staff, including the treating physicians.[91] Under a "split admission" or "visiting consultant" contract, the patient can choose to have separate contracts with the hospital and the doctor(s) who treat her, where the hospital is responsible for nursing and other ancillary treatments, but is not responsible for the physician's medical treatment, and vice versa.[92] Contract also plays an important role in determining who bears the liability for errors resulting from outpatient services. Patients with public insurance who visit doctors in private practice have the same rights under contract as a private patient paying from their own pocket, and patients who receive outpatient care in hospitals are deemed by German law to have formed contracts only with the chief physician managing that department, and not with the hospital who owns the facilities.[93] Physicians who operate a "joint practice," where they hold themselves out as a specialist unit in which each member is capable for treating the patient, are jointly and severally liable under contract for the damage caused by any one of the members of the group.[94]

In Italy, the specific features of tort and contract liability in the field of medical malpractice described before, in section 2.2, have shaped the rules concerning direct and vicarious liability. Prior to 1988, victims of medical error caused by physicians employed by hospitals could bring a suit against the physician in tort only, since no contract was held to exist between the patient and doctor (the only exception being the cases in which there was an agreement between them prior to the patient's recovery). In turn, the hospital, as the employer of the physician, could be sued in contract or tort (under art 1228 CC, or under art 2049 CC, respectively). Since 1988, direct liability in contract against physicians who had no direct contract with their patients, has been developed under a number of doctrines ranging from the idea that the patient is a third-party beneficiary of the employment contract

[91] Stauch (n 19) 11.
[92] Petry (n 6) 257–258.
[93] Petry (n 6) 259–260.
[94] See BGH 29 June 1999, VersR 1999, 1241 and BGH 4 December 2001, VersR 2002, 233, cited by Petry (n 6) 260.

between the physician and the hospital[95] to the idea that there exists a "social contact" (*contatto sociale*) which arises when the physician accepts the responsibility to provide medical care to the patient (similar to the German concept of *Schutzpflichten*).[96] Under such a regime, hospitals could be held jointly and severally liable for tortious and contractual liabilities of their employed physicians through vicarious liability, while individuals could be held directly liable for injuries caused by others if the duties imposed on them under tort or contract required them to exercise diligence in the supervision of others.[97]

The adoption of law no. 24 of 2017 has, however, changed the legal landscape. Under the new rules, doctors are liable in tort, unless they entered in a contract with the patient.[98] By contrast, public and private health care institutions are

> directly and vicariously liable in contract, respectively under art 1218 and 1228 of the Italian Civil Code, for the fault of professionals working within the institutions themselves, even if the professionals were chosen by the patient and are working as independent contractors.[99]

Moving to France, the rules of *respondeat superior* developed by French courts before the PRL have survived its passage.[100] Regardless of whether the healthcare provider is employed by a public or private institution, French courts continue to hold the employer vicariously liable for the employee's negligent acts (unless the latter caused the injury while acting *ultra vires*, a category which not only includes sexual misconduct—to take an obvious example—but also refusing to treat a patient or concealing an error).[101] By contrast, the healthcare provider (be she employed by a public or a private entity) is not personally liable for her negligence as long as she is performing a duty assigned by the employer.[102] Rules are different when the healthcare provider

[95] Scarso & Foglia (n 24) 335–336.
[96] Scarso & Foglia (n 24) 342.
[97] Thus, a physician could be held liable under tort or contract for failure to supervise the team (équipe) under his control and member of the team can be held liable under tort or contract for failure to intervene to prevent another member of the team from carelessly harming the patient. Scarso & Foglia (n 24) 340.
[98] Art 7(3), Law no 24 of 2017.
[99] Art 7(1), Law no 24 of 2017.
[100] Binet (n 43) 234–237.
[101] G'sell-Macrez (n 4) 1104; Binet (n 43) 234–237.
[102] Simon Taylor, *Medical Accident Liability and Redress in English and French Law* (CUP 2015) 162; G'sell-Macrez (n 4) 1104; Binet (n 43) 235–237.

is a not an employee of the public or private institution. In such a case, the practitioner responds personally for the injury she caused. Thus, even when a hospital retains the (not employed) healthcare provider's services, it cannot be held liable, unless it somehow acted negligently in its selection of, and/or coordination with the healthcare provider.[103]

3. Grounds of Liability

In general, the kinds of wrongs that occur in medical malpractice fall into two types: "treatment malpractice" and "disclosure malpractice." The former is the result of medical procedures that do not meet the standard of care required by law, and the latter is the result of procedures performed upon the patient without her consent.[104] One might want to add as a third category liability for injuries which result to the patient from medical hazards without proof of a failure by the medical provider to meet the standard of care, such as those which are now handled by an alternative compensation scheme under the PRL,[105] but these forms of strict liability should be seen as just one type of treatment malpractice, where all injuries caused from the treatment are in principle the responsibility of the defendant.

In each branch of malpractice the tort systems have had to provide answers to a slightly different set of questions. In treatment malpractice the courts must determine (a) the scope of the medical provider's obligation—that is, to whom the provider might be liable; (b) the standard of care required to fulfill the obligation; (c) factual and legal causation of the injury. In disclosure malpractice the courts must determine (a) what counts as adequate consent; (b) what counts as adequate disclosure; (c) factual and legal causation. Each of these sets of questions may bring with it their own special doctrines of proof, including burden-shifting doctrines. In this chapter we discuss only some of these questions, namely those that fall under (a) and (b) in each form of malpractice. Questions of causation are dealt with in a more accurate way in Chapter VII.

[103] G'sell-Macrez (n 4) 1103–1104.
[104] Giesen (n 27) 72.
[105] See section 2.2 in this chapter.

3.1. Treatment Malpractice

The discussion in sections 2.2. and 2.3 contrasting the role of tort and contract law among the various jurisdictions in this survey provides an initial answer to the question concerning the nature of the obligation in treatment malpractice. In all the systems reviewed, tort actions, when they are allowed, are almost always based in negligence (including vicarious liability for negligence) while contract actions are allowed on the basis of basic rules of contract, which divide, predictably, between the common law, where the exchange of consideration is paramount, and the civilian systems, where contract obligations are unproblematically extended to third parties and others with whom no exchange of consideration with the provider was possible. A partial exception is France, which, as noted, has now a medical malpractice regime which is technically neither contract nor tort.

The content of the obligation will vary, at least at first glance, on the nature of the obligation, that is, whether it is in tort or contract, and it may vary within different national tort and contract schemes. As already mentioned, the first source of variation may be less dramatic than appearances might suggest. For all systems that allow contract actions, the content of the contract obligation is strikingly similar, in that it is based on the obligation to "provide medical services according to the applicable standards of care."[106] In all the systems that allow tort actions, the negligence standard drawn from everyday life—to take the care expected of a reasonable person under the circumstances—must be qualified, since "circumstances," as it is

[106] Koch (n 70) 642. Almost all of the civilian systems test whether the medical contract has been breached against a negligence-like "obligation of means" standard. As noted in the text, however, the content and nature of the medical obligation might be affected by the form of service promised by the medical provider. In Germany, for example, where the provider agrees with the plaintiff to provide a medical apparatus, or to provide a well-organized and managed workplace (such as a laboratory or operating room), courts assume that reasonable care is tantamount to the successful operation of the equipment or the adequacy of the workplace provided (Stauch (n 19) 45). This is because the defendant is held to be capable of "mastering" the technical risks inherent in these activities, whether by taking precautionary measures against failure or by providing better training to staff (this is what the Germans call *voll beherrschbare Risiken*: "fully masterable risks"). See also § 630h I BGB, according to which "[a]n error is to be presumed to have been committed by the treating party if a general treatment risk has materialised which was fully manageable for the treating party and which led to the injury to the life, limb or health of the patient." The only way for the defendant to escape liability would be to prove that it was impossible to fulfill the contractual obligation (BGH 11 December 1990, NJW 1991, 1543, as well as Stauch (n 19) 38). For instance, where a patient suffered brain damage because of the mechanical breakdown of the system providing oxygen, the court noted that the doctrine of *Dienstvertrag* (obligation of means) did not apply and that the defendant was under a obligation of result, i.e., that the health provider had guaranteed to the patient "safe technical equipment during the treatment" (BGH 11 October 1977, NJW 1978, 584; see also Stauch (n 19) 45).

used here presupposes a certain level of care based on expert training and experience.[107] The content of the tort duty has to be determined by reference to professional standards.[108] The variations among different systems for ascertaining these standards is discussed in section 3.1.2.

Another important qualification concerns the scope of obligation. Typically, the medical provider's obligation will be very easy to ascertain in either tort or contract. The decision to treat a patient, which is almost always the product of mutual assent (but not always, as in the case of unconscious persons), is enough to clearly define for the provider to whom she owes a duty of care in tort in both the common law and civilian systems. The situation of contracts is only slightly more complex, since the common law countries, as we will see, are more restrictive in the scope of protection under contract law than the civilian systems.[109] However, in both tort and contract, the scope of the obligation may sometimes be unusually difficult to ascertain. This will be discussed in the following section.

3.1.1. Scope of Obligation (and the Beginning of Life)

While the scope of liability may be clearly indicated by the healthcare provider's subjective assent to form a physician/patient relationship, it may extend further. For example, does a physician owe a duty to a person whom she examines on behalf of another, such as an employer or an insurer? American courts have typically denied such claims under tort law.[110] English courts have held that such a duty exists under tort, while civilian courts find that an obligation in contract law may extend beyond the party who makes the contract.[111]

What about injuries to persons not yet in existence when the malpractice occurs, such as a fetus injured *in utero*? American courts initially refused to recognize a right of action in negligence (toward a physician or anyone else), claiming that there was no person to whom a duty was owed.[112] This position reversed in the middle of the twentieth century, so that now injuries done to a fetus who is then born alive are actionable by the newborn child.[113] This was

[107] Dobbs, Hayden, & Bublick (n 72) 417, 423–426.

[108] Stauch (n 19) 27; Giesen (n 27) 77. On the determination of such standards, see also Chapter II, sections 6–9.

[109] Horton Rogers (n 21) 187; Koch (n 70) 641.

[110] See, eg, *Lee v New York*, 162 AD2d 34 (NY App Div 1990) (no duty) and *Martinez v Lewis*, 969 P2d 213 (Colo 1998) (same).

[111] Giesen (n 27) 15–17.

[112] *Dietrich v Northhampton*, 138 Mass 14 (Mass 1884).

[113] See, eg, *Bronbrest v Kotz*, 65 F Supp 138 (DDC 1946). The trend in the United States has been to extend the duty to plaintiffs injured by negligence that occurred before they were conceived: cf

a topic of some controversy in the English courts, and the matter was settled by the passage of the Congenital Disabilities (Civil Liability) Act 1976, which provided that a child injured while *in utero* could sue once born.[114] Claims for prenatal harm have not been nearly as controversial for civilian systems as for the common law systems. As early as 1953 a German court permitted a suit by a child against a physician who committed malpractice against the child's mother by negligently transfusing blood tainted with syphilis before the conception of the child, resulting in both the mother and child becoming infected.[115] Despite not even existing when the carelessness took place, the child could sue in tort for an invasion of its "absolute right" in life and health.[116] Similarly, in France and Italy, in cases of post-conception damage (i.e., where a physician injures a fetus in the course of the procedure), the resulting child has long been allowed to sue the physician for tort and received pecuniary and non-pecuniary damages.[117]

The scope of the medical provider's obligation to persons not yet born becomes more controversial when the injury caused by the provider is not to the bodily health of the plaintiff (that is, taking them from a state of health to a state of disability), but causing her damage as a result of the child being born at all. Two classes of victims may be harmed by a careless healthcare provider in these cases: the parent and the child. *(i)* In wrongful birth cases, the putative obligation runs between the healthcare provider and the parents of the child who has been born (either with or without a disability).[118] *(ii)* In wrongful life cases, the putative obligation runs between the healthcare provider and the child who was born disabled. The child's claim is that the negligence of the healthcare provider caused the child's parents either to conceive the child or to fail to terminate the pregnancy that led to his birth.[119]

Albala v New York, 54 NY2d 269 (NY 1981) (no duty to plaintiff born with defect due to preconception injury to mother) and *Empire Casualty Co v St Paul Fire & Marine Ins Co*, 764 P2d 1191 (Colo 1988) (finding duty to plaintiff born with defect due to preconception carelessness).

[114] See Walter van Gerven, Pierre Larouche, & Jeremy Lever, *Cases, Materials and Text on National, Supranational and International Tort Law* (Hart 2000) 91.

[115] BGH 20 December 1952, BGHZ 8, 243, NJW 1953, 416; see also van Gerven, Larouche, & Lever (n 114) 80 and Cees van Dam, *European Tort Law* (2nd edn, OUP 2013) at 199.

[116] BGH 20 December 1952, BGHZ 8, 243; NJW 1953, 416. The same reasoning applied to a child who was injured *in utero* when his mother was hit in a car accident, the child's suit in tort was allowed under § 823: BGH 11 January 1972, BGHZ 58, 48.

[117] Cf Conseil d'État 27 September 1989, D 1991.80, cited in van Gerven, Larouche, & Lever (n 114) 114–115; and, in Italy, Cass 22 November 1993, no 11503, Giur it 1995, I, 1, 318.

[118] See Ronen Perry, "It's a Wonderful Life" (2008) 93 Cornell LR 329, 332.

[119] Ibid at 331.

(i) Wrongful birth. There are a variety of wrongful birth cases, and it is impossible in this chapter to classify them comprehensively from a comparative perspective. They all share the common feature that the parent alleges that, but for the negligence of the healthcare provider, they would not have become a parent. The negligence might have been in connection with information the healthcare provided (or was under a duty to provide) that misled the parent into thinking that they could have a healthy child if they conceived or carried a child to term, or it may have been in connection with an effort by the parent to prevent conception or to terminate a pregnancy. These cases, while raising difficult questions of damages, are relatively uncontroversial from the perspective of obligation.

In tort, the duty of the physician to perform a task relating to controlling fertility (eg, a sterilization) or lowering the risk associated with pregnancy (eg, monitoring the health of mother and fetus during the pregnancy) runs to the parent(s) just as any other duty to provide professional medical services runs to a patient. Almost all United States jurisdictions whose courts have considered the question permit wrongful birth claims when they involve the loss of an opportunity for a mother (or parents) to avoid the birth of a child (even a healthy child) due to faulty pre-conception sterilization.[120] In these cases, the debate has focused on damages, and there is a diversity of approaches. Where the child is born healthy, many states have awarded medical expenses and emotional distress damages associated with pregnancy and childbirth but *not* the costs of raising the unexpected child to adulthood.[121] A smaller number have permitted the recovery of the cost of raising the child as well, while others have allowed this heading of damages to be "off-set" by the emotional benefits received by the parent(s).[122] Where the child is born disabled, there is no question among courts that the parent(s) should receive at least the *additional* cost of raising the child given the disability compared to raising a child without a disability.[123]

[120] See *Emerson v Magendantz*, 689 A2d 409 (RI 1997) (reviewing cases).

[121] *MA v United States*, 951 P2d 851, 855, no 8 (Alaska 1998) (reviewing cases).

[122] *MA v United States*, 951 P2d 851, 855, no 8 (Alaska 1998) (reviewing cases). The additional emotional distress of the parent(s) resulting from raising a disabled child is also subject to the same off-set. See *Lodato ex rel Lodato v Kappy*, 353 NJ Super 439, 448 (App Div 2002).

[123] See *Keel v Banach*, 624 So 2d 1022, 1030 (Ala 1993) (reviewing cases). For a different approach, holding under general tort principles that, having breached a duty to the parents and caused the disabled child to be born, the defendant must bear the whole cost of its upbringing, see *Robak v United States*, 658 F2d 471 (7th Cir Ill 1981).

The English approach to wrongful birth has followed a pattern similar to the United States. After some early cases suggesting that wrongful birth claims for the cost of maintaining a healthy child would be allowed,[124] the House of Lords rejected a wrongful birth claim for the maintenance of a healthy child born as a result of a negligently performed vasectomy in *McFarlane v Tayside Health Board*.[125] The mother could collect damages only for her pain and suffering and loss of earnings connected with and surrounding the pregnancy. The question of whether maintenance for a healthy child should be paid in a wrongful birth case was answered in the negative by the House of Lords in *Rees v Darlington Memorial Hospital*.[126] The claimant in these proceedings (Ms Rees), suffering from a severe and progressive visual disability, felt unable to discharge the ordinary duties of a mother, and for that reason wished to be sterilized. She made her wishes known to a consultant employed by the appellant NHS Trust, who carried out a sterilization operation but did so negligently, and the claimant conceived and bore a son, normal and healthy. The claimant's disability remained. She claimed as damages the cost of rearing the child. The Court of Appeal held that she was entitled to recover the additional costs she would incur so far as they would be attributable to her disability.[127] The House of Lords overturned the decision and awarded the mother only a conventional sum (15,000 pounds) for she has been denied, through the negligence of a third party, the opportunity to live her life in the way that she wished and planned.[128] In another case, in which a general practitioner failed to properly test a pregnant woman to see if she was a carrier of hemophilia, and the child was later born suffering with both hemophilia and autism, the English Court of Appeal partially overturned the High Court's decision entitling the mother (who would have undergone a termination if she was made aware of the son's hemophilia) to recover the costs associated with her son's

[124] See, eg, *Thake v Maurice* [1986] QB 644 (CA) and *Benarr v Kettering Health Authority* [1988] 138 NLJ 179 (QBD).

[125] [2000] 2 AC 59 (HL).

[126] *Rees v Darlington Memorial Hospital* [2003] UKHL 52.

[127] [2002] EWCA Civ 88, [2003] QB 20.

[128] Ibid. See also Lord Scott's speech in *Parkinson v St. James and Seacroft University Hospital NHS Trust* [2001] EWCA Civ 530; Stauch (n 19) 16–17; and, more recently, *ARB v IVF Hammersmith & Another* [2018] EWCA Civ 2803 (CA). The case arose from a claim for breach of contract against a clinic. The clinic implanted an embryo containing plaintiff's/appellant's gametes into a woman, from whom the former had by that date separated (although they had used the clinic earlier to conceive and birth a prior child). The clinic failed to obtain the man's written or informed consent to the procedure and it proceeded on the basis of a signature on the relevant form which the judge found had been forged by the woman. The father succeeded on all aspects of his primary case against the clinic for breach of contract, but judges of both instances held that he could not recover damages for the cost of the (healthy) child's upbringing.

hemophilia *and* autism (which were quantified as amounting to, respectively, £1,400,000 and £7,600,000).[129] According to the Court of Appeal, the scope of the risk accepted by the defendant doctor was limited to the losses arising out of the child's hemophilia, and did not extend to all the risks associated with the pregnancy.[130]

In Germany, the benefits of approaching medical malpractice through a contract lens become clear in cases of wrongful birth, which have usually been analyzed under § 278 BGB. The first benefit of this approach is that the plaintiff's purpose for contracting with the medical provider gives content to the obligation owed. The court takes the "*Schutzzweck der Norm*," or the protective purpose of the contract law rule, to determine whether the breach of obligation is related to the injury suffered by the parent(s).[131] Thus, where the plaintiff was negligently sterilized, German courts find malpractice depending on the goal of the sterilization—if it was to avoid a feared birth defect, then the medical provider is deemed in breach of contract only if the failed sterilization produces a child with that defect, but if the sterilization was to avoid having any children at all, then the provider is deemed in breach of contract if even a healthy child is born.[132] Along the same lines, where a plaintiff had contracted with a provider for one purpose unrelated to the possible termination of a pregnancy, the negligent failure of the provider to give information which would have led the plaintiff to terminate her pregnancy is deemed not to be a breach of § 278 BGB, even if it results in a disabled child.[133] In this case, an expectant mother went to have a rash examined and mentioned her pregnancy to the physician, who then negligently failed to recognize that the rash was a symptom of rubella. The child was born disabled as a result of the rubella, and the mother sued, claiming she would have terminated the pregnancy had she been cautioned of the risk of rubella to her child. But because the physician had not been consulted with the purpose of assisting in the pregnancy, his contract did not extend to providing the mother with information useful to her to decide whether to terminate the pregnancy.[134]

129 *MNX v Khan* [2017] EWHC 2990 (QB).

130 *Khan v MNX* [2018] EWCA Civ 2609 (eventually allowing the plaintiff to recover only for the costs associated with the hemophilia, that is, £1,400,000).

131 See Stauch (n 19) 20.

132 BGH 15 February 2000, NJW 2000, 1782. This is, in fact, similar to the approach suggested by Lord Scott in *Parkinson v St James and Seacroft University Hospital NHS Trust* (n 128).

133 BGH 21 December 2004, NJW 1995, 1609.

134 Stauch (n 19) 21.

The language of contract also helped the BGH address the challenge raised by the Constitutional Court in 1993 that allowing for damages in wrongful birth cases would be inconsistent with the German Constitution because it would require the courts to violate their duty "to honour every human being in its existence" by treating the disabled child's life as "damages."[135] In a decision a year later allowing parents who had sought to avoid the birth of a second disabled child through preconception genetic testing, the BGH noted that the contract at issue was "geared to prevent economic burdens incurred from the birth of children."[136] Granting damages on the contract breach implied nothing about the value of the plaintiff's disabled child—"damages" are the maintenance costs, not the child itself, whose value can exist in a "non-economic" sense.[137] The Constitutional Court seemed to accept this contract-based reasoning in 1997 when it reviewed two cases, one involving the wrongful birth of a healthy child and the other involving the wrongful birth of a disabled child, and in both cases the defendants were found to have breached their contract obligations to the parents.[138]

In France, giving birth to a healthy child because of a doctor's negligence in performing a sterilization procedure or in advising the parents after the procedure is carried out, is no injury at all. The position of the French courts on this point has always, and still is, neat: the birth of a child cannot, by itself, be conceived as a harm that can be legally compensated.[139]

More flexible has been the approach of French judges to cases where the child was born disabled. Before the end of the twentieth century, French administrative and ordinary courts were in agreement that physicians could be contractually held liable for wrongful birth with regard to both parents, when a doctor's negligence in failing to provide the mother with adequate prenatal treatment or advice resulted in the birth of a child with serious genetic disorders.[140] However, after the *Cour de cassation* pronounced the *Perruche* decision,[141] extending compensation to the disabled child as well, the PRL intervened to reform the entire matter. Leaving aside, for the time being, the claim of the disabled child (on which we will focus later in the

[135] BVerfG 28 May 1993, NJW 1993, 1751 (translation in Markesinis, Bell, Janssen (n 32) 246).

[136] BGH 16 November 1993, NJW 1994, 788 (translation in Markesinis, Bell, Janssen (n 32) 247).

[137] BGH 16 November 1993, NJW 1994, 788 (translation in Markesinis, Bell, Janssen (n 32) 248).

[138] BVerfG 12 November 1997, NJW 1998, 519. It must be noted that this decision was made by a different panel of the Constitutional Court than the panel that issued the 1993 decision.

[139] Cass civ 25 June 1991, D 1991, Jur, 566.

[140] Conseil d'État 14 February 1997, JCP 1997, II, 22828; Cass civ 26 March 1996, RTD civ 1996, 623.

[141] Cass civ (Plenary) 17 November 2000, JCP 2001, I, 286; see also below in the text.

chapter), the PRL sought to provide a statutory framework for the parents' claims in wrongful birth actions. Accordingly, parents who, had they discovered the child's disability in time would have resorted to abortion, can assert a claim against the health provider.[142] Yet, for the establishment of liability, it is required that the health provider acted with gross negligence (*faute caractérisée*), and it is expressly provided that parents may claim compensation only for their own losses; they may not claim compensation for the cost arising out in connection with the care of the disabled child.[143]

Italian law has long followed a path close to the French one. For years, the Court of cassation has been adamant in its determination that the birth of an unwanted, healthy child cannot be considered an injury.[144] Recently, however, the same court has changed its position, recognizing that a doctor who does not properly perform an abortion or sterilization procedure, or does not adequately inform the patient of the risks of failure of the procedure, is liable to the parents for the expenses they will incur for the upbringing of the unwanted child, since the doctor injured their right of self-determination as to responsible procreation.[145]

Like their French colleagues, Italian judges have been historically more prone to accept the parents' claims with regard to children born disabled. Since the end of the 1990s, mothers who could demonstrate that they would have terminated the pregnancy if they had been informed of the child's impairment in time by their medical practitioner, were awarded compensation for the emotional and physical distress they suffered, plus the pecuniary losses associated with the growth of a disabled child.[146]

(ii) Wrongful life. Wrongful life has been widely rejected by almost all of the systems reviewed within this book. Only a handful of American states allow a child to claim damages for itself against a healthcare provider whose

[142] See art L114-5 (3) of the Code of Family and Social Action.

[143] See below, n 159.

[144] Cass 8 July 1994, no 6464, NGCC 1995, I, 1107.

[145] See Cass 24 October 2013, no 24109, Resp civ prev 2014, 898; Cass 5 February 2018, no 2675, Resp civ prev 2018, 639. Lower courts were admitting such actions since the 1990s: see Trib Milan 20 October 1997, Danno resp 1999, 82, as well as the decisions cited in Bénédict Winiger, Helmut Koziol, Bernhard A Koch, & Reinhard Zimmermann (eds), *Digest of European Tort Law. Essential Cases on Damage* (Springer 2011) 886, fn 28.

[146] Cass 24 March 1999, no 2793, Giur it 2000, 43; Cass 1 December 1998, no 12195, Giur it, 1999, 2038. The same type of damages is awarded to fathers of disabled children (Cass 10 May 2002, no 6735, Foro it 2002, I, 3115) and, and, as far as non-pecuniary losses are concerned, to siblings as well (Cass (Plenary) 2 October 2012, no 16754, Foro it 2013, 1, I, 181). On family members' right to compensation for non-economic damages in case of injury to a close relative, see also Chapter V.

negligence caused it to be born with a disability.[147] England rejected a claim for wrongful life in *McKay v Essex AHA*, with the court questioning whether the child really suffered any injury at all and noting that the child was not owed a duty under the 1976 Congenital Disabilities Act.[148]

The German *Bundesgerichtshof*'s treatment of this issue has been among the most carefully developed from a philosophical and jurisprudential point of view. In a claim quite similar to *McKay*, the German court allowed the parents of a child who had been born disabled to claim economic damages but rejected any claim by the child himself.[149] The court handled the parents' claims under contract law and then turned to the child's claim in tort:

> A direct *duty*, enforceable by an *action in tort*, to prevent the birth of a child on the ground that in all probability it will be affected by an infirmity which makes its life appear "valueless" in the eyes of society or in its own presumed opinion (for which naturally no evidence can be produced) would be alien to the duties sanctioned by the law of tort [...] No such duty exists.[150]

Until very recently, Italian courts rejected a wrongful life claim, on the ground that allowing the child compensation would have implied asserting the protection of a nonexistent right not to be born.[151] In 2012 the Third section of the Court of cassation, while reaffirming that there is no such a thing as a right not to be born, overturned its previous judgments, recognizing that the disabled child may sue in tort the physician and/or the hospital whose negligence has prevented her mother from exercising her right of abortion. According to the Court of cassation, the child's loss did not consist in the lost chance of not having been born, but in the impaired living conditions in which she was forced by the defendants' failure to act with due care.[152] In 2015, however, a further *revirement* by the plenary of the Supreme Court

[147] For the United States, see *Turpini v Sortini*, 643 P2d 954 (Cal 1982), *Procanik v Cillo*, 478 A2d 755 (NJ 1984), and *Harbeson v Parke-Davis, Inc*, 656 P2d 483 (Wash 1983); note that these decisions limit the plaintiff to economic damages and did not allow pain and suffering to be awarded. For a review of the case law and legislative efforts to allow recovery, see Perry (n 118) 335–345.

[148] *McKay v Essex AHA* [1982] QB 1166. Criticism of the damages portion of this decision can be found in Tony Weir, "Wrongful Life—Nipped in the Bud" (1982) 41 Cambridge LJ 225.

[149] BGH 18 January 1983, BGHZ 86, 240; JZ 1983, 447.

[150] BGH 18 January 1983, BGHZ 86, 240; JZ 1983, 447 (translation in Markesinis, Bell, Janssen (n 32) 241–242).

[151] Cass 14 July 2006, no 16123, Dir fam pers 2007, 137; Cass 29 July 2004, no 14488, Foro it 2004, I, 3327.

[152] Cass 2 October 2012, no 16754, Foro it 2013, 1, I, 181.

(on the basis of a thorough comparative review of the United States, English, German and French position on the matter) made it clear that the Italian legal system does not recognize the right not to be born, thus shutting again the door on wrongful life claims.[153]

The story about the rise and fall of wrongful life in France illustrates yet again the differences in the protection offered, before the passage of the PRL, by private and administrative courts (the former hearing trials for liability in private practice, and the latter hearing trials about liability in the public medical sector[154]). Wrongful life was championed by the *Cour de cassation* and opposed by the *Conseil d'État*. In 1996 the *Cour de cassation* held, in a case with facts identical to the English, German and Italian cases reviewed earlier, that a disabled child whose birth could have been prevented could sue for wrongful life.[155] The *Conseil d'État* pushed back, rejecting a wrongful life claim a year later.[156] In 2000 the *Cour de cassation* reiterated its commitment to wrongful life in the *Perruche* case and then again in five more decisions in 2001.[157] Criticism of *Perruche* mounted from various parts of society, including both physicians who feared malpractice liability and disabled rights groups who, in their turn, worried that the ruling could reinforce negative stereotypes against the disabled.[158] The PRL harmonized French law's approach to wrongful life by adopting the Conseil d'État's position and rejecting the idea that a medical professional owes any obligation to a child to take reasonable steps to ensure that they would not be born disabled.[159]

153 Cass (Plenary) 22 December 2015, no 25767, Resp civ prev 2016, 152.

154 Dominique Thouvenin, "French Medical Malpractice Compensation since the Act of March 4, 2002: Liability Rules Combined with Indemnification Rules and Correlated with Several Kinds of Proceedings" (2011) 4 Drexel LR 165, 170.

155 Cass civ 26 March 1996, D 1997, Jur, 35, and see discussion in van Gerven, Larouche & Lever (n 114) 116–118. Wrongful life was accepted by a French criminal court even where the child was not disabled in a case where the child sued a rapist for the wrongful life produced by the rape. Cass crim 4 February 1998, JCP 1999.II.10178, cited by van Gerven, Larouche & Lever (n 114) 118.

156 Conseil d'État 14 February 1997, JCP 1997.II.22828. See van Gerven, Larouche & Lever (n 114) 118.

157 See Cass (Plenary) 17 November 2000, JCP 2000, II, 10, 438 (*Perruche*) and the cases cited by Perry (n 118) 343.

158 Perry (n 118) 343 and Conseil d'État 14 February 1997, JCP 1997.II.22828.

159 The PRL also moved France into a more restrictive position with regard to wrongful life compared to any other system examined in this book. Before the *Perruche* decision (n 157) there could be no cause of action for the cost of maintenance in the event of the birth of a healthy child due to negligent sterilization, but in the event of the birth of a disabled child there could be damages for both the cost of maintenance and *préjudice moral* for the distress of the parent(s). See Taylor (n 23) at 104–105. After 2002 these remaining forms of wrongful life actions were limited even further, so that to receive compensation the parent(s) must prove an elevated degree of fault (*faute caractérisée*) and may receive only *préjudice moral*, not the cost of maintenance. See art L114-5 (3) of the Code of the Family and of Social Action, as amended, and, in the literature, Taylor (n 23) 105–106.

3.1.2. Standard of Care

As we mentioned in Chapter II, sections 6–9, there is a great deal of agreement among the various systems examined in this book over the actual criteria for determining defendants' standards of care. This holds true also for the definition of the standard of care required of medical providers, whether in tort or contract. The jury instructions[160] in one of England's leading cases on this question, *Bolam v Friern Hospital Management Committee*, put it well:

> [W]here you get a situation which involves the use of some special skill or competence, then the test as to whether there has been negligence or not is not the test of the man on top of a Clapham omnibus, because he has not got this special skill. The test is the standard of the ordinary skilled man exercising and professing to have that special skill.[161]

This is very similar to the characterization of the standard of care under French law: "A fault will be considered as any defect in conduct that normally diligent and competent doctor placed in the same circumstances as the person who made the error would have avoided."[162] American, German, and Italian courts have all said very much the same thing.

In the United States, in medical malpractice, the professional standard asks the fact-finder only to determine whether the defendant's conduct conformed to the medical standard or medical custom in the relevant community.[163] The definition of the "relevant community" in the United States had at one time allowed some variation based on geographical location to take into account the very large differences in training in far-flung communities, but this practice, known as the "locality rule," has generally been discarded for a rule that defines the standard of care against an objective measure of similar localities, the state, or nationally.[164] Although the United States relies in theory on lay judgment to determine whether the standard has been met in any particular case, US judges play a crucial role in establishing the standard of care for the jury by deciding which experts proffered by the parties may testify.[165] This means that the evaluation by the court of the relevance of an expert based on

160 At that time medical negligence cases were still trials by jury.

161 *Bolam v Friern Hospital Management Committee* [1957] 2 All ER 118, 122 (per Justice McNair).

162 Taylor (n 23) 101, citing Cass civ 6 June 2000, RDSS 2000, 750.

163 Dobbs, Hayden, & Bublick (n 73) 417–426; Dobbs (n 73) 633.

164 See, eg, *Jordan v Bogner*, 844 P2d 664 (Colo 1993) and *Fitzmaurice v Flynn*, 167 Conn 609 (Conn 1975).

165 *Locke v Pachtman*, 446 Mich 216 (Mich 1994).

her background and proposed testimony can control a medical malpractice case in the United States in ways that may seem quite similar to England and civilian systems.

The control over the definition of the standard of care exercised by American judges may be similar in kind to that exercised in other systems, but it is still limited by the fact that in most cases judges are obliged to define the standard of care by the practices "employed by the medical profession generally" and not what individual doctors would have done or what the court would have thought to have been the most prudent course of action.[166] England, until 1998, when *Bolitho v City and Hackney Health Authority*[167] was decided, had somewhat the opposite situation—a minority or a handful of experts finding the defendant's conduct consistent with "accepted practice" was often enough to warrant dismissal of a case.[168] *Bolitho* established that the court was not bound by medical experts who are genuinely of the opinion that the defendant's treatment or diagnosis accorded with sound medical practice.[169] Instead, it could exercise independent judgment to determine whether the expert opinion has a "logical basis." This gives the trial judge in England even more latitude than that given to federal judges in the United States under *Daubert v Merrell Dow Pharmaceuticals, Inc.*, which requires judges to exclude testimony which is not the product of sound "scientific methodology."[170] Bolitho opens the door—theoretically at least—for the court to find a breach of the standard of care in the face of substantial expert opinion supporting the defendant's conduct.[171] While it could be argued that the *Bolitho* court adopted a stance close to that of Judge Hand in *TJ Hooper*,[172] as a practical matter, this door, while open, has rarely been

166 See *Johnson v Riverdale Anesthesia Assocs PC*, 563 SE2d 431 (Ga 2002) (reversed on other grounds in *Condra v Atlanta Orthopaedic Group*, 681 SE2d 152 (Ga 2009). This general principle has exceptions, such as when personal practices are deemed relevant for purposes of impeachment (eg, ibid, as well as Chapter II, section 9) or in the rare case when the court substitutes its own judgment for that of the medical profession, which is what happened in *Helling v Carey*, 519 P2d 981 (Wash 1974). *Helling* had been deemed an exceptional departure from the basic rule. See Elizabeth A Weeks, 'Beyond Compensation: Using Torts to Promote Public Health' (2007) 10 J Health Care L&Pol'y 27, 44–46; Eric E Fortess & Marshall B Kapp, "Medical Uncertainty, Diagnostic Testing, and Legal Liability" (1985) 13 L, Med & Health Care 213, 215.

167 [1998] AC 232 (HL).

168 Stauch (n 19) 40, citing *De Freitas v O'Brien* [1995] PIQR P281 (CA).

169 *Bolitho v City and Hackney Health Authority* [1998] AC 232 (HL) at 241.

170 509 US 579 (US 1993). *Daubert* has significantly influenced state evidence law as well. See *Condra* (n 166).

171 Stauch (n 19) 41–42.

172 60 F2d 737 (2d Cir 1932):

Indeed in most cases reasonable prudence is in fact common prudence; but strictly it is never its measure; a whole calling may have unduly lagged in the adoption of new and available devices. It

used, for the simple reason that English courts are very likely to defer to the body of expert opinion.[173]

The approach on the continent is not significantly affected by the shift in focus from tort to contract. In Germany, for example, a judge must rely on the testimony of experts and cannot rely upon her own opinion.[174] Yet German courts have wide discretion in assessing the reliability of experts' opinion, such as when the BGH found that expert testimony about experienced dentists' common practice to work with needles unattached to string (to prevent them from falling into the patient's throat) was insufficient to establish the reasonableness of that practice, which was described as unsafe by some dentistry textbooks.[175] This statement from the BGH does seem to adopt the position of the *Helling* court[176]—an outlier in America—rather than the more deferential approach of most American courts:

> [T]he fact a given practice is customary will not be sufficient to negative negligence if at the same time there is a failure to do all that is necessary, according to the rules and experience of medical science, to safeguard the patient from bodily harm.[177]

In France, the contract of care traditionally required the healthcare provider to exercise "conscientious and attentive care and, subject to exceptional circumstances, in line with what is known by science."[178] The PRL frames the standard of care as a right inherent in the patient's status and not as an obligation owed by contract, but the assessment of the conduct of the healthcare provider is virtually the same, with the only difference (if it can be called that)

never may set its own tests, however persuasive be its usages. Courts must in the end say what is required. Ibid at 739.

[173] The *Bolitho* court itself recognized this limitation when it noted that:

> It is only where a judge can be satisfied that the body of expert opinion cannot be logically supported at all that such opinion will not provide the bench mark by reference to which the defendant's conduct [is] to be assessed. *Bolitho v City and Hackney Health Authority* [1998] AC 232 (HL) at 243.

[174] BGH 9 January 2018, NJW 2018, 2730; BGH 17 September 1985, VersR 1985, 1187.

[175] BGH 27 November 1952, NJW 1953, 257. See also § 630a II BGB, which provides that, "[u]nless agreed otherwise, the treatment must take place according to the medical standards that are generally recognised at the time of the treatment."

[176] See above, n 166.

[177] BGH 13 October 1964, NJW 1965, 345 translated and cited in Stauch (n 19) 44.

[178] Cass civ 24 November 1987, D 1989, Somm, 61, quoted in G'sell-Macrez (n 4) 1198.

being an explicit addition of language relating to negligence in "prevention, investigation, or treatment."[179]

A similar standard is applied to doctors by Italian courts, according to which healthcare providers are liable for violating the ordinary standard of care relating to professional preparation, scrupulous attention, and adequate training.[180] In cases where the performance of the medical obligation entails the solution of uncommon technical complications, healthcare professionals can avail themselves of the limitation of liability provided for—explicity, in Italy—by art 2236 of the Civil Code, thus answering only for intentional or reckless injuries. Such a limitation, however, only applies to problematic cases such as those where "different diagnostic and therapeutic methods or surgical techniques are still discussed among medical scientists" and the damage occurred despite scrupulous attention paid by the physician in diagnosing and treating the disease.[181]

Under Italian law, like in France and Germany, medical negligence may also amount to a criminal offense under the heading of unintentional manslaughter or injury.[182] The rule is of special significance because of its procedural implications: German, French, and Italian criminal courts have the ability to award compensation to the victim through a combined action by which a provider can be criminally convicted and the victim can obtain damages directly from the criminal court, thereby benefiting from the results of investigations and trials carried out at public expenses.[183]

[179] See art L1110-5, para 1, *Code de la Santé Publique*:

> Any person, given his health and the emergency response that it requires, is entitled to receive the most appropriate care and to receive treatment whose effectiveness is recognized and which guarantees the best safety in light of established medical knowledge. Acts of prevention, investigation, or treatment should not, in the state of medical knowledge, make him take risks that are disproportionate to the expected benefits (quoted in G'sell-Macrez (n 4) 1198).

Under French Law, also corporations can be criminally responsible along with the natural persons who work for them. See Katrin Deckert, "Corporate Criminal Liability in France," in Mark Pieth & Radha Ivory (eds), *Corporate Criminal Liability. Emergence, Convergence, and Risk* (Springer 2011) 147–176.

[180] Cass 18 October 1994, no 8470, Giust civ mass 1994, 1235.

[181] Cass 19 May 2004, no 9471, Danno resp 2005, 23 (translation in Claudia diMarzo, 'Medical Malpractice: The Italian Experience' (2012) 87 Chi-Kent LR 53, 66).

[182] Cp § 222 of the German Penal Code; art 221-6, 222-19, and 222-20 of the French Penal Code; art 589 of the Italian Penal Code.

[183] Cp § 406 of the German Code of Criminal Procedure; art 85 of the French Code of Criminal Procedure; art 75 of the Italian Code of Criminal Procedure. See Matthew Dyson, "Tort and Crime," in Mauro Bussani & Anthony J Sebok (eds), *Comparative Tort Law. Global Perspectives* (2nd edn, EE 2021) 84, 87–91.

3.2. Disclosure Malpractice

In the United States a healthcare provider (usually a physician) must give a patient material information about the risks of a procedure.[184] The procurement of consent to a medical procedure by misrepresentation or duress amounts to the tort of battery.[185] Negligent failure by a physician to provide material information where the patient's consent is sought may result in the medical malpractice claim commonly referred to as *informed consent*.[186] Yet, a handful of courts may still allow a patient to sue in battery instead of informed consent.[187]

In a case of informed consent, the patient does not have to show that the healthcare provider performed the procedure negligently. The wrong to the patient is not that the procedure was done carelessly, or without the patient's consent, but that it was done without the patient's *informed* consent. Still, in almost all American jurisdictions, a necessary element of an informed consent claim is a personal injury, and this distinguishes it from battery by a healthcare provider, where dignitary harm alone[188] would satisfy the injury requirement of the tort.[189]

In disclosure malpractice, the scope of the obligation is straightforward—the duty is owed to the person the physician is treating. The content of the obligation—what must be disclosed—can be mapped along two ends of a spectrum in the United States. On one end of the spectrum is the "professional" standard, which holds that a physician has a duty to disclose what a "reasonable physician in the community of like training" would customarily disclose.[190] On the other end of the spectrum is the more modern "prudent patient" standard, which sets the duty to disclose by reference to what a reasonable patient, "in what the physician knows or should know to be the patient's position, would be 'likely to attach significance to the risk [...]' in deciding to forego [treatment]."[191] The professional standard is seen as more

[184] Dobbs, Hayden, & Bublick (n 72) 429.

[185] See, eg, *Rains v Superior Court*, 150 Cal App 3d 933 (Cal App 1984).

[186] Peter H Schuck, 'Rethinking Informed Consent' (1994) 103 Yale LJ 899.

[187] See, eg, *Fox v Smith*, 594 So2d 596 (Miss 1992).

[188] I.e., in this case, the mere fact of having being treated without consent.

[189] See *Canesi v Wilson*, 158 NJ 490 (NJ 1999). For some skepticism about this distinction, see Aaron Twerksi & Neil Cohen, 'Informed Decision-making and the Law of Torts: The Myth of Justiciable Causation' (1988) U Ill LR 607; see also § 19 of the Restatement Third of Torts: Intentional Torts to Persons.

[190] *Largey v Rothman*, 110 NJ 204, 209 (NJ 1988), citing David W Louisell & Harold Williams, *Medical Malpractice*, vol 2 (Bender & Co 1987) § 22.08 at 22–23.

[191] *Largey v Rothman*, 110 NJ 204, 211–212 (NJ 1988), quoting *Canterbury v Spence*, 464 F2d 772, 787 (DC Cir 1972), cert den, 409 US 1064, 93 SCt 560, 34 LEd2d 518 (1972).

protective of defendant physicians, not only because it (theoretically, at least) directs the jury's attention toward considerations that may be more salient to a physician than a patient, but also because, as a matter of trial practice, the professional standard, like any other standard of care in medical malpractice, is determined by reference to customary practice among physicians, and not by reference to what a jury might themselves conclude would be reasonable, all things considered.

The same common law categories of battery and informed consent occupy approximately the same analytical space in England as in the United States. Misrepresentation and the complete failure to provide any information at all to the patient before obtaining consent for treatment may open the door to a suit in intentional tort, but any other failure of communication is remedied through negligence.[192] The standard of care required in disclosure malpractice in England has long fallen closer to the professional standard than the prudent patient standard, at least as a matter of technical law. The 1985 case *Sidaway v Board of Governors of Bethlem Royal Hospital* involved a failure to disclose a risk of partial paralysis in an operation intended to relieve neck pain.[193] The majority adopted the *Bolam* approach[194] and held that the fact that the doctor was following a practice accepted among medical professionals in his community would defeat the plaintiff's claim.[195] Despite the fact that this holding was not reversed until 2015, the *Sidaway* standard was often applied in ways that make it look much more like the prudent patient standard rather than the professional standard.[196] Finally, in 2015, the UK Supreme Court expressly overruled *Sidaway* and its application of the *Bolam* test to failure to inform, holding that

> [a] person can of course decide that she does not wish to be informed of risks of injury (just as a person may choose to ignore the information leaflet enclosed with her medicine); and a doctor is not obliged to discuss the risks inherent in treatment with a person who makes it clear that she would prefer not to discuss the matter. Deciding whether a person is so disinclined may involve the doctor making a judgment; but it is not a judgment

[192] Stauch (n 89) 98–99.
[193] [1985] AC 871 (HL).
[194] See above, n 161.
[195] *Sidaway v Board of Governors of Bethlem Royal Hospital* [1985] AC 871 (HL) 888.
[196] See Stauch (n 19) 105 ("in the last decade or so English law has undeniably moved towards a greater acceptance of the patient's right to know," in part because "medical practice has shifted in the direction of greater disclosure").

> which is dependent on medical expertise. It is also true that the doctor must necessarily make a judgment as to how best to explain the risks to the patient, and that providing an effective explanation may require skill. But the skill and judgment required are not of the kind with which the Bolam test is concerned; and the need for that kind of skill and judgment does not entail that the question whether to explain the risks at all is normally a matter for the judgment of the doctor.[197]

On this basis, the Supreme Court stressed that the doctor is under a duty to take reasonable care,

> to ensure that the patient is aware of any material risks involved in any recommended treatment, and of any reasonable alternative or variant treatments. The test of materiality is whether, in the circumstances of the particular case, a reasonable person in the patient's position would be likely to attach significance to the risk, or the doctor is or should reasonably be aware that the particular patient would be likely to attach significance to it.[198]

Civilian approaches to disclosure malpractice differ in two ways from the common law approach. First, consistent with what has already been noted in relation to treatment malpractice, a physician who fails to receive informed consent before invading the body of his patient is violating contract obligations as well as committing a tort. Second, given that civilian systems do not emphasize the distinction between intentional torts and negligence, the concern displayed in American and English law for establishing the boundary between intent, misrepresentation, and informed consent is of little importance. In Germany, this means that a physician's failure to disclose a material risk of a procedure is treated the same as a physician's failure to respect the scope of consent (see new §§ 630d and 630e BGB).[199] In Italy, long before doctors' information duties were enshrined in Law no. 219 of 2017, courts have acknowledged that the failure of physicians to properly

[197] *Montgomery v Lanarkshire Health Board* [2015] UKSC 11, para 85 (per Lords Keer and Reed).
[198] Ibid at para 87 (per Lords Keer and Reed).
[199] Stauch (n 19) 101. Both failures, in theory, could result in criminal liability under § 223 of the Criminal Code (StGB)) and in civil liability under §§ 278 and 823 I BGB: Stauch (n 19) 101. In the 1957 *Myom* decision, a physician was held to have acted criminally by failing to tell a patient that an operation to remove a cyst might lead to a full hysterectomy. BGH 28 November 1957, NJW 1958, 267 (268).

inform patients about medical risks and to obtain their consent entailed the liability of the former to the latter.[200] In France, the contract duty to obtain consent based on informed consent was subsumed into the PRL in 2002 (and is nowadays enshrined in articles L1111-2 and L1111-4 of the *Code de la Santé Publique*), although before the PRL there was some indication that the *Cour de cassation* had adopted the view that the obligation of a physician to obtain informed consent was based in tort on former art 1382 (current art 1240) CC.[201]

By contrast, the civilian systems are quite similar to the common law systems in terms of the content of the obligation in disclosure malpractice. Still, it is worth noting that, broadly speaking, the civilian systems moved toward the prudent patient end of the spectrum earlier and more fully than the common law systems. This can be seen most dramatically in Germany, where the courts never adopted the professional standard for disclosure malpractice. Once a duty to warn about possible risks was recognized by the courts, the standard that was adopted was that of the reasonable patient (*verständiger Patient*).[202] But the reasonable patient standard, in the hands of some courts, proved too conservative for some critics, since it exonerated doctors who refused to tell patients about risks which the doctor deemed were too remote or peculiar to matter to a "reasonable" patient, even if these risks mattered to the plaintiff.[203] Consequently, German courts have held that a physician should "disclose all risks specifically associated with a given treatment that could theoretically influence the particular patient's decision."[204] In 2013, the judicial developments were codified in § 630e I BGB, which now provides:

> [t]he treating party is obliged to inform the patient of all and any circumstances which are relevant to consent. This includes in particular the nature, extent, implementation, anticipated consequences and risks involved in the measure, as well as its necessity, urgency, suitability and prospects for success with regard to the diagnosis or the therapy. Alternatives to the measure must also be referred to in the information if

200 See Cass 20 August 2013, no 19220, Rass dir farm 2013, 780; Cass 13 January 1997, no 364, Foro it 1998 I, 586.
201 G'sell-Macrez (n 4) 1101.
202 Stauch (n 19) 108.
203 See BGH 24 June 1980, NJW 1980, 2751.
204 Stauch (n 19) 108. See BGH 15 February 2000, NJW 2000, 1784 (1785) ("in principle this means that, on occasion, extremely rare risks have to be disclosed").

> several equally medically indicated, customary methods may lead to significantly different strains, risks or chances of recovery.

The information should be communicated in clear terms and in good time so as to allow a well-considered decision by the patient. In case of controversy, the physician has the burden to prove that she properly acquired the patient's consent and that the information provided was full, timely, and understandable.[205]

Since the 1990s, in Italy, consent to medical treatment has been seen as part of individuals' constitutional right to freedom of choice and personal inviolability under article 32 (2) of the Constitution, which states that nobody may be forced to undergo any medical treatment, unless when it is provided by law.[206] These interpretative developments were elevated into a statute in 2017. According to Law no. 219 of 2017, "no medical treatment can commence or continue in the absence of the patient's free and informed consent, except when it is provided by law,"[207] and that

> every person has the right to be fully, timely and clearly informed about her health condition, her diagnosis and prognosis, the benefits and the risks associated with the treatment proposed, the possible alternatives and the consequences of the refusal of exams and treatments.[208]

The Law no. 219 of 2017 does not explain who has the burden of prove the completeness, timeliness, and clarity of the information provided to the patient and the latter's consent to the treatment concerned. Italian courts, however, have long held that it is for the practitioner to prove that she provided adequate information and obtained the patient's consent.[209]

After 1998, France moved toward a position very similar to Germany's and Italy's. At the beginning of the new century, the *Cour de cassation*,[210] followed by the administrative courts,[211] held that a physician must inform the patient

205 § 630h II BGB. The requirements that the information should have are listed in § 630e BGB.
206 See the decisions quoted above, n 200.
207 Art 1(1), Law no 219 of 2017.
208 Art 1(3), Law no 219 of 2017.
209 See, for instance, Cass 13 January 1997, no 364, Foro it 1998, I, 586; more recently, Cass 21 June 2018, no 16336, Resp civ prev 2018, 1872.
210 Cass civ 9 October 2001, Bull civ I, no 252; Cass civ 7 October 1998, Bull civ I, nos 287, 291.
211 G'sell-Macrez (n 4) 1101.

of all risks, even exceptional ones. In 2016, the issue has been extensively regulated by the *Code de la santé publique*, which states that

> [a]ny person is entitled to be informed about her health condition. The information should cover the exams, treatments and preventive actions that are proposed to the patient, their usefulness, their possible emergency, their consequences, the ordinary and ordinarily foreseeable serious risks that are associated with them, as well as the other possible alternatives and their foreseeable consequences in the case of a refusal.[212]

Like in Italy and Germany, "[i]n the event of a dispute, it is up to the physician to prove that the information was provided to the patient according to the law."[213]

[212] Article L1111-2 para 1 *Code de la Santé Publique*, inserted by the *Loi* n° 2016–87.
[213] Article L1111-2 para 7 *Code de la Santé Publique*.

IV

Non-economic Damage and Primary Victims

1. The Notion of Non-economic Damage and Its Plaintiff

Non-economic damages might be best understood in contrast with economic damages, which are losses that can be directly traced to a market value. Non-economic losses refer to losses that have no easily calculable market value.[1] Although the specific components have changed over the years, non-economic damages[2] have always been at the center of the stage in both the common law and the civil law tort debate.[3] Indeed, all the legal

[1] Anthony J Sebok, "Translating the Immeasurable. Thinking About Pain and Suffering Comparatively" (2006) 55 De Paul LR 379, 383.

[2] Terminology is not uniform across European civil law jurisdictions. The French and Spanish legal systems employ the term "moral damage": "*dommage moral*", "*daño moral*." In Germany (§ 253 BGB), Italy (art 2059 Civil Code), and Portugal (art 496 Civil Code), the civil codes speak of "*Schaden, der nicht Vermögensschaden ist*," "*danno non patrimoniale*," and "*danos não patrimoniais*," respectively. Art 299 of the Greek Civil Code uses the term "intangible damage." § 1325 ABGB refers to "*angemessenes Schmerzengeld*" (damages for pain and suffering), while the 5 Chapter 1 § of the Swedish Tort Liability Act (*skadeståndslagen*, SKL) deals with compensation for "pain, affliction, and other permanent impairments," which is commonly called "*ideellt skadestånd*." See Christian von Bar, *The Common European Law of Torts* (II, OUP 2000) 164, fn 957.

[3] Robert L Rabin, "Pain and Suffering and Beyond: Some Thoughts on Recovery for Intangible Loss" (2006) 55 DePaul LR 359, 362–367; Jeffrey O'Connell & Rita J Simon, "Payment for Pain & Suffering: Who Wants What, When and Why?" (1972) U Ill L Forum 1, 83–109; Bénédict Winiger, Helmut Koziol, Bernhard A Koch, & Reinhard Zimmermann (eds), *Digest of European Tort Law. Essential Cases on Damage* (de Gruyter 2011) 493–718.

Common Law and Civil Law Perspectives on Tort Law. Mauro Bussani, Anthony J. Sebok, & Marta Infantino, Oxford University Press.
DOI: 10.1093/oso/9780195368383.003.0004

systems recognize the legal notion and distinguish it as an autonomous form of damage. The category includes such diverse damages as compensation for physical pain, mental suffering, bereavement, disfigurement as a harm in itself, loss of bodily functions, loss of enjoyment of life, embarrassment, as well as for infringement of personality, privacy rights, of the rights to liberty and not to be discriminated.

This and the following chapter will not be able to address one by one all the particular situations that may ground a claim for non-economic damage. We will focus on the overall nature and main features of this damage and on the different ways the jurisdictions under review approach its recoverability.

Another preliminary refinement is in order: a fundamental distinction is to be drawn between "primary" and "secondary" victims of non-economic damage. A primary victim can be defined as one who suffers non-economic damage after being directly injured, either physically or personally.[4] A "secondary victim" suffers non-economic damage as a consequence of simply being informed about or witnessing an accident, which involves another. The secondary victim may have suffered a psychological reaction brought about by being informed of another's death or injury in particular circumstances. Or the reaction can be triggered by witnessing an accident where another is injured, or is at risk of being injured, even if the injury does not materialize. The "witness" may be present at the event itself, see it relayed through television or hear about it on the radio, or come on the scene of the accident in its immediate aftermath.[5] In all these occurrences the question arises whether, and if so under what circumstances, someone being informed about, or

[4] Simon Deakin & Zoe Adams, *Markesinis & Deakin's Tort Law* (8th edn, OUP, 2019) 109–110.

[5] Deakin & Adams (n 4) 111. The terminology of "primary" and "secondary" victims is quite uncommon in the United States, but is widely employed in England to distinguish victims who are actually injured or exposed to a danger of physical injury, and bystanders who are not exposed to any danger and yet suffer a shock because of their relationship with the victims: see Mark Lunney, Donal Nolan, & Ken Oliphant, *Tort Law: Text and Materials* (6th edn, OUP 2017) 354–359; Donal Nolan & John Davies, "Torts and Equitable Wrongs," in Andrew Burrows (ed), *English Private Law* (3rd edn, OUP 2013) 927, 958–961; Basil S Markesinis, Michael Coester, Guido Alpa, & Augustus Ullstein, *Compensation for Personal Injury in English, German and Italian Law. A Comparative Outline* (CUP 2005) 52–53. The distinction is not limited to England. The French legal system adopts it too, for example when using the concept of *dommage par ricochet*: see, eg, Walter van Gerven, Pierre Larouche & Jeremy Lever, *Cases, Materials and Text on National, Supranational and International Tort Law* (Hart 2000) 61 and 127, and Suzanne Garland-Carval, "France," in WV Horton Rogers (ed), *Damages for Non-Pecuniary Loss in a Comparative Perspective* (Springer 2001) 87, 97. Italian lawyers and courts rely on the notion of secondary victims to identify those who are entitled to bereavement damages (while no distinction between primary and secondary victims is made in cases of nervous shock: see below, sections 3.2 and 4 in this chapter). The Germans do not adopt the precise terminology of "primary" and "secondary" victims, but the functional equivalent is implied in the doctrinal categories of bystander nervous shock (*Schockschäden Dritter*): Basil S. Markesinis, John Bell, & André Janssen, *Markesinis's German Law of Torts* (5th edn, Hart 2019) 235–236.

witnessing to another's suffering or death, can claim damages for immediate or subsequent psychological pain and suffering.

After some general remarks of common interest to primary and secondary victims (section 2), this chapter will deal with compensation to primary victims of their non-economic losses, while the next chapter will discuss compensation to secondary victims.

2. Restrictions on Recovery

The main concern that some jurisdictions are very sensitive to is represented by the theoretical incommensurability of pain and suffering. In this perspective, what pushes a few Western jurisdictions (i.e., the German and the common law ones) to retain special limitations on recovery is a twofold argument. The first reason is grounded on the impossibility of repairing past pain or alleviating future loss of enjoyment of life by provision of money damages.[6] The other argument hinges on the need to avoid encouraging or validating "undue" sensitivity, as well as easily fabricated and/or exaggerated claims, and the associated "floodgates" problem[7] (even though, one should note, any possible concern about the impact of pain and suffering litigation on the court's docket is rather to be seen as a concern about the amount of the awards, and not about the number of claims, at least when the latter are dependent on correlative claims of physical injury).

By contrast, Italian and French legal systems present an appearance of maximum permissiveness and indifference to the strong policy arguments usually made elsewhere against recovery, and do not impose any a priori check upon the judge's free sense of what harm is recoverable.

Moreover, all systems in our study permit recovery when non-economic damage is inflicted on a victim the wrongdoer intended to harm. Thus, it would be difficult to say whether the nature of the interest or the nature of the fault is the more important factor in the equation. Indeed, we will find out that it would be essentially misguiding to assign such priorities, because

[6] Rabin (n 3) 365; Joseph A Page, "Reflections on Pain-and-Suffering Damages in the United States," in Aurelia BC Colombi Ciacchi, Christine Godt, Peter Rott, & Lesley J Smith (eds), *Haftungsrecht im dritten Millennium—Liability in the Third Millennium. Liber Amicorum Gert Brueggemeier* (Nomos 2009) 193, 201–203, 209–210.

[7] Deakin & Adams (n 4) 112–113.

the recovery is really the outcome of many other interacting factors as well.[8] Not the least of these are many meta-legal considerations, such as the size of the plaintiff class and the potential scope of the damages, which have varying degrees of cogency in actual contexts. Through the study of these factors in their liability context, we will understand why the rules on recovery operate selectively and situationally, never mechanically.

3. Compensation for Primary Victims

As to what we have called "primary victims," we said that the above contrasting attitudes do not follow the familiar common law/civil law divide, for both legal families are in their turn split inside themselves over the issue. We will now delve in more detail into the reasons explaining the split.

3.1. Civil Law

In the civil law world one can easily detect two different general tendencies, at least at first sight.

The first approach is the most liberal one. The French *Code civil* does not distinguish between economic and non-economic damage: the definition of damage in articles 1240 and 1241 (former articles 1382 and 1383) of the Code is deemed to comprise both types of damage. The only conditions for recovery are that the damage must be certain, direct, and not bearing on an unlawful interest.[9] Another approach is followed by the legal systems whose

[8] As we already made it clear, in general terms, in Chapter II, sections 4–7, and will do in Chapter VI, especially sections 6–8 and Chapter VII, section 4.

[9] Similarly, in Spain, that non-economic damage is recoverable under the general clause of art 1902 of the Civil Code was established as early as at the beginning of twentieth century (STS 6 December 1912, CLJCiv no 95) and the rule has not changed ever since (von Bar (n 2) 165, fn 963). A slightly different approach makes recovery dependent on the decisive influence borne upon the case by some specific factual evidence, concerning either the wrongdoer's state of mind, or the intensity of plaintiff psychological impairment. Austrian judges, for instance, award damages for pain and suffering only if the defendant acted with intent or gross negligence—and if the law does not exclude compensation of non-economic damage (see Christian von Bar, *The Common European Law of Torts* (I, OUP 1998) 633; Helmut Koziol, "Mitigation of Damages under Austrian Law and Ideas for Future Regulations," in Jaap Spier (ed), *The Limits of Liability. Keeping the Floodgates Shut* (Kluwer 1996) 53, 57). Under art 496(1) of the Portuguese Civil Code ("Any non patrimonial damage which, due to its severity, warrants legal protection is indemnifiable"), non-economic harm can only be taken into account for the assessment of damages when it is severe: hence it is neither the type of tort that is important, nor the nature of the impaired interest, but rather the degree of the victim's mental suffering: von Bar (n 2) 172.

civil codes allow compensation for non-economic damage only if expressly provided for by the law. This is the basic rule in Germany (§ 253 BGB) and Italy (art 2059 Civil Code),[10] even though, as we see immediately below, over time both jurisdictions have moved away from their basic rules.

In Italy, the restrictive rule of article 2059 of the *Codice civile*, whereby compensation of nonmaterial injury is limited to instances provided by law, has been recently reinterpreted by higher courts rulings. The Court of cassation[11] and the Constitutional Court[12] have given a new meaning to art 2059 CC, distinguishing two kinds of non-economic damage: one directly connected to the victim's health (and then the award is grounded on predefined judicial tables[13]), the other—whose amount is determined by the judge according to the circumstances of the case—framed as either a loss of amenities or the experience of pain and suffering, and compensable through reference to art 2 of the Italian Constitution, protecting "the inviolable rights of the person, as an individual and in the social groups where human personality is expressed."

In Germany the general rule is now to be found in § 253 BGB, which states the non-compensability of non-pecuniary headings of harm, and that exceptions from this basic rule require explicit legislative authorization. By far the most important regulation of that kind is set forth by the second paragraph of the same § 253 BGB (formerly § 847 BGB[14]). It grants compensation for non-pecuniary damage as a consequence of any claim on the grounds of

[10] The same approach is shared by Finland (5 Chapter 2 §, 2 c §, 2 d §, and 6 § of the Tort Liability Act—SKL), Sweden (5 Chapter 1 and 6 § of the Tort Liability Act—SKL), Greece (art 299 Greek Civil Code), and the Netherlands (art 6:95 BW): von Bar (n 2) 20, 164, 171–172. In particular, in the Netherlands, article 6:106 (1) BW specifies that the primary victim is entitled to compensation for "other harm" (i.e., nonmaterial damage), to be equitably determined, if one of the following requirements are met: (a) the wrongdoer inflicted the injury intentionally; (b) the victim suffered bodily harm, injury to honor or reputation, or was otherwise injured in her person; (c) the harm to the memory of the deceased was inflicted upon one of a specified number of relatives, provided that the same injury would have entitled the deceased to compensation had she still been alive. The most frequent instance of "other harm" is the one referred to under (b), which includes pain and suffering or reduction in the enjoyment life resulting from interference with the victim's body and health: van Gerven, Larouche, & Lever (n 5) 128–129.

[11] Cass 31 May 2003, no 8828, Foro it I, 2003, I, 2272.

[12] Constitutional Court 11 July 2003, no 233, Foro it 2003, I, 2201.

[13] See below, section 6.

[14] The 2001 Act on the Modernization of the Law of Obligations, which entered into force in 2002, repealed § 847 BGB and replaced it with § 253 BGB. Any violation of any of the interests enumerated in § 253 II BGB automatically entitles the victim to non-pecuniary damages, irrespective whether liability is based on negligence or on a strict liability regime (or is claimed under a contract). This takes German rules closer to Italian and French ones, whereby non-pecuniary damages are generally available in strict liability cases on the same basis as they are in negligence cases. See Christian von Bar, *Non-Contractual Liability Arising out of Damage Caused to Another* (München 2009) 329–331.

an injury to the body, freedom, health, or sexual self-determination of the claimant—and case law has a long time ago added to the list the case of infringement of personality rights.[15] Therefore, to a large extent, the technical relation of rule and exception is in Germany converted into its opposite.[16]

3.2. Common Law

On the common law side, the picture also reveals inner differences. These are already recognizable as to the ways the legal systems frame the issue.

In England, damages for non-pecuniary loss are available even in the absence of a physical injury where the plaintiff can demonstrate she suffers a negligently inflicted psychiatric injury, or where the tort results in intentional invasion of the plaintiff's personal sphere.[17] Despite the distinction between the two principle heads of non-pecuniary loss—pain and suffering and loss of amenities of life—being well established in English law, the general practice of the courts is to make a global award and not to sub-itemize the damages.[18] But when the plaintiff suffers a mental distress, or "injury to feelings," because of the manner in which the defendant committed the wrong or of the defendant's conduct subsequent to the wrong, English courts may award the so-called aggravated damages—that is, damages that are meant to compensate for the "shock, distress, outrage and similar emotions experienced by the claimant."[19]

[15] At least since BGH 25 May 1954, BGHZ 13, 334.

[16] Markesinis, Coester, Alpa, Ullstein (n 5) 60.

[17] Rachael Mulheron, "Rewriting the Requirement for a 'Recognized Psychiatric Injury' in Negligence Claims" (2012) 32 Ox J Leg Stud 77–112. Compensation for this kind of damage is also possible in cases of nuisance affecting immovable property, but recovery is confined to householders, on a view that the tort is aimed at protecting land (*Hunter v Canary Wharf* [1997] AC 655). Such a claim, however, has been recognized in cases against public authorities as available to a wider range of people, on the basis of a breach of the Human Rights Act 1998 (*Marcic v Thames Water Facilities* [2002] EWCA Civ 64).

[18] Law Commission, *Damages for Personal Injury: Non-Pecuniary Loss*, Law Com no 140 (1995), para 2.4, at http://www.lawcom.gov.uk/app/uploads/2016/08/No.140-Damages-for-Personal-Injury-Non-Pecuniary-Loss-A-Consultation-Paper.pdf.

[19] *Ashley v Chief Constable of Sussex Police* [2007] 1 WLR 398, para 10; see also Law Commission, *Aggravated, Exemplary and Restitution Damages*, Law Com no 247 (1997), para 2.1, at lawcom.gov.uk/project/aggravated-exemplary-and-restitutionary-damages/. The nature of such damages, whether compensatory or punitive, is much questioned: cf Michael Tilbury, "Aggravated Damages," 71 Current Leg Probls 215–244 (2018); John Murphy, "The Nature and Domain of Aggravated Damages," 69 Cambridge LJ 353–377 (2010); Anthony J Sebok & Vanessa Wilcox, "Aggravated Damages," in Helmut Koziol & Vanessa Wilcox (eds), *Punitive Damages: Common Law and Civil Law Perspectives* (Springer 2009) 257–274.

Other types of damage have been addressed by the legislature. This is—for instance—the case of harassment damages and loss of expectation of life (associated with a personal injury). As to the former, s. 3 (2) of the Protection from Harassment Act 1997 now provides that, in case of harassment, "damages may be awarded for (among other things) any anxiety caused by the harassment and any financial loss resulting from the harassment." With regard to the loss of expectation of life associated with a personal injury, the Administration of Justice Act 1982 (chapter 53), s. 1 (1) (a) makes that such loss cannot be considered as an independent form of damage. But, if the expectation of life of the victim of a personal injury has been reduced by the injuries sustained, s. 1 (1) (b) of the same Act mandates courts, in assessing damages in respect to pain and suffering, to "take account of any suffering caused or likely to be caused to him by awareness that his expectation of life has been so reduced."

In the United States, every state jurisdiction allows recovery for negligently inflicted emotional harm when it stems from a compensatable physical injury to the same person. It should however be noted that, since the mid-1970s, several states have attempted to limit the size of these awards by enacting caps and ceilings for pain and suffering awards, especially in medical malpractice cases (many of which have been invalidated by courts as being unconstitutional).[20]

Outside this "parasitic" dimension of the non-economic damage (on which we will come back to in the following section), United States courts' reasoning and rhetoric have developed divergent tendencies. Amid this variety, two lines of exceptions to the general rule that an actor is not liable for negligent conduct that causes only emotional harm were developed. The first one, called "impact" rule, was based on cases in which an actor's negligent conduct created a danger of bodily harm and caused some impact, however slight, to the person seeking recovery. Later, courts admitted recovery also in cases in which the actor's negligent conduct did not actually cause any impact but created a danger of bodily harm ("zone of danger" rule). Today, the only shared agreement can be found in that the plaintiff can recover if the defendant created a danger of bodily harm to him (or to a close relative), and

[20] Robert L Rabin, "Intangible Damages in American Tort Law: A Roadmap" (2016) Stanford Public Law Working Papers, at ssrn.com/abstract = 2727885, para I (B) (3). On medical malpractice in the United States, see Chapter III, section 3.1.

a normally constituted person would suffer, and the plaintiff in fact suffered, severe distress.[21]

Beyond the negligence realm, since the mid-twentieth century another tort came to be recognized as a cause of action. This can be represented as an extension of the idea that mental tranquility, and not just physical security, warrants legal protection. The new tort is called "intentional infliction of emotional distress" (IIED),[22] although some courts refer to it as the "tort of outrage,"[23] since it imposes liability on an actor who, by means of outrageous conduct, intentionally or recklessly causes severe emotional distress to another.

The American Law Institute first endorsed the IIED cause of action in a 1948 "Supplement" to the Restatement First of Torts of 1939, whose § 46 provided that: "[o]ne who, without a privilege to do so, intentionally causes severe emotional distress to another is liable (a) for such emotional distress, and (b) for bodily harm resulting from it." According to the Supplement's reporter, Dean Prosser, the expression "without [...] privilege" was meant to block use of the tort against those who induced severe emotional distress in others simply by insisting on their legal rights (such as landlords menacing defaulting tenants of eviction, or creditors threatening to foreclose on property securing unpaid loans).[24] In 1965, when the provision was published as § 46 of the Restatement Second of Torts, the expression "without a privilege" was replaced by the requirement of "extreme and outrageous conduct." The same requirement was then maintained by the 2010 Restatement Third

[21] See now Restatement Third of Torts—Liability for Physical and Emotional Harm (PEH), 2010, §§ 47 and 48; see also Dan B Dobbs, Paul T Hayden, & Ellen M Bublick, *Torts and Compensation, Personal Accountability and Social Responsibility for Injury* (8th edn, West 2017) 628–638. A similar tort exists under the federal common law: see *Consolidated Rail Corporation v Gottshall*, 512 US 532 (US 1994) (joined cases), where the Court upheld the claim under the Federal Employers' Liability Act of plaintiff Gottshall, a railroad worker who developed severe depression and post-traumatic stress disorder following an episode in which a co-worker died at work, insofar as the defendant's negligence placed him in immediate risk of physical injury. The same Court, however, denied the claim of plaintiff Carlisle, a railroad worker who suffered severe emotional distress because he had been subjected to unreasonably stressful working conditions, insofar as the plaintiff failed to satisfy the zone-of-danger requirement. See also Chapter V, section 4.1.

[22] Rabin (n 3) 369. See also ibid at fn 40: "IIED is a particularly interesting tort because it mirrors the evolving social attitudes about the extent to which one is expected to have a thick skin in dealing with the occasional insults and indignities that are a part of everyday life. The baseline has certainly shifted towards greater protection of psychic distress, but not without continuing reservations." Cf *Wallace v Shoreham Hotel, Corp*, 49 A 2d 81 (DC 1946) (refusing to recognize liability for a public insult in a restaurant), with *Wishnatsky v Huey*, 584 NW2d 859 (ND Ct App 1998) (similarly refusing to recognize liability, a half-century later, for rudeness in barring entry to a private meeting).

[23] John CP Goldberg, Leslie C Kendrick, Anthony J Sebok, & Benjamin C Zipursky, *Tort Law: Responsibilities and Redress* (5th edn, Wolters Kluwer 2021) 775.

[24] Willam L Prosser, "Insult and Outrage" (1956) 44 Cal LR 40, 49–50.

of Torts—Liability for Physical and Emotional Harm (PEH), which also extended the scope of the cause of action to the protection from reckless behavior. Section 46 of the Restatement Third of Torts—PEH now reads:

> An actor who by extreme and outrageous conduct intentionally or recklessly causes severe emotional harm to another is subject to liability for that emotional harm and, if the emotional harm causes bodily harm, also for the bodily harm.

An argument can be made that, prior to the adoption of the IIED cause of action by American jurisdictions, damages for purely dignitary injuries (that is, injuries consisting in the mere infringement of the victim's dignity or personality) were already captured by the institution of punitive damages. Punitive damages, which have been a traditional feature of common law jurisdictions, were sometimes awarded in significant amounts even when there was slight or no actual damage caused by the defendant. As Judge Richard Posner noted in the *Mathias v Accor Motor Lodge* opinion,[25] there are two possible interpretations of this traditional remedy. One is that punitive damages in "low damages" cases are really a stealth form of emotional distress compensation for hard-to-measure dignitary harms. The other is that they were introduced for a quasi-public function, that is, to provide deterrence where compensatory damages would be inadequate. It is important to recognize that IIED's emergence is significant regardless of whether both, either, or neither of these interpretations of punitive damages is correct. IIED created a new ground of liability that did not previously exist. Before the establishment of IIED in its present form, a court inclined to award punitive damages in a case involving pure intentionally inflicted emotional distress would have been barred from doing so unless it could have linked the distress to an independent intentional tort, such as battery, assault, or false imprisonment.[26]

4. Unconsciousness, Survival, and Death

A further issue is raised when a person survives a tortiously caused physical accident, but her senses are permanently lost. Most legal systems make

[25] *Mathias v Accor Econ Lodging, Inc*, 347 F3d 672, 675–677 (7th Cir 2003).
[26] Prosser (n 24) 44.

compensation available to this kind of plaintiffs. Nominal reference can be made to either pain and suffering or loss of amenities, but the point still is that England,[27] Germany,[28] France,[29] and Italy[30] recognize such a non-economic damage recoverable with a certain largess. It is in most of the jurisdictions in the United States that the situation is different: for the plaintiff to recover, she is required to show both duration and consciousness of the pain and suffering.[31] This doctrine leads to the paradoxical result that the "greater the degree of brain injury inflicted by a (negligent) defendant, the smaller the award the plaintiff can recover in general damages."[32]

A different issue arises when the victim, conscious or not, dies after the injury. From a comparative perspective, one can observe that the basic rule for the victim's death is that her survivors, as successors, may continue or lodge the tort actions that the victim would have been entitled to raise, standing in her shoes. At least theoretically, these claims are distinct from those which survivors may lodge for their own losses—such as for the loss of the decedent's contributions to their lives, or for their own pain and suffering. While the former (successors' tort actions for the victim's loss) are in all respects treated as if the deceased herself made them, the latter (survivors' tort actions for their own loss) are considered derivative claims, that is, claims by secondary

[27] In these cases, the heading of recoverable non-economic damage is "loss of amenities of life." Courts have held that damages can be awarded even where a claimant is unconscious, to compensate her for the actuality of her deprivation: "If a [claimant] has lost a leg, the court approaches the matter on the basis that he has suffered a serious physical deprivation no matter what his condition or temperament or state of mind may be": *H West & Son v Shephard* [1964] AC 326, HL, at 365. However, if unconscious victims might recover for their loss of amenities (insofar as "the fact of unconsciousness does not [...] eliminate the actuality of the deprivations of the ordinary experiences and amenities of life which may be the inevitable result of some physical injury": ibid at 349), they cannot claim damages for their pain and suffering, since damages of this kind "depend for their existence upon an awareness in the victim" (ibid). Though this approach has been criticised, the Law Commission has recommended no change in the law: see Law Commission, *Damages for Personal Injury: Non Pecuniary Loss*, Law Com no 257 (1998), para 2.19, at lawcom.gov.uk/app/uploads/2015/03/lc257_Damages_Personal_Injury_Non-pecuniary_Loss.pdf.

[28] BGH 13 October 1992, BGHZ 120 1, NJW 1993, 781 (compensation because of a brain injury caused at birth by medical malpractice). See also BGH 12 May 1998, NJW 1998, 2741 (awarding compensation to a victim of a traffic accident who survived ten days, being initially conscious for half an hour) and BGH 6 December 1994, NJW 1995, 783 (awarding compensation to a victim of a traffic accident who died fifty-one days after the accident being mostly all the time without consciousness). On this point, see also Markesinis, Bell, & Janssen (n 5) 198–199.

[29] Cass civ 28 June 1995, Bull civ 1995, II, no 224; Cass civ 22 February 1995 (two decisions), D 1995, Somm 233 ("*'L'état' végétatif d'une personne humaine, n'excluant aucun chef d'indemnisation, son préjudice doit étre réparé dans tous ses éléments*": ibid at no 3).

[30] Cass 6 October 1994, no 8177, Giur it 1995, I, 1534. The same holds true in Spain: SAP Pontevedra 3 March 2006, JUR 2006\118502; SAP Toledo 17 January 2006, JUR 2006\54657.

[31] See David W Leebron, "Final Moments: Damages for Pain and Suffering Prior to Death" (1989) 64 NYU LR 256, 268.

[32] *McDougald v Garber*, 504 NYS2d 383, 386 (NY 1986).

victims. As such, we will discuss them in the next chapter. Here, the focus is on the claim brought on behalf of the deceased.

The starting point is that only the claims vested in the deceased before her death can be transferred to the successors. This means that (a) only those identified by each legal system as successors of the deceased may stand in the latter's shoes, and (b) successors may claim damages for the victim's non-economic losses only if the deceased has experienced pain and suffering prior to death. If death is instantaneous, no survival action exists at all, because no damages occurred prior to the decedent's death.[33] Yet how long does the victim have to survive for pain and suffering to be considered an item of damage?

In Europe—from Berlin to Toulouse, from London to Palermo—the issue finds the same pragmatic solution, which can be summarized in three sentences:[34] Successors may inherit the claims of the deceased subject to the length and conditions of survival; if there is an interval between the accident and the death, then the estate will be able to claim the non-pecuniary items of damage for that period; where injury and death are close enough to be appreciated as a single occurrence, compensation for non-pecuniary loss cannot be awarded.[35] Even though, in a few European jurisdictions there are some additional requirements to be met in order to allow the claim to be part of the estate,[36] Germany, France, Italy, and England do not impose any of such formalities.[37]

[33] von Bar (n 14) 402–406.

[34] In a minority of jurisdictions, such as Estonia and Ireland, the claim for non-pecuniary damages dies with the victim. In Estonia, claims of compensation for non-economic loss are deemed to be personal, and therefore not transferrable to the estate under the Law of Succession Act of 2008, § 2 ("An estate does not include the rights and obligations of the bequeather which pursuant to law or by their nature are inseparably bound to the person of the bequeather"). In Ireland, s 7 (2) of the Civil Liability Act 1961 expressly states that "[w]here [...] a cause of action survives for the benefit of the estate of a deceased person, the damages recoverable for the benefit of the estate of that person shall not include exemplary damages, or damages for any pain or suffering or personal injury or for loss or diminution of expectation of life or happiness."

[35] von Bar (n 14) 402; see also Ulrich Magnus & Jörg Fedtke, "Germany," in Horton Rogers (ed) (n 5) 115; Galand-Carval (n 5) 97; Giovanni Comandé & Francesco D Busnelli, "Italy," in Horton Rogers (ed) (n 5) 135, 144–145.

[36] Some legal systems require a formal step to be taken by the deceased when she was still alive, such as a lawsuit brought before a court: this is the case in Greece (according to art 933 of the Greek Civil Code, "[t]he claim for moral reparations is not transferable and does not pass to the heirs, unless it has been acknowledged by contract or an action on it has been commenced"); in Poland (under art 449 of the Polish Civil Code, "[t]he claims provided for in articles 444–448 cannot be disposed of unless they are already due and payable and have been recognized in writing or awarded in a final and non-revisable court decision"); and in Spain (STS 3 December 1999, RAJ 1999 (5), no 8532, 13363; STS 24 June 1997, RAJ 1997 (3), no 5208, 7978). Other jurisdictions require a "notification" by the victim to the wrongdoer about the former's claim for reparation (this is the case in the Netherlands: see Art 6:106 (2) BW) or an assertion by the victim of her claim against the injurer or the latter's insurer still others (for instance, in Sweden and Finland: see, respectively, 6 Chapter 3 § SKL and 7 Chapter 3 § SKL).

[37] Consequently, it is especially in these jurisdictions that the determination of how long the injured person has to live for the estate to be entitled to claim compensation for her pain and suffering,

In the United States, damages recoverable in survival actions provide the decedent's estate with compensation for any harm that the decedent suffered up to the moment of her death. As such, most states permit recovery in survival actions for pain and suffering experienced by the decedent prior to death, an element of damages that, where recognized, might support substantial damage awards (assuming that death was not instantaneous).[38]

5. Contractual Remedies

Non-economic damage can also arise from nonperformance or misperformance of a contractual obligation (eg, a catering provider breaches the obligation of arranging the service on the wedding she had been hired for; a veterinary misperforms his duties, killing the animal she was supposed to take care of). The conditions on which such a claim is granted, or rejected, however, are quite different across the legal systems.

One can start with recalling that in Europe there exist two common models shaped by European Union law, and related to specific contractual settings. The first pattern is provided by art 14(2) of the Package Travel Directive,[39] according to which "the traveller shall be entitled to receive appropriate compensation from the organiser for any damage which the traveller sustains as a result of any lack of conformity." As the whereas (34) of the Directive makes clear, "[c]ompensation should also cover nonmaterial damage, such

becomes an issue for the trier. By contrast, in the legal systems where a legal action, a notification or an assertion is required (see n 36), the time needed to take these steps works as an implicit answer to the question, screening out claims arising from events in which the time span between injury and death is too short to allow the parties to fulfil those requirements. It should however be noted that, under German law, claims for infringement of personality rights are not inheritable: see BGH 23 May 2017, NJW 2017, 3004; BGH 29 April 2014, NJW 2014, 2871.

[38] Sebok (n 1) 344. See, for example, *Nelson v Dolan*, 230 Neb 848 (1989).

[39] Directive (EU) 2015/2302 of the European Parliament and of the Council of 25 November 2015 on package travel and linked travel arrangements (a similar provision was contained in the repealed Council Directive 90/314/EEC of 13 June 1990 on package travel, package holidays, and package tours, whose art 5 (1) read: "1. Member States shall take the necessary steps to ensure that the organizer and/or retailer party to the contract is liable to the consumer for the proper performance of the obligations arising from the contract [...]"). For the statutory rules implementing the provision mentioned in the text, see art L211-16 of the *Code du tourisme* in France, § 651n of the BGB in Germany, art 46 of the Legislative Decree no 79 of 2011 in Italy, s 16(3) of the Package Travel and Linked Travel Arrangements Regulations 2018 in the United Kingdom.

as compensation for loss of enjoyment of the trip or holiday because of substantial problems in the performance of the relevant travel services."[40]

The other model comes from EU legislation aiming to prevent racial, ethnic, and gender-specific discrimination in employment law. Amid other legal instruments, integrating or supplementing national legislation already in force,[41] art 18 of the Directive 2006/54/EC[42] reads: "Member States shall introduce into their national legal systems such measures as are necessary to ensure real and effective compensation or reparation as the Member States so determine for the loss and damage sustained by a person injured as a result of discrimination [...] in a way which is dissuasive and proportionate to the damage suffered." The reference to "real and effective," as well as to "dissuasive" compensation has been interpreted as consistent with the statutory aims only to the extent that it includes recovery of non-economic damage.[43]

The tendency gradually emerging in EU law to grant compensation for non-economic loss in contract law is echoed in some, but by no means in all, national European contract law regimes. There are at least four approaches one can sort out: the first can be dubbed "liberal," the second "cautious ex ante," the third can be defined as "cautious ex post," and the fourth "conservative" (with exceptions).

In the liberal group we find, as usual, France. In the French legal system, indeed, the principle that the "moral damage" suffered by the contractual obligee represents compensable damage, is not questioned.[44] For instance,

[40] Before the enactment of Directive EU/2015/2302, the compensation claim ensured by art 5 (1) of the Directive 90/314/EEC (above n 39) was expressly interpreted by the Court of Justice as allowing not only recovery of non-economic damage as a consequence of breaches of contract which lead to damage to health, but also non-economic damage as a consequence of holiday pleasure missed out on: ECJ 12 March 2002, C-168/00, *Simone Leitner v TUI Deutschland GmbH & Co KG* [2002] ECR I-2631, at curia.europa.eu.

[41] For a survey of these texts, cf Everlyn Ellis & Philippa Watson, *EU Anti-Discrimination Law* (2nd edn, OUP 2012); Samantha Besson, "Fundamental Rights and European Private Law," in Mauro Bussani & Franz Werro (eds), *European Private Law. A Handbook* (I, Stämpfli 2009) 7–40; Dagmar Schiek, Lisa Waddington, & Mark Bell, *Cases, Materials and Text on National, Supranational and International Non-Discrimination Law* (Hart 2007).

[42] Directive 2006/54/EC of the European Parliament and of the Council of 5 July 2006 on the implementation of the principle of equal opportunities and equal treatment of men and women in matters of employment and occupation (whose contents reproduce former art 5 (2) of the Directive 2002/73/EC of the European Parliament and of the Council of 23 September 2002 on the implementation of the principle of equal treatment for men and women as regards access to employment, vocational training and promotion, and working conditions). As to the statutory rules implementing the provision mentioned in the text, see art L1134-8 of the *Code de travail* in France, § 15 of the *Allgemeines Gleichbehandlungsgesetz* (AGG) in Germany, art 37 of the Legislative Decree no 198/2006 in Italy, s 124 of the Equality Act 2010 in the United Kingdom.

[43] Christian von Bar & Ulrich Drobnig (eds), *The Interaction of Contract Law and Tort and Property in Europe* (Sellier 2004) 101.

[44] Vernon V Palmer, "The French Awakening in the Nineteenth Century," in Vernon V Palmer (ed), *The Recovery of Non-Pecuniary Loss in European Contract Law* (CUP 2015) 58–74. This is also

there is no doubt, in France, that the death of an animal, caused by its keeper's negligence, causes the owner of the animal (economic as well as) affective harm, which may be compensated under contract law rules.[45]

The cautious ex ante approach is exemplified by the German rules. German contract law only recognizes liability for nonmaterial damage in cases of infringement of an interest that is protected by § 253 II BGB—that is, injury to body, health, freedom, or sexual self-determination. Once this requirement is met, however, the road to recovery is open. A well-known example is that of the man who, prior to undergo an operation which would result in sterility, had his sperm frozen. Some years later, when he wished to father children, he discovered that the sperm had been negligently destroyed by the hospital where it was deposited. The plaintiff was awarded damages for pain and suffering.[46]

A cautious ex post stance is taken by Italian law. Until some years ago, the issue of recoverability in contract of non-economic damage was scarcely mentioned by case law, thanks to frequent concurrence of actions regarding contractual and tortious liability. Consequently, for the Italian judge very few occasions actually existed to expressly elaborate on this question. However, the standard view embraced by courts was that the scope of fairly agreed-upon contractual rules cannot be diverted by an indiscriminate recourse to the tort law remedies. The balance point between this attitude and the instances brought forward by the aggrieved party was found in that that Italian case law limited purely contractual recovery to cases in which misperformance or nonperformance of contractual obligations led to an egregious infringement of a right to life, body, or liberty.[47] However, in the last thirty years, the expansion of the notion of recoverable non-economic

the case in Spain. Art 1106 of the Spanish Civil Code does not exclude the compensation of such damage, and its recoverability in contract law actions is well-established since a Supreme Court's decision in 1984: STS 9 May 1984, RJ 1984, 2403. See also Josep Solé Feliu, "El daño moral por infracción contractual: Principios, modelos y derecho español," InDret 1/2009, 19.

[45] Cass civ 16 January 1962, D 1962, 199. It may be worth recalling that in France the owner, being in contract with the keeper, would not have any claim in tort against the keeper herself.

[46] BGH 9 November 1993, BGHZ 124, 52 (at that time, however, damages were awarded in tort under § 847 BGB—whose wording is now to be found in § 253 II BGB). On the German approach, see also Vernon V Palmer, "European Contractual Regimes: The Contemporary Approaches," in Palmer (ed) (n 44) 106–107. One has to note that in Germany no compensation is allowed for cases of death of a beloved pet: see Florian Wagner-von Papp, "Germany—Case 4," in Palmer (ed) (n 44) 239–240.

[47] See Cass 19 January 1977, no 261, Giur it 1978, I, 1, 1791; Cass 27 February 1980, no 1376, Giur it 1980, I, 1459; Cass 14 May 1987, no 4441, Giust civ 1987, I, 1628; see also Miquel Martìn-Casals, "The Borderlines of Tort Law," in Miquel Martìn-Casals (ed), *The Borderlines of Tort Law. Interactions with Contract Law* (Intersentia 2019) 713, 731.

damage in tort has triggered a parallel and consistent development in contract law. Nowadays, moral damages in the contractual sphere are permitted whenever the defendant's breach of contract infringed a constitutional right: from human dignity to physical integrity, from protection of family, to sanctity of home.[48] Yet there are remnants of the previous cautious approach. For instance, Italian courts may in principle award non-pecuniary damages in case of the death of a pet,[49] but are generally reluctant to award nonmaterial damages resulting from damage to property other than beloved animals.[50]

England takes a conservative approach. Non-economic damages are in principle not awarded for breach of contract. However, some exceptions have been carved out in the exclusionary rule, provided that certain requirements are met. First of all, non-economic damage can be awarded where the "very object of a contract is to provide pleasure, relaxation, peace of mind or freedom from molestation,"[51] and the breach is one that results in that not occurring. The classic examples include package holiday contracts, when the facilities contracted for were not available at a holiday resort.[52] In the same vein, non-economic damages have been awarded for the breach of a building contract to construct a swimming pool at a private house, being the contract described as one for a pleasurable amenity,[53] and for the breach of contract caused by a surveyor who failed to advise his client that a property that the latter intended to purchase for his retirement was likely to be significantly affected by aircraft noise.[54] The same solution may in principle apply also

[48] Palmer (n 44) 98–99.

[49] See, among others, Cass 25 February 2009, no 4493, Resp civ prev 2009, 1013.

[50] See the cases cited in Marta Infantino, "Italy—Case 4," in Palmer (ed) (n 44) 229–232.

[51] *Watts v Morrow* [1991] 1 WLR 1421 per Bingham LJ at 1445.

[52] *Jarvis v Swan Tours Ltd* [1973] QB 233.

[53] *Ruxley Electronics Ltd v Forsyth* [1996] AC 344. Facts were as follows: The plaintiffs entered into a contract with the defendants for the construction of a swimming pool at their house. The contract provided for the pool having a maximum depth of seven feet and six inches. Yet, as built, the maximum depth of the pool was only six feet. The plaintiffs sought to recover as damages for breach of contract the cost of demolition of the existing pool and of construction of a new one of the required depth. Since the pool as constructed was perfectly safe to dive into, there was no evidence that the shortfall in depth had decreased the value of the pool. The House of Lords therefore held that the plaintiffs were not entitled to the cost of cure, but that their personal preference for a deeper pool entitled them to damages for loss of amenity. As von Bar & Drobnig (n 43) 106, note, it is likely that this extension was made "only because in the circumstances of the case the contract breaker would otherwise have escaped all liability since there was no financial loss, the pool as built was of no less value than the one contracted for and just as suitable, and it was a situation where an order requiring it to be changed to that contracted for was not available as unjustifiably economically wasteful. In effect a rather nominal sum was awarded for inconvenience."

[54] *Farley v Skinner (No 2)* [2001] UKHL 49. Plaintiff's claim as to the diminution of value of the property by reason of the negative effect of aircraft noise was rejected since the purchase price coincided with the open market value of the property after taking into account aircraft noise. Yet the

to a breach of contract causing the death of an animal, provided that the contractual arrangement was intended to ensure the animal's owner peace of mind that her animal was adequately kept and looked after.[55] A second line of exceptions is given by contracts whose purpose is to provide relief to an existing state of stress. This has been the case of contracts for legal services. Thus, solicitors who had failed to obtain protection for their client being molested by a man had to compensate her for the mental distress and upset caused by the continued molestation.[56] Similarly, some solicitors who conducted a criminal case in such a poorly manner to cause a psychiatric injury to their client, have been held liable to pay non-economic damages to him.[57]

An approach similar to the English one is adopted in the United States, where courts have manifested a long-standing reluctance to award non-economic damages in contract.[58] Here too, however, there are some exceptional situations where such damages are recoverable.

First of all, under federal civil rights statutory law, an employee subject to an unlawful and intentional discriminatory act by her employer might claim damages not only for her future pecuniary losses, but also for her "emotional pain, suffering, inconvenience, mental anguish, loss of enjoyment of life, and other nonpecuniary losses."[59] Thus, awards for pain and suffering are available to victims of sexual harassment at the workplace under federal civil rights law.[60] Outside the realm of employment relationships, a line of cases is related to the manners in which the breach occurred. When the defendant acts outrageously at the time of the breach—think of bad faith contract performance—damages for mental distress may be recoverable insofar as the court recognizes that the defendant has not merely breached the contract, but that

House of Lords awarded compensation to the plaintiff for distress: "if the cause is no more than disappointment that the contractual obligation has been broken, damages are not recoverable even if the disappointment has led to a complete mental breakdown. But, if the cause of the inconvenience or discomfort is a sensory (sight, touch, hearing, smell, etc.) experience, damages can, subject to the remoteness rules, be recovered" (Ibid at 85, per Scott J).

[55] Dorota Leczykiewicz, "United Kingdom—Case 4," in Palmer (ed) (n 44) 241–243.

[56] *Heywood v Wellers* [1976] QB 466, per James LJ.

[57] *McLoughlin v Grovers* [2001] EWCA Civ 1743.

[58] See Ronnie Cohen & Shannon O'Byrne, "Cry Me a River: Recovery of Mental Distress Damages in a Breach of Contract Action—A North American Perspective" (2005) 42 Am Bus LJ 97—also for an assessment of the similar approach taken by Canadian jurisdictions.

[59] 42 USC § 1981a, letter (b) (3).

[60] See Douglas M. Staudmeister, "Grasping the Intangible: A Guide to Assessing Nonpecuniary Damages in the EEOC Administrative Process," (1996) 46 Am U LR 189.

she has done so in a way that requires additional punishment.[61] Another set of circumstances permitting recovery for mental distress is when the breach is of such kind as that serious emotional disturbance was a particularly likely result.[62] Common examples are (as elsewhere) holiday contracts,[63] and (as in England) ill-performed contracts for building new homes (presenting thereby substantial defects),[64] and legal malpractice claims. For example, in *Hanumadass v Coffield, Ungaretti & Harris*,[65] at issue was the conduct of an attorney representing a physician in a malpractice claim. The attorney settled the claim on behalf his client, but neglected to advise the physician of the settlement. As a result, the physician needlessly worried about the claim for six years before learning it had been settled. The plaintiff was awarded non-economic damages on the basis of the sheer foreseeability of the injury.[66]

6. Factors Shaping the Award

Damages awards for non-economic loss take the form of a lump sum payment and/or of regular annuities. The structure and amount of these awards are connected to the nature of the injury: physical, emotional or psychological, or some combination thereof.

The amount of recoverable money differs considerably from system to system, which is also due to a variable emphasis as to which aspects of non-pecuniary loss are relevant, although everywhere an important guideline for the courts is to look at how precedent decisions treated similar cases.[67] This practice fulfills the principle of equal treatment and serves the purpose of legal consistency, facilitating the predictability of judicial solutions and the reaching of extrajudicial settlements.[68]

[61] See, for example, *Brown v Fritz*, 699 P2d 1371 (Id 1985). In other cases, the disturbance accompanies a bodily injury, and in such cases, typically medical malpractice cases, the victim's claim is regarded as a tort action. See Restatement Second of Contracts, 1981, § 353, cmt a, as well as Chapter III, section 2.2.

[62] *Hanumadass v Coffield, Ungaretti & Harris*, 724 NE2d 14 (Ill 1999).

[63] *Vick v National Airlines*, 409 So 2d 383 (La 1982).

[64] *Taylor v Burton*, 708 So 2d 531 (La Ct App 1998).

[65] *Hanumadass v Coffield, Ungaretti & Harris* (n 62).

[66] Ibid at 18. The plaintiff's choice between tort, contract, and fiduciary duty does not control the damages available in legal malpractice in the United States. See ibid at 18 ("included within the rubric of legal malpractice are claims grounded in breach of contract, negligence, and breach of fiduciary duty").

[67] Cees van Dam, *European Tort Law* (2nd edn, OUP 2013) 360–362.

[68] Markesinis, Coester, Alpa, & Ullstein (n 5) 67.

By contrast, the variations can be sorted out according to whether (a) or not (b) the plaintiff's claim for non-economic damage stems from a physical injury.

(a) Even if in most European countries lawmakers do not officially adopt any tariffs for compensation for pain and suffering, there is a quite widespread agreement among European national courts, at least in personal injury cases, on that the amounts awarded in similar cases should more or less be consistent one another. This is why personal injury awards are gathered and processed in non-statutory tables to serve as guidelines.[69] A further consequence of this is that the more the awarded amount diverges from these standards, the more reasons the judge has to give for his decision.[70]

In Germany, the so-called *Schmerzensgeldtabellen* list the range of compensation that has been awarded and for what injury.[71] In England the Judicial Studies Board created a Working Party to develop and constantly update—on the basis of new decisions and in light of intervening inflation—a set of guidelines for assessing damages in personal injury cases.[72] French and Italian courts require plaintiffs to present their claims for pain and suffering in terms of a medically standardized "point system" measuring the severity and the likely duration of the plaintiffs' injuries. Courts then calculate the amount of compensation to be paid with the help of judicially made *barèmes*, that is, tables translating the victims' "points" in money, having regard to the victims' age.[73]

[69] See Denise Amran, "Identifying and Calculating Personal Injury Damages in Ireland, Italy, France and Belgium: Recent Debates between Scholars, Judges and Practitioners," in Eoin Quill & Raymond J Friel (eds), *Damages and Compensation Culture. Comparative Perspectives* (Hart 2016) 113, 118–122; Stephen D Sugarman, "Tort Damages for Non-Economic Losses: Personal Injury," in Mauro Bussani & Anthony J Sebok (eds), *Comparative Tort Law. Global Perspectives* (2nd edn, EE 2021) 305, 315–318.

[70] Markesinis, Coester, Alpa, & Ullstein (n 5) 67.

[71] See, eg, Andreas Slizyk, *Schmerzensgeldtabellen 2022* (18th edn, Beck 2022). On these *Tabellen*, see also Markesinis, Bell, & Janssen (n 5) 198–199; van Dam (n 67) 363.

[72] Judicial College, *Guidelines for the Assessment of General Damages in Personal Injury Cases* (15th edn, OUP 2019), on which see also Sugarman (n 69) 323–324.

[73] Cf for instance Benoît Mornet, "L'indemnisation des préjudices en cas de blessures ou de décès" (2021), at www.m-reynier.fr/post/barème-mornet-l-indemnisation-des-préjudices-en-cas-de-blessures-ou-de-décès-edition-2021 and Tribunal of Milan, "Tabelle per la liquidazione del danno non patrimoniale" (2021), at tribunale.milano.it. On the current French and Italian approach, see also Amran (n 69) 118, 122; Markesinis, Coester, Alpa, & Ullstein (n 5) 17–18; Sebok (n 1) 389. In France, the *décret n° 2020-356 du 27 mars 2020 portant création d'un traitement automatisé de données à caractère personnel dénommé « DataJust »* has authorized the Ministry of Justice to apply artificial intelligence tools to public repositories of civil decisions in order, *inter alia*, to "elaborate

In the United States, appellate courts are divided as to whether the amount of prior awards should influence them in reviewing challenges to damages awarded in personal injury cases. Some jurisdictions refuse to look at earlier cases, while others allow judges to use previously decided cases as guidelines. What is uncontested, in any case, is that jurors are not allowed to consider past awards, so as to preserve "the ideal of individualized justice, to be rendered on the basis of the unique experience of the particular plaintiff."[74] As it is clear, however, this practice also "creates the risk of variance in award levels for the same general types of harm."[75]

(b) Much less uniformity is to be found outside physical injury litigation. In cases of dignitary torts (that is, in cases involving an infringement of the victim's dignity or personality), the variance in the awards is great across (and many times within[76]) jurisdictions.

On the one hand, legal systems have different understandings of what constitutes an infringement to dignity and personality, and of how the latter should be remedied—an understanding which is strictly dependent upon the possibility of redressing non-economic loss through symbolic, general, presumed, punitive and/or restitutionary damages, as well as upon the availability of other remedies (such as preventive injunctions and restrictive orders).[77] On the other hand, the quest for standardization is countered, within every legal system, by the relevance assigned, in this field, to the specific circumstances of each case—such as the defendant's

guidelines for assessing damages in personal injury cases" (art 1(1), n° 2, *décret n° 2020-356*). In Italy, it is to be noted, the heading of "non patrimonial damages," in cases of personal injury, covers all the different kinds of damage that common law jurisdictions would compensate under such headings as "loss of amenities of life," damage to the aesthetic appearance of the victim, damage to the general working capacity, including temporary and permanent disability. See Markesinis, Coester, Alpa, Ullstein (n 5) 84–95; Guido Alpa, "Personal Injury. Features of the Italian Legal System," in Mauro Bussani (ed), *European Tort Law. Eastern and Western Perspectives* (Stämpfli 2007) 153–223.

74 Page (n 6) 193, 212.

75 Ibid. The American approach may create an incentive for plaintiffs to appeal to common stereotypes about the gravity of hedonic losses due to physical disability, which may be tactically useful in litigation, but reinforces those stereotypes in the community. See Samuel R Bagenstos & Margo Schlanger, "Hedonic Damages, Hedonic Adaptation, and Disability" (2007) 60 Vand LR 745.

76 David A Logan & Michael D Green, "The Protection of Personality Rights against Invasions by Mass Media in the United States of America," in Helmut Koziol & Alexander Warzilek (eds), *The Protection of Personality Rights against Invasions by Mass Media* (Springer 2006) 383; von Bar (n 2) 176.

77 Gert Brüggemeier, Aurelia BC Colombi Ciacchi, & Patrick O'Callaghan, "A Common Core of Personality Protection," in Gert Brüggemeier, Aurelia BC Colombi Ciacchi, & Patrick O'Callaghan (eds), *Personality Rights in European Tort Law* (CUP 2010) 568, 571–572.

degree of blameworthiness and her possible lucrative intent, the severity of the attack, the gravity of the subjective and objective consequences for the plaintiff, the parties' social status and their relationship vis-à-vis each other, and so forth.[78]

6.1. Peculiar Conditions of the Victim

Two other interrelated factors are to be taken into account when studying compensation for non-economic damage. The first is relevant regardless of whether the non-economic damage is related to a physical injury; and it is the well-known basic rule that the causal contribution of the victim to the harm she claims compensation for (including pain and suffering), leads to a reduction in the award of damages.[79] The other factor can be seen, to a certain extent, as a counter-corollary of the former: we refer to the widespread acknowledgment of the rule according to which, if the tortfeasor is liable for the full extent of the victim's personal injury, the former is obliged to compensate the latter's non-economic damage even if she did not know of a particular predisposition to injury of the victim. As we will see right below, the rule finds variable applications, and most of the times it is discarded when actions normally considered insignificant have extremely serious consequences.[80]

In Italy, the "take-your-plaintiff-as-you-find-her" rule is opposed by scholars,[81] and nevertheless applied by judges, regardless of the nature, psychological or physical, of the plaintiff's previous conditions.[82] In France and in the United States, psychological predispositions generally receive less judicial consideration—and sometimes their assessments lead to deny recovery—than physical predispositions.[83] In Germany, preexisting damage or

[78] von Bar (n 2) 176–177.

[79] On this rule, see also Chapter II, section 9 and Chapter VII, section 1.

[80] Markesinis, Bell, & Janssen (n 5) 68–70; Michael D Green, "The Third Restatement of Torts in a Crystal Ball" (2011) 37 Wm Mitchell LR 993, 1000; Deirdre M Smith, "The Disordered and Discredited Plaintiff: Psychiatric Evidence in Civil Litigation" (2010) 31 Cardozo LR 749, 763–771; J. Stanley Mc Quade, "The Eggshell Skull Rule and the Related Problems in Recovery for Mental Harm in the Law of Torts" (2001) 24 Campbell LR 1, 3, 35; von Bar (n 2) 484; Anthony M Honoré, "Causation and Remoteness of Damage," in *International Encyclopedia of Comparative Law* (Mohr 1971), vol XI, ch 7, 131.

[81] Pietro Trimarchi, *Causalità e danno* (Giuffrè 1967) 90–91; for further references, see Marta Infantino, *La causalità nella responsabilità extracontrattuale* (Stämpfli-ESI 2012) 143–149.

[82] As to psychological predispositions, see Cass (labor division) 9 April 2003, no 5339, Not giur lav 2003, 422; with regard to physical fragilities, see Cass (labor division) 5 November 1999, no 12339, NGCC 2000, I, 661.

[83] See, in France, Cass civ 20 June 1985, Bull civ 1985, 125; Cass civ 17 May 1990, as reported in Bénédict Winiger, Helmut Koziol, Bernhard A Koch, & Reinhard Zimmermann (eds), *Digest*

injury may justify an increase or a reduction of damages depending upon each individual case—most of the decisions which have taken into account an existing predisposition, however, are characterized by a careful weighing of all aspects of the circumstances of the case;[84] therefore, a definite qualification of predisposition as a factor which increases or decreases the amount of damages is very hard to draw.[85]

In England, it is true that a hypersensitive victim does not recover damages unless it is found that a person of "average backbone," under the circumstances, would have suffered the same kind of psychological harm. Yet, once this requirement is met, the rule is that the defendant "takes the plaintiff as she finds her," and therefore the unusually sensitive claimant can recover in full.[86] This implies that the defendant has to answer for the consequences of the plaintiff's predispositions, even if the latter is extremely vulnerable.

7. A Quantitative Survey

As we said, usually compensation of non-pecuniary loss takes the form of a lump sum, which, especially when the physical impairment is considered particularly severe, can be coupled with a periodical payment.

One of the possibilities to compare legal systems in this respect is to look at the amounts paid for pain and suffering arising from one of the most severe kinds of physical injury, such as quadriplegia, although one should also keep in mind the caveats mentioned above about the actual comparability of the awards.

of European Tort Law. Essential Cases on Natural Causation (Springer 2008) 512–513; Cass com 4 December 2001, Bull civ 2001, IV, 194 (all with regard to psychological conditions); cf Cass crim 30 January 2007, Rec D 2007, 868; Cass crim 27 March 1957, Bull crim 1957, 290; (as to physical conditions). In the United States, cf *Stoleson v United States*, 708 F 2d 1217 (7th Cir 1983) (mental predisposition); *Vosburg v Putney*, 80 Wis 523, 50 NW 403, 27 Am St Rep 47 (Wis 1891) (physical predisposition). The American Law Institute has definitively embraced the equal treatment of mental and physical predisposition under the "eggshell rule." See Restatement of Torts—PEH, Section 31, cmt b, Reporters' Notes and Stephen P Calandrillo & Dustin E. Buehler, "Eggshell Economics: A Revolutionary Approach to the Eggshell Plaintiff Rule" (2013) 74 Ohio State LJ 375, 385.

84 Cf for instance BGH 29 February 1956, BGHZ 20, 137 and BGH 11 November 1997, NJW 1998, 810.

85 See a detailed survey of the cases quoted in the previous footnotes, as well as of further case law, in Markesinis, Coester, Alpa, & Ullstein (n 5) 75–77 (where it is also underlined that in Germany the victim can be found comparatively negligent if she has not taken reasonable measures to protect herself against her vulnerability); Markesinis, Bell, & Janssen (n 5) 68–70.

86 See Deakin & Adams (n 4) 232–234. See also Lord Parker in *Smith v Leech Brain Co* [1962] 2 QB 405, 414, and *Page v Smith* [1966] AC 155.

As to quadriplegia, according to a study published by Stephen D. Sugarman in 2015,[87] the highest sum of compensation for non-pecuniary loss awarded by an English judge (and expressed in USD) is of $ 436,000 (€ 409.000). The highest reported German award for *Schmerzensgeld* in such cases is currently $ 655,000 (€ 614,000), while the Italian record is set by an award of $ 1,093,000 (€ 1,024,000).[88]

These amounts show that, though some jurisdictions (such as England and Germany) are generally considered to be less liberal toward claimants than others, the sums awarded by the former might be generous. In these jurisdictions, "[t]he chance of getting compensation is lower but when one is successful the compensation is higher. In other words, the top of the compensation pyramid is higher but the base, that is, the number of people compensated, is smaller."[89]

In a previous study carried out in 2006,[90] Stephen D. Sugarman compared awards for pain and suffering in the United States and in Europe (combining data from twenty European jurisdictions), and elaborated the following table.[91]

Cross-National Award Size Comparison Comparing United States Median Pain and Suffering Awards with European Awards

(1 Euro= $ 1.333)	**US Medians in $ 1000s**	**US Medians in € 1000s**	**Europe Medians in € 1000s**	**Europe Range in € 1000s**
Finger	137	100		
Arm			38	10–66
Leg	1000	750	41	10–166
One Eye	500	375		
Blindness	4500	3375	65	22–235
Quadriplegia	3400	2550	92	15–250

[87] Sugarman (n 69) esp 323–324 and 334. See also the previous researches carried out by the same author (Stephen D Sugarman, "A Comparative Look at Pain and Suffering Awards, Presentation at Clifford Symposium on Pain and Suffering" (2006) 55 DePaul LR 412), as well the Europe-wide comparative overview of personal injury awards provided by David McIntosh & Marjorie Holmes (eds), *Personal Injury Awards in EU and EFTA Countries* (3rd edn, Kluwer 2003).

[88] Other European jurisdictions recognize relatively less large sums. For instance, the highest awards for quadriplegia awarded in the Netherlands, Sweden, and Denmark were, respectively, for $ 133,000 (€ 125,000), $ 62,000 (€ 59,000), and $ 29,000 (€ 27,000). See Sugarman (n 69) 319.

[89] van Dam (n 67) 365.

[90] Sugarman, A Comparative Look (n 87) 399.

[91] Ibid at 418, Table 14.

What do these numbers tell us? Essentially, they highlight how the average amounts awarded for pain and suffering in the United States are significantly greater than those recognized in Europe. As noted by the author of the table above, this result holds true "when looking at averages as well as the full range of European awards." Indeed, "these data show that the United States median awards are enormously larger than the highest predicted awards for similar injuries in Europe, notwithstanding the great diversity of award levels throughout Europe. More specifically, the median pain and suffering award in the United States for quadriplegia was more than twenty-five times greater than the predicted award for quadriplegia in the median European nation and more than ten times the highest predicted European award. For loss of a leg, the median American award, even taking into account a wider range of leg injuries including the perhaps lesser injury of a loss below the knee, was nearly twenty times the predicted award in the median European nation, and more than four times the highest predicted award. Indeed, the loss of a finger in the United States tends to generate almost three times the median European nation pain and suffering award for loss of an arm. Loss of one eye in the United States tends to attract more for pain and suffering than does total blindness in Europe."[92]

One has to recall, however, that the above difference in the level of the awards in the United States is influenced, perhaps by a pervasive private insurance market, most likely by the absence of a full-fledged public health service, and certainly by the absence of the jury in European civil proceedings.[93] In Europe, the amount of compensation is assessed by a judge, whose mentality, social milieu, and personal income are most of the times comparable with those of higher-ranking civil servants.[94] Thus, "middle class values and economic perceptions determine the assessment of damages. Attempts at the arbitrary redistribution of wealth, as one finds (or is said to find) in American jury awards, are totally unknown [...] in the law of tort of continental Europe."[95]

[92] Sugarman, A Comparative Look (n 87) 418–419.

[93] This holds true on the European continent as well as in England: see Chapter I, section 8.

[94] Markesinis, Coester, Alpa, & Ullstein (n 5) 17; John G Fleming, *The American Tort Process* (Clarendon Press 1988) 224–225.

[95] Markesinis, Coester, Alpa, & Ullstein (n 5) 17.

V

Recovery of Secondary Victims for Economic Harm and Emotional Distress

1. The Problem of "Secondary" Victims

Every accident can produce multiple victims. This can happen most simply when a defendant's tortious conduct creates a risk that harms one or more persons in the same way, such as when a careless driver strikes a car with four passengers. There are multiple "primary" victims, and each of the passengers can claim a direct right to recovery based on the harm suffered by each of them independently and separately.

Multiple victims can arise out of an accident indirectly, too. A single tortious act may produce a heterogeneous set of risks that affect different victims in different ways. This type of situation may be easily illustrated by the case where a careless driver strikes a car, and then the driver of the car that was struck responds in an unreasonable fashion and strikes a pedestrian crossing the road. The injury caused by the defendant to the passengers in the first scenario arises from a different risk than the injury caused to the pedestrian, even though the two risks are connected to the same careless act. A third variation of this problem can be illustrated by considering the claim

Common Law and Civil Law Perspectives on Tort Law. Mauro Bussani, Anthony J. Sebok, & Marta Infantino, Oxford University Press.
DOI: 10.1093/oso/9780195368383.003.0005

by a rescuer injured by the defendant's careless act while trying to help the pedestrian in the second example. The harm caused by the defendant to the rescuer arises from yet another and different risk than the harms caused to the passengers and pedestrian, even though this risk is also connected to the same careless act.

It is conventional to say that the passengers in the first variation are direct victims of the defendant's careless act and to describe the rescuer in the third as an indirect victim.[1] The pedestrian in the second variation may be a direct or indirect victim; one could argue the point either way.[2]

In cases of personal injury and property damages, it makes very little difference where one draws the line between direct and indirect harms, since every tort system examined in this book would treat each of these examples as raising a question of liability of the defendant to the victim as a *primary* victim.[3] Where indirect harm cases hinge on physical injury to the person or property of the plaintiff, these cases are treated like cases of direct harm, which is not saying that they do not pose difficult questions of both duty and causation. For example, it is worth noting that the third variation involving liability by a defendant to rescuers is treated as a problem of causation in Germany and one of duty in the United States, sometimes with opposite results.[4] However, within both the common law and the civil law tort systems, indirect harm cases that do not involve personal injury and property of the plaintiff are denominated under special categories and decided under ad hoc sets of rules.

These cases most often concern plaintiffs who claim compensation for the indirect economic and non-economic harm they suffered as the indirect result of a physical injury to somebody else's person or property. There is a diverse range of such claims for indirect injuries, and not all of them can be usefully discussed together.

[1] See Gert Brüggemeier, *Common Principles for Tort Law. A Pre-Restatement of the Law* (BIICL 2004) 97–104 ("Direct Harm and Indirect Third Party Injury"). The third variation is the classic problem of a defendant's duty to a foreseeable rescuer. See, eg, *Wagner v International Railway Co*, 133 NE 437 (NY 1921), where Cardozo J famously held that "danger invites rescue." See also Basil S. Markesinis, John Bell, & André Janssen, Markesinis's German Law of Torts (5th edn, Bloomsbury 2019) 68–69.

[2] The second variation parallels the structure of the famous American case of *Palsgraf v Long Island Railway Co*, 248 NY 339 (NY 1928).

[3] On the notion of "primary" victims vis-à-vis "secondary" ones, see Chapter IV, section 1.

[4] Compare BGH 30 June 1987, BGHZ 101, 215 (where a mother was able to recover from a negligent physician whose malpractice obliged her to donate a kidney to her daughter) with *Moore v Shah*, 458 NYS2d 33 (App Div 1982) (where, under similar circumstances, the court found that there was no duty and rejected liability). See also Markesinis, Bell, 7 Janssen (n 1) 68–69.

One of the most typical illustrations of these claims for "indirect injuries" is that of family members pursuing recovery for the indirect pecuniary and emotional harm caused by the death of their loved ones. As we will see in the next Chapter (devoted to pure economic losses), all the tort systems under review allow for indirect pecuniary harm in cases involving the death of a family member, whether under the heading of wrongful death statutes (in the United States and England) or of *Reflexschaden/ricochet* damage in Germany, France, and Italy.[5] Yet, although the obligation to compensate family for pecuniary loss is analytically related to the obligation to compensate them for their non-pecuniary losses caused by the primary victim's death or injury, divergence still looms large as far as recovery for the latter harms is concerned (see section 3 in this chapter).

Another recurring scenario for these kinds of harms involve nervous shock suffered by bystanders who witness an accident. In these cases, the direct victim is the person injured in the accident and the indirect victim is the person who, by observing the direct victim, suffers a psychic injury. In cases of bystanders' nervous shock, the problem of how to handle emotional upset and psychological disturbances in the absence of any physical contact (a problem that, as we saw in Chapter IV, every tort law system has struggled with, even with regard to primary victims) is further magnified by the position of the plaintiff as a *secondary*, rather than primary, victim. As the German Federal Court put it in the well-known "*Schockschäden*" case of 1971, "it is a matter of common knowledge that the pain, grief, and fright arising from a very negative experience can have a very marked effect" on the secondary victim, but that alone does not make it a loss compensable in tort, absent certain specific conditions (such as an invasion of personality rights or a sexual assault).[6] Without something more, these psychic harms are "*allgemeines Lebensrisiko*": part of life's general risks, and uncompensable even if caused by a tortious act.[7]

But cases of indirect harm are also those where someone suffers an indirect economic loss as a consequence of an injury to somebody else's person or property, such as cases where a driver negligently kills the star player of a soccer club, whose profits plummet,[8] and where A carelessly damages B's

[5] See also below, section 3, as well as Christian von Bar, *The Common European Law of Torts* (II, OUP 2000) 191.

[6] BGH 11 May 1971, BGHZ 56, 163.

[7] Markesinis, Bell, & Janssen (n 1) 231.

[8] These are the facts of Cass (Plenary) 26 January 1971, no 174, Giur it, 1971, I, 1, 681 (the so-called *Meroni* case), on which see Chapter VI, section 5.3.

electrical cable and C suffers a loss because B cannot sell C electricity.[9] In theory, one could call the plaintiffs in these indirect pure economic loss cases "secondary victims,"[10] although as a matter of convention, no one does. Yet, as Bruggemeier notes, there is no significant conceptual difference between the *Meroni* and *Spartan Steel* fact patterns and those underlying wrongful death claims by surviving family members.[11]

We have chosen to follow convention and treat cases of indirect pure economic loss separately from the cases discussed in this chapter. Here, the term "secondary victims" will be used, according to ordinary language, to identify with claims by family members and other persons closely connected with the primary victim for non-pecuniary (or non-economic) losses caused by the primary victim's injury.[12] Therefore, in this chapter we will consider claims by secondary victims to include two kinds of indirect losses: emotional distress of family members for the death of their loved ones (section 3), and nervous shock suffered by a family member or a bystander when someone dear or near dies or is injured (section 4). Two connected caveats, however, are in order.

The first caveat relates to the fact that the line between primary and secondary victims is often blurred not only between legal systems, but also within them. As we said at the beginning of this section, the qualification of victims as being primary or secondary depends on a variety of factors, ranging from linguistic habits to conventional ways of framing injuries and torts, which often lack coherence and systematization even within the boundaries of a single jurisdiction.

The second caveat is referred to the equally muddy separation between emotional distress and nervous shock. The distinction is well entrenched in England and German legal language ("bereavement"/"nervous shock," *Angehörigenschmerzensgeld/Schockschäden*), perfectly understandable to an American lawyer (who however might speak in both cases of "emotional

[9] These are the facts of *Spartan Steel and Alloys Ltd v Martin & Co Ltd* [1973] QB 27, on which see Chapter VI, section 5.4.

[10] In civil law systems such cases are often referred to as "ricochet" cases. See Vernon V Palmer & Mauro Bussani, "The Present Study," in Vernon V Palmer & Mauro Bussani (eds), *Pure Economic Loss: New Horizons in Comparative Law* (Routledge 2009), 7, 16. See also Chapter VI, section 3.

[11] Brüggemeier (n 1) 97–102.

[12] See Chapter IV, section 1. See also John G Fleming, "Distant Shock in Germany (and Elsewhere)" (1972) 20 AJCL 485. Indeed, in this context, the definition of "secondary" victim may encompass family members and other persons closely connected with the primary victim for non-pecuniary (or non-economic) losses caused by the primary victim's non-lethal injury. A different issue arises when the primary victim, initially injured by the tortfeasor, eventually dies and her successors step into her shoes to claim damages on her behalf: on this point, see Chapter IV, section 4.

distress") and substantially unknown to French and Italian legal practice. Yet, even in the jurisdiction recognizing the two categories, the divide between them is often hard to draw. We retain the distinction inasmuch as we believe that, by entailing different regimes, it remains useful for our purposes of description and explanation.

2. Death in the Family: Recovery for Secondary Victims' Economic Losses

As we just mentioned, and as we will see in more detail in the next Chapter, in all the systems herein studied, surviving family members can recover their indirect economic losses stemming from the death of a loved one. Of course, differences still exist as to the identity and standing of the secondary victims, as to the amounts awarded, and as to the legal basis for the awards. Since the recognition of such losses is tightly related to (and not always easily distinguishable from) the overall development of rules about family members' entitlement to bereavement damages, it is worth recalling here the principles that govern compensation to family members for their economic losses in case of death of a loved one.

While the English common law, until about 1850, almost never authorized causes of action for negligence resulting in death,[13] in 1846 the Lord Campbell's Act entitled the "wife, husband, parent and[/or] child" of a person who was wrongfully killed to obtain compensation for damages where the deceased had such a right at the time of her death.[14] Lord Campbell's Act was repealed in 1976 by the Fatal Accidents Act, which nowadays allows a wider spectrum of plaintiffs[15] to recover economic damages from the person

[13] A partial exception came from the rule that permitted an action for trespass on the case per quod consortium amisit (literally, "a trespass whereby [plaintiff] lost the company of his wife") by husbands for injuries caused to their wives by the wrongful act of another: William Blackstone, *Commentaries on the Law of England* (III, 16th edn, Strahan 1825) 140. Loss of consortium was recognized very early in the history of the common law. See, eg, *Guy v Livesey* [1618] 79 Eng Rep 428 (KB). However, the window for loss of consortium suits by husbands was closed by the 1808 decision of *Baker v Bolton* [1808] 1 Camp 493, which declared that, "[i]n a civil court, the death of a human being [cannot] be complained of as an injury."

[14] On the reasons underlying its adoption, see Rande W Kostal, *Law and English Railway Capitalism 1825–1875* (OUP 1994) 289–290. On such developments, see also Chapter VI, section 5.4.

[15] The list of dependents set out in s 1 (3) of the Fatal Accidents Act 1976 (as amended), include spouses, civil partners, and cohabitants of the deceased, as well as the latter's parents, children, brothers, sisters, aunts and uncles, and any person who is the issue of a brother, sister, uncle or aunt of the deceased.

who caused the deceased's death for "the injury resulting from the death."[16] A similar pattern has occurred in the United States, where the American states, shortly after the approval of the Lord Cambell's Act, followed the English lead by enacting their own "wrongful death" statutes.[17] The statutes were (and still are) diverse in their particulars, but they typically ushered in two broad changes in tort law. First, they allowed tort litigation to proceed after the death of the primary victim, enabling the decedent's estate to claim compensation for any harm that the decedent suffered up to the moment of her death.[18] Second, they created a new action on behalf of certain persons defined by the statutes themselves (and most often identified with the deceased's spouses and minor children), who were presumed to have suffered as a result of the death of the primary victim—in a sense, creating through statute a new class of indirect primary victims.[19]

In Germany, similarly to what happens in a number of other European jurisdictions,[20] § 844 II BGB entitles the persons to whom the primary victim owed a legal duty to provide support (such as parents, spouses, born and unborn children[21]) to receive "the payment of an annuity to the extent that the person killed would have been obliged to provide maintenance for the presumed duration of her life." By contrast, France and Italy handle the right of recovery by secondary victims of economic damages resulting from the death of a loved one through the general clauses of tort liability.[22] Subject

[16] S 3 (1) of the Act.

[17] Dan B Dobbs, Paul T Hayden, & Ellen M Bublick, *Torts and Compensation, Personal Accountability and Social Responsibility for Injury* (8th edn, West 2017) 666.

[18] Damages ordinarily recoverable in survival actions include medical expenses incurred by the deceased prior to her death (which may be nonexistent, if death was instantaneous) (*Warner v McCaughan*, 77 Wash2d 178 (Wash 1969)), lost earnings between the time of injury and the time of death (*Printy v Schwantes*, 40 Wis2d 418 (Wis 1968)), and funeral expenses (which, although incurred after death, are commonly viewed as obligations of the estate of the deceased: *McGowan v Estate of Wright*, 524 So2d 308 (Miss 1988); *Estate of Kronemeyer v Meinig*, 948 P2d 119 (Colo App 1997)). Most states nowadays also permit recovery in survival actions for pain and suffering experienced by the decedent prior to death, assuming death was not instantaneous: *Nelson v Dolan*, 434 NW2d 25 (Neb 1989). On the latter issue, see also Chapter IV, section 4.

[19] Dobbs, Hayden, & Bublick (n 17) 666–681. Wrongful death damages go to the persons named in the statute and not the primary victim's estate; therefore they are not subject, for example, to the whims of a testator nor to the rights of the primary victim's creditors: John CP Goldberg, Leslie C Kendrick, Anthony J Sebok, & Benjamin C Zipursky, *Tort Law: Responsibilities and Redress* (5th edn, Wolters Kluwer 2021) 469–470.

[20] Such as Austria, Greece, the Netherlands, Poland, and Switzerland: see § 1327 ABGB (Austria), art 922 CC (Greece), art 6:108 BW (Netherlands), art 446 CC (Poland), and arts 45 and 47 Code of Obligations (Switzerland).

[21] Stepchildren who have not been legally adopted, fiancé(e)s, and romantic partners whom the primary victim has not been married are thus excluded from the scope of §§ 844 II and 845 BGB. See Markesinis, Bell, & Janssen (n 1) 200.

[22] Suzanne Garland-Carval, "France," in Ulrich Magnus (ed), *Unification of Tort Law: Damages* (Kluwer 2001) 77, 86; Francesco D Busnelli & Giovanni Comandé, "Italy", ibid, 134–136. The same

to these general rules, the main limitation on whether someone could claim economic damage as a secondary victim, in Italy and France, comes from principles of "causality and attributability."[23] Under such view, non-marital partners can qualify as secondary victims,[24] as well as relatives outside the nuclear family, provided that they were relying on the primary victim for economic support.[25]

One way of viewing the difference between the approach adopted by the United States, England, and Germany, on the one hand; and France and Italy, on the other hand, is that the latter treat all economic loss as part of the same problem and tend to permit a broader set of persons to recover, while the former focus on the triangular nature of the relationship between the secondary victim, the defendant, and the primary victim, and seek to define a rule of recovery that is based on the special relationship between the primary victim and the secondary victim.

3. Death in the Family: Recovery for Secondary Victims' Emotional Distress

Whether to allow family members and alike to recover for their emotional distress presents an additional problem. Should the right to recovery for these losses be treated under the same rules that govern other recoverable losses (such as economic losses), or should special rules, based on the quality of the relationship between the primary and secondary victim determine the right to recovery? And if the latter, which qualities of the relationship should matter? As we shall see, the systems we review answer this question in a way that tends to fit the patterns we just set out with regard to economic losses.

approach applies in other countries, such as Belgium and Spain: see Herman A Cousy & Anja Vanderspikken, "Belgium," in Magnus (ed), *Unification of Tort Law,* 27–28; Miquel Martín-Casals, Jordi Ribot, & Josep Solé, "Non-Pecuniary Loss under Spanish Law," in WV Horton Rogers (ed), *Damages for Non-Pecuniary Loss in a Comparative Perspective* (Kluwer 2001) 192–194.

[23] von Bar (n 5) 194. Under such logic, compensation can go beyond bonds of affection to other bonds, especially bonds of business interests.

[24] Cf Cass (mixed division) 27 February 1970, *Gaudras v Dangeraux*, D 1970, 201 and Cass 28 March 1994, no 2988, Giur it 1995, I, 1, 1366.

[25] See Busnelli & Comandé (n 22) 117, 129 and 134, n 59. This fits with the European trend that extends the right to recovery for maintenance to unmarried partners: Ulrich Magnus, "Comparative Report on the Law of Damages", in Magnus (ed) (n 22) 185, 211 ("[t]he majority [of European countries] also allow the surviving partner of a stable and lasting relationship such a claim").

With the exception of a growing number of states which have begun to liberally interpret their wrongful death statutes, the United States does not recognize a right to recover for negligent infliction of emotional distress in cases of death of a loved one. England and Germany permit damages for emotional distress arising from the death of a primary victim only under special circumstances denoted by the relationship, while France and Italy allow for recovery for the same distress under the general liability clauses to be found in their civil codes.

3.1. The United States and England

In the United States the traditional rule was that the emotional distress suffered by secondary victims caused by the death of a loved one was not a compensable injury.[26] This rule has never been enforced consistently, given that, even before the advent of wrongful death statutes, at least some secondary victims (husbands) could recover for the emotional pain experienced when their wives were tortiously killed under the common law action of loss of consortium, which in principle allowed husbands to recover for injuries caused to their wives by the wrongful act of another.[27] Still, modern courts distinguish between the non-pecuniary injuries compensated by loss of consortium, which they equate with the reduced quality of life suffered by a family member after the primary victim's death, and emotional distress, which is limited to the pain, anguish, and grief naturally induced in the secondary victim upon learning of the death.[28] The former may be allowed under loss of consortium (or wrongful death statutes that allow recover for loss of companionship) while the latter can only be pursued in those states that permit recovery for mental anguish or distress. As the Texas Supreme Court explained,

> [m]ental anguish represents an emotional response to the wrongful death itself. Loss of society, on the other hand, constitutes a loss of positive benefits which flowed to the family from the decedent's having been a part of it. Mental anguish is concerned "not with the benefits [the beneficiaries]

[26] Dobbs, Hayden, & Bublick (n 17) 628.

[27] See above, n 13, as well as John G Culhane, "Even More Wrongful Death: Statutes Divorced from Reality" (2005) 32 Fordham Urb LJ 171, 190 (2005).

[28] See *Krouse v Graham*, 562 P2d 1022 (Cal 1977).

> have lost, but with the issue of compensating them for their harrowing experience resulting from the death of a loved one." Loss of society asks, "what positive benefits have been taken away from the beneficiaries by reason of the wrongful death?" Mental anguish damages ask about the negative side: "what deleterious effect has the death, as such, had upon the claimants?"[29]

Texas belongs to the significant, yet still minority, of states that permit recovery for mental anguish *and* loss of society under its wrongful death statute.[30] Typical of the majority is Nebraska, which rejected a grieving mother's claim for compensation for her grief upon losing her seventeen-year-old son.[31] The son had been killed in a very gruesome fashion, but the mother did not witness the death. The court allowed her to sue for the "economic value" of the loss of the son's companionship to her, but not for her "mental suffering or bereavement" resulting from her son's death. It should be noted that, as the personal representative of her son's estate, the court did allow the mother to sue on *his* behalf for the emotional distress that *he* suffered before he died (the son had been aware for a number of seconds that he was going to suffer a serious injury that would have led him to die).

England has settled the issue in a direct way. Under Lord Campbell's Act, it was for the jury to specify a wrongful death claimant's damages.[32] In theory, then, the jury was empowered to award surviving family members compensation not only for economic loss but also for their bereavement. The practice was made explicit in 1982 when (after the jury had been made irrelevant) the Fatal Accident Act of 1976 was amended to allow a very limited set of secondary victims to collect damages for bereavement in the amount set by the statute.

Two features about the English approach are noteworthy.

First, the Act deliberately provides bereavement damages to a much more limited set of secondary victims: only the wife, husband, civil or cohabiting partner of the primary victim, and the parents if the primary victim was a minor[33] (in the latter case, the sum awarded to the parents shall be divided equally between them[34]). Second, compared to the United States, the amount

[29] *Moore v Lillebo*, 722 SW2d 683, 687–688 (Tex 1986).

[30] See Andrew J McClurg, "Dead Sorrow: A Story about Loss and a New Theory of Wrongful Death Damages" (2005) 85 BU LR 1, 25–26, fns 131–133.

[31] *Nelson v Dolan*, 434 NW2d 25 (Neb 1989).

[32] *Franklin v South Eastern Railway* [1858] 157 ER 448.

[33] S 1A (2) Fatal Accidents Act.

[34] S 1A (4) Fatal Accidents Act.

awarded for bereavement is relatively modest (£15,120).[35] It must be noted that, as in the United States (and elsewhere[36]), "loss of services" and such items as the loss of the "caring services by a parent to child," may fall within the heading of pecuniary damages, where they are not constrained by the limitation on bereavement damages.[37] However, in the United States, where mental anguish is awarded under the wrongful death statutes, the amount is not defined by the statutes themselves, but rather awarded by juries and can therefore vary depending on the vagaries of trial practice. While no state has attempted to standardize mental anguish damages for secondary victims, the September 11 Victims Compensation Fund (VCF) provides an interesting point of comparison. The special master of the VCF, Kenneth Feinberg, was asked by the US Congress to create a statutory alternative compensation program which potential plaintiffs could enter instead of suing airlines whom they believed were partially responsible for allowing the terrorist attacks of 9/11 to occur.[38] Feinberg was ordered by Congress to base the program on existing rules of tort law, which included the nation's various wrongful death statutes. His solution was unusual; he decided to give to each member of the primary victim's family the same amount of money for their non-pecuniary damages: $100,000 for the spouse and each dependent of the deceased victim.[39] As one observer noted, given that these figures would include loss of services as well as mental anguish, the amount awarded to a primary victim's family consisting of a surviving spouse and three young children for their claims as secondary victims ($400,000) might seem too low by modern American standards.[40] Nonetheless, mental anguish compensated by the $100,000 awarded far exceeds the amount awarded for bereavement in England.[41]

[35] S 1A (3) Fatal Accidents Act.

[36] See above, section 2.

[37] Mark Lunney, Donal Nolan, & Ken Oliphant, *Tort Law: Text and Materials* (6th edn, OUP 2017) 948, and see *Franklin v South Eastern Railway* [1858] 157 ER 448.

[38] Anthony J. Sebok, "What's Law Got to Do With It? Designing Compensation Schemes in the Shadow of the Tort System" (2013) 53 DePaul LR 501, 502–503.

[39] Final Rule, September 11th Victim Compensation Fund of 2001, § 104.44, 67 Fed Reg at 11,246.

[40] Marshall S Shapo, "Compensation for Victims of Terror: A Specialized Jurisprudence of Injury" (2003) 36 Ind LR 237, 246 (2003).

[41] Recall that in jurisdictions where non-economic damages for wrongful death are linked to loss of services, older spouses by definition receive less than younger spouses (since they have fewer years of lost services), and that even in those jurisdictions which permit non-economic damages to be awarded for grief, it is possible that an older spouse will receive less on the grounds that they will suffer fewer years of grief. See Goldberg, Kendrick, Sebok, & Zipursky (n 19) 465–467.

3.2. Germany, France, and Italy

The rule in Germany used to be very restrictive with regard to the emotional distress suffered by secondary victims resulting from grief or bereavement: until 2017 the secondary victim had no right to recovery for non-economic losses under § 844 II BGB.[42] In 2017, however, a legislative reform added to § 844 a third section, according to which survivors who, at the time of the primary victim's death, were in a particularly close relationship with her, are entitled to recover (on the top of the annuity mentioned by § 844 II[43]) a "reasonable monetary compensation" for their emotional distress against the tortfeasor.[44] If such a close relationship is presumed where the survivor was the spouse, the civil partner, a parent, or a child of the deceased, the new § 844 III BGB does not provide any indication about what a "reasonable monetary compensation" should be.[45]

This is not to say that, prior to 2017, German law never recognized that grief can cause a compensable loss. As early as in 1931 a mother's right to recovery for the loss of her earning capacity caused by grief at the death of her son in an automobile accident was permitted.[46] The court distinguished between a claim for "indirect" damages, which the mother could collect only under § 844 II BGB (wrongful death), and damage to bodily health (and therefore the capacity to earn), for which the mother could claim under § 823 I BGB: "It is normally to be expected that a fatal accident of her child will greatly excite the mother emotionally, and it is not unusual if a grave emotional excitement of this kind results in a nervous breakdown which affects the capacity to work."[47] As Markesinis notes, the mother in this case is a secondary victim, yet the Reichsgericht treated her claim for damages under § 823 I BGB as identical to that of a primary victim.[48] Thus, the key step to recovery by a secondary victim before the recent reform was to show an invasion of health, thus bringing the claim under § 823 I. This was clearly established by the Federal Court in 1971 when it held that a widow could only

[42] Basil S Markesinis, Michael Coester, Guido Alpa, & Augustus Ullstein, *Compensation for Personal Injury in English, German and Italian Law. A Comparative Outline* (CUP 2005) 81.

[43] On which see above, in this chapter, section 2.

[44] The reform was brought by the *Gesetz zur Einführung eines Anspruchs auf Hinterbliebenengeld* of 17 July 2017, BGBl I 2017 S 2421.

[45] It is suggested a rule of thumb of € 10,000 per each eligible beneficiary: Markesinis, Bell, & Janssen (n 1) 200.

[46] RG 21 September 1931, RGZ 133, 270, in Markesinis, Bell, & Janssen (n 1) 233.

[47] Quoted in Markesinis, Bell, & Janssen (n 1) 234.

[48] Markesinis, Bell, & Janssen (n 1) 235.

claim damages outside of § 844 BGB if she could prove that she "not only experienced the normal reactions of pain, grief and depression, but also directly suffered a "traumatic" injury to her physical and psychical health."[49] Even after the introduction of the new § 844 III, the action grounded on § 823 I BGB is still available to family members in case of death of their beloved ones, but to obtain recovery they are required to prove that they suffered a psychological impairment with relevant medical effects and imposing medical treatment.[50] It is not sufficient, for instance, to demonstrate that, after the accident, the alcohol addiction of the deceased's wife has worsened.[51]

The treatment of secondary victims who suffer emotional distress as a result of a tort to a primary victim in France is very different than the approach adopted by Germany and common law jurisdictions. This is because the French handle the losses of this group of secondary victims, whom they call *victimes par ricochet*, like primary victims.[52] The most important and practical consequence of this is that, with regard to secondary victims, the French rules for the recovery of non-economic losses are largely identical to the rules that govern economic losses.

As early as in 1931 the *Cour de cassation* awarded bereavement damages to a spouse, noting that the injury was compensable under former art 1382 (now art 1240) of the Civil Code due to "an affectionate *interest* arising because of a blood relationship or a relationship by marriage linking the victim of the harmful act" with the spouse.[53] These damages are not limited to what the Americans call loss of society/consortium although they certainly include that. This head of damages, known as *préjudice d'affection*, relates to the "distress and sorrow" felt by the secondary victim as a result of the death of the primary victim, covering (but not limited to) the loss of future pleasant experiences that the secondary victim could be expected to have with the primary victim.[54] Secondary victims who could claim *préjudice*

[49] BGH 11 May 1971, BGHZ 56, 163, NJW 1971, quoted in Markesinis, Bell, & Janssen (n 1) 224.

[50] Markesinis, Bell, & Janssen (n 1) 32–33; see also BGH 5 February 1985, BGHZ 93, 351; BGH 11 May 1971, BGHZ 56, 163. It goes without saying that a claim for *Schockschäden* under § 823 I BGB may be pursued only by persons closely related to the primary victim: Markesinis, Coester, Alpa, & Ullstein (n 42) 82.

[51] Markesinis, Coester, Alpa, & Ullstein (n 42) 82.

[52] Suzanne Garland-Carval, "France," in WV Horton Rogers (ed), *Damages for Non-Pecuniary Loss in a Comparative Perspective* (Springer 2001) 93; and Walter van Gerven, Pierre Larouche, & Jeremy Lever, *Cases, Materials and Text on National, Supranational and International Tort Law* (Hart 2000) 126.

[53] Cass Req 2 February 1931, DP 1931.I.38 (translated in van Gerven, Larouche, & Lever (n 52) 127, n 193)

[54] Garland-Carval (n 22) 83; see, for instance, Cass civ 24 October 2019, Gaz Pal 2020, no 2, 30. This conclusion is further strengthened by the fact that *préjudice d'affection* is rebuttably presumed

d'affection include partners in an unwed couple, fiancé(e)s, godchildren, and illegitimate children.[55] Suzanne Galand-Carval has observed that a backlash against the court's application of the rules of *préjudice d'affection* has developed as a result of the perception that "it has become rather frequent for distant relatives (aunts, uncles, cousins) to ask for, and get, damages for moral suffering."[56] Galand-Carval also noted that, as of 1994, the amounts awarded were not very great ("25,000 francs for a brother or sister, 50,000 for a child, 75,000 for a spouse"[57]). One might wonder whether this still holds true as of today. In 2018, a review of the compensation criteria adopted by the Compensation Schemes for Terrorism Victims ("Fond de Garantie pour le Terrorisme International") showed that the latter awarded "a minimum of € 7,000 for the *préjudice d'affection* suffered by a grand parent who did not have regular contacts with his deceased grandchild and a maximum of € 35,000 for the *préjudice d'affection* suffered by the spouse, partner or parent of the deceased if the latter was less than 26 years old."[58]

The state of the art is similar, but the awards are much higher, in Italy. Under Italian law, family members and the like, in case of death of their beloved ones, can recover their economic and non-economic losses under the general clause of art 2043 of the Civil Code, which covers all economic damage, and under art 2059 c.c., which allows for the award of non-economic damages. At first sight, the Italian system apparently lies in between the French and German approach: while the French Civil Code poses no limitation to the award of *préjudice d'affection*, art 2059 of the Italian Civil Code makes compensation for non-economic losses conditional upon a violation of the law, in a way similar to that adopted by § 253 BGB.[59] Yet, the

for members of the primary victims' family. See van Gerven, Larouche, Lever (n 52) 127. However, it is interesting in this regard that a wife's recovery for *préjudice d'affection* may be rebutted by showing that she was intending to divorce her husband before the accident occurred. Cass civ 7 October 1992, Resp civ ass 1992, 434, cited in Garland-Carval (n 52) 91.

[55] van Gerven, Larouche, Lever (n 52) 127 and Garland-Carval (n 22) 83.

[56] Garland-Carval (n 52) 93. According to the Bellet Commission, in 1979 the average number of relatives compensated for their moral suffering in fatal cases was 5.3, and "it was not infrequent to see cases where damages were awarded to ten relatives": Garland-Carval (n 52) 93, n 13. See also CA Lyon 16 December 1988, JCP 1990.II.21510, *L'Olympique Lyonnais v Fuster*, in which the court ordered damages for *préjudice d'affection* to be paid to the parents and five adult siblings after the death of a man due to the negligence of the operators of a stadium. See van Gerven, Larouche, & Lever (n 52) 127.

[57] Garland-Carval (n 52) 93, n 13. One Euro has been made equal to approximately 6.56 French francs.

[58] Cour des comptes, "La prise en charge financière des victimes du terrorisme," December 2018, 47, at ccomptes.fr/system/files/2019-01/20190130-Indemnisation-victimes-terrorisme.pdf.

[59] Francesco D Busnelli & Giovanni Comandé, "Italy," in Rogers (ed) (n 22) 135, 140.

textual similarity between § 253 BGB and art 2059 of the Civil Code is actually more illusory than real, since the former is traditionally applied in a cautious manner, while the latter has come to be interpreted broadly.

Under the current reading of art 2059 of the Italian Civil Code, the notion of recoverable non-economic loss includes any damage associated with the infringement of a constitutionally protected right. When the victim proves that she suffered a medically diagnosed illness, of physical or psychological nature, as a result of an infringement of her (constitutionally protected) right to health, she can claim damages for her *danno biologico* ("biological damage").[60] Moreover, in case of infringement of a constitutionally protected right (*danno per la lesione di un interesse costituzionalmente protetto*) other than health, such as the right to a family life, the victim does not need a medical diagnosis to claim compensation (as a stand-alone item, or in addition to *danno biologico*) for any mental distress that causes her a serious discomfort.[61]

Therefore the current state of the law is that, following the death of a loved one, secondary victims who suffer a diagnosable mental disease and/or a severe emotional discomfort can sue under art 2059 c.c. for *danno biologico* and/or damage to a constitutionally protected interest.[62] The placement of non-economic losses under art 2059 CC could suggest a right to recovery by secondary victims for emotional distress somewhat more limited than what is provided under the French approach seen before. But the difference is more theoretical than functional: on the ground, both systems permit the recovery of bereavement damages to family, and both systems have expanded the sphere of loved ones who qualify under the general clauses of the civil codes, including non-married partners.[63]

Further, the Italian system is more generous than the French one. As we said in the previous Chapter (section 6), when a primary victim can prove she suffered a medically diagnosable (physical or psychic) illness, her compensation will be determined according to the judicially made guidelines that translate the victims' "injury points" into a monetary amount, taking into

[60] On this notion, see also Chapter I, section 5; and Chapter IV, section 6.

[61] Emanuela Navarretta & Elena Bargelli, "Italy," in Helmut Koziol & Barbara Steininger (eds), *European Tort Law 2005* (Springer 2006) 382, 387–388.

[62] Constitutional Court (order) 22 July 1996, no 293, Danno resp 1996, 697, quoted by in Busnelli & Comandé (n 22) 124.

[63] See, eg, Cass 28 March 1994, no 2988, Giur it 1995, I, 1, 1366; see also Trib Rome 9 July 1991, Riv giur circ trasp 1992, 138 (victim had a wife and a mistress who was also awarded *danno morale*).

account the severity and duration of the illness and the victim's age.[64] The same guidelines set out a list of secondary victims who are presumed to suffer emotional distress in case of the death of a family members, and provide for the amount to be awarded to each of them. According to the most recent version of the guidelines, spouses, civil partners, and unmarried cohabitants are entitled, in case of death of their companion, to bereavement damages that range between € 168,000 and € 336,000. The same amount is recognized to each child for the death of a parent and to each parent in case of death of their child. Each grandparent, brother, and sister of the deceased are entitled to a sum between € 24,000 and € 146,000.[65] Simply because the guidelines only mention spouses (and spousal equivalent), children, parents, grandparents, brothers, and sisters as possible beneficiaries for emotional distress awards does not mean that other categories of people—such as uncles, aunts, step-parents and step-children, long-time roommates, and so forth—cannot claim compensation for the emotional harm they suffered as a consequence. They can, provided that they can prove they suffered a medically diagnosed serious emotional distress. In such a case, the court will have a large degree of discretion in assessing their damages.[66]

4. Bystanders as Secondary Victims in Nervous Shock Cases. Concerns and Indifference

As we just saw, there is a great diversity among common law and civil law systems as to the availability of emotional distress that rises only to the level of bereavement or *pretium doloris* for secondary victims—many jurisdictions in the United States do not allow it, while it is allowed by statute in England and Germany and permitted generously by codes and courts in France and Italy. In the jurisdictions that do permit it, the circumstances under which they may be awarded also follow a distinct pattern: the secondary victims entitled to bereavement or *pretium doloris* are those persons who foreseeably would grieve if the primary victim was killed.

[64] See Milan Tribunal, "Tabelle per la liquidazione del danno non patrimoniale" (2021), at tribunale.milano.it. See also Chapter IV, section 6.

[65] See Milan Tribunal (n 64) 51.

[66] See, for instance, Cass 13 July 2018, no 18568, available at dejure.it, where the Court of cassation allowed a couple to recover damages for the emotional distress they suffered for the wrongful death of an old lady who (was not their relative, and yet) had lived for fifteen years with them and was considered by the entire family as a putative aunt.

The same pattern—with the caveats we introduce below—repeats itself as to the right to recovery by secondary victims for nervous shock—that is, the trauma and possible psychic injury suffered by seeing or hearing an accident to another person. All the jurisdictions seem to permit recovery for the trauma and psychological disturbances caused by an injury to a family member or someone who falls within a sphere of family-like affection. The justification for this seems to be that these secondary victims belong to the set of persons who would foreseeably suffer nervous shock if the primary victim was killed or (in a handful of jurisdictions) injured.

The variations within the systems have to do with whether courts will insist on specific elements (such as contemporaneous observation of the primary victim's injury or medical evidence of the psychological trauma), but not really with the underlying principle that only the nervous shock suffered by a secondary victim who has a bond of affection with the primary victim is a loss recognizable by the various national tort systems.

The point, however, is that the notion of nervous shock is deeply embedded in the jurisdictions historically bound to look at tort law taking for granted that only specific rights or duties matter, and that new forms of loss have to carve out their way in the preestablished grid of duties and right to be admitted to recovery.

This is why there is little point to discussing nervous shock cases as a separate topic in French and Italian tort laws. Historically, the French have neither explicitly distinguished these cases as a matter of duty, as do the Americans and English, nor as a matter of injury, as do the Germans. As Garland-Carval puts it, "the question of compensation for nervous shock has never been debated as such in France."[67] Under art 1240 (former art 1382) of the Civil Code, all losses suffered, whether economic, bereavement, or arising from nervous shock after witnessing another person's suffering an injury, are treated the same. The rules that come into play to award or deny recovery are the usual ones, concerning fault (or the "act of a thing" under art 1242 Code civil), causation, and damages.[68] Under Italian tort law, too, nervous shock cases are not recognized per se, insofar as, under the general clauses of liability, any loss fitting the requirements of articles 2043 and 2059 of the Civil Code is recoverable.[69] Italian courts have consistently held that the death of a relative can produce a shock which affects the health of the victim. In a 1994

[67] Garland-Carval (n 22) 83.
[68] Garland-Carval (n 22) 79.
[69] See above, section 3.2 in this chapter.

decision, the Constitutional Court explained that the shock arising from the same event—the death of a family member—can produce *both* a physical disease and a "psychological upsetting that constitutes subjective moral damage"[70]—and both of them are forms of non-economic loss that can be compensated under article 2059 c.c.[71] In the case of death of a beloved one, family members are therefore entitled to damages for their *danno biologico*, if they suffered a diagnosable mental disease, and, in any event, to the usually quite generous awards for their damage to a constitutionally protected interest—no matter what the circumstances of death were and whether they were close or not to the place of accident.[72]

Being that said, and dealing with another split not between but across legal traditions, we will first present the common law solutions and then the ones resulting from the civil law jurisdiction that shares the Anglo-American concerns about this kind of damage.

4.1. The United States

One small but important remark on the treatment in the United States of secondary victims who suffer nervous shock (that, in the American legal jargon, is dubbed "indirect" emotional distress or emotional harm) concerns the treatment of secondary victims where the primary victim was the subject of an intentional tort such as battery. This is, of course, a consequence of the common law's practice of emphasizing the distinction between intentional torts and negligence as a ground of liability, something which not all civil law systems do explicitly.[73]

The Restatements Second and Third of Torts approach the issue through the lens of "indirect" emotional distress (which has then become "emotional harm" under the Restatement Third). According to § 46 of the Restatement Second of Torts, a defendant is liable for the emotional distress caused to a

[70] Constitutional Court 27 October 1994, no 372, Foro it 1994, I, 3297, cited in Busnelli & Comandé (n 59) 139. See also ibid at 143 (in cases of a primary victim's death "[r]elatives can claim their own moral suffering and *danno biologico, but the latter if—and only if—they show its actual existence (an illness clearly evidenced by medical doctors) causally linked with their relative's death*" [emphasis added]).

[71] See above, section 3.2 in this chapter.

[72] Constitutional Court (order) 22 July 1996, no 293, Danno resp 1996, 697, and Constitutional Court 14 July 1986, no 184, Foro it 1986, I, 2053, quoted by in Busnelli & Comandé (n 22), respectively at 124 and 139.

[73] von Bar (n 5) 262–71.

secondary victim if the defendant engages in an intentional tort against the primary victim, and if (a) the defendant was substantially certain—but did not desire—that the secondary victim would suffer extreme emotional distress and (b) the secondary victim (i) was a family member of the primary victim or (ii) suffered bodily harm as a result of the emotional distress suffered.[74] Unlike the rules allowing for recovery for emotional distress resulting from a negligent injury caused by the defendant to the primary victim, liability for emotional distress in cases of intentional torts can follow even if the primary victim suffered no personal injury, provided she is a family member. The same holds true under § 46 of the Restatement Third of Torts—Physical and Emotional Harm (PEH), whose comment m "limits recovery for emotional harm to "bystanders" who are close family members and who contemporaneously perceive the event." One might argue, however, that given the requirement that the defendant had to be at least "substantially certain" of the consequences of his actions upon the emotional well-being of the secondary victim, this takes the problem out of the realm of the true secondary victim, and the family member who suffers the emotional distress is really the "primary" victim of the defendant's tort, albeit an indirect primary victim, per the discussion at the beginning of this chapter. From the civil law perspective, the answer would most likely be to view the plaintiff in a § 46 case as a primary victim, since regardless of the defendant's subjective intent, the loss to a family member was at least foreseeable—and therefore from the perspective of civil law systems, cases that fall under § 46 might properly belong in Chapter IV of this book.

A clear case of a claim for nervous shock by a secondary victim arises in American tort law under the tort of negligent infliction of emotional distress, or NIED.[75] As we saw in Chapter IV,[76] the history of American common law was to exclude these claims in their entirety, with a few ad hoc exceptions,[77] under the doctrines known as the "impact rule" and the "zone of danger rule,"

[74] See Restatement Second of Torts, § 46 cmt a, and *Christensen v Superior Court (Pasadena Crematorium of Altadena)*, 820 P2d 181 (Cal 1991).

[75] Dobbs, Hayden, & Bublick (n 17) 624. See *Amaya v Home Ice, Fuel & Supply Co*, 379 P2d 513 (Cal 1963), overruled by *Dillon v Legg*, 441 P2d 912 (Cal 1968).

[76] See Chapter IV, Section 3.2.

[77] For instance, a telegraph operator was held liable for the injury caused by the negligent failure to deliver information about the death of a loved one (*Stuart v Western Union Tel Co*, 66 Tex 580 (Tex 1885)). American common law also recognizes liability for the mishandling of a corpse. See Restatement Second of Torts, § 868: "One who intentionally, recklessly or negligently removes, withholds, mutilates or operates upon the body of a dead person or prevents its proper interment or cremation is subject to liability to a member of the family of the deceased who is entitled to the disposition of the body".

which limited liability for trauma to primary victims who were either *contacted* physically by the defendant (under the impact rule) or were in a "zone of danger" where they *could have been contacted* by the defendant (under the zone of danger rule).

Under the "bystander test," first developed by the California Supreme Court in *Dillon v Legg*, a secondary victim was owed compensation by the defendant who harmed a primary victim if three "guidelines" were satisfied (either jointly or in some combination). The three guidelines were that the secondary victim (1) was near the scene at which the primary victim suffered a personal injury (or was threatened with a personal injury by the defendant); (2) was contemporaneously aware of the personal injury or threat; and (3) was closely related to the primary victim.[78] This test, by its own admission, was not supposed to serve as a rule in which each of the three elements were taken as necessary conditions. The court's chief argument was negative—it was trying to justify its rejection of the zone of danger rule (discussed in Chapter IV, section 3.2) in a case where the plaintiff, the mother of the primary victim (a girl struck by a car), was just far enough away from the primary victim that she was not in danger herself of being struck by the car, while another plaintiff, the sister of the girl struck by the car, was standing next to the primary victim and could therefore be in danger of being struck by the defendant's car (but was not). As the court noted, unless it abandoned the zone danger rule in this case the sister could recover for her pure emotional distress, but the mother could not, a result it found to be "anomalous." Instead of "artificial abstractions which bar recovery contrary to general rules," the court called for the application of "factors [...] which will determine whether [this kind of loss] was *reasonably* foreseeable."[79]

A majority of the states now follow one or another version of *Dillon*.[80] However, a number of courts have rejected the bystander rule. Perhaps most notably, the year after *Dillon* was decided, the New York Court of Appeals refused to adopt the bystander rule in a case where a mother contemporaneously heard a car strike her two year old daughter, thus denying recovery to the mother.[81] The court did not focus on the difference between seeing and hearing an accident (which was not a central issue in *Dillon*, either) nor even on the difficulties of weeding out fraudulent claims. The problem, in its eyes,

[78] *Dillon v Legg*, 441 P2d 912 (Cal 1968).
[79] *Dillon v Legg*, 441 P2d 912 (1968) (emphasis in the original).
[80] Goldberg, Kendrick, Sebok, & Zipursky (n 19) 862–864.
[81] *Tobin v Grossman*, 249 NE2d 419 (NY 1969).

was that in *Dillon* the court created a new duty. In zone of danger cases—even the case of the sister in *Dillon* against the driver—the plaintiff can be described as a primary victim vis-à-vis a risk of physical contact. But neither mother, in neither the California nor the New York scenarios, had been wronged by the defendant with regard to their physical security: "[*Dillon*'s] solution does not depend upon advances in medical science, namely, that mental traumatic causation can now be diagnosed almost as well as physical traumatic causation. The question is profounder than that, because there is now urged the creation of a new duty and therefore an entirely new cause of action."[82]

Leaving aside the risk of fraudulent claims, the chief policy concern that critics of *Dillon* presented was that it would open the door to a very large number of new claims for emotional distress, given the diversity of circumstances under which accidents can occur and persons can experience distress.[83] It was not clear from *Dillon*, and some of the cases that followed it, whether the three factors it listed were exemplars of a general principle of foreseeability or were to be taken as the boundary markers of a new but limited duty designed to protect a very specific set of interests (eg, distress arising from the shock of seeing a family member injured). A good example of the debate over this question can be found in the one case where the United States Supreme Court considered the question of the right of secondary victims to recover for emotional distress, *Consolidated Rail Corp v Gottshall*.[84]

In *Gottshall*, the United States Supreme Court was asked to interpret a federal law that preempted state tort law concerning injuries suffered by railroad workers. The effect of the law was to move these tort cases to federal court, where they would be decided under a uniform federal common law which was based on a variety of sources such as the language of the statute (which was not very informative on the question of emotional distress, having been

[82] *Tobin v Grossman*, 249 NE2d 419 (NY 1969). New York later expanded *Tobin*'s zone of danger rule so that it conditionally permits bystander emotional distress damages under limited circumstances. In *Bovsun v Sanperi*, 61 NY2d 219 (1984) it allowed close family members *who were in the zone of danger* to sue for the trauma they suffered watching another close family member suffer physical injuries, in addition to the trauma they suffered from fearing their own (unrealized) physical injury. The court stood by its defense in *Tobin*, noting that in *Bovsun* "the recovery allowed [...] is not conceptualized as a new, discrete cause of action but as an element of damages cognizable in a familiar action in negligence for personal injuries." *Bovsun* at 233, n 12.

[83] Justice Burke, dissenting in *Dillon*, warned that the bystander rule would "throw us 'into the fantastic realm of infinite liability'" (*Dillon* at 928 (per Burke J), quoting from *Amaya v Home Ice, Fule & Supply Co*, 59 Cal 2d 295 at 315 (Cal 1963)—the case which *Dillon* overturned).

[84] 512 US 532 (1994).

written in 1908) and general principles of common law. The case involved two separate cases from the same court of appeals. In one case, a railroad worker (Gottshall) suffered severe emotional distress because he saw a co-worker (who was a close friend) die at the worksite due to the negligence of their employer.[85] In rejecting the worker's claim, the court did not deny the credibility and reality of his emotional distress, nor did it hold that, as a matter of fact, it was unforeseeable to the defendant employer that a worker might suffer extreme emotional distress upon witnessing the gruesome death of a co-worker. But, argued the court, the facts that made the case compelling from a moral point of view—that the plaintiff was a good friend of the primary victim and that the defendant forced the plaintiff to resume working for hours within sight of the dead body of the primary victim—were relevant only if the common law had adopted foreseeability test for the duty owed to secondary victims with regard to emotional distress. But the common law—even California, according to the court—had not.[86] The reasoning offered by the US Supreme Court recalled the reasons offered by New York's highest court for rejecting the bystander rule:

> The common law consistently has sought to place limits on this potential liability by restricting the class of plaintiffs who may recover and the types of harm for which plaintiffs may recover. This concern underlying the common-law tests has nothing to do with the potential for fraudulent claims; on the contrary, it is based upon the recognized possibility of *genuine* claims from the essentially infinite number of persons, in an infinite variety of situations, who might suffer real emotional harm as a result of a single instance of negligent conduct.[87]

The court therefore held that the plaintiff could recover only as a primary victim—and then remanded the case to the trial court to determine whether the worker could sue the employer under the zone of danger rule, under the

[85] In the other case a railroad worker (Carlisle) suffered severe emotional distress because he had been subjected to unreasonably stressful working conditions as a dispatcher. Carlisle was awarded $ 386,000 by a federal jury, which was upheld on appeal. The Supreme Court reversed the judgment on the grounds that under common law principles, Carlisle did not meet any test for recovery as a primary victim—he was neither subject to an injurious physical contact not put in danger of an injurious physical contact as a result of the defendant's negligence. See also Chapter IV, section 3.2.

[86] Arguably, the forseeability test has been adopted in a few states. See *Sacco v High Country Indep Press, Inc*, 896 P2d 411 (Mont 1995) and *Camper v Minor*, 915 SW2d 437 (Tenn 1996).

[87] 512 US 532, 552 (1994) (emphasis in the original).

theory that the risk of physical injury that had felled his friend threatened him as well.

The United States Supreme Court was correct, at least as far as its analysis of California. By the 1980s, the *Dillon* guidelines had turned into rules. In *Thing v La Chusa*,[88] the claim by a mother who heard but did not see her child fatally injured (a set of facts ironically identical to *Tobin v Grossman*[89]) was rejected by the California Supreme Court because she did not contemporaneously see the injury to the primary victim. Not all courts adopted the same three conditions in their version of the bystander rule, but of the three, a consensus has emerged that, to be recoverable, the emotional distress should result from seeing or learning about the death of someone whom is a member of one's family, not a stranger or a co-worker.[90] There is greater variation as to whether the secondary victim must actually see the primary victim get injured.[91] A consensus exists that the primary victim must have actually suffered a substantial injury resulting in either death or serious physical injury, although it is not clear whether a court would permit a claim by a secondary victim such as a parent, who believed, reasonably but falsely, that the primary victim had suffered a substantial injury due to the defendant's negligence and had suffered extreme emotional distress as a result.[92]

Thing and the jurisdictions that have followed it have added a fourth rule, which is that the secondary victim must have sustained a serious emotional injury—that is, "a reaction beyond that which would be anticipated in a disinterested witness and which is not an abnormal response to the circumstance."[93] This almost certainly arises in response to the fact that in the period between *Dillon* and *Thing*, the law of emotional distress for primary victims liberalized so that physical symptoms of harm are no longer required in most jurisdiction.[94] "Serious emotional distress which results from witnessing a

[88] 771 P2d 814 (Cal 1989).

[89] See above, nn 81–82 and accompanying text.

[90] See, eg, *Bowen v Lumberman's Mut Cas Co*, 517 NW2d 432 (Wis 1994) (secondary victim must be a spouse, parent, child, grandparent, or sibling of primary victim) and *Groves v Taylor*, 729 NE2d 569, 572 (Ind 2000) (same).

[91] See *Ferriter v Daniel O'Connell's Sons, Inc*, 413 NE2d 690 (Mass 1980) (the secondary victims' emotional distress claims was predicated on viewing the injured person at the hospital rather than at the scene of the accident; the court reversed the lower court's summary judgment against the claimants for mental anguish).

[92] "To a sensitive parent, witnessing a minor injury to his or her child could produce an emotional response and result in serious injury. Nevertheless, under those circumstances, a cause of action for bystander emotional distress will not lie." *Clohessy v Bachelor*, 237 Conn 31 at 53 (Conn 1996).

[93] *Thing v La Chusa*, 48 Cal 3d 644 (Cal 1989).

[94] On such developments, see Chapter IV, section 3.2.

closely related person critically injured or killed can be, in some cases, as debilitating and as severe as a physical injury."[95] While it would have been possible to preserve the physical manifestation rule in only those cases involving severe emotional distress for bystanders, it is not clear whether that would have served the same function as the other tests imposed by *Thing*, specifically the requirement of a close family relationship and contemporaneous observation of the injury, especially considering the fact that the worker in *Gottshall* did credibly testify that he suffered physical manifestations following the shock of seeing his friend die at their workplace. The point is now clarified by comment i of § 48 of Restatement Third of Torts—PEH. According to § 48,

> [a]n actor who negligently causes sudden serious bodily injury to a third person is subject to liability for serious emotional harm caused thereby to a person who:
> (a) perceives the event contemporaneously, and
> (b) is a close family member of the person suffering the bodily injury.

As cmt. i explains, early case-law often required a plaintiff to prove a physical manifestation of the alleged emotional harm in order to establish that the emotional harm was genuine. Other courts have rather abandoned this requirement, relying instead on a jury's ability to determine whether emotional harm is genuine. This is also the position embraced by the comment, according to which there is "no requirement of resulting physical consequences of the emotional harm."

4.2. England

England recognized some version of the bystander rule much earlier than the United States. In 1925 in *Hambrook v Stokes Bros* a mother was allowed compensation for the emotional distress she suffered when she experienced—but did not see—her children run over by a negligently handled wagon.[96] The

[95] *Heldreth v Marrs*, 188 W Va 481, 490 (W Va 1992).

[96] [1925] 1 KB 141. The plaintiff saw the wagon pass before her toward where she knew her children to be and she heard a large crash; she was later informed that one of her children had been injured by the wagon. For an even earlier precedent, see also *Wilkinson v Downton* [1897] 2 QB 57, where the court recognized that a woman suffered a compensable injury when she was told, falsely,

court made precisely the same argument made by the *Dillon* court sixty-three years later: that it would be arbitrary to allow the mother to be compensated as a primary victim were she to suffer trauma as a result of fear for her own safety and not allow her to be compensated as a secondary victim for the emotional distress she suffered as a result of fear for the safety of her children. Yet the English court's rejected an almost identical claim in *Bourhill v Young* where the woman was not related to the primary victim, thus following the same pattern of limiting the duty of care with regard to the emotional distress of secondary victims only to those circumstances in which the nervous shock created by the defendant arose from a separate and independent tort against someone with whom the secondary victim shared a family relation.[97]

The English courts have expanded on their version of the bystander rule in a series of recent decisions. The first, *McLoughlin v O'Brien*, reaffirmed the holding in *Hambrook*, and adopted three guidelines to help ascertain the foreseeability of the risk imposed by the defendant on the secondary victim in language similar to *Dillon*, which it quoted.[98] The court held that the duty should depend on the "class of persons" to whom the secondary victim belonged (family as opposed to strangers); the proximity of the secondary victim to the accident; and "the means by which the shock is caused."[99] Like *Dillon*, *McLoughlin* has been seen as a progressive decision whose "liberalizing" promise has been limited by later decisions.[100]

In *Alcock v Chief Constable of South Yorkshire*, the House of Lords applied the *McLoughlin* guidelines in ways that suggest that the availability of damages for emotional distress in England is only slightly more liberal than in those American jurisdictions that have adopted the bystander rule.[101] The case involved a terrible accident in which ninety-six people died due, in part, to the negligence of the police in controlling a crowd at a stadium. Numerous

that her husband had been "smashed up" in an accident and that she had to rush to see him; her suffering was deemed to be compensable because it was associated with a disturbance of the body.

97 [1943] AC 92. It may be added that within family relations, according to the High Court, a family member does not owe a duty of care to other family members in circumstances where her self-inflicted injuries caused the other family members psychiatric injury: *Greatorex v Greatorex* [2000] 1 WLR 1970.

98 [1983] AC 410.

99 Lunney, Nolan, Oliphant (n 37) 342.

100 Markesinis, Bell, & Janssen (n 1) 236.

101 [1992] 1 AC 310. For a criticism of *Alcock*, see Nicholas J Mullany, "Negligently Inflicted Psychiatric Injury and the Means of Communciation of Trauma—Should it Matter," in Nicholas J Mullany & Allen M Linden (eds), *Torts Tomorrow: A Tribute to John Fleming* (LBC Information Services 1998) 162–220.

important cases involving the law of emotional distress arose from the hundreds of personal injury suits that followed the tragedy. In *Alcock* the issue was the claims of secondary victims—parents, siblings, unmarried partners of those who were at the stadium—who saw the tragedy unfold on television, or who traveled to the stadium to claim the bodies of their loved ones afterward. The House of Lords applied the "proximity of relationship" guideline in a strict fashion. First, it made clear that emotional distress has to be proven, although the court granted that "the closest ties of love and affection [could] be presumed from the fact" that a secondary victim was the primary victim's father or fiancé.[102] Secondly, while the court did not retreat to the position that a secondary victim has to contemporaneously witness the accident in time and space, it did hold that some of the secondary victims were either too far away or came too late to qualify as bystanders. Thus, the families' members who came after the tragedy to claim the bodies of their loved ones could not claim nervous shock for themselves,[103] at best they could receive bereavement damages under the Fatal Accidents Act.[104] Furthermore the court held that a perception that an accident was occurring was not enough, despite the fact that the perception in this case was the observation of the tragedy in real time on live television. The court held that "shocks sustained by reason of [the broadcast] cannot found a claim."[105]

As to the emotional distress itself, after *Alcock* its recoverability in English practice resembles the position adopted by many American jurisdictions rejecting the requirement that a plaintiff must prove physical manifestations to prove emotional distress.[106] In *Alcock* the court assumed that the law's treatment of defendants who cause emotional distress differs according to the different duties owed to primary and secondary victims, and not by the degree of intensity or discomfort experienced by the victims.[107] In both cases, the plaintiff must complain of something more than "ordinary"

[102] [1992] 1 AC 310.

[103] See Lunney, Nolan, & Oliphant (n 37) 347–351. This outcome was anticipated by *Ravenscroft v Rederaktiebolaget Transatlantic* [1992] 2 All ER 470 (CA) (the plaintiff, who was unaware of injury to her child when he was struck by a truck and did not see him die, claimed that the nervous shock was produced when she saw his body in the hospital hours later. Her suit for nervous shock was dismissed). Cf with the American case *Ferriter v Daniel O'Connell's Sons, Inc*, 413 NE2d 690 (Mass 1980), above n 91.

[104] See above, section 2 in this chapter.

[105] [1992] 1 AC 310 (although the court kept the door open to the possibility that under some circumstances a simultaneous broadcast might give rise to a shock that could be recognized by the law). See also *Jones v Wright* [1991] 3 All ER 88.

[106] See Chapter IV, section 3.2.

[107] Markesinis, Coester, Alpa, & Ullstein (n 42) 54.

fear or grief,[108] but as a secondary victim she must plead what English law now calls "psychiatric injury."[109] This is how the *Alcock* court described the mental shock suffered by secondary victims, which, unlike many other cases involving primary victims, does not typically arise from a fear for their own personal safety:

> It is classified as an anxiety disorder. It follows on a painful event, which is outside the normal human experience [...] these symptoms may be experienced in the form of sleep difficulty, irritability or outbursts of anger, problems with memory or concentration, startle responses, hyper vigilance and over-reaction to any reminder of the event [...] All those in whom post-traumatic stress disorder was identified appear to have undergone a personality change, the significant features of which [included] being moody, irritable, forgetful and withdrawn within themselves [and] frequent unprovoked outbursts of anger and quarrelsome behavior were reported.[110]

The difference between the duties owed to primary and secondary victims in England matters precisely because the English courts have held that liability for psychiatric injury can arise through a variety of ways in the case of primary victims, while it can only arise for secondary victims through the narrow set of conditions discussed above, including that the psychiatric injury must arise from a shock to the secondary plaintiff.[111] So, for example, a spouse's claim for the psychiatric injury incurred as a result of her taking care of the loved one seriously injured in an accident was rejected because the court found that she did not suffer her psychiatric injury through a shocking experience.[112] Applying the "*Alcock* control mechanisms" in a slightly different combination, a police officer who suffers psychiatric injury as a result of participating into a rescue at a stadium cannot sue as a secondary victim, although he may have suffered extreme distress as a result of being

[108] *Vernon v Bosley (No 1)* [1997] 1 All ER 577 (CA), cited in van Gerven, Larouche, & Lever (n 52) 106.

[109] Markesinis, Coester, Alpa, & Ullstein (n 42) 51.

[110] [1992] 1 AC 310 at 317.

[111] Lunney, Nolan, & Oliphant (n 37) 361–362. In later decisions the courts have come to refer to this as the "*Alcock* control mechanisms." See *White v Chief Constable of South Yorkshire* [1998] 3 WLR 1509; and *Paul & Anor v Royal Wolverhampton NHS Trust* [2020] EWHC 1415 (QB).

[112] *Jaensch v Coffey* [1984] 155 CLR 549 at 569 (per Brennan J), cited with approval in *Alcock* [1992] 1 AC 310, 403. According to Brennan J, shock means "the sudden sensory perception – that is, by seeing, hearing or touching – of a person, thing or event, which is so distressing that the perception of the phenomenon affronts or insults the plaintiff's mind and causes a recognisable psychiatric illness" (*Jaensch v Coffey* [1984] 155 CLR 549 at 567).

present when others suffered severe physical injuries and death, because he was a stranger to the primary victims.[113] The police officer's only hope to be compensated for his psychiatric injury, assuming it was a foreseeable consequence of the defendant's negligence, would be to bring a claim as a primary victim—something which the House of Lords said he cannot do, since it held in *White v Chief Constable of South Yorkshire* that police rescuers are not owed a duty by the defendants (the police department) to forbear from causing them foreseeable extreme emotional distress arising from their reasonable performance of the rescue, even if the rescuer responds to an emergency created by their employer.[114]

4.3. Germany

As explained in section 3.2, the German law of *Schockschäden* allows a secondary plaintiff to claim compensation for non-pecuniary harm under § 253 BGB when she can demonstrate that the harm suffered by the primary victim caused an injury to the secondary victim's health under § 823 I BGB—in other words, when she is able to qualify as a "primary" victim.[115] This principle was established as early as 1931[116] and was subsequently reaffirmed on multiple occasions.[117] By health, as explained above, the Germans mean something a little more restrictive than the English concept of "psychiatric injury" after *Alcock*. The Federal Supreme Court, worrying that suits for *Schockschäden* would undermine the primacy of the economic secondary victim rights established in §§ 844 and 845 BGB, held in 1989 that psychiatric injuries must be something more than "recognized by medical science," and must display "an obvious pathology . . . seen by the general public as injuries to the body

[113] *White v Chief Constable of South Yorkshire* [1998] 3 WLR 1509.

[114] *White v Chief Constable of South Yorkshire* [1998] 3 WLR 1509. The court recognized that this put police officers in an anomalous position from other employees, but justified it by suggesting that it would be intolerable from a policy perspective to treat police officers "better" than many bystanders who may have acted similarly, in terms of providing aid and suffering as a result.

[115] Alternatively, the victim might claim recovery for her non-pecuniary harms under §§ 823 II and 826 BGB, but, even under such causes of action, there remains a marked suspicion of German courts toward requests for compensation of emotional distress: see Nils Jansen, David Kästle-Lamparter, & Lukas Rademacher, "Germany–Case 15," in Marta Infantino & Eleni Zervogianni (eds), *Causation in European Tort Law* (CUP 2017) 521–522; Anthony M Honoré, "Causation and Remoteness of Damage," in *International Encyclopedia of Comparative Law* (Mohr 1971) vol XI, ch 7, 132.

[116] RG 21 September 1931, RGZ 133, 270; JZ 1929, 914, in Markesinis, Bell, & Janssen (n 1) 233.

[117] See BGH 11 May 1971, BGHZ 56, 163 and BGH 17 April 2018, NJW 2018, 3250, BGHZ 218, 220.

or health" of the plaintiff.[118] The court went on to say that the scheme set up in the BGB

> would be undermined if those types of psychological and mental effects resulting from the experience of the death of a close relative amounted to recoverable injury to health under § 823 I BGB *simply because they are recognized by medical science.*[119]

As in other jurisdictions, the contemporaneous observation of the death—especially the murder—of a close relative easily meets the test set out by the BGH.[120] Further, provided that a sufficiently serious and long-lasting psychological impairment is proven, a close relative might also claim non-pecuniary damages where she has not directly witnessed the death or serious injury of the primary victim, but she has been informed about the latter's death or serious injury.[121]

The amount of damages awarded in these cases has traditionally been low. In a case in which two teenage brothers witnessed the fatal shooting of their mother, they were awarded each around 10,000 German marks (ca. € 5,000).[122] Where a father found his ten-year-old son at the scene of the accident and spoke to him before the son died later the same day, the court considered non-pecuniary damages of 1,000 DM (ca. € 500) sufficient for the father.[123] Yet, there recently appears to be a trend to higher awards: for instance, in a case in which the parents and two brothers of a young boy witnessed the latter drowning after he was sucked into a defective water pump next to a waterslide, the BGH confirmed the lower instance courts' decision to award € 20,000 to each of the four family members.[124]

It is interesting to note that the German courts are willing to distinguish between the nature and quality of the nervous shock of primary and

[118] BGH 4 April 1989, NJW 1989, 2317 (in Markesinis, Bell, Janssen (n 1) 230); see also van Gerven, Larouche, & Lever (n 52) 88.

[119] BGH 4 April 1989, NJW 1989, 2317 (in Markesinis, Bell, & Janssen (n 1) 229) (emphasis added).

[120] See, eg, OLG Nuremberg 27 February 1998, NJW 1998, 2293 (two children witnessed mother's murder and were compensated for damage to their health due to shock); see also Florian Wagner-von Papp, "Germany—Case 6.2," in Vernon V Palmer (ed), *The Recovery of Non-Pecuniary Loss in European Contract Law* (CUP 2015) 177, 180–181 and von Bar (n 5) 80, n 398, and cases therein collected.

[121] Cf BGH 6 February 2007, NJW-RR 2007, 1395; BGH 5 February 1985, NJW 1985, 1390.

[122] OLG Nuremberg 27 February 1998, NJW 1998, 2293.

[123] KG Berlin 10 November 1997, NZV 1999, 329.

[124] BGH 18 July 2006, NZV 2006, 69.

secondary victims. A primary victim seeking non-economic damages under § 253 BGB for "reduction in well-being" (*Wohlgefühl*) or happiness (*Lebensfreude*) would not have to show that their hedonic loss was severe.[125] This can be illustrated by the following case, where the plaintiff, a motorist, was involved in an accident where a pedestrian negligently crossed the road and was struck by the plaintiff.[126] The pedestrian was killed and the plaintiff was injured. In the suit that followed, against the pedestrian's estate, the plaintiff's claim for non-economic damages, arising from the emotional distress he experienced when he struck the defendant, was challenged by the defendant's estate on the grounds that, since the plaintiff was not a close relative of the person (the defendant) whose accident he saw, he could not sue for *Schockschäden*. The court rejected the defendant's argument, noting that the plaintiff was not suing as a secondary victim but as a primary victim of the defendant's negligence, since it was foreseseeable to the pedestrian that his carelessness would cause emotional distress to the driver who ran into him. This case is interesting for many reasons, but at this point the chief thing we want to point out is that, had the plaintiff been a "true" secondary victim—that is, a bystander who had merely seen the defendant get run over—it is hard to imagine that the BGH would have allowed the claim. In fact, it is easy to see that a court would have held that watching a stranger get hit by a car is precisely one of the "everyday risks of life" which does not properly fall under § 823 BGB.[127]

Like the English and the American rules, German ones have embodied a somewhat functional attitude toward the set of persons who may by secondary victims in *Schockschäden* cases. The shock must be "*verstandliche*" or "understandable" from a social point of view; and the shock of strangers is never understandable from the perspective of the BGB.[128] Lower courts have said that only relatives may be secondary victims in *Schockschäden* cases,[129] but there has been recognition of the possibility of expanding the set to include fiancé(e)s and partners in a "serious love relationship."[130]

German rules for nervous shock differ in content (if not in form) from the rules adopted by the United States and England in their treatment of

125 van Gerven, Larouche, & Lever (n 52) 79.
126 BGH 12 December 1985, NJW 1986, 777 (in Markesinis, Bell, & Janssen (n 1) 235).
127 See Markesinis, Bell, & Janssen (n 1) 235.
128 Markesinis, Bell, & Janssen (n 1) 233.
129 LG Tübingen 29 November 1967, NJW 1968, 1187 and OLG Stuttgart 21 July 1988, NJW-RR 1989, 477; see Ulrich Magnus & Jörg Fedtke, "Germany," in Rogers (ed) (n 22) 109, 111.
130 LG Frankfurt 28 March 1969, NJW 1969, 2286 and see and Markesinis, Bell, & Janssen (n 1) 33.

proximity. Ever since the earliest case in 1931, Germans have been less interested in geographical proximity between the secondary victim and the primary victim than the Americans or the English.[131] As a result, the cases of relatives suing for nervous shock arising from recovering the dead or injured bodies some period of time after the accident which injured the primary victim would not be dismissed in Germany for reasons of lack of proximity as they were in *Alcock* and *Ravenscroft*. This may be a consequence—it has been fairly noted—of the fact that in Germany the "severity" requirement sometimes does the work that in other tort systems is done by other doctrines.[132]

[131] Markesinis, Bell, Janssen (n 1) 231 (noting the decision of BGH 5 February 1985, BGHZ 93, 351, where a woman was permitted to sue for *Schockschäden* despite the fact that she was told of her husband's serious traffic accident while on a ship far away).

[132] See Markesinis, Bell, &Janssen (n 1) 33 ("German courts tend to approach problems of nervous shock in terms of causation (rather than duty)"). For instance, in a case in which a mother, after the death of her adult son in a road accident, attempted to recover her *Schockschäden* as well as the cost of a cruise on the Mediterranean which she cancelled due to the her son's sudden death, the Federal Court rejected all her claims, holding—not that the case did not meet the proximity requirement, but—that she did not establish an injury to her health as required by the special rules for secondary victims seeking compensation for nervous shock: BGH 4 April 1989, NJW 1989, 2317 (in Markesinis, Bell, & Janssen (n 1) 228).

VI
Compensation for Pure Economic Loss

1. Introduction

When the comparative tort law vessel leaves the safe harbor of physical injuries, where everywhere is more or less stable and neat, it soon faces the fogs and winds of many different issues. Some of them have been dealt with in the previous two chapters; another is compensation for pure economic losses.

In any jurisdiction the recoverability of pure economic loss stands at the cross point of many crucial questions, such as these: Is this kind of interest to be protected? If this is the case, as a matter of policy should the recovery of pure economic loss be the domain principally of the law of contract? If the latter is not the case, how far can tort liability expand without imposing excessive burdens upon individual activity?[1]

This chapter pursues the goal of sketching possible answers to these questions from a comparative law perspective.[2] Thus, we will first outline the

[1] Peter Benson, "The Basis for Excluding Liability for Economic Loss in Tort Law," in David G Owen (ed), *The Philosophical Foundations of Tort Law* (OUP 1995) 427, 431. See also David Howarth, "Three Forms of Responsibility: On the Relationships Between Tort Law and the Welfare State" (2001) 60 Cambridge LJ 553.

[2] This chapter is largely based on two research projects conducted in the first decade of this century by Professors Vernon Valentine Palmer and Mauro Bussani. See Mauro Bussani & Vernon V Palmer

Common Law and Civil Law Perspectives on Tort Law. Mauro Bussani, Anthony J. Sebok, & Marta Infantino,
Oxford University Press.

DOI: 10.1093/oso/9780195368383.003.0006

notion and the factual situations where this loss is likely to occur (sections 2 to 4). Then we will look through comparative lenses at the spectrum of national approaches to this kind of damage, offering a focused analysis on the discrete ways of dealing with the issue (sections 5 to 5.5). The final part of the chapter sets the outcomes of the comparative survey against the basic arguments for and against an exclusionary rule (sections 6 to 9).

2. Pure and Consequential Economic Loss

What is clear in the transnational definition of "pure economic loss" is the negative cast and the economic character of this loss. In countries where the term is explicitly used its meaning is essentially explained in a negative way. It is an economic loss without antecedent harm to plaintiff's person or property. Here the word "pure" plays a central role, for if there is economic loss that is connected to damage to person or property of the plaintiff then the latter is called *consequential* economic loss and the whole set of damages

(eds), *Pure Economic Loss in Europe* (CUP 2003); Vernon V Palmer & Mauro Bussani, *Pure Economic Loss: New Horizons in Comparative Law* (Routledge-Cavendish 2008)—but see also Vernon V Palmer, A Comparative-Law Sketch of Pure Economic Loss, in Mauro Bussani & Anthony J Sebok (eds), *Comparative Tort Law. Global Perspectives* (2nd edn, EE 2021) 284–304. The first research was developed within "The Common Core of European Private Law" Project (Mauro Bussani & Ugo Mattei, General Editors)—and covered thirteen European jurisdictions: Austria, Belgium, England, Finland, France, Germany, Greece, Italy, the Netherlands, Portugal, Scotland, Spain, and Sweden. The second research resulted from the preparation of the General Report on Pure Economic Loss presented at the 7th World Congress of the International Academy of Comparative Law (2006), in Utrecht, the Netherlands. The study covered twenty-two jurisdictions: Austria, Belgium, England, Finland, France, Germany, Greece, Italy, the Netherlands, Portugal, Scotland, Spain, Sweden, Canada, Croatia, Denmark, Israel, Japan, Poland, Quebec, South Africa, and the United States.

The approach followed in these researches was not to make any supposition in advance about the nature or definition of pure economic loss. A neutral, fact-based questionnaire was allowed to flush out the rules and responses of each national system. Therefore the questionnaire mixed into the facts instances of property damage, personal injury, and other infringements that particular traditions may regard as absolute rights (i.e., rights opposable to the world at large—*erga omnes*). In this way the research was attempting to clarify the gray zones that exist between recoverable and non-recoverable loss. Consistent with the Common Core factual methodology, the questionnaire alleged mere facts and avoided the use of what could be classified as legal artifacts such as the expression "pure economic loss" itself. Because there is no recognition of the term in some systems, and in any event less than complete consensus about its meanings in others, the research rigorously excluded all use of the term in the hypotheticals. These are the same reasons that account also for the choice of not referring to any pigeonhole framework (such as the ones used, eg, by Izhak Englard, *The Philosophy of Tort Law* (Darmouth 1993)211–213; Benson (n 1) 427–458; see also Hein Kötz, "Economic Loss in Tort and Contract" (1994) 58 RabelsZ 423; Peter Cane, "Economic Loss in Tort and Contract" (1994) 58 RabelsZ 429) in presenting the study of the cases.

may be recovered.[3] Consequential economic (sometimes also termed parasitic[4]) loss is recoverable because it presupposes the existence of physical injuries, whereas pure economic loss strikes the victim's wallet and nothing else.[5]

Thus, before going any further it will be useful to give some specific examples of the factual situations usually subsumed under the label "pure economic loss."

3. The Standard Cases

Broadly speaking, pure economic loss arises out of the interdependence of relationships and interests. These relationships are sometimes two-dimensional and other times three-dimensional. A taxonomy of the principal ways in which this loss arises within such relationships will surely not exhaust all the conceivable ways in which such damage may arise. But the real interest here lies in tracing the most recurrent and typical patterns which we call the "standard cases." With these provisos in mind, one may set forth four categories that seem to be functionally and relationally distinct.[6]

(i) Ricochet loss. Ricochet loss classically arises when physical damage is done to the property or person of one party and that loss in turn causes the impairment of a plaintiff's right—certain authors call this situation

[3] Perhaps another way to describe pure economic loss is to say it does not arise as a consequence of some earlier physical loss, and it is not a court's substituted valuation of physical loss. It goes without saying that there may be some hesitancy to recognize trivial physical losses as a pathway to recover predominantly economic loss. See, eg, *Lloyd's Leasing Ltd v Conoco*, 868 F2d 1447 (5th Cir 1989). Walter van Gerven, Jeremy Lever, & Pierre Larouche, *Cases, Materials and Text on National, Supranational and International Tort Law* (Hart 2000)68, speak of a "worsening of one's overall economic position (loss of profit, diminution in the value of property, etc.) that is not directly consequential upon injury to the person or damage to a particular piece of property."

[4] For this usage, § 766c, cmt b, Restatement Second of Torts ("When recovery is allowed, the loss of expected profits or other pecuniary loss may, in an appropriate case, be recovered as 'parasitic' compensatory damages").

[5] In Sweden, where the legislator states that only victims of crimes may recover for pure economic loss, the Tort Law Act (SKL), 1 Chapter 2 §, defines the notion exactly in these terms: "In the present act, 'pure economic loss' (*ren förmögenhetsskada*) means such economic loss as arises without connection to personal injury or property damage to anyone." See Walter van Gerven, Jeremy Lever, Pierre Larouche, Christian von Bar, & Geneviève Viney (eds), *Cases, Materials and Text on National, Supranational and International Tort Law: Scope of Protection* (Hart 1998)44.

[6] For a longer taxonomic list consisting of eight categories, see William Bishop & John Sutton, "Efficiency and Justice in Tort Damages: The Shortcomings of the Pecuniary Loss Rule" (1986) 15 J Leg Stud 347, 360–361. Benson's taxonomy consists of five situations, two of which he calls "exclusionary situations." His three other situations are called "non-exclusionary." See Benson (n 1) 427–430.

"relational economic loss."[7] A direct victim sustains physical damage of some kind, while plaintiff is a secondary victim who incurs only economic harm.

To illustrate, A has a contract to tow B's ship. C's negligent act of sinking the ship makes it impossible for A to perform his contract and thus deprives him of expected profits. A's financial loss is the ricochet effect of C's negligence toward B. This loss is purely economic since no property interest of A's has been impaired.[8] Ricochet loss can also arise from the impairment of an employment contract. For instance, B is a key employee in A's business or sporting team. C's negligent driving leads to B's death or incapacity, thus causing A's team or business to lose profits and revenues. Here B's injury is physical, but A's loss is purely financial.[9]

(ii) Transferred loss. Here C causes physical damage to B's property or person, but a contract between A and B (or the law itself) transfers a loss that would ordinarily be B's onto A. Thus, a loss ordinarily falling on the primary victim is passed on to a secondary victim. The transfer of the loss from its "natural" to an "accidental" bearer differentiates this from a case of ricochet loss where the damage in question is not transferred but is a distinct damage to the interests of the secondary victim. These transfers frequently result either by operation of law or from leases, sales, insurance agreements, and other contracts that separate property rights from rights of use or specifically reallocate risk bearing.

To illustrate, A is time charterer of a ship owned by B. The day before the time charter is to go into effect, and while the ship is in B's possession, C negligently damages the ship's propeller, thus necessitating repairs and a two-week delay, which causes A to lose all use of the ship. Here B suffers property damage and ordinarily B as owner would recover for the consequential loss of the ship's use, but the right of use—and the risks related to it—were

[7] See this terminology and analysis in Robby Bernstein, *Economic Loss* (I, 3rd edn, Longman 2013) 789–1003; Ronen Perry, "The Economic Bias in Tort Law" (2008) Ill U LR 1573; Bruce P Feldthusen, *Economic Negligence* (3rd edn, Carswell 2000)193–258; Peter Benson, "The Problem with Pure Economic Loss" (2009) 60 So Cal LR 823.

[8] The example closely follows *La Société Anonyme de Remorquage à Helice v Bennets* [1911] 1 KB 243.

[9] Cass (Plenary) 26 January 1971, no 174, *Torino Calcio SpA v Romero*, Giur it 1971, I, 1, 681. See also *Spartan Steel and Alloys v Martin & Co Ltd* [1973] QB 27. Concern about the indeterminate number and size of the claims for losses is often associated with cases falling within this category.

transferred to A by the boat charter. So, A's loss is purely pecuniary because he has no antecedent property loss.[10]

An equivalent result is reached when the transfer occurs by operation of law. For instance, B, A's employee, may be injured by the negligent driving of C and thus find himself unable to work for three months. Nevertheless, a statute requires A to continue to pay B's salary, even though no work is received in return. Thus, what ordinarily would have been B's loss is statutorily transferred to A as a combined result of C's negligence and the effects of the pay continuation statute.[11]

(iii) Closures of public markets, transportation corridors, and public infrastructures. Here economic loss arises without a previous injury to anyone's property or person. There may be physical damage, but it is to "unowned resources" that lie in the public domain.[12] A single negligent act may necessitate the closure of markets, highways, and shipping lanes which no private person owns, yet the closure inflicts economic loss directly on individuals whose livelihoods closely depend upon the use of these facilities.

To illustrate, C negligently allows infected cattle to escape from his premises, and the government must order all cattle and meat markets to close. As a result, broad classes of plaintiffs will suffer pure economic loss, from cattle raisers who are unable to sell or deliver their stock, to butchers who are unable to obtain supplies.[13] A similar chain of loss may arise when C negligently spills chemicals into the river, and all traffic on the waterway is suspended for two weeks during a cleanup effort. As a result, shippers must take more expensive overland routes, and marinas, boat suppliers, hotel operators, and commercial fishermen in the area suffer severe economic loss[14]—the BP

[10] The illustration is based upon *Robins Dry Dock v Flint*, 13 F2d 3 (2d Cir 1926), 275 US 303 (1927). For an evaluation of the role this landmark admiralty case has had on the economic loss rule in the United States, see Vernon V Palmer, "The Great Spill in the Gulf... and a Sea of Pure Economic Loss: Reflections on the Boundaries of Civil Liability" (2011) 116 Penn State LR 105.

[11] Transferred loss cases are liability neutral from the perspective of the tortfeasor and could allay fears of indeterminate liability. Another usual argument in favor of an award of compensation is that the tortfeasor who is clearly liable to the primary victim should not benefit from the accidental operation of rules which by pure chance exclude him from liability. According to von Bar, the concept of transferred loss is intended "to prevent someone appealing to rules whose purpose is not to protect that person, but to protect others": Christian von Bar, *The Common European Law of Torts* (I, OUP 1998) 510–511.

[12] Victor P Goldberg, 'Recovery For Economic Loss Following the Exxon Valdez Oil Spill' (1994) 23 J Leg Stud 1, 37.

[13] See *Weller v Foot & Mouth Disease Research Inst* [1966] 1 QB 569.

[14] See, eg, *Louisiana ex rel Guste, v M/V Testbank (The Testbank)*, 752 F2d 1019 (5th Cir 1985).

oil spill in the waters of the Gulf of Mexico is another example, but on a far greater scale, of pure economic losses stemming from damage to "unowned" resources.[15]

(iv) Reliance upon flawed data, advice, or professional services. Those who furnish advice, prepare data, or render services concerning financial matters often understand that the information will be supplied to a client and then relied upon by third persons with whom they have no contractual relation. If the advice, data, or services are carelessly compiled or executed, this may not only breach the provider's contract with his/her client but cause a relying third party to sustain pure pecuniary loss.

For instance, C, an accountant, carelessly conducts an audit of B, a publicly traded company, and vastly overstates the company's net financial worth. Relying upon the accuracy of the audit, investor A buys shares in B at twice their actual value. Here A's loss arises not in consequence of physical damage to B, but on the basis of misplaced reliance.[16] Similarly, erroneous information about a client's solvency may lead to financial losses. Thus A, before extending credit to B, takes the precaution of asking C (the merchant bank where B kept its account) for an assessment of B's creditworthiness. C carelessly replies that B is "good for its ordinary engagements" (when in fact B would soon go into liquidation) and thereby influences A to advance credit and to lose a large sum.[17] Here A's loss is purely financial, not because it ricochets off or is transferred from someone else's physical damage, but because it arises directly from A's

[15] See below, section 5.5 in this chapter.

[16] According to Tony Honoré, economic losses based upon someone's "reliance" pose a causation issue which is different in kind than causation in the context of physical damage. His discussion seems pertinent to the concern of some that this category of pure economic loss opens the floodgates of liability. When a person is said to "rely" on another's statement, he or she often has two or more (typically many more) reasons or motives for reaching a decision and acting on it. The question whether A's statement "caused" B's response is highly indeterminate. A potential investor in Eldorado Mines, for instance, may be influenced by a false statement in a prospectus as well as by advice from his stockbroker, by his own review of the company books, and so forth. How may we say that from among all these reasons it is the false statement in the prospectus that "caused" his financial loss? See Anthony M Honoré, "Necessary and Sufficient Conditions in Tort Law," in Owen (ed) (n 1) 382–383. See also Michael Coester & Basil S Markesinis, "Liability of Financial Experts in German and American Law: An Exercise in Comparative Methodology" (2003) 51 AJCL 275 (2003).

[17] These facts are taken from the well-known case of *Hedley Byrne & Co v Heller & Partners Ltd* [1964] AC 465 (HL). For other instances of pure economic harm from incorrect information, see Case 18 ("Wrongful Job Reference"), in Bussani & Palmer (eds) (n 2) 469–482, and Case 7 ("Ruined Credit"), in Palmer & Bussani (eds) (n 2), 83–84, 106–107, 126–127, 155–158, 178–179, 211–213, 252–254, 273–274, 292–293. As to the possible recovery of the pure economic loss caused by a credit rating agency, see below, section 5.5 in this chapter.

reliance. Professional services for a client may also cause pecuniary loss to a non-client. B, an elderly man, asks C, his lawyer, to prepare a will in which he will leave USD 100,000 to A, a friend of B. C takes no action for six months, whereupon B dies intestate and A thereby receives nothing.[18] A's loss, again, is purely economic.

4. Pure Economic Loss and Loss of a Chance

To the above taxonomy let us add an obvious, and yet important distinction. Examples given so far would suggest that financial injury may take two distinguishable forms. It may relate to the existing as opposed to the anticipated wealth of the victim. In the first sense, plaintiff's present wealth may be simply depleted by poor financial advice, or by wasting time and petrol taking overland routes because of the closure of a waterway. In the second sense, plaintiff may instead lose that which s/he was entitled, or expected to acquire, such as a testamentary legacy lost because of a defectively drawn instrument, or a sport club's reduced gate receipts due to the accidental death of the club's star player. Sometimes, however, when an expectation is destroyed *in utero* (and proof that it would have materialized is difficult, for instance: a public commission unlawfully rejects a candidate's application for a job or a fellowship),[19] it is called the loss of a chance.[20]

As between these types of wealth, it is the loss which is only expected (and therefore hard to prove) that presents the sharpest question for tort systems to deal with. This is true also in the realm of pure economic loss. The difficulty is not simply that the demand for proof is more exigent—by definition expectancies explore a future that only might have occurred. The difficulty also concerns the appropriateness of affording protection in tort. In countries where the recovery of pure economic loss is barred by an exclusionary

[18] See, eg, *White v Jones* [1995] 2 AC 207 (HL); *Ross v Caunters* [1980] Ch 297.

[19] See, eg, Conseil d'État 12 November 1965, Leb 1965, 613: "*le réquérant, évincé d'un concours auquel il se serait présenté avec des chances sérieuses de succès en raison de ses titres et travaux, a subi un préjudice*".

[20] As to the debate, see Claudio Lombardi, *Causation in Competition Law Damages Actions* (CUP 2020)94–98 (as to French and Italian law); Nils Jansen, 'The Idea of a Lost Chance' (1999) 19 Ox J Leg Stud 271 (discussing German and English solutions); John CP Goldberg, Leslie C Kendrick, Anthony J Sebok, & Benjamin C Zipursky, *Tort Law: Responsibilities and Redress* (5th edn, Wolters Kluwer 2021) 284–292 (for the United States experience).

rule of tort law, there is a tendency to say that most wealth expectancies should be protected in contract.[21] For instance German courts are generally unable to approach the question through tort, but at the same time they unreluctantly stretch contractual concepts to make defendant liable to plaintiff, though there is no actual contract between the parties—a long-standing attitude eventually sanctioned by the legislator in 2001.[22] By contrast, when an economic expectation receives legal protection in tort, as in principle it does under French law, plaintiff may end up being compensated to the same extent *as if* she were protected by a contract with the tortfeasor.[23]

From a comparative point of view, whenever legal systems show these attitudes it becomes difficult to tell where tort ends and contract begins. In all these circumstances we seem to be once more at the frontier where functions meet and merge, for though it has been theorized that contract "creates" wealth whereas tort only protects that which we already have,[24] the notion of pure economic loss presents a challenge to traditional views about the relationship between the two concepts.

[21] Note, for example, the tense unease in the following statement from a British judge: "I do not consider that damages for loss of an expectation are excluded in cases of negligence arising under the principle in Hedley Byrne, simply because the cause of action is classified as tortious. Such damages may in principle be recoverable in cases of contractual negligence; and I cannot see that, for present purposes, any relevant distinction can be drawn between the two forms of action" (per Lord Goff of Chieveley in *White v Jones* [1995] AC 207). On this subject, see also Jane Stapleton, "The Normal Expectancies Measure in Tort Damages" (1997) 113 LQR 257; Helen Reece, "Loss of Chances in the Law" (1996) 59 Mod LR 188.

[22] Most of these "stretches" have indeed been embodied in the reform of many BGB provisions carried out by the Act on the Modernization of the Law of Obligations (*Gesetz zur Modernisierung des Schuldrechts*)—in BGBl 29 November 2001, I, no 61, 3138. This Act, effective as from 1 January 2002, has deeply affected the portion of legal landscape which concerns our topic. It codified, for instance, both the principles of culpa in contrahendo (see § 311 II and III as well as § 241 I BGB) and of the "contract with protective effects for third parties" (see § 311 III BGB). For a general discussion of the reform, see, *e multis*, Reinhard Zimmermann, *The New German Law of Obligations: Historical and Comparative Perspectives* (OUP 2005); Claus-Wilhelm Canaris (ed), *Schuldrechtsmodernisierung* (Beck 2002); Peer Zumbansen, "The Law of Contracts," in Joachim Zekoll (ed), *Introduction to German Law* (Kluwer 2002) 193.

[23] See Mauro Bussani & Vernon V Palmer, "Editors' Comparative Comments to Case 18," in Bussani & Palmer (eds) (n 2) 483, regarding the distinction to be made between cases in which the lost chance is to be understood as an autonomous loss, and cases in which the concept is invoked as an equitable means of proving a loss. See also Goldberg, Kendrick, Sebok, & Zipursky (n 20) 291.

[24] Anthony M Weir, "Complex Liabilities," in *International Encyclopedia of Comparative Law* (Mohr 1976) vol XI, ch 6, 5 ("Contract is productive, tort law protective").

5. The Regimes at Work

Comparative law research shows that the question of the recoverability of pure economic loss is not just a civil law versus common law issue.[25] As we will see, civil law countries are themselves divided, not from the common law, but between themselves and the common law. The various differences and similarities across these systems have little to do with the "legal families" matrix in which they happen to be placed. Instead, there is a broad spectrum of approaches, methods, and policies at work in the different jurisdictions when they deal with pure economic loss. Below, we offer some details about this spectrum of differences.

5.1. France: A Counterintuitive Liberalism?

The general formula *neminem laedere*, "injure no one," is the basis of article 1240 (former article 1382) of the *Code Napoléon*, which reads, "[a]ny act whatever of a man which causes damage to another ("*Tout fait quelconque de l'homme qui cause à autrui un dommage*") obliges him by whose fault it occurred to make reparation."[26] Article 1241 (former article 1383) adds that "[e]ach one is liable for the damage he causes not only by his own act but also by his negligence or imprudence." Because of its encompassing reach as well as its indeterminate potential, this unitary principle does not screen out recovery for pure economic loss. It does not set forth a numerus clausus of protected interests: the legislator imposes no a priori check upon the judge's free sense of what constitutes recoverable harm.[27] Therefore the question whether causing pure economic loss is a source of tortious liability becomes a judicial question, a matter of jurisprudence and the advice of doctrine. Put another way, the protection of pure economic loss in France must be viewed as an outcome for which there is no external, preexisting concept of unlawfulness concerning this loss to determine or to exclude liability.

Nevertheless, the seamless quality of the general provision is not necessarily the determinant formant of a liberal or conservative approach to our

[25] This is not the first time the analysis drives us to reach this conclusion. See Chapter IV, sections 2, 3, 5, 7 on non-economic damage and Chapter VII, sections 2–3 on causation.

[26] As we said above, Chapter I, section 3, the law no 2016–131 reforming contract law in the Civil Code changed the numeration of the chapter on tort, but left its content untouched.

[27] According to a German scholar, of all the European codes, "the French Code Civil gives the courts the least guidance": von Bar (n 11) 22.

subject. Behind virtually identical façades, national courts have been capable of reaching diametrically opposite results. For instance, judicial thought may become imbued with an "implied" list of absolute rights, restrictively conceived in accordance with metalegal formants like internal history, social policy and justice. In that event, the tort system, despite a *façade de libéralisme*, may approach the question of pure economic loss little differently from systems in which the legislator has deliberately controlled recovery through crafted solutions. French doctrine in the nineteenth century did exactly this. All French authors of the first half of the nineteenth century, and many thereafter, thought that arts 1382 and 1383 (current arts 1240 and 1241) of the *Code civil* contained the kind of solution which the German BGB adopted later in §§ 823–826—thereby limiting liability for injuries to certain enumerated rights.[28]

In twentieth-century France, however, a new orientation emerged. The same text now sustains an expansive law of tort in which harm not only to absolute (*erga omnes*) rights but to almost any legal interest, including a purely economic interest, is unlawful and therefore recoverable.[29] Under the prevailing view, the prohibition on causing harm is the general rule, and the instances in which one is at liberty to cause harm are exceptions. Arts 1240 and 1241 (former arts 1382 and 1383) have consistently been found not to contain any a priori limitations on the scope or nature of protected rights and interests, nor to contain an a priori class of protected persons. Thus there has been no difficulty in admitting the recovery of economic loss of victims by ricochet, whether it be the loss of profit suffered by a subtenant of business premises because of the failure by the owner to perform the maintenance

[28] The historical evolution of French delictual thought is traced by Rodolfo Sacco, "Legal Formants: A Dynamic Approach to Comparative Law, Installment II" (1991) 39 AJCL 359. As Sacco indicates, the articles of the Code civil were originally understood by the doctrine as applying to interference with "absolute rights" of the victim or to statutory standards of conduct protecting victims' rights. This rights-based position was fundamentally restated by Planiol who attempted to draw up "a table" of legal obligations protected by former art 1382 (now art 1240). He defined fault as the breach of a "pre-existing obligation" and wrote that (former) art 1382 did not mean "any act whatsoever" but only an act illegitimate in character: Marcel Planiol, *Traité elémentaire de droit civil* (II, 11th edn, Pichon 1931) 285–290.

[29] According to Zweigert and Kötz, today in France "it is immaterial whether the harm complained of by the plaintiff is physical harm to person or property or not. Indeed the very idea of "purely economic loss" is not to be met with in judgments or books; liability under art 1382 Code civil [now art 1240] attaches to a person even if his negligence affects nothing but the plaintiff's future income or business prospects". Konrad Zweigert & Hein Kötz, *An Introduction to Comparative Law* (transl Anthony M Weir, 3rd edn, OUP 1998) 617.

duties provided in the latter's contract with the original tenant,[30] the expenses of a father forced to make repeated voyages to the bedside of his son who was injured in Greece through defendant's negligence,[31] or the expenses of an unmarried cohabiting partner of the injured victim.[32] Besides, the general principle of faute controls the obligation of the tortfeasor to pay for secondary victim's loss of her husband/partner's income in a fatal accident in the same way that it controls the obligation to pay the primary victim's lost future earnings were he to live but be permanently disabled.[33]

While the unlawfulness question may have disappeared from view, it may possibly be operating at a different level, the level of judicial policy working tacitly within rather capacious notions. Indeed, the French judge retains at least some rough concept of unlawfulness, for there are still areas where a person is free to cause harm, including pure economic harm, without incurring liability. An entrepreneur may deliberately set up business next door to a business competitor and through fair competition drive him into bankruptcy.[34] A partnership could not recover for deals that failed to be concluded when the company president who was negotiating them was negligently injured.[35] A creditor whose borrower was negligently killed could not recover from the tortfeasor the sums which the decedent could not repay.[36] The

[30] Cass civ (Plenary) 6 October 2006, D 2006, 2825 (holding that a third party making a claim on the grounds of extra-contractual liability can rely on a breach of contract if the latter has caused damage to the third party).

[31] Cass civ 20 December 1960, D 1961.141.

[32] See van Gerven, Lever, Larouche, von Bar, & Viney (n 3) 144–146. On the same lines, but with regard to the economic loss suffered by a woman who gave up her job to provide nursing care for her son, left severely disabled after the accident caused by the defendant, see Cass civ 14 April 2016, D 2016, n°16, 895.

[33] Suzanne Galand-Carval, "France," in Ulrich Magnus (ed), *Unification of Tort Law: Damages* (Kluwer 2001) 77, 86. The principle has been extended primarily to non-marital relationships. The so-called "concubine suit" of 1970 involved a woman who lived together with the primary victim. The fact that the primary victim had not divorced his wife, and (at the time) the illegality of the primary victim's actions (adultery) seemed to have concerned the lower court. The Court of cassation was however straight in recognizing that (former) art 1382 of the Civil Code "does not require [...] that there is a legal relationship between the deceased and the plaintiff" (Cass (mixed division) 27 February 1970, *Gaudras v Dangeraux*, D 1970, 201 (our transl)). See also Chapter V, sections 3.2 and 4.

[34] See Marie Malaurie-Vignal, *Droit de la concurrence interne et européen* (8th edn, LDGJ 2019) no 387.

[35] Cass civ 12 June 1987, JCP 1987.IV.286.

[36] Cass civ 21 February 1979, JCP 1979.IV.145. On similar facts, see Cass civ 25 June 1975, Bull civ II, 195. Basil S Markesinis, 'La politique jurisprudentielle et la réparation du préjudice économique en Angleterre: une approche comparative' (1983) 35 RIDC 31, 45–46, argues that the case decided in 1979 by the French Court of cassation affords an excellent example of a concealed policy to place limits upon the recovery of pure economic loss via the manipulation of causal requirements. The plaintiff's debtor was killed in a car accident and the debtor's heirs refused to accept succession to the estate. Accordingly, the succession could not pay the debts of the deceased, including the debt owed to the plaintiff, so the plaintiff sought redress from the tortfeasor responsible for the car accident. The

reasoning in these cases seems unexceptional: the harm was not considered a "certain" or "direct" consequence of the negligent act. These instances, however, are exceptions that have been carved away from the general presumption in favor of actionability, and they only emerge from an inductive search of the case law. Obviously a latent concern with saddling excessive liability upon the tortfeasor may have influenced these pronouncements, but no one can be sure.

From a comparative perspective France's accent on inclusiveness holds great interest. It presents an appearance of maximum permissiveness toward pure economic loss as well as an appearance of maximum indifference to the strong policy arguments usually made elsewhere against its recovery.[37] Bernard Rudden draws attention to the paradox that "the French seem to ignore almost all of Cardozo's warnings without suffering ill effects."[38] Against all predictions that the sky will fall, French judges are serene. To those who argue that the floodgates of liability must be firmly closed, the French experience must simply appear counterintuitive.

5.2. Italy's Revolution

In Italy the legislator does not expressly require the violation of an absolute right for liability to be imposed, but at the same time the judge is required to find that the injury was "wrongful" (according to art 2043 of the Civil Code, "[a]ny intentional or negligent act that causes a wrongful injury [*danno ingiusto*] to another obliges the person who has committed the act to pay damages"). As a matter of principle it is evident that no textual distinction is made between physical damage and pure economic losses. Both could qualify as an unjustified type of injury. By leaving the notion of an

Court of Appeal ruled, however, that the plaintiff's loss should not be viewed as the "certain" result of the defendant's act and it was thus unrecoverable. In view of the length of time for repayment and the risks that the debtor might discontinue his work, the anticipated repayment was aleatory. The *Cour de cassation* quashed this decision, ruling that repayment of a loan of money is never aleatory in a juridical sense, and returned the case to another Court of Appeal. The court of *renvoi* in turn ruled that while the loss was certain, it was not "direct," since the refusal of the heirs to accept the debtor's succession broke the chain of causation with a nova causa interveniens. CA Bordeaux 17 May 1977, D 1978, I.R.34, and this decision was confirmed by the *Cour de cassation* (Cass civ 21 February 1979, quoted above).

[37] There is hardly any specialized literature on this subject within France and almost no internal criticism of its liberal attitude.

[38] Bernard Rudden, "Torticles" (1991–1992) 6/7 Tulane Civ L Forum 105, 107.

"unjustified" injury open, the legislator grants the Italian judge a good deal of interpretive power.

Until the mid-twentieth century, the standard doctrine maintained that an injury is unjustified whenever there is an infringement of an absolute right of the victim, particularly the rights to property, liberty, life or reputation.[39] Only in such cases would the tortfeasor be bound to pay damages. However, the list of absolute rights has never been viewed as a limitation in the case of intentional torts, because it has always been recognized that any form of damage proceeding from an intention to harm could be recoverable.[40] From a comparative perspective, the standard doctrine was therefore quite similar to the German one regarding tort liability under BGB §§ 823–826.

In the 1960s a sustained scholarly effort made it possible to enlarge the scope of tort liability.[41] The old meaning given to "wrongful injury" based upon the violation of a victim's absolute right gave way to recognition of various "protected interests." The turning point came in a Supreme Court (*Corte di Cassazione*) ruling in the early 1970s. In *Meroni*,[42] the Court held that a creditor can recover damages for the pecuniary losses he suffered from an injury to his debtor. It was the case of a famous soccer player who was killed in a car accident. The soccer team, Torino Calcio SpA, sued for damages alleging an economic loss.[43] The creditor had only a relative right (a right *in personam*) derived from the contract. No absolute right of the plaintiff/creditor had been invaded by the tortfeasor. Nevertheless, the Supreme Court stated that—in principle—the team could recover damages: from then on it was clear that the old doctrine had collapsed.

Besides the cases where an employee is injured, this "Meroni" doctrine is now broadly used whenever a right in personam is infringed. For instance, non-marital partners who live like spouses can claim their pure economic

[39] See, eg, Giorgio Giorgi, *Teoria delle obbligazioni nel diritto moderno italiano* (V, 7th edn, Cammelli 1909) 215; and cf Rodolfo Sacco, "L'ingiustizia di cui all'art 2043" (1960) Foro pad I, 1420; Mauro Bussani, *L'illecito civile* (ESI 2020)171–203.

[40] For details, see Paolo Cendon, *Il dolo nella responsabilità extracontrattuale* (Giappichelli 1976) *passim*, esp 21–23, 250–255.

[41] Cf, eg, Sacco (n 39) 1420; Piero Schlesinger, "L'ingiustizia del danno nell'illecito civile" (1960) Jus 336; see also Stefano Rodotà, *Il problema della responsabilità civile* (Giuffrè 1964); Francesco D Busnelli, *La lesione del credito da parte di terzi* (Giuffrè 1964).

[42] Cass (Plenary) 26 January 1971, no 174, *Torino Calcio SpA v Romero*, Giur it 1971, I, 1, 681. The case is known not by the name of the parties, but by the name of the soccer player fatally injured in the accident.

[43] The Court held the principle stated above, but the team did not succeed in recovering damages because the evidence of an actual damage was not deemed satisfactory.

losses under art 2043 *Codice civile*.[44] Defendant has been held liable, and compensation for pure economic losses has been granted in cases where an artist negligently assured the authenticity of a painting to a buyer, thus convincing the latter to purchase a mere counterfeit,[45] or when investors acquired shares of ownership in a close-to-bankruptcy company, relying on the inaccurate assertions of the authority for the financial markets as regards the safe financial situation of the company, for the losses the investors suffered when the company went bankrupt.[46]

Thus, in spite of the wide and long-standing debate about the meaning of "danno ingiusto," current Italian operative rules do not now differ very much from the positions taken in France.[47] As a matter of principle, no distinction is made between physical harm and economic losses: both of them may represent a "wrongful injury." The limiting factor for the recovery of pure economic loss is rather to be found in the (scholarly and) judicial views requiring the plaintiff to show special blameworthiness in the conduct of the defendant.[48]

5.3. Germany: Narrow in Tort but Wide in Contract

The German legal system seems to deny even preliminary access to damages for pure economic loss. This prophylactic role is vested in a text that envisions liability only for injuries to certain enumerated rights. According to § 823 I of the BGB, individuals are liable if they willfully or negligently injure "the life, body, health, freedom, property or other right" of the victim. Deliberately excluded from this list is any reference to injuries of a purely financial kind. It is therefore undisputed that, as a basic rule, pure economic loss is not recoverable in tort. Compensation may be obtained in tort in some exceptional

[44] Cass 28 March 1994, no 2988, Giur it 1995, I, 1, 1366. Italy's pragmatism extends beyond the marital/non-marital divide to include the extended family as well: relatives outside the nuclear family can receive financial damages provided that the secondary victim may prove that she was relying on the primary victim for economic support. See Francesco D Busnelli & Giovanni Comandé, "Italy," in Magnus (ed) (n 33) 117, 129, and 134, fn 59. As to the non-economic damages this class of plaintiffs can be entitled to, see Chapter V, section 3.2.

[45] Cass 24 May 1982, no 2765, Foro it 1982, I, 2864.

[46] Cass 25 February 2009, no 4587, Giust civ mass 2009, 312.

[47] The general clause in the French code is effectively the same as the old Italian code of 1865, before its renovation in 1942.

[48] See Bussani (n 39) 367–377; Marta Infantino, *La causalità nella responsabilità extracontrattuale. Studio di diritto comparato* (Stämpfli 2012)201–202, 211–213, 226.

situations, but the plaintiff must find a cause of action in some provision other than § 823 I BGB.[49]

On the surface, German tort law rules have changed little since their enactment more than a century ago. The real change has been accomplished through case law. While this is certainly not a phenomenon peculiar to German law,[50] nevertheless it is worth stressing if we are to understand a system that attempted a rigid legislative solution.

For instance, German law requires the violation of a right (an "absolute" one) but new rights have been added to the traditional set through interpretation. In this way German law developed the so-called right of the established and ongoing commercial enterprise (*Recht am eingerichteten und ausgeübten Gewerbebetrieb*) to protect an enterprise from unlawful interferences with matters particular to its business, such as its brand, its marketing activities, or its creditworthiness.[51] Something similar happened to § 823 II BGB, where wording about the infringement of "a statute intended for the protection of others" became a vehicle to compensate pure financial losses arising out of such infringement, provided that the type of loss can be included within the sphere of the statutory aim.[52] But this is not all. § 826 BGB provides that a person is liable if s/he intentionally causes harm to another in a manner contrary to public policy. To understand the subjective requirements of this provision, it is not deemed necessary that "the defendant actually intended to cause harm"; it will be enough "if he was conscious of the possibility that harm might occur and acquiesced in its doing so."[53] The role this rule plays

[49] For example, under § 824 BGB, which provides that a person who declares or publishes, contrary to the truth, a statement which is likely to endanger the credit earnings or prosperity of another is liable for "any damage" arising therefrom, even if he does not know of its untruth but should know of it. Here the protection against pure economic loss is the crux of the rule, but its scope is narrowed by the privilege granted to the author of the communication in § 824 II BGB: according to this section, the author of the communication is not liable if he was unaware of the untruthfulness of his statement, and he or the recipient of his communication had a "justified interest" in the communication itself. On this subject, and for further references see, in English, van Gerven, Lever, & Larouche (n 3) 189.

[50] Toward the end of the nineteenth century, French courts developed a case law imposing liability in cases arising from making a void contract, seduction, misleading information, unfair competition, and so forth—all pursuant to a code that left open the meaning of "*dommage*" and the interests to be protected (see above, n 28). The courts in Germany, at the same time, felt the need to impose liability in the same types of cases, so that the legislator, in drafting the code, was able to enumerate the cases in which liability would be imposed: Sacco (n 28) 362, n 35.

[51] On this notion, see Basil S Markesinis, John Bell, & André Janssen, *Markesinis's German Law of Torts* (5th edn, Bloomsbury 2019) 12, 19, 37, 49; Cees van Dam, *European Tort Law* (2nd edn, OUP 2013) 88; Mathias Reimann, "Germany - case 2," in Bussani & Palmer (eds) (n 2) 200–202.

[52] von Bar (n 11) 45–49.

[53] Zweigert & Kötz (n 29) 463. For instance, following the so-called Dieselgate scandal, many buyers of Volkswagen cars carrying the defective device brought contract law actions against sellers, as well as tort law actions against Volkswagen claiming damages in the amount of the purchase

with regard to our issue can be appreciated if one looks at the factual situations to which it has mainly been applied. These are, for example, participating as a third person in a breach of contract committed by a contracting party, delaying someone's bankruptcy in order to obtain personal benefit at the expense of other creditors, giving false information, or omitting to give information in circumstances where there is a duty to give it.[54]

Further, Germany has written into its code a specific right to recovery by family members who suffer a pecuniary loss due to the death of the primary victim.[55] Sections 844 II and 845 BGB do not specify the biological identity of the secondary victims entitled to recovery, but define them in terms of legal obligations elsewhere in the law: only persons to whom the primary victim owed a legal duty to provide support will qualify. This has been interpreted to include spouses, children, and parents.[56] Stepchildren who have not been legally adopted, fiancé(e)s, and romantic partners whom the primary victim has not married are excluded from the scope of § 844, a result which is harsher than French and Italian ones, but not that different from the rule adopted in common law countries (see below, sections 5.4 and 5.5 in this chapter).[57]

In solving questions of pure economic loss, contract remedies are more widely employed in Germany than in other countries. The reason for contract's enlarged role is probably twofold. On the one hand, apart from rules permitting the concurrence of tort and contract actions, tort law is considered too weak and narrow to safeguard all financial interests that merit

price against surrender of the car. The ensuing individual and collective tort law actions were framed either under § 823 II BGB for violation of § 263 of the German Penal Code on commercial fraud, or under § 826 BGB (Wolfgang Wurmnest & Merlin Gömann, "Germany," in Ernst Karner & Barbara C Steininger (eds), *European Tort Law Yearbook 2019* (de Gruyter 2020) 205, 210–221; Jens Kleinschmidt, "Germany," in Ernst Karner & Barbara C Steininger (eds), *European Tort Law Yearbook 2018* (de Gruyter 2019) 221, 225–227); also claims based on § 826 BGB were occasionally upheld by courts: OLG Köln 3 January 2019, MDR 2019, 222. See also BGH 25 May 2020, NJW 2020, 1962; BGH 30 July 2020, NJW 2020, 2798.

[54] Karl Larenz & Claus-Wilhelm Canaris, *Lehrbuch des Schuldrechts* (13th edn, Beck 1994) 276. See other references in Christian von Bar, "Liability for Information and Opinions Causing Pure Economic Loss to Third Parties: A Comparison of English and German Case Law," in Basil S Markesinis (ed), *The Gradual Convergence* (CUP 1994) 104.

[55] The same solution is adopted by many other European countries, such as Austria, Greece, the Netherlands, Poland, and Switzerland: cf § 1327 ABGB (Austria), art 922 CC (Greece), art 6:108 BW (Netherlands), art 446 CC (Poland) and arts 45 and 47 of the Code of Obligations (Switzerland). In 2017 a new paragraph III was added to § 844 BGB to cover also secondary victims' non-economic losses: see Chapter V, section 3.2.

[56] See Markesinis, Bell, & Janssen (n 51) 199–200.

[57] See also Chapter V, sections 3.2 and 4.3.

legal protection. On the other hand, contract claims may seem to be a relatively safer path to those who dread unleashing the floodgates of tort, since there is certainly less danger of boundless damages occurring in a breach of contract situation. For whatever reason, courts and scholars certainly expanded the sphere of contractual liability beyond the limits marked by the BGB. This was accomplished through the exploitation of various devices, including the greater ease of establishing breach of contract rather than fault (§ 282 BGB),[58] and the stronger regime of vicarious liability in contract (§ 278 BGB) rather than in tort (§ 831 BGB).[59] The range of contractual duties was also stretched both to include "implied" duties of care, so that liability might arise not only from the violation of the parties' express obligations but also the breach of a host of judicially imposed duties of care, and to absorb judicial doctrines (such as *culpa in contrahendo*) into the BGB.[60]

The most important innovation of all, however, was that courts and commentators lowered the privity barrier in contract and applied these duties in favor of those who are not parties to any contract. The principal instrument in this regard is the "contract with protective effects for third parties" (*Vertrag mit Schutzwirkung zugunsten Dritter*), which brings strangers to a contract under its umbrella and permits them to sue a promisor for breach of one of the contract's secondary obligations, notably (for our subject) some breach causing purely financial harm to the plaintiff.[61] The function of the contract with protective effects is arguably tort-like in that the protected third party need not stand in a close personal relationship to the promisor nor be specifically identified in advance. At the same time it is operationally

[58] According to § 282 BGB, the party to a contract who breaches her contractual duty to "take into account the rights, legal interests and other interests of the other party" as set forth under § 241 II BGB, is per se liable to the other party, i.e., with no need for the latter to establish the former's fault.

[59] While § 278 BGB imposes a strict liability rule upon the principal for the harm caused by her employees, § 831 BGB is a fault-based rule, which relieves the principal from liability for the acts of her employees if the former can demonstrate she has exercised reasonable care in the selection and supervision of the latter. On the differences between the two regimes, see Markesinis, Bell, & Janssen (n 51) 123–127; see also Chapter III, section 2.3.

[60] See also above, n 22. Under this doctrine contractual duties may arise as soon as the parties set up a pre-contractual "contact," thus well before any contract is concluded and even when none is ever in fact concluded.

[61] See Mathias Reimann, "Germany – case 13" and "Germany – case 17," in Bussani & Palmer (eds) (n 2) 393–395 and 463–464 (devoted respectively to "Subcontractor's Liability" and "Auditor's Liability"). See also Miquel Martìn-Casals, "The Borderlines of Tort Law," in Miquel Martìn-Casals (ed), *The Borderlines of Tort Law. Interactions with Contract Law* (Intersentia 2019) 713, 748–749; Basil S Markesinis, Hannes Unberath, & Augustus Johnston, *The German Law of Contract. A Comparative Treatise* (2nd edn, Hart 2006) 186–216.

free of the "absolute rights" requirement of German tort law and permits recovery of purely financial harm.[62]

All these rules are firmly established today to the extent that most of them have been included in the reform of the law of obligations recently adopted[63] and, as a result, many cases that an English, American, Italian, or French lawyer would consider solely a matter of tort law are actionable in Germany in contract.

5.4. England's Cautious and Opportunistic Judges

The English façade tends to make a continental lawyer think more of the criminal law (where all crimes are typically nominate) than the law of tort.[64] Most of these torts arose in defense of protecting a plaintiff's life, limb, and property and are far removed from affording relief for pure economic loss. There are, to be sure, a series of intentional economic torts, notably actions for deceit; interference with trade; inducing breach of contract, passing off, misfeasance in public office;[65] intimidation and conspiracy; and if the defendant has intentionally caused such loss, the claim for pure economic loss may fit into one of these pigeonholes. If the loss was occasioned by negligence, however, these actions are unavailable. The plaintiff's chief recourse must therefore be to the tort of negligence.

The generic tort of negligence would appear, at first glance, to hold great promise for the recovery of pure economic loss. Animated by the "neighbor principle" which *Donoghue v. Stevenson* announced in 1932,[66] this tort has been compared to a general clause covering all forms of negligent behavior. But this is generally true within the realm of protection from physical harm

[62] It is not the only possibility under German law. Another institution of possible application in this field is the so-called *Drittschadensliquidation* which may be described as a quasi-contractual judge-made doctrine that allows a creditor to a contract to claim in contract for loss resulting from its breach, even though the loss falls not upon him but upon a third party. Markesinis, Bell, & Janssen (n 51) 102–103.

[63] See above, n 22.

[64] The language of the common law has always made a connection between civil and penal redress. "We 'commit' a tort as we 'commit' an offense. We can be 'guilty' of either or both; and all our crimes are nominate": Rudden (n 38) 126.

[65] Cf Sue Arrowsmith, *Civil Liability and Public Authorities* (Earlsgate Press 1992). See *David v Abdul Cader* [1963] 1 WLR 834 (PC); and, obiter, *X (some minors) v Bedfordshire County Council* [1995] 3 All ER 353 (HL); *Three Rivers DC and Others v Governor and Company of the Bank of England* [2000] 2 WLR 1220 (HL).

[66] See also Chapter I, section 7, and Chapter VIII, section 3.

(bodily injury or damage to property). Negligence is not primarily applicable to the compensation of pure economic loss.[67] This means that the nature of the plaintiff's damage controls the existence of a duty to avoid causing it. Indeed, the common law as a matter of policy begins with the proposition that there is, as a rule, no duty of care to avoid causing pure economic loss.

This deep misgiving is based upon an instinctive fear of wide liability, customarily expressed by recourse to the floodgates metaphor or the "nightmare scenario," but more fundamentally by a cautious case-by-case approach which studies the economic and social implications of each extension. As is usual in common law jurisdictions, judges are willing to impose a "duty of care" only when satisfied on utilitarian grounds that, in the particular case brought before them, it is socially and economically convenient to do so. The occasions upon which such a duty is recognized in England are exceptional; are highly fact-sensitive; cover narrow fact situations; and may be increased in the future only if the courts find it "fair, just and reasonable" to do so.[68] The exceptions began with *Hedley Byrne & Co Ltd v. Heller & Partners* (a case in which the defendant bankers, who had negligently given incorrect information about a company's creditworthiness, were held liable for the pure economic loss suffered by the plaintiff when the latter, relying upon that information, invested in the company, which shortly afterwards went bankrupt)[69] and then multiplied. The general principle of no liability for pure economic loss survives, but with a number of exceptions that thus far are limited to negligent misstatements made and relied upon (in a context of "virtual" contract),[70] negligent interference with the performance of a contract,[71]

[67] *Murphy v Brentwood District Council* [1991] AC 398 (HL).

[68] On the meaning of this phrase, which reserves judicial options for future development (in marked contrast to the more principled methodology announced in *Anns v Merton London Borough Council* [1978] AC 278), see, eg, *Caparo Industries Plc v Dickman* [1990] 2 AC 605.

[69] [1964] AC 465.

[70] *Hedley Byrne* [1964] AC 465. One should be aware, however, that if, after a misrepresentation, the parties actually enter into a contract with each other, it is doubtful whether there is any practical need to resort to the rule of Hedley Byrne, since liability may end up being based on contract under s 2 (1) Misrepresentation Act 1967. The text provides that "[w]here a person has entered into a contract after a misrepresentation has been made to it by another party thereto and as a result thereof he has suffered loss, then, if the person making the misrepresentation would be liable to damages in respect thereof had the misrepresentation been made fraudulently, that person shall be so liable notwithstanding that the misrepresentation was not made fraudulently, unless he proves that he had reasonable ground to believe and did believe up to the time the contract was made that the facts represented were true." See Bussani & Palmer (eds) (n 2) 140–141 and fn 66; see also von Bar (n 11) 449.

[71] *Junior Books v Veitchi* [1983] 1 AC 520. This Scottish case, however, has been disapproved in almost every later English case. Jane Stapleton, "Duty of Care Factors: A Selection from the Judicial Menus," in Jane Stapleton & Peter Cane (eds), *The Law of Obligations. Essays in Honour of J. Fleming* (OUP 1998) 59, 80 and fn 82–83; JM Thomson, "A Prophet Not Rejected in His Own Land" (1994) 110 LQR 361 (1994).

negligent defamation in the writing of a reference for a former employee,[72] professional negligence in the drawing up of a will,[73] and breach of statutory duty.[74] In cases of wrongful death, statutory law specifically provides that some of the deceased's dependents—a notion that was traditionally limited to the spouse, parent and child of the decedent only, but that now includes (also) civil partners and unmarried co-habitants—might claim compensation for the economic loss they suffered.[75]

What appears characteristic and consistent in these exceptions is the limited quantitative exposure of the defendant to a defined number of plaintiffs, or even better, a single plaintiff. The danger of unbounded financial repercussion is avoided. The total liability can be calculated in advance as not exceeding the value of a lost legacy, a lost job or investment, a wrongful death. The plaintiff is an individual specified ex ante—the potential legatee of a will,

[72] *Spring v Guardian Assurance PLC* [1993] 3 All ER 273 (CA).

[73] *White v Jones* [1993] 3 All ER 481(CA), [1995] 2 WLR 187 (HL).

[74] For relevant references, see von Bar (n 11) 328–329.

[75] For the list of dependants in this respect, see s 1 (3) of the Fatal Accidents Act 1976. See also Chapter V, sections 2, 3.1, and 4.2. The historical precedent of this Act was Lord Campbell's Act, which was adopted by the Parliament in 1846. Until the enactment of Lord Campbell's Act, English law almost never authorized causes of action for negligence resulting in death. This surprising gap emerged from a confluence of several common law rules. Common law observed the maxim *actio personalis moritur cum persona* (a "personal" cause of action dies with the person). The tort action died with the plaintiff or defendant because "neither the [representatives of the deceased] plaintiff have received, nor those of the defendant have committed, in their own personal capacity, any manner of wrong or injury" (William Blackstone, *Commentaries on the Law of England* (III, 16th edn, Strahan 1825) 302). True, in the early history of common law (see, eg, *Guy v Livesey*, 79 Eng Rep 428 (KB 1618)), one rule seemed to point toward an exception to the actio personalis maxim, allowing husbands to pursue an action for trespass on the case *per quod consortium amisit* (literally, "a trespass whereby [plaintiff] lost the company of his wife": Blackstone, *Commentaries*, 140) in case of their wives' wrongful death. Yet this right—per se unavailable to women—was often a matter more of theory than practice, because husbands faced a significant practical barrier to bringing such claims arising from the interaction between criminal and tort law. Under the criminal law of the seventeenth, eighteenth, and early nineteenth centuries, all crimes that constituted "felonies" were punishable by forfeiture to the Crown of all the felon's assets (John H Baker, *Introduction to English Legal History* (5th edn, OUP 2019)562–568). Most felonies also earned the criminal the death penalty. Premeditated killings and killings arising from recklessness constituted one class of felonies subject to these penalties. The death penalty and the total forfeiture rule eliminated the practical point of a loss of consortium suit by a husband who might otherwise seek compensation via a tort suit against a person who killed his wife. By 1800, then, the state of English law was roughly as follows: (1) the death of the victim precluded any tort action on behalf of the victim for her injuries, and (2) although husbands in theory could sue for the wrongful killing of their wives, the felony merger rule actually barred the success of any tort law suits for intentional and reckless killings. Even the small window for loss of consortium suits by husbands was then closed by the 1808 decision of *Baker v Bolton*, where, confronted with a tort claim by a husband for the negligent killing of his wife, the court declared summarily that, "[i]n a civil court, the death of a human being [cannot] be complained of as an injury" (*Baker v Bolton* [1808] 1 Campb 493, at 1033 per Lord Ellenborough). Around the 1830s, the rapid development of the railways and the escalation of railway deaths generated an increasing dissatisfaction with the common law bar on tort actions for negligently caused deaths, which led to the enactment of Lord Campbell's Act (Rande W Kostal, *Law and English Railway Capitalism 1825–1875* (OUP 1994)289–290).

a former employee, a specific investor or a deceased's dependent—whose interests are very distinctly contemplated by the defendant at close range. But the presence of other factors which demonstrate a closer degree of proximity between the parties than mere foreseeability of economic harm may be insisted upon, such as defendant's "assumption of responsibility" for the plaintiff's economic well-being coupled with the plaintiff's reliance upon it.[76] The class of claimants is thereby limited, as if an invisible privity paradigm structured the resulting bond in tort.

It may be noted that although actions may be brought concurrently, a contract action cannot be used in these circumstances for there is no "consideration" and therefore no contract between plaintiff and defendant. Given its insistence on consideration, England's rigid contract law cannot protect legal strangers against such losses. It was therefore faced with the choice either to expand its tort law opportunistically or to deny these actions altogether.[77]

The English judges express their pragmatism in an open manner. Policy decisions are not cloaked behind a particular view of causation or of *culpa*, as we have already noticed in several continental systems. The unlawfulness issue is isolated as a preliminary policy decision. Thus in English law, the façade of judge-made tort law approaches the inner reality of the process.

5.5. The United States: A Flexible Consensus

For the purposes of this chapter, the analysis of United States law on the recoverability of pure economic loss can start with the Restatement Second of Torts. Section 766C of the Restatement bars the compensation of this loss, if negligently inflicted, with wording that echoes the ruling of a famous federal case,[78] and has become ever since fairly common in the legal debate. It reads, "[o]ne is not liable to another for pecuniary harm not deriving from physical

76 The phrase "assumption of responsibility" originates in *Hedley Byrne* (nn 69–70) at 528 (Lord Devlin) It seems to make recourse to an underlying contract model to earmark occasions when it is appropriate to impose a duty of care. See Lord Goff's opinion in *Henderson v Merrett Syndicate Ltd* [1995] 2 AC 145, [1994] 3 All ER 506, discussing the role played by voluntariness of the assumption of responsibility and of reliance upon it. See also Stathis Banakas, "Liability for Incorrect Financial Information: Theory and Practice in a General Clause System and in a Protected Interests System" (1999) 7 ERPL 261, 270–272.

77 Basil S Markesinis, "An Expanding Tort Law—The Price of a Rigid Contract Law" (1987) 103 LQR 354.

78 *Robins Dry Dock & Repair Co v Flint*, 275 US 303 (2d Cir 1926). See, eg, Herbert Bernstein, "Civil Liability for Pure Economic Loss under American Tort Law" (1998) 46 AJCL 111.

harm to the other, if that harm results from the actor's negligently (a) causing a third person not to perform a contract with the other, or (b) interfering with the other's performance of his contract or making the performance more expensive or burdensome, or (c) interfering with the other's acquiring a contractual relation with a third person."

This no-liability rule has been extended to many other areas of the law of torts,[79] so that the so-called pure economic loss rule is now understood as a denial of liability for the negligent infliction of any of such losses. That is the general position taken by most of the American scholars and courts; as put by § 1 of the Restatement (Third) of Torts, "[a]n actor has no general duty to avoid the unintentional infliction of economic loss on another."[80]

This is not the entire picture, though.

First of all, avenues to recovery are kept open in some lines of cases where the fear of indeterminate and excessive liability is seen, on a practical matter, quite low. The loss of earnings by the plaintiff who takes care for her injured spouse is recoverable to the extent of the market value of the services rendered.[81] Since the late nineteenth century, the American states followed the English lead by enacting their own wrongful death statutes.[82] These statutes allowed tort litigation to proceed after the death of the primary victim, with representatives of the deceased party taking over the litigation with what are known as survival actions.[83] The same statutes that created survival actions

[79] See for all David Gruning, "The United States," in Palmer & Bussani (eds) (n 2) 134, 139–161; more recently, Anthony J Sebok, 'The Failed Promise of a General Theory of Pure Economic Loss: An Accident of History?' (2012) 61 DePaul LR 615.

[80] § 1 (1) Restatement (Third) of Torts: Liability for Economic Harm (2020). The rule applies in most of the cases transnational debate places under the pure economic loss label. There is no recovery indeed, eg, for the workers who lost their job because the cutting of electrical cables has caused employer's plant to shut down, nor in the cases concerning the injury to a key employee of the plaintiff. No compensation for pure economic loss is available to the lessee of a ship negligently damaged by a third party, nor for the (entirety of the) losses incurred by a wife who must abandon her employment in order to care for her injured husband. See Gruning (n 79) 143–145, 148–150.

[81] See Gruning (n 79) 148–150. See also Restatement Second of Torts, § 693 (Action by One Spouse for Harm Caused by Tort Against Other Spouse).

[82] Dan B Dobbs, Paul T Hayden, & Ellen M Bublick, *Torts and Compensation, Personal Accountability and Social Responsibility for Injury* (8th edn, West 2017) 666. See also above, n 75.

[83] Dobbs, Hayden, & Bublick (n 82) 666–681; see also Chapter V, section 3.1. Damages recoverable in survival actions have a fairly narrow aim: to provide the decedent's estate with compensation for any harm that the decedent suffered up to the moment of her death. As such, compensation flowing from these actions is often quite modest, typically being limited to medical expenses incurred by the deceased prior to her death (which may be nonexistent, if death was instantaneous) (*Warner v McCaughan*, 77 Wash2d 178 (Wash 1969)), lost earnings between the time of injury and the time of death (*Printy v Schwantes*, 40 Wis2d 418 (Wis 1968)) and funeral expenses (which, although incurred after death, are commonly viewed as obligations of the estate of the deceased: *McGowan v Estate of Wright*, 524 So2d 308 (Miss 1988); *Estate of Kronemeyer v Meinig*, 948 P2d 119 (Colo App 1997)). Other pecuniary harms, including loss of future income, are not compensable in survival actions. The

have also authorized wrongful death claims by certain family members (usually spouses and minor children) for at least some of the harms they have suffered by virtue of the wrongful killing of the decedent. If conduct would have amounted to a tort had the victim been injured, it constitutes "wrongful" death when death rather than injury results. In contrast to survival actions, wrongful death actions do not seek to impose liability for the decedent's losses prior to death. Instead, they compensate immediate family members for the losses that they have suffered because of the decedent's death.[84] Further, in some jurisdictions, it is a finding that the plaintiff was "particularly foreseeable" by the defendant at the time of her negligence that can lead to an award of damages for pure economic losses. For example, in a case in which the defendant was found negligently responsible for a fire which caused the temporary evacuation of the surrounding area, where plaintiff had its business facilities, plaintiff recovered the pure economic loss due to the discontinued business.[85] But courts can allow compensation also when they find the contract between defendant and plaintiff's co-contractant was "intended to affect" the plaintiff. This can be the case when the defendant contractor delays the renovations of the owner's building and plaintiff, whose restaurant leased space in that building, is unable to reopen the restaurant at the expected time, and therefore suffers economic losses.[86] As to the construction sector, in particular, research conducted over 465 disputes, adjudicated by State Appellate courts from 1970 to 2005, shows that not less than 126 cases ended with the award of pure economic loss damages to the plaintiff—with an in increasing trend since the mid-'90s.[87]

theory is that a dead person herself does not suffer from being deprived of future gains: Goldberg, Kendrick, Sebok, & Zipursky (n 20) 468.

[84] This is why wrongful death claims are "indirect" in nature. Wrongful death damages go to the persons named in the statute and not the primary victim's estate: Goldberg, Kendrick, Sebok, & Zipursky (n 20) 469–470. See also Chapter V, section 3.1.

[85] *People Express Airlines, Inc v Consolidated Rail Corp*, 495 A2d 107 (NJ 1985) at 116–118. As to the series of cases presenting problems similar to those addressed by *People Express*, cf *532 Madison Avenue Gourmet Foods, Inc v Finlandia Center, Inc*, 711 NYS2d 391 (App Div 2000) (affirming liability) with *Goldberg, Weprin & Ustin, LLP v Tishman Construction Corp*, 713 NYS2d 57 (App Div 2000) (rejecting liability). See also Gary T. Schwartz, "American Tort Law and the (Supposed) Economic Loss Rule," in Bussani & Palmer (eds) (n 2) 94, 105–108; Goldberg, Kendrick, Sebok, & Zipursky (n 20) 138–140; and, straightforwardly considering *People Express* an outlier in United States case law, Robert L Rabin, "Respecting Boundaries and the Economic Loss Rule in Tort" (2006) 48 Ariz LR 857, 858.

[86] *J'Aire Corp v Gregory*, 598 P2d 60 (Cal 1979) at 63. See also *Venore Transportation Co v M/V Struma*, 583 F2d 708 (4th Cir 1978).

[87] See Anthony Niblett, Richard A Posner, & Andrei Shleifer, "The Evolution of a Legal Rule" (2010) 39 J Leg Stud 325–358.

A further and larger path to recovery is opened when plaintiff's loss is due to negligently performed professional services. A number of rules make it possible that auditors, lawyers, or insurance brokers would be responsible for the pure economic losses negligently inflicted to third persons with whom they had no contractual tie.[88] Although there may be specific requirements that must be met in certain states that are not clearly imposed in others,[89] still it seems fair to say that in many situations—provided indeterminate and excessive liability is excluded—plaintiffs may recover losses caused by negligent professionals.

But many other roads may lead to a compensation for pure economic loss in the United States. Under private nuisance law, for example, it is possible for plaintiffs to recover the reduction in value of her land when defendant's (noninvasive) activity carried on outside plaintiff's land is found to threaten a future harm. This can be the case of defendant's stored explosives that create a reasonable fear;[90] when a halfway house in a residential neighborhood presents a serious danger that convicted felons on early release can cause harm;[91] or when toxic materials contaminate a nearby land (again, without any invasion of plaintiff's property).[92]

Federal statutory law offers further significant insights, straightforwardly allowing compensation for pure economic loss, for instance, in case of infringement of intellectual property rights and trademarks.[93] Further, the language of the Dodd-Frank Wall Street Reform and Consumer Protection Act, concerning credit rating agencies' liability is promising. Section 933 (b) (2) states: "In the case of an action for money damages brought against a credit

[88] See in general Gruning (n 79) 150–158; Catherine M Sharkey, "Tort Liability for Pure Economic Loss: A Perspective from the United States and Some Comparative European Insights" (2016) 7 JETL 237–271; Anita Bernstein, "Keep It Simple: An Explanation of the Rule of No Recovery for Pure Economic Loss" (2006) 48 Ariz LR 773, 787; Dobbs, Hayden, & Bublick (n 82) 1082–1102 (on auditors and lawyers); see also § 4 Restatement (Third) of Torts: Liability for Economic Harm (2020) (establishing an exception to the "pure economic loss rule" when a a client sues a professional for malpractice).

[89] For example, Mississippi and Wisconsin require a showing that the plaintiff's reliance upon the published audit was foreseeable by the defendant. See Gruning (n 79) 137.

[90] *Comminge v Stevenson*, 76 Tex 642, 13 SW 556 (Tex 1890); *Cumberland Torpedo Co v Gaines*, 201 Ky 88, 255 SW 1046 (Ky 1923) (depreciation of value due to fear, not fear itself is the basis).

[91] *Arkansas Release Guidance Foundation v Needler*, 252 Ark 194, 477 SW2d 821 (Ark 1972).

[92] *Gray v Westinghouse Elec Corp*, 624 NE2d 49 (Ind Ct App 1993) (PCBs in adjacent landfill); *Allen v Uni-First Corp*, 151 Vt 229, 558 A2d 961 (Vt 1988); *Exxon Corp v Yarema*, 69 Md App 124, 516 A2d 990 (Md 1986) (nearby groundwater contaminated, recovery without invasion if this substantially reduced plaintiff's use and enjoyment).

[93] See, respectively, the Copyright Act of 1976, 17 USC §§ 101–1332, esp § 504; the Patent Act of 1952, 35 USC §§ 271–297; and, in particular, the Lanham (Trademark) Act of 1946, 15 USC §§ 1051–1129).

rating agency or a controlling person under this title, it shall be sufficient, for purposes of pleading any required state of mind in relation to such action, that the complaint state with particularity facts giving rise to a strong inference that the credit rating agency[violated their duties] knowingly or recklessly."[94] Notwithstanding the cause of action is not open to negligence claims, the plaintiff's path to recovery is no longer substantially precluded as it was in the past when United States courts, because of First Amendment and other regulatory protections, would be unable to recognize the de facto regulatory power of rating agencies within the market and ended up equating their ratings to mere opinions, thereby imposing liability on the agencies only when they were found causing the harm intentionally.[95]

In summary, despite the façade of no-recovery, American law displays conspicuous exceptions. In addition to the recoverability of intentionally inflicted pure economic loss,[96] and under some special applications of private nuisance law, compensation may be allowed in the significant area of liability for negligently rendered professional services, for specific types of losses not arousing any fear of "liability in an indeterminate amount for an indeterminate time to an indeterminate class,"[97] in a relevant percentage of construction disputes, and, under statutory law,[98] even when the likely result

[94] 15 USC 78u–4(b)(2)(A).

[95] Mauro Bussani, "Credit Rating Agencies' Accountability: Short Notes on a Global Issue" (2010) 10(1) *Global Jurist* 1–13, also (in a version updated as of August 2011) at ssrn.com/abstract=1515285; Mauro Bussani, "La responsabilité des agences de notation de crédit. Brèves remarques sur un enjeu global" (2013) 65 RIDC 239–258.

[96] See John G Fleming, *The Law of Torts* (8th edn, The Law Book Company Ltd 1992)694–695; Catherine M Sharkey, "In Search of the Cheapest Cost Avoider: Another View of the Economic Loss Rule" (2017) 85 U Cin LR 1017, 1018.

[97] *Ultramares Corporation v Touche* (1931) 255 NY 170 at 179 (per Cardozo CJ). See also Vincent R Johnson, "The Boundary-Line Function of the Economic Loss Rule" (2009) 66 Wash & Lee LR 523 at 530–534 (2009).

[98] Besides the examples above (nn 94–95), what is still worth the mention is the Oil Pollution Act of 1990 (33 USC § 2701 and ff) ("OPA"), enacted in response to the Exxon Valdez oil spill (on the ensuing litigation, eg, Ronen Perry, "Economic Loss, Punitive Damages, and the Exxon Valdez Litigation" (2011) 45 Ga LR 409; Ronen Perry, 'The Deepwater Horizon Oil Spill and the Limits of Civil Liability" (2010) 86 Wash LR 1). Under OPA, a person may obtain compensation for pure economic loss from a party responsible for a spill if she can prove that her loss is due to the injury, destruction, or loss of real property, personal property, or natural resources, irrespective of whether she owns that property or those resources (33 USC § 2702(b)(2)(E)). This statutory language is best understood to allow recovery by those claimants who can prove that they have suffered pure economic loss because a spill has rendered physically unavailable to them property or resources they put to commercial use (see, eg, *Sekco Energy, Inc v M/V Margaret Chouest*, 820 F Supp 1008 (ED La 1993)). Thus, if a spill were to deprive commercial fishermen of expected profits by killing fish they ordinarily would catch and sell, or by causing authorities to bar the fishermen from accessing those fish for a period of time, the fishermen would be entitled to recover. By contrast, operators of beach resorts in areas physically unaffected by a spill, even though suffering economic loss because of a general downturn in tourism resulting from the spill, are not entitled to recover under OPA (see John CP Goldberg, "Liability for Economic Loss in Connection with the Deepwater Horizon Spill"

is precisely liability in an indeterminate amount and to an indeterminate class.[99]

One could even say, to use Gary Schwartz's words, that "no single rule can even begin to determine how all such [pure economic loss] cases should be decided."[100] What the above survey makes clear, however, is (a) that the erosion of the unitary no-recovery rule was not driven by a clear-cut desire to build an opposite, pro-plaintiff rule, but may be attributed to a "pragmatic" case-by-case approach, oriented by openly verbalized and case-tailored policy choices; and (b) that beyond its exclusionary façade, American law is much less stingy toward victims of pure economic loss than most of its oracles are inclined to admit.[101]

(2010) 30 Miss C LR 335, 337). But see also § 8 Restatement (Third) of Torts: Liability for Economic Harm (2020) on public nuisance, according to which "[a]n actor whose wrongful conduct harms or obstructs a public resource or public property is subject to liability for resulting economic loss if the court concludes that the claimant's losses are distinct in kind from those suffered by members of the affected community in general." On public nuisance's "innovative" use as a means of recovering purely financial losses between non- contracting parties when the "pure economic loss rule" would bar recovery, Catherine M Sharkey, "Public Nuisance as Modern Business Tort: A New Unified Framework for Liability for Economic Harms" (forthcoming 2021) 70 DePaul LR.

[99] See also the critical discussion of the class actions aiming (and of case law allowing) to "extract" recovery in tort for pure economic losses under state consumer protection laws, in L Brickman, *Lawyer Barons. What Their Contingency Fees Really Cost America* (CUP 2011) esp 185–199.

[100] Schwartz (n 85) 119. See also ibid at 108–118, for the discussion of other cases that have led to compensation for pure economic loss: by professional laboratories issuing "false positive" results for drug or alcohol tests of existing or potential employees, and by adoption agencies for the economic losses suffered from the adopting families because of agencies' failure to disclose information about the physical or mental health problems of the adopted children.

[101] As is well known, however, it is not only legislation and case law that shape legal expectations and behaviors. Private practices have a role in it, and indeed an even larger cleft into the exclusionary wall could be brought about by the legal aftermath of the so-called Deepwater Horizon Spill. What has been called the greatest oil spill in history, and certainly the largest in the American history, began with an explosion on April 20, 2010, some 41 miles off the Louisiana coast. The accident occurred during the drilling of an exploratory well by the Deepwater Horizon, a mobile offshore drilling unit under lease to BP (formerly British Petroleum) and owned by Transocean. BP established a $ 20 billion compensation fund (which operated outside the statutory compensation scheme set up under OPA—above n 97), that disbursed compensation through a claims facility: the Gulf Coast Claims Facility (GCCF), acting for and on behalf of BP Exploration & Production Inc. in fulfilling BP's statutory obligations as a "responsible party" under the Oil Pollution Act of 1990 (gulfcoastclaimsfacility.com). Claims filed with the GCCF were adjudicated in accordance with the rules and procedures set forth by the facility itself, allowing "individuals and businesses that have incurred damages as a result of the Spill" to claim compensation for "lost earnings or profits and loss of subsistence use of natural resources" (gulfcoastclaimsfacility.com/faq#Q7). In 2012, however, in the wake of widespread criticism against the way the GCCF was administered by its manager, Kenneth Feinberg, BP replaced the settlement of claims through the GCCF with a court supervised settlement program, covering $9.6 billion of the original $20 billion, under the supervision of a court-appointed claims administrator, Patrick Juneau (deepwaterhorizoneconomicsettlement.com/). Parties reached an agreement upon a "Economic and Property Damages Settlement" which became final in 2014 and covered "economic loss and property damage claims related to the Deepwater Horizon Incident, including claims for seafood compensation, business economic loss, individual economic loss, loss of subsistence" (cert.gardencitygroup.com/dwh/fs/faq?.delloginType=faqs#Q6). For a detailed analysis of the

6. The Exclusionary Rules and Its Discontents. The "Floodgates"

To better understand, from a comparative perspective, most of the domestic arguments about the recoverability of pure economic loss, the results of this brief survey are to be set against the fundamental reasons which are usually presented in support of an exclusionary rule. Naturally these arguments are developed by jurists in legal systems which take the position that such losses should not be generally recoverable in tort. Needless to say, different theoretical approaches, as well as the experience of other countries, suggest certain counterarguments, which will be equally worth of mention.

Exploring the reasons underpinning the exclusionary rule, however, one should start with the so-called floodgates argument. This is the most important of the arguments, because it is not only pervasive but has proved persuasive in many quarters. It usually links up with and reinforces the other arguments. Among the jurisdictions under review, Germany and common law countries share similar concerns about the danger of excessive liability entailed by pure economic loss claims. In this context, a closely connected explanation for the exclusionary rule has to do with the fear of open-ended liability and derivative litigation, that is, the extension of liability for the remote consequences of a wrongful act. The common premise of this argument is that in a complex economy, pure economic losses are likely to be serially linked to one another. Damage to a particular good, for example, often generates losses that affect several downstream individuals and firms who would have utilized the good as an element in their production process, and so on. In such a world of economic networking, it becomes necessary to set reasonable limits to the extent to which remote economic effects of a tort should be made compensable.[102]

legal aftermath of the BP Oil Spill, see Catherine M Sharkey, 'The BP Oil Spill Settlements, Classwide Punitive Damages, and Societal Deterrence' (2015) 64 DePaul L Rev 681–710; Samuel Issacharoff & D Theodore Rave, 'The BP Oil Spill Settlement and the Paradox of Public Litigation' (2014) 74 La LR 397; Myriam Gilles, "Public-Private Approaches to Mass Tort Victim Compensation: Some Thoughts on the Gulf Coast Claims Facility" (2012) 61 DePaul LR 419; Palmer (n 10) 105. Besides its practical results, what may be interesting to test in the future is whether this scheme will be able to lend itself as a model for future emergencies, and to what extent the exclusionary rule may be challenged by the combined impact of the OPA and the BP rules, and on the ground of what arguments. As we saw for other jurisdictions, change of expectations, approaches, legal culture, and tort law rules is a process that takes time, but it never is beyond the horizon.

[102] Fears of open-ended liability arguments have a well-established doctrinal lineage. See Nils Jansen, "Duties and Rights in Negligence: A Comparative and Historical Perspective on the

Thus, though not always noticed, there are actually two distinct strands to the floodgates argument, and it is helpful to separate them. The *first* strand is the belief that to permit recovery of pure economic loss in some cases would unleash an infinity of actions that would burden if not overwhelm the courts. If defendant's negligence necessitates the closure of trading markets or shuts down all commerce traveling a busy motorway, there may be hundreds, perhaps thousands of persons who would be financially damaged. Assuming a large number of these cases reach the courts, there would be administrative chaos. The justice system could not cope with the sheer numbers of claims.

The *second* strand is the fear that widespread liability would place an excessive burden upon the defendant who, for purposes of the argument, is treated as the living proxy of human initiative and enterprise. The potentially staggering liability would be out of all proportion to the degree to which defendant was negligent. It is also said that it is manifestly impossible for defendant to predict in advance how many ricochet economic loss claims she might face when, for example, she injures the property of a primary victim. Whether there is a small or large class of secondary loss sufferers depends, fortuitously, upon the number of parties with economic interests linked to the exploitation of the property.[103]

The danger of disproportionate consequences resulting from minor blameworthiness is of course an issue of fairness no matter what kind of damages have been caused,[104] but some scholars believe that the danger is exacerbated in pure financial loss cases.[105] Financial harm is assumed to have

European Law of Extra-contractual Liability" (2004) 24 Ox J Leg Stud 443. Rudolf von Ihering's statement, "Where would it all lead if everyone could be sued!" is a famous rendition of this general concern. Rudolf von Jhering, "Culpa in contrahendo" (1861) 4 *Jahrbücher für die Dogmatik des heutigen römischen und deutschen Rechts* 1, 12–13.

[103] The rationales of predictability and practicality are discussed, eg, in Bernstein (n 7) 726–774.

[104] See Jeremy Waldron, "Moments of Carelessness and Massive Loss," in Owen (ed) (n 1) 387.

[105] The harm has often been compared to the recovery of damages for nervous shock, since there too the loss can be "pure" as opposed to consequential, and there too the danger of reverberating impacts is commonly given as a reason for restrictive rules (on nervous shock, see also Chapter V, section 4). The analogy, however, must not be pressed too far. Courts in nervous shock cases have been troubled by a number of rather different concerns, particularly the difficulty of defining the threshold harm (what degree of shock should be cognizable? what manifestation of the harm should be required?) and the difficulty of detecting false or fraudulent claims. In the case of pure economic loss, however, the problem of defining the threshold of the harm is minimal (the threshold of financial damage always begins at zero); the factual existence of the loss is objectively demonstrable and its measurement and proof are not easy but perhaps less problematic. The threat of fraud is also of less concern because such loss is arguably free of the danger that claimants may simulate her symptoms. Accordingly, economic loss is less easily feigned than the manifestations of nervous shock. The most important similarity between the two areas is rooted in judicial concern about expanding liability in favor of an indeterminate number of plaintiffs, for indeterminate amounts of damages.

a greater propensity to travel far and wide. It has often been pointed out that the laws of Newton do not apply on the road to financial ruin.[106] Physical damage has at least a final resting point, while financial harm is not slowed down by gravity and friction.[107]

7. A Contingent Dogma

In assessing the cumulative weight of the argument, there are a number of considerations to bear in mind. To begin with, it should be remembered that the floodgates argument has never purported to be a scientific claim nor a claim based upon comparative law research. It is not very easy to test whether the dire prophecy of the "nightmare scenario" is dream or reality. Is it founded on blind conservatism or does it have a rational basis?[108] For instance, the central assertion that physical damage is different from financial damage because it is more contained and judicially manageable seems increasingly difficult to understand[109] in view of today's mass torts, which sometimes—as we said above—involve innumerable physically injured victims asserting claims sometimes amounting to billions of dollars.[110] This

[106] Weir (n 24) 9–10. This was also the view of Fleming James who stated that the "physical consequences of negligence usually have been limited, but the indirect economic repercussions of negligence may be far wider, indeed virtually open-ended": James Jr Fleming, "Limitations on Liability for Economic Loss Caused by Negligence: A Pragmatic Appraisal" (1972) 25 Vand LR 43, 45. On these issues, see also, in this volume, Chapters IV, esp section 3; V; and VII, esp sections 2.2 and 3.2.

[107] See, however, Jane Stapleton, "Legal Cause: Cause-in-Fact and the Scope of Liability for Consequences" (2001) 54 Vand LR 941, 974: "The reference to the laws of physics reflects a long-standing fallacy in traditional running down cases that control of liability for consequences can be achieved by some 'billiard ball' notion of the laws of physics. That is, this reference rests upon the faulty notion that claims for physical damage, whether to person or property, are inherently limited by the laws of physics which teach that physical forces will ultimately come to rest. After I have run you over and broken your leg, we have come to rest in a crude sense. Yet if you later suffer negligent treatment at a hospital that damages your other leg, the law may well say this injury is within the appropriate scope of my liability for consequences. What is doing the work in this judgment is not some inherent limit on my liability set by the law of physics but a judgment about the appropriate scope of liability for consequences in light of, among other things, the perceived purpose underlying the recognition of the obligation in the first place" [footnotes omitted].

[108] For example, in 1939 William Prosser cuttingly observed: "[i]t is the business of the law to remedy wrongs that deserve it, even at the expense of a 'flood of claims'; and it is a pitiful confession of incompetence on the part of any court of justice to deny relief upon the ground that it will give the courts too much work to do" (William L Prosser, "Intentional Infliction of Mental Suffering: A New Tort" (1939) 37 Mich LR 874, 877).

[109] The point is repeatedly emphasized by Bernstein (n 78) 126–128.

[110] It should be noted that comparative tax law shows that damages awards for personal injuries usually go tax-free, like any other physical damage to property that is to be considered non-income bearing. The opposite solution prevails, however, whenever recovery is meant as restoration of taxable income. See Enrico Marello, "The Western Approach to Taxation of Damages: The

would suggest that the law is normally content (or not reluctant at all) to impose liability even though the potential plaintiff class is large. It would certainly sound very odd if the defendant could argue that s/he should not owe a duty because s/he would have too many victims.[111] But it is certain that the justification for a no-recovery rule based upon a supposed difference in ripple effect or in the sheer size of the plaintiff class is hard to reconcile with the recovery of extremely large economic losses resulting from negligently caused physical injury.[112]

The geographical distribution of the floodgates argument is another interesting facet of its development. While a perennial in some soils and climates, the argument has failed to take root in others. There is no agreed upon explanation why this occurs. One might say that the theme resonates better in particular legal cultures, but what makes one culture or legal infrastructure more receptive to this theme than another? The answer is not clear. Until research is available, the question is open to speculation and to discussion of interesting clues. Consider England, where the floodgates argument has enjoyed significant success. Should we be surprised that a historically small, close-knit coterie of judges may be sensitive to the question of administrative overload? Does institutional structure and conditioning play a role in this question? Another relevant issue may be to investigate the way in which broad arguments of this kind circulate in international channels. The ruling ideas of influential exporting legal cultures (not merely substantive law ideas, but "soft" formants such as the conventional wisdom and dominant policy arguments) clearly have extraterritorial scope and impact. It does not seem accidental that in countries where English and German legal cultures had a decisive sphere of influence, historically speaking (eg, English influence in Commonwealth countries and the United States; Germanic influence in Austria and Portugal), the floodgates argument has been received almost

Substitution Myth," in Mauro Bussani (ed), *European Tort Law. Eastern and Western Perspectives* (Stämpfli 2007) 121.

[111] For example, the judgment in *Griffiths v British Coal Corporation* [1998] EWHC 2008 (QB) upheld a large personal injury claim. It produced a settlement of £2 billion for the benefit of 100,000 ex-miners suffering from a range of chest illnesses, a sum considerably higher than the one the government received from the privatisation of the coal industry: see Stapleton (n 107) 962. In a slightly different context, this reasoning was set out in a dissent in *Riss v New York*, 22 NY2d 579, 585 (1968): "It is not a distortion to summarize the essence of the city's case here in the following language: 'Because we owe a duty to everybody, we owe it to nobody.' Were it not for the fact that this position has been hallowed by much ancient and revered precedent, we would surely dismiss it as preposterous."

[112] See, eg, Stapleton (n 71) 65–66.

unquestioned. It is interesting that in other countries one vainly searches for any trace or mention of floodgates anxiety.[113] As stated earlier, the subject deserves an open-minded approach and deeper investigation.

8. Values, Resources, Blame

Another argument against recovery of pure economic loss is cast in terms of social values. It maintains that intangible wealth is not and should not be treated on the same level as protecting bodily integrity or even physical property. People are more important than things, and things are more important than money.[114] Our legal interest in liberty, bodily integrity, land, possessions, reputation, wealth, privacy, and dignity are all good interests, "but they are not equally good." The law protects the better interests better.[115] And so "a legal system which is concerned with human values (and the law is supposed to reflect the proper values of society) would be right to give greater protection to tangible property than to intangible wealth."[116] The exclusionary rule could then be a reflection of the lower value ascribed to unreified wealth.[117]

It is important to notice that this view—besides being at odds with the impact finance has, and the role it plays upon global, national and individuals' economies—has a silent premise: these interests must be ranked because the law *cannot* simultaneously protect all interests fully. Even if one accepts, for

[113] Yet things may not be so simple. How does one explain developments in jurisdictions like Japan where the floodgates argument is rather muted and moderate, yet the Civil Code is considered German-inspired and the country's public law and judicial organization bear a heavy American imprint? See Vernon V Palmer & Mauro Bussani, "The Present Study," in Palmer & Bussani (eds) (n 2) 7, 46–47; Yoshihisa Nomi, "Japan," ibid, 71–87; Vernon V Palmer & Bussani, "Surveying the Results," ibid, 303, 304–306.

[114] The argument has been made in England that "[t]he philosophy of the market place presumes that it is lawful to gain profit by causing others economic loss [...]. Certainly there seems to have developed an understanding that economic loss at the hands of others is something we have to accept without legal redress, unless caused by some specifically outlawed conduct such as fraud or duress" (*The Aliakmon* [1985] 2 All ER 44, 73, per Lord Goff).

[115] Law and economics makes this argument slightly differently. Many cases of economic loss to one party involve an offsetting economic gain to another, and the law should not trouble itself with wealth transfers that do not affect aggregate welfare. See William Bishop, "Economic Loss in Tort," (1982) 2 Ox J Leg Stud 1, 1; Richard A Posner, "Common-Law Economic Torts: An Economic and Legal Analysis," (2006) 48 Ariz LR 735, 740.

[116] Anthony M Weir, *A Casebook on Tort* (10th edn, Sweet & Maxwell 2004) 6.

[117] If this were in fact the case, then one might expect legal systems to care much more than they do about memories, sentiments, personal well-being, and all the other values that for the most part represent the only real wealth of a person (and, probably, more aligned with the layperson's notion of "human values").

sake of argument, that wealth is less important than other values, still there would be no justification for a rule restricting its recovery unless we had to do so in order to protect other, more meritorious interests. Thus, the theoretical point is persuasive to the extent one is ready to agree on that (1) there is indeed a finite limit to the law's ability to protect interests, and (2) giving full protection to pure economic interests would clearly exceed that capacity and therefore impinge on other protections or the interests of third persons.

The first point may be less controversial than the second. No one doubts that resources are finite: judicial resources are not unlimited; tort liability cannot be extended indefinitely without stifling human initiative; and responsible defendants can be bankrupted by financial claims that leave claims for bodily injury unsatisfied. It may be argued, therefore, that if pure economic loss were freely protected and allowed to compete on an equal footing with other, worthier claims for limited resources, the effect might be to crowd out 'better' interests and leave them unsatisfied. That conclusion depends, however, on the answer to the second point, namely whether those limits would be surpassed by a presumption of recoverability. The answer to this question again seems to be conjectural since it ultimately depends to some extent upon the same unverified assumptions inherent in the floodgates rationale. It also raises the question how countries like France and Italy, which follow a rule of presumptive recovery of economic loss, have managed to avoid what the floodgates argument predicts. Is their experience proof that the argument is a gross exaggeration of the consequences, or does their experience tend to prove that these countries are simply using other means of controlling those consequences?[118]

There is an additional question. The exclusionary rule is associated with the negligence standard. All systems, however, permit recovery when pure financial loss is inflicted intentionally. Thus, the exclusionary rule cannot be simply seen as an abstract ordering of interests but as a rule tied to the gradations of blame (and to the statistical occurrence of lawsuits lodged under the intention heading). As it occurs for the liability for non-economic loss, it would be difficult to say whether the nature of the interest or the nature of the fault is the more important factor in the equation. Indeed, it would be essentially misguiding to assign such priorities because the rule, when it is applied and to the extent that it is a rule, is really the outcome of many other

[118] See above, sections 5.1 and 5.2 in this chapter, for the discussion of French and Italian tort law rules, respectively.

interacting factors as well.[119] Only through study of these factors in their liability context one understands why the alleged exclusionary rule operates selectively and situationally, never mechanically, and indeed leaves untouched a number of defined situations where one may even speak of a limited core of protection for pure economic loss.

9. Things (May) Change

Some scholars assert as a historical matter that pure economic loss has traditionally been left unprotected by the law. If the assertion were generally true, it may have important normative implications for the present and the future. Professor Kötz deduces a teleological point from the study of the past: The primary *purpose* of the law in England and Germany, he maintains, has "always been" to provide protection against personal injuries and harm to physical property. Pure economic loss seems left out of historical development, at least in those two countries.[120]

Whether these views do justice to the past, however, is open to question. James Gordley, who explored the history of pure economic loss in some detail, notes that many early civilians said that a plaintiff could recover if he suffered "damage" and damage meant simply a diminution of the economic value of his assets. They did not distinguish between loss of a physical asset and other kinds of loss. They occasionally put cases in which the plaintiff would recover what we today would regard as pure economic loss—though the prominent scholar cautions that they did not know or use this term and did not recognize an autonomous category by that name.[121] For instance, there was the dependent's action for loss of support due to wrongful death, which clearly existed on the continent in Grotius's time. This was in effect an action for the recovery of pure economic loss sustained by wife and children, but it was not referred to in those terms. Evidence of this kind would suggest that there never was a per se rule against compensation for pure economic

[119] For a nuanced attempt to use various factors in a sliding scale to explain the lesser protection given to pure economic loss, see Helmut Koziol, "Wrongfulness under Austrian Law," in Helmut Koziol (ed), *Unification of Tort Law: Wrongfulness* (Kluwer 1998) 11, 29–30.

[120] Kötz (n 2) 428.

[121] James Gordley, "The Rule Against Recovery in Negligence for Pure Economic Loss: An Historical Accident," in Bussani & Palmer (eds) (n 2) 26–29 (also for the citations to the views of Durandis, Baldus, Brunnemann, Lauterbach, and Grotius).

harm in the civilian tradition.[122] Indeed, Gordley's account characterizes the rise of the exclusionary rule both in England and Germany as a late development of the nineteenth century[123] and the peculiar outgrowth of analytical thinking and rising capitalism. He concludes that the rule is an "accident" of legal history, not a pervasive feature of it, nor necessarily of the future.

[122] See Reinhard Zimmermann, *Law of Obligations: Roman Foundations of the Civil Law Tradition* (Clarendon Press 1996) 1024–1025; Vernon V Palmer, "The Fate of the General Clause in a Cross-Cultural Setting: The Tort Experience of Louisiana" (2000) 46 Loy LR 535, 551.

[123] Insurance practices tend also to show the late development of the rule. Development of business interruption insurance, often called "consequential loss insurance," belongs to the late nineteenth century, and even now the availability of such insurance is still limited. A prevalent restriction is that interruption insurance is essentially "follow-on" coverage to another insured peril, such as fire. Under the wording of standard fire policies, there is no compensation for interruption unless it results from a fire. This is not really compensation for pure economic loss, however, but rather compensation for parasitic loss. See Bill W Dufwa, "Insurance in a European Tort Law Perspective," in Bussani (ed) (n 95) 133; Christian Lahnstein, "Pure Economic Loss and Liability Insurance," in Willem H van Boom, Helmut Koziol, & Christian A Witting (eds), *Pure Economic Loss. A Comparative Perspective* (Springer 2004) 162–166.

VII
Causation

1. The Silence of the Codes

Notwithstanding causation plays wherever a key role in the adjudication of tort law cases,[1] its notion is not explicitly addressed by most legislators.

This is no surprise in Anglo-American law. In England and in the United States statutory references to causation are scanty, and even when the requirement is mentioned it is formulated in very loose terms, or with regard to very specific circumstances.[2] But the same remark holds true for codified

[1] In the comparative law literature see, eg, HLA Hart & Tony (Anthony) M Honoré, *Causation in the Law* (2nd edn, CUP 1985); René Rodière & Michel Pédamon (eds), *Faute et lien de causalité dans la responsabilité délictuelle. Etude comparative dans les pays du marché commun* (Pédone 1981); Anthony M Honoré, "Causation and Remoteness of Damage," in *International Encyclopedia of Comparative Law* (Mohr Siebeck 1971) vol XI, ch 7; more recently, see Marta Infantino, "Causation Theories and Causation Rules," in Mauro Bussani & Anthony J Sebok (eds), *Comparative Tort Law. Global Perspectives* (2nd edn, EE 2021) 264–283; Marta Infantino & Eleni Zervogianni (eds), *Causation in European Tort Law* (CUP 2017); Bénédict Winiger, Helmut Koziol, Bernhard A Koch, & Reinhard Zimmermann (eds), *Digest of European Tort Law. Essential Cases on Natural Causation* (Springer 2007); Jaap Spier (ed), *Unification of Tort Law: Causation* (Kluwer 2000).

[2] In England, one should look to statutory provisions such as s 3(1) of the Compensation Act 2006, which reads: "This section applies where (a) a person ("the responsible person") has negligently or in breach of statutory duty caused or permitted another person ("the victim") to be exposed to asbestos; (b) the victim has contracted mesothelioma as a result of exposure to asbestos; (c) because of the nature of mesothelioma and the state of medical science, it is not possible to determine with certainty whether it was the exposure mentioned in paragraph (a) or another exposure which caused the victim to become ill; and (d) the responsible person is liable in tort, by virtue of the exposure mentioned in paragraph (a), in connection with damage caused to the victim by the disease (whether by reason of having materially increased a risk or for any other reason)." In the United States, a good reference comes from the Oil and Pollution Act 1990, 33 USC § 2703(a): "A responsible party is not

Common Law and Civil Law Perspectives on Tort Law. Mauro Bussani, Anthony J. Sebok, & Marta Infantino, Oxford University Press.
DOI: 10.1093/oso/9780195368383.003.0007

jurisdictions, where the black letter words used by legislators to set out the general architecture of tort law systems usually give little guidance about what causation is, and how it should be assessed.[3]

In France, for instance, the Civil Code contains a causation rule only in the contract law domain. According to art 1231–4 (former art 1151) of the Civil Code, damages extend only "to the direct and immediate consequences of the breach of contract." Judges and scholars consider the rule applicable to tort law as well, and it is upon this rule that they start grounding their arguments.[4]

In Italian law the role played by French jurists is taken up by the Civil Code itself. Art 2056 of the Italian *Codice civile* declares tort law causation dependent on a provision laid down for the breach of any obligation (art 1223), whereby compensation is allowed for any damage that is an immediate and direct consequence of the breach. In the same Title of the *Codice*, covering the general law of obligations, one finds art 1227, which reduces the amount of damages according to the comparative fault of the injured, and imposes upon the plaintiff the duty of mitigating the loss. Under the tort law section of the Code, art 2055 provides for joint and several liability in cases involving multiple tortfeasors.[5]

In Germany, three Civil Code provisions concern causation issues. They are §§ 254, 830, and 840 BGB. The former, included in the "*Allgemeiner Teil*"

liable for removal costs or damages under section 1002 [33 USC § 2702] if the responsible party establishes, by a preponderance of the evidence, that the discharge or substantial threat of a discharge of oil and the resulting damages or removal costs were caused solely by [...] an act of God." Worth reminding are also the statutes that, in the majority of American states, modify the common law doctrine of joint-and-several liability: see Gary T Schwartz, "Causation under US Law," in Spier (n 1) 123–124.

[3] Honoré (n 1) 11, fn 91.

[4] See Geneviève Viney, Patrice Jourdain, & Suzanne Carval, *Les conditions de la responsabilité* (4th edn, LGDJ 2013) 252–253; Christophe Quézel-Ambrunaz, *Essai sur la causalité* (Dalloz 2010) 450–452.

[5] Moreover, a few provisions on causation in the Italian penal code are generally deemed applicable to tort law as well (cf Pietro Trimarchi, *Causalità e danno* (Giuffrè 1967) 21; Marta Infantino & Eleni Zervogianni, "The European Ways to Causation," in Infantino & Zervogianni (eds) (n 1) 93–95). According to art 40 of the Italian Penal Code,

> [n]o one shall be punished for an act designated by law as an offence if the harmful or dangerous event on which the existence of the offence depends was not a consequence of his own act or omission. Failing to prevent an event which one has a legal obligation to prevent shall be equivalent to causing it.

Art 41 of the same Code reads as follows:

> [t]he presence of pre-existing, simultaneous or supervening causes, even though independent of the act or omission of the offender, shall not exclude a causal relationship between his act or omission and the event. Supervening causes shall exclude a causal relationship when they were in themselves sufficient to bring about the event.

of the Code laying down the private law general rules and therefore applying also to tort law, sets forth the comparative fault and mitigation of damage rules. §§ 830 and 840 BGB, located in the tort law title of the same book, cover cases involving multiple tortfeasors, with § 830 applying to jointly committed torts and § 840 establishing joint and several liability in case of multiple contributions to the harm.[6]

All the above-mentioned codes were adopted between the 1804 (the French Civil Code) and the 1942 (the second Italian unitary Civil Code). Civil codes and code-like statutes adopted in European countries after the Second World War display a trend toward the increase of statutory attention to problems of causation. In the civil codes and equivalent texts enacted in the second half of the twentieth century, statutory rules about causation have multiplied.[7]

[6] For a comment on these provisions, cf Basil S Markesinis, John Bell, & André Janssen, *Markesinis's German Law of Torts* (5th edn, Bloomsbury 2019) 407–408, 412, and Ulrich Magnus, "Causation in German Tort Law," in Spier (ed) (n 1) 63, 66.

[7] For instance, a tort law provision of the 1964 Polish Civil Code, art 361 (1), specifies that compensation is granted only for damages that were "adequately" connected to the defendant's behavior: see Ewa Bagińska, "Overview of Polish Private Law. Tort Law and Property Law," in Mauro Bussani & Ugo Mattei (eds), *Opening Up European Law* (Stämpfli 2007) 233, 241. The 1992 Dutch Burgerlijk Wetboek contains express provisions on joint and several liability in cases of "indeterminate" causation (that is, cases where an unknown member of a group of people causes a harm which could have been prevented by the other members of the same group: art 6:166 BW), and of "concurrent" causes (i.e., when the harm appears to be the result of different factors, for each of which a different person is responsible, but it remains unclear to what extent: art 6:99 BW). See Christian von Bar, Non-Contractual Liability Arising out of Damage Caused to Another (Sellier 2009) 786–787. The two scenarios just mentioned were considered by subsequent legislatures as well. To make a few illustrations, art 186 (4) of the Slovenian Law of Obligations of 2002, § 2915 (1) of the Czech Civil Code of 2012, and s 6:524 (4) of the Hungarian Civil Code of 2013 provide for joint and several liability in cases of indeterminate causation (cf Christian von Bar, Non-Contractual Liability Arising out of Damage Caused to Another (Sellier 2009) 785; Marta Infantino & Eleni Zervogianni, "Summary and Survey of the Results", in Infantino & Zervogianni (eds) (n 1) 632; Ádám Fuglinszky, "Risks and Side Effects: Five Questions on the "New" Hungarian Tort Law' 2 ELTE L J 199, 206–207 (2014)), while joint and several liability for concurrent causation is imposed, eg, by art 138(1) of the Estonian Law of Obligations of 2002, art 1.370 of the Romanian Civil Code of 2009 and the same s 6:524 (4) of the Hungarian Civil Code of 2013 (on these provisions, cf Christian Alunaru & Lucian Bojin, "The Tort Law Provisions of the New Romanian Civil Code" (2011) 2 JETL 103; Janno Lahe & Tambet Tampuu, "Estonia," in Winiger, Koziol, Koch, & Zimmermann (eds) (n 1) 429–430; Fuglinszky, above in this n, 206–207). In the draft tort law reform published in 2017 by the French Ministry of the Justice, at least seven provisions dealt with causation-related problems: see Projet de réforme de la responsabilité civile, March 2017, at http://www.justice.gouv.fr/publication/Projet_de_reforme_de_la_respons abilite_civile_13032017.pdf, arts 1239–1240, 1253–1256, 1265. Similar considerations apply to the legislative bill for tort law reform now pending before the French Parliament: see arts 1236–1237, 1239, 1250–1251, 1253–1256 of the *Proposition de loi n° 678*, at senat.fr/leg/ppl19-678.html. See also Chapter I, section 3, n 30.

2. Two-Stage Causation

Rather than focusing on the myriad of causal problems that might arise in tort law cases—such as issues of comparative negligence, multiple (intentional and negligent) contributions to the harm, apportionment between tortfeasors, effect of natural hazards, and distribution of the evidentiary burden—, this chapter focuses on the fundamental principles that, in every legal system, come into play in causal assessments. As we will see, jurisdictions differ not only in the theories they rely upon, but also in the way in which these theories are interpreted, applied, and mixed with one another.

There is an exception, though. A unanimous agreement can be found on that, differently from criminal law, in tort law there is no abstract liability for merely endangering someone's interest without actually harming it.[8] To illustrate: two drivers, A and B, carelessly throw half-filled, jumbo-sized paper cups of coffee out of their car windows as they drive on a public street. The cup thrown by A splatters on the windshield of nearby driver Z, which causes Z to crash his car into a tree. The fly of the cup thrown by B gives Z a fright but does not hit his car, and Z keeps driving safely, while the cup falls harmlessly on the ground. Both A and B were careless in the same way, and both A and B can be sued for littering, but A alone is subject to liability in negligence, because only A's carelessness actually caused injury to another.[9]

Beyond this point, interpretive roads sometimes overlap, sometimes diverge.

[8] This holds true in both civil law and common law jurisdictions: see, eg, Gert Brüggemeier, *Common Principles of Tort Law: A Pre-Statement of the Law* (BIICL 2004) 53, and John CP Goldberg, Leslie C Kendrick, Anthony J. Sebok, & Benjamin C. Zipursky, *Tort Law: Responsibility and Redress* (5th edn, Wolters Kluwer 2021) 245.

[9] The illustration is taken from Goldberg, Kendrick, Sebok, Zipursky (n 8) 245, 250. A related issue, on which legal systems do diverge, however, is whether the plaintiff's fear of developing an illness in the future (typically after exposure to a toxic substance) could be viewed as an injury in itself. Reasonable fear of developing an illness in the future has been deemed to be a compensable injury in the United States (*Wetherill v University of Chicago*, 565 F Supp 1553 (ND Ill 1983); *Norfolk & Railway Company v Ayres*, 538 US 135 (US 2003)), in Italy (Cass, 13 May 2009, no 11059, Riv giur amb, 2009, 1005) and in France (Cass civ (Plenary) 5 April 2019, D 2019, 922; Cass soc 3 March 2015, Droit social 2015, 360; Cass soc 11 May 2010, JCP Social 2010, 1261), while is not considered as a recoverable injury in England (*Johnston v NEI International Combustion Ltd* [2007] UKHL 39; *Rothwell v Chemical & Insulating Co Ltd* [2006] EWCA Civ 27) and in Germany (BGH 2 April 2014, VIII ZR 19/13). On this issue, cf Paola Monaco, *Sostanze tossiche e danni. Profili di diritto globale, europeo e nazionale* (Editoriale Scientifica 2020); Cristina Corgas-Bernard, "Le préjudice d'angoisse: État des lieux" (2014) Rev jur Ouest 29–34; Andrew R Klein, "Fear of Disease and the Puzzle of Futures Cases in Tort" (2002) 35 UC Davis LR 966–1004; John CP Goldberg & Benjamin C Zipursky, "Unrealized Torts" (2002) Va LR 1626, 1664–1667.

Across the ocean and the Channel, a general distinction is made between interpretive techniques that aim to establish factual/natural causation (also known as cause-in-fact or actual cause), and techniques devoted to the assessment of legal causation or proximate cause (or scope of liability), which aim to elaborate on the factual chain to determine if and to what the extent liability should be imposed under the circumstances.[10]

In English and American law, the causation issue is openly approached through a two-pronged test. The first stage, which is expected to focus on the so-called "cause in fact" (England) and "factual/actual cause" (United States), essentially concerns whether the defendant's activity was a but-for condition of the loss. The second stage—that of "remoteness of damage" (England) and of "proximate cause"/"scope of liability" (United States)—is usually presented as centered, in England, on whether the link between the conduct and the ensuing loss was sufficiently close, and, in the United States, on whether there is something about the causal connection between defendant's activity and plaintiff's loss that warrants freeing the defendant from liability.[11]

Though less openly, the two-stage causation divide is implicitly employed in the civilian jurisdictions as well. Germans distinguish between "*haftungsbegründende Kausalität*" (literally, "causation establishing liability") and "*haftungsausfüllende Kausalität*" ("causation implementing liability"),[12] a division which to a large extent corresponds to the Italian separation between "*causalità in fatto*" and "*causalità giuridica.*"[13] Rarely mentioned by case law, the distinction between the "*lien entre le fait du défendeur et le dommage initial*" and the "*lien entre le dommage initial et ses conséquences ultérieures*" is occasionally acknowledged by French legal literature.[14]

10 From the common law world, see, in comparative perspective, Hart & Honoré (n 1) 85–87; Anthony M Weir, "Recent Developments in Causation in English Tort Law," in *De tous horizons. Mélanges Xavier Blanc-Jouvan* (Société de législation comparée 2005) 887–889; Jane Stapleton, "Legal Cause: Cause-in-Fact and the Scope of Liability for Consequences" (2001) 54 Vand LR 941, 945, 957–958. As to continental Europe, see Jaap Spier & Olav A Haazen, "Comparative Conclusions on Causation," in Spier (n 1) 127–134; Christian von Bar, *The Common European Law of Torts* (II, OUP 2000) 437–468.

11 See, respectively, Anthony M Weir, *An Introduction to Tort Law* (2nd edn, OUP 2006) 71–72, 83–85, and Joseph A Page, *Torts. Proximate Cause* (Aspen 2003) 4–7. As we will see below in section 3 in this chapter, in the United States causation is generally held to be a question for the jury, subject to the judge's power to decide issues as a matter of law: Goldberg, Kendrick, Sebok, & Zipursky (n 8) 273–274.

12 Magnus (n 6) 63–64.

13 Gino Gorla, "Sulla cosiddetta causalità giuridica: 'fatto dannoso e conseguenze'" (1951) Riv dir comm I, 405–415.

14 Viney, Jourdain, Carval (n 4) 265–268; Quézel-Ambrunaz (n 4) 206–207.

According to these civil law partitions, which are only partially overlapping with those in use in common law countries, the first segment of causation ties the tortfeasor's activity to the victim's injury, while the second segment brings together the injury and the assessment of damages that stemmed from that injury.[15] Yet, it should be noted that French scholars and courts often fail to overtly distinguish the two causation stages, and that, in Germany and in Italy, the distinction is strongly emphasized by legal scholarship, but routinely forgotten by courts.[16]

All national approaches show that the causation inquiry is expected to be performed (in both stages) by applying to the case at hand a wide array of formulas that in all jurisdictions are available to evaluate causal connections. We will now see in more detail what these formulas are, and how they work.

2.1. First Stage: Facts and Nature

In order to establish "factual" causation, all jurisdictions tend to apply a quite homogeneous test, which is called "but-for" in common law countries and "condicio sine qua non" in the civil law world.[17] According to this test, the defendant is the cause of the plaintiff's damage when, in the absence of the former's wrongful activity, the latter would not have suffered the same harm.[18]

[15] See the authors mentioned above, nn 12–14. The same approach is not entirely unknown in common law jurisdictions: see Richard W Wright, "The Grounds and Extent of Legal Responsibility" (2003) 40 San Diego LR 1425, 1445–1446 (2003).

[16] Jonas Knetsch, *Tort Law in France* (Wolters Kluwer 2021) 131–134; Magnus (n 6) 64; Francesco D Busnelli & Giovanni Comandè, "Causation under Italian Law," in Spier (ed) (n 1) 82.

[17] The theory is also known as "Äquivalenztheorie" in Germany (Markesinis, Bell, & Janssen (n 6) 61–62), "teoria dell'equivalenza" in Italy (Michele Graziadei & Davide Migliasso, "Italy," in Koziol, Koch, Zimmermann, & Winiger (eds) (n 1) 35, 38), and "équivalence des conditions" in France (Suzanne Galand-Carval, "Causation under French Law," in Spier (n 1) 53, 54–55).

[18] von Bar (n 10) 437–447. The formula might equally apply to omissions, but it is often held that causation assessments are carried out differently, according to whether the wrong is inflicted by an active misconduct or by an omission: cf Hart & Honoré (n 1) 138–141; von Bar (n 10) 218–223. In this regard, three refinements are in order, though: (a) in many cases distinguishing acts from omissions is far from being easy, since what might be defined as an omission can be conceptually turned into an act (and vice versa), depending on how the defendant's behavior is framed; (b) in common law jurisdictions the distinction among "acts" and "failures to act" becomes usually relevant under the (theoretically antecedent) "duty-test" stage (see Goldberg, Kendrick, Sebok, & Zipursky (n 8) 85–93; Anthony M Weir, *A Casebook on Tort* (10th edn, Thomson 2004) 97–89; see also Chapter II, section 5); and (c) the positive/negative nature of the conduct is only one of the elements—and not necessarily the most important one—to be taken into consideration when assessing causation (Douglas Hodgson, *The Law of Intervening Causation* (Ashgate 2008) 129).

As a general matter, the test adequately assists the court to make a selection among the possible causes of the plaintiff's harm and filtering out the factors bearing no relationship with it. But there are situations whose factual settings make it impossible for the test to work properly, either because of the uncertainty surrounding the events or because of the concurrence of multiple sets of conditions that were each actually or potentially sufficient to cause the harm. In many jurisdictions, such cases call for more "relaxed" criteria to refine or substitute the but-for/condicio sine qua non test with other formulas—such as the French doctrine of the "*perte d'une chance*," or the English "material contribution to the risk" test, or the United States "substantial factor" test and market share liability rule.

The French notion of "*perte d'une chance*," which is usually understood by French scholars as an exception to the principle of certainty of damage,[19] might be useful in overcoming the uncertainty surrounding (not only the existence and the extent of the damage, but also) the causal relationship between the defendant's wrong and plaintiff's injury.[20] Much more limited is the scope of the English principle of liability for "material contribution to the risk" (i.e, increase of the risk) that the claimant would suffer an injury. The principle applies only to exceptional cases—most often, cases of wrongful exposure to toxic substances—where an evidential gap made it impossible to draw a certain inference that the breach of duty had caused the harm at issue.[21]

In the United States, the "substantial factor" test originally appeared in the Restatement First of Torts, and was then expanded in the Restatement Second, where it featured in two of the main provisions on causation, §§ 431[22] and 432 (2).[23] In the mind of the drafters of the Restatement Second,

[19] Quézel-Ambrunaz (n 4) 154–174; François Chabas, "La perte d'une chance en droit français," in Olivier Guillod (ed), *Développements récents du droit de la responsabilité civile* (Centre d'études juridiques européennes 1991) 131.

[20] Quézel-Ambrunaz (n 4) 163–169.

[21] Jane Stapleton, "Asbestos in UK Courts," in Miquel Martín-Casals & Diego M Papayannis (CUP 2016) 87; Sandy Steel, "Sienkiewicz v Greif and Exceptional Doctrines of Natural Causation" (2011) 3 JETL 294, 295; Marc Stauch, "'Material Contribution' as a Response to Causal Uncertainty: Time for a Rethink" (2009) 68 Cambridge LJ 27.

[22] According to § 431:

> [An] actor's negligent conduct is a legal cause of harm to another if (a) his conduct is a substantial factor in bringing about the harm.

[23] The rule set forth by § 432 (2) is as follows:

> [i]f two forces are actively operating, one because of the actor's negligence, the other not because of any misconduct on his part, and each of itself is sufficient to bring about harm to another, the actor's negligence may be found to be a substantial factor in bringing it about.

the test—which is satisfied if "the defendant's conduct has such an effect in producing the harm as to lead reasonable men to regard it as a cause"[24]—was to serve two different goals. The first was to help establish "factual" causation in an unusual set of cases, known as multiple sufficient causes, in which causation of plaintiff's injury can be traced back to two or more factors, each of which would have been sufficient to cause the entire harm. The second goal of the test was to graft onto the standard but-for test a proximate cause restriction that would bar the assignment of responsibility to a defendant whose carelessness turns out to be (deemed) as a trivial—that is, non-substantial—but-for cause of the plaintiff's injury.[25] However, precisely because the Restatement Second used the "substantial factor" to try to kill two very different birds with one stone, it turned out to be needlessly confusing and of limited guidance in judicial practice. This explains why the Restatement Third of Torts—Liability for Physical and Emotional Harm (PEH), eliminated the phrase "substantial factor." What had once been its relevance to the first stage—its handling of "overdetermined" causation—is now handled under the test for multiple sufficient causes.[26] The other job performed by the expression "substantial factor"—to manage trivial but-for causes in the second stage—is now covered by § 36 of PEH ("Trivial Contributions to Multiple Sufficient Causes").[27]

On a different side of the picture, the drafters of the Restatement Third, PEH, decided not to include any rule on the so-called "market share liability" theory, another theory developed in the United States with regard to the specific set of circumstances occurring when a person is harmed by a product whose manufacturer cannot be identified. According to the theory, which was originally conceived as a remedy for those injured by a pharmaceutical

[24] § 431 Restatement Second of Torts, cmt a.

[25] Goldberg, Kendrick, Sebok, & Zipursky (n 8) 309–310.

[26] See § 27 of the Restatement Third of Torts—PEH (essentially reproducing § 432 of the Restatement Second of Torts):

> [i]f multiple acts occur, each of which under § 26 alone would have been a factual cause of the physical harm at the same time in the absence of the other act(s), each act is regarded as a factual cause of the harm.

On the reasons underlying the abandonment of the "substantial factor" test as the driving doctrine in ordinary cases, see also Restatement Third of Torts—PEH, § 26, cmt j, and § 28, cmt b. On the new version of the test, see Anthony J Sebok, "Actual Causation in the Second and Third Restatements: Or, the Expulsion of the Substantial Factor Test," in Infantino & Zervogianni (eds) (n 1) 68–83.

[27] With the demise of the phrase "substantial factor," the but-for test and the scope of the risk theory (on which see below, section 2.2.2, in this chapter), are now the appropriate legal standards against which to determine actual causation and the scope of liability problem, respectively: see §§ 26 and 29 of the Restatement Third of Torts—PEH.

known as DES (the acronym of "diethylstilbestrol"), a plaintiff unable to identify the manufacturer of the product that caused her injury can recover on a proportional basis from each of the manufacturers that might have supplied the product.[28] The "market share liability" theory has been pleaded by plaintiffs seeking compensation for injuries allegedly caused by asbestos, tobacco, handguns, lead-based paint, latex gloves, blood clotting factors, and many other products.[29] Yet, the theory has had virtually no application beyond the DES cases, and even its application to DES claims has been vigorously contested in many states.[30] Further, the original DES cases featured an unusual set of conditions that are rarely seen in combination outside of that context, such as: (1) the existence of reasons unrelated to the plaintiffs that rendered evidence of product identification unavailable; (2) the ability of the plaintiffs to bring before the court a group of defendants that occupied (most of) the market of the product; (3) the availability of at least some reliable data on market share; and (4) the fact that the products sold by the defendants were generic and fungible[31] in terms of their design specifications, their manufacture, and their propensity to cause the same illness among differently situated victims.[32] Because of the "declining significance of the

[28] Goldberg, Sebok, Kendrick, & Zipursky (n 8) 319–331.

[29] Goldberg, Sebok, Kendrick, & Zipursky (n 8) 328–330. European courts too have confronted DES cases, but have ended up establishing defendants' collective liability on the basis of different doctrines. Cf the Dutch opinion of Hoge Raad 9 October 1992, NJB 1994, 535, where collective liability was grounded upon art 6:99 BW (on which see above, n 7; for a comment to the decision, see Ewoud Hondius, "A Dutch DES Case: Pharmaceutical Producers Jointly and Severally Liable" (1994) 2 ERPL 409) with the French decisions Cass civ 24 September 2009 (two opinions), D 2010, 49, and Cass civ 28 January 2010, Resp civ assur 2010, comm 80, which established defendants' joint and several liability by reversing the burden of proof of causation, thereby imposing upon the defendants the burden of proving that they did not cause plantiffs' injuries (on this case law, see Patrice Jourdain, "Une nouvelle présomption de causalité, au profit cette fois des victimes du DES ou distilbène" (2010) D 111).

[30] Cf *Sutowski v Eli Lilly & Co*, 696 NE2d 187 (Ohio 1998); *Wood v Eli Lilly & Co*, 38 F3d 510 (SD Fla 1994); *Gorman v Abbott Laboratories*, 599 A2d 1364 (RI 1991); *Tidler v Eli Lilly & Co*, 271 US App DC 163, 851 F2d 418 (DC Cir 1988); *Mulcahy v Eli Lilly & Co*, 386 NW2d 67 (Iowa 1986); *Zaft v Eli Lilly & Co*, 676 SW2d 241 (Mo 1984); *Mizell v Eli Lilly & Co*, 526 FSupp 589 (DSC 1981); *Namm v Charles E Frosst & Co, Inc*, 178 NJ Super 19, 427 A2d 1121 (App Div 1981); *Morton v Abbott Laboratories*, 538 FSupp 593 (MD Fla 1981).

[31] *Sindell v Abbott Laboratories*, 607 P2d 924 (Cal 1980).

[32] Goldberg, Kendrick, Sebok, & Zipursky (n 8) 329. Perusing state courts' decisions accepting market share liability in DES cases, one can find several nuances of the theory. For instance, in *Sindell v Abbott Labs* (607 P2d 924, 928 (Cal 1980)), the California Supreme Court held that the burden of proof that the drug did not cause the plaintiffs' injury was to be placed on every and each defendant. From any defendant who could not disprove causation the plaintiff could recover a percentage of damages equal to the defendant's percentage share of the "relevant" market for DES. *Sindell* left unresolved the question of what the "relevant" market was, and how the market share was to be determined. Relying on *Sindell*, Florida courts specified that market share should be calculated at the geographically narrowest level, such as the state or preferably the county in which the plaintiff's mother purchased DES. They went so far as to affirm that, "[w]here it can be determined that the DES ingested by the mother was purchased from a particular pharmacy, that pharmacy should be

issue,"[33] there was little reason for the drafters of the Restatement Third—PEH—to draw specific rules on market share liability within the provisions on causation. The doctrine thus goes unmentioned in the Restatement Third.

The theories and rules just mentioned are supposed to refine or substitute the condicio sine qua non/but-for test in cases of uncertain or overdetermined causation. But even in cases in which the appreciation of causation is affected neither by the uncertainty of the evidentiary framework, nor by the overdetermination of causes, the condicio sine qua non/but-for test is well known for its limits. Such a test is generally unable to screen out consequences which are too remote in time and space from the defendant's activity, or more closely related to some other intervening factor, or too unusual and freakish to link their occurrence of the defendant's conduct. The latter circumstances are therefore targeted by the so-called second stage of the causation inquiry.

2.2. Second Stage: Law and Policy

Once the first step is completed, courts are expected to assess whether the link between the conduct and the ensuing loss is sufficiently close, and which of the but-for conditions of the plaintiff's harm could also be deemed to be its causes in a legal sense.

There is no generalized answer as to the question of how such a task should be performed. In the jurisdictions under review, many theories have arisen in the attempt to develop a formula applicable in every case in which causation is at issue. These theories are dubbed with a variety of labels: adequacy, reasonable foreseeability, scope of the rule, sphere of risk, directness

considered the relevant market" (*Conley v Boyle Drug Co*, 570 So2d 275, 284 (Fla 1990)). To the contrary, Michigan courts decided that the notion of relevant market refers to the national market rather than its share of the market in the state in which the plaintiff's mother resided at the time of ingesting DES. Further, for Michigan courts defendants who were unable to exonerate themselves were subject (not to market share, but) to joint and several liability (*Abel v Eli Lily & Co*, 418 Mich 311, 343 NW2d 164 (Mich 1984), claiming to apply rules on actions in concert, and not the market share liability theory). Courts in New York accepted their Michigan colleagues' view that the relevant market was the national market for DES (*Hymowitz v Eli Lilly & Co*, 539 NE2d 1069, 1078 (NY 1989)). But New York judges also created an irrebuttable presumption on causation under which each defendant was held liable to each DES plaintiff in proportion to its share of the national market, the only possible exculpation for the manufacturer being the proof that it did not actually participate in the national marketing of DES for pregnancy use (*Hymowitz v Eli Lilly & Co*).

[33] Restatement Third of Torts—Physical and Emotional Harm, § 28, cmt p.

of the damage, and so forth. Some of these labels are most often used in the common law jurisdictions, while others take the forefront of the debate in the civil law world. We will briefly summarize the state of the art of these formulas, starting with the civil law tradition.

2.2.1. Civil Law

A theory that is broadly referred to in civil law countries,[34] especially in negligence cases, is the foreseeability theory, according to which the injured party can be compensated only if the harm she incurred was but-for caused by, and foreseeable to the defendant. As is immediately clear from the definition, this theory tends to overlap causation assessments with those centered on the elements of fault and damage. Foreseeability is indeed a multifaceted notion, flexible enough to be employed: to draw the causation perimeter, to substantiate or deny findings of fault, to determine the extent of the damage to be compensated. Needless to say, no matter for what purpose is foreseeability called into play, the mainstream attitude is to expunge from it any subjective approach (according to which what should be assessed is the foreseeability of the harm by the alleged tortfeasor). Instead, the test is understood as an objective one under which causation can be established if a reasonable person in the tortfeasor's position would have foreseen the harm at the time of the wrong.[35] Under this test it becomes immaterial what the alleged tortfeasor personally did or could foresee.[36]

Equally widespread across civilian jurisdictions[37] (and across liability regimes) is the recourse to the theory which relies upon the driving force of the couple of adjectives "direct"/"indirect" in order to include/exclude the recoverability of losses classified accordingly.[38] Under this theory, the defendant can only be considered the cause of that harm which is the immediate consequence of her activity. She cannot be held liable for indirect consequences, even though they were but-for caused by her activity. The

[34] A formal exception is France, where art 1231–3 of the Civil Code (according to which, when the breach of contract is unintentional, damages are recoverable only for losses which were foreseeable at the time of the conclusion of the contract) is—in principle—held not to be applicable to causation issues in tort law disputes. See for all Quézel-Ambrunaz (n 4) 452. As to common law jurisdictions, see below, section 2.3.

[35] Honoré (n 1) 56.

[36] The limits within which the "objective" test may prove useful are illustrated: see Chapter II, sections 9–12.

[37] The theory is close to the English and American notions of "remoteness of damage" and "proximate cause": see below, section 2.3.

[38] Honoré (n 1) 40.

argument in favor of this way of limiting liability is presented as follows: (i) the initial harm caused by the tortfeasor's conduct may often occasion (i.e., it may be a condition of) a further harm or a third party's wrongful behavior; (ii) there may then be a long sequence of harms related to one another as condition and consequence; (iii) yet, liability must stop somewhere, and should not extend to harm which, besides the tortfeasor's conduct, have been caused by some other act or event.[39]

By contrast, the "adequacy" or "adequate cause theory," another test commonly employed in continental Europe,[40] is based on a probability assessment.[41] It can be formulated either in a positive or in a negative way. According to the former, the conduct of the defendant is the adequate cause of the damage if it significantly increased the objective probability that that damage occurred (that is to say, if an average observer, under the circumstances in which the wrong occurred, would have predicted the occurrence of the damage). Under the negative formulation, the defendant's behavior is not the adequate cause of the damage if (according to the same average observer) that behavior could produce the harm only under particularly unique and quite improbable circumstances that substantially deviate from the predictable and normal course of events.[42]

More openly rooted in policy arguments[43] is the "scope of the rule" theory, which is widely applied in Germany, less common in Italy, and rarely, if ever, mentioned by French scholars and judges.[44] According to this formula, plaintiff may recover only for damages deemed to be within the range of consequences whose occurrence the infringed rule is meant to avoid. Such a theory displays its highest relevance in legal systems, such as the German one, where the infringement of the "*Schutz eines anderen bezweckenden Gesetzes*" ("a statute intended for the protection of other": § 823 BGB II, 1st sentence) is a statutory requirement to be met to get recovery (beyond the narrow limits marked by § 823 I). Even though this doctrine can be seen as a

[39] Honoré (n 1) 41.

[40] Quézel-Ambrunaz (n 4) 73–81; Galand-Carval (n 17) 54–55; Mauro Bussani, *L'illecito civile* (ESI 2020) 649–650; Markesinis, Bell, & Janssen (n 6) 52–53; Magnus (n 6) 65. The test remains essentially unknown to common law jurisdictions.

[41] Honoré (n 1) 49; Walter van Gerven, Pierre Larouche, & Jeremy Lever, *Cases, Materials and Text on National, Supranational and International Tort Law* (Hart 2000) 453.

[42] van Gerven, Larouche, Lever (n 41) 397. The test applies under no-fault liability regimes as well: Honoré (n 1) 55, 146–147.

[43] Honoré (n 1) 60.

[44] Cf Markesinis, Bell, & Janssen (n 6) 68; Magnus (n 6) 65; Trimarchi (n 5) 67–68, 70, fn 26, 73, fn 29; Quézel-Ambrunaz (n 4) 141–153.

useful device for German plaintiffs to overcome the need of proving the infringement of an absolute right, its reverse side is that it easily allows courts to reject a claim because, in their view, the plaintiff's loss, or the plaintiff herself, are not covered by the umbrella of the statutory rule(s) breached by the defendant.[45]

Still different is the line of reasoning based on the concept of "sphere of the risk" (this test too is frequently employed in Germany and less commonly relied upon in France and Italy).[46] According to this theory, an activity may be deemed the cause of an event when the latter represents the realization of the risks typically associated with that activity. In the negative, the theory excludes that an activity may be considered as the cause of an event when the latter can be seen more as the realization of a "general risk associated with existence" than as the realization of the particular risk associated with the defendant's activity. The consideration for the "general risk" factor stems from the assumption that everyone must bear the risks that are ordinarily run in her own life and business, and cannot simply pass it onto others. It follows that whenever the occurrence of damage represents no more than the realization of a risk which is deemed to be one that lies within the plaintiff's sphere, the latter would not recover. For instance, a policeman should bear the ordinary risks related to the pursuit of criminals.[47] It is only if the fugitive, by the features of his fight, has "in a reprehensible manner provoked the pursuer to a reaction which endangers himself,"[48] that the ensuing harm suffered by the plaintiff could be thought to lie outside the sphere of a policeman's ordinary risk and included into the sphere of the risk created by the criminal's escape.

2.2.2. Common Law

The common law approaches to the second stage are basically the same ones we just reviewed in the civil law world, although they are sometimes known by different labels.

Common lawyers are familiar with the foreseeability theory, according to which causation, in particular in negligence cases, can be established only if the defendant should have anticipated the occurrence of the harm.

[45] Infantino & Zervogianni (n 7) 605.

[46] Markesinis, Bell, & Janssen (n 6) 66; Magnus (n 6) 77; Quézel-Ambrunaz (n 4) 421–427; Pietro Trimarchi, *Rischio e responsabilità oggettiva* (Giuffrè 1971) 9–12.

[47] BGH 13 January 1976, NJW 1976, 568.

[48] BGH 12 March 1996, BGHZ 132, 164, reported in Markesinis, Bell, & Janssen (n 6) 357, 359.

Like in civil law countries, the test is met only if a reasonable person in the defendant's position would have foreseen the plaintiff's damage as a consequence of her activity. Moreover, like in civil law, in common law foreseeability may be employed for many purposes: to solve causal problems, to evaluate defendant's carelessness, to assess the duty relationship between her and the plaintiff.[49]

Equally widespread is the recourse to the couple of adjectives "proximate"/ "remote[50] (the equivalent of the civil law "direct"/"indirect" couple). On a superficial reading, the language of "proximate" and "remote" suggests that liability should attach to carelessness causing injury only if the former is sufficiently close to the latter in time or space, and it should be excluded when there is no temporal or spatial proximity between the carelessness and the injury.[51] However, notions of spatial or temporal distance do not accurately convey the substance of the proximate cause requirement, at least as it is invoked by modern courts. Many injuries complained of in negligence are compensated although they result from careless acts that took place hundreds or even thousands of miles from the locus of the plaintiff's injury, or that took place years before the plaintiffs' injury emerged.[52] In other terms, the proximate cause/remoteness of damage theory is to be mainly understood as a limit to the extent to which it is appropriate or fair to trace backward the causes of harm[53]—thus eventually revisiting at the "second" stage the results produced by the but-for test at the "first" stage.

Within the common law framework, a special attention deserves a set of rules that mostly apply in the United States.

The "scope of the risk" rule was "codified" in the Restatement Second of Torts, § 442B (as regards intervening causes),[54] and today it is embodied

[49] See above, section 3.1 in this chapter, as well as Hart & Honoré (n 1) 255; Honoré (n 1) 56–57; see also Schwartz (n 2) 123; John G Fleming, "The Passing of Polemis" (1961) 39 Can Bar R 489, 519, 522; Glanville Williams, "The Risk Principle" (1961) 77 LQR 179, 190–191; Frederick Pollock, "Liability for Consequences" (1922) 38 LQR 165; Joseph H Beale, "The Proximate Consequences of an Act" (1920) 33 Harv LR 633.

[50] As said above, in section 2 in this chapter, the American legal language speaks of "proximate cause," while in England the focus is on "remoteness of damage."

[51] Goldberg, Kendrick, Sebok, & Zipursky (n 8) 337.

[52] Think, for example, of the famous case *MacPherson v Buick Motor Co*, 217 NY 382 (NY 1916) (on which see also Chapter VIII, section 2); or think of *Aldridge v Goodyear Tire & Rubber Co*, 34 FSupp 2d 1010 (D Md 1999), where the fact that the defendant's employees developed various diseases many years after their retirement did not prevent the Court from finding a "proximate" relationship between their diseases and the use of toxic chemicals in the defendant's factory.

[53] Honoré (n 1) 4, 45; more recently, Goldberg, Kendrick, Sebok, & Zipursky (n 8) 336.

[54] Restatement Second of Torts, § 442B:

> [w]here the negligent conduct of the actor creates or increases the risk of a particular harm and is a substantial factor in causing that harm, the fact that the harm is brought

in § 29 of the Restatement Third of Torts—PEH.[55] Under this theory—be it strict or based on fault—"an actor should be held liable only for harm that was among the potential harms—the risks—that made the actor's conduct tortious."[56] As to the risks that are to be regarded as having been introduced by the defendant, the answer is necessarily framed in terms of probability. Only unusual and exceptional risks, and risks stemming from unexpected intervening factors, may be excluded from the defendant's sphere of liability, and then only under very specific rules that limit the general principal of the scope of the risk adopted by the Restatement.[57]

3. The Two Stages and the Role of the Fact-Finder

There is a good deal of internal overlapping between the causation formulas employed within both civil law and common law jurisdictions. The comparative law issue to be highlighted is neither the difficulty of identifying the area of application of each formula, nor any diversity depending on national views of the technicalities attached to each theory. The point is that any attempt to draw clear boundaries between the above-mentioned formulas, or to find out which formula outperforms the others in the selection of legally relevant causes, has so far been prompted either by the desire of promoting one test over the others, or by a Leibnizian aspiration of rules that could be mechanically applied to achieve predictable results. Desire and aspiration are foreign to the present inquiry. Rather, what is to be underlined is that traditional approaches to causation originate from a common trans-Atlantic attitude that, hegemonic at its normative core, often fails to fulfill its own promises. Such a failure involves both the two-stage distinction and the explanatory value assigned to tests and theories. We will deal in this section with the limits of the customary partition of the causation inquiry into two

> about through the intervention of another force does not relieve the actor of liability, except where the harm is intentionally caused by a third person and is not within the scope of the risk created by the actor's conduct.

55 Restatement Third of Torts—PEH, § 29:

> [a]n actor's liability is limited to those physical harms that result from the risks that made the actor's conduct tortious.

56 Restatement Third of Torts—PEH, § 29 cmt c. See also Honoré (n 1) 58. This is also known as the "risk rule."

57 Restatement Third of Torts—PEH, § 29 cmt o ("manner of harm") and cmt p ("extent of harm) and § 34 ("Intervening Acts and Superseding Causes") and see Honoré (n 1) 60.

stages, and will devote the following sections to the analysis of the challenges that tort law adjudication poses to causation formulas.

Under the division of causation assessment in two phases lies the assumption that the first stage of inquiry is simply technical or evidentiary, while the second one is truly legal, and fueled by policy-based arguments.[58] Yet in many cases such an assumption appears ill-founded. On the one hand, carrying out any factual inquiry entails (different technical and/or policy-driven ways of) sifting the potentially legal causes from the unlimited sequences of physical correlations. On the other hand, issues that come under the rubric of legal cause are often affected by both considerations for the relations between particular events in time and space,[59] and by considerations of policy, such as which of the parties is best placed to shift the loss in question, or which outcome will best promote loss prevention in that context in the future.[60]

The uneasiness of isolating two different moments in the assessment of causation is further made clear by the way in which American and European courts put the distinction at work. On both sides of the Atlantic it is up to the judge to draw the line between facts and law. But in the United States the divide between factual and legal issues retains a special meaning: the latter are for the judge only, while the former are for the jury whenever the judge thinks that reasonable people could differ as to what the material facts of the case are.[61] With regard to causation, this implies that the jury would usually determine issues of factual causation as well as issues of proximate cause, insofar as they involve disputed facts, while matters of law always rest upon the judge. What should be stressed, however, is that the application of such principles is a matter of judicial discretion. It is always up to the judge to disentangle factual from questions of law, and to determine which facts the jury, as a matter of law, should be allowed to decide. Actually, what often happens

[58] Richard W Wright, "Acts and Omissions as Positive and Negative Causes," in Jason W Neyers, Erika Chamberlain, & Stephen GA Pitel (eds), *Emerging Issues in Tort Law* (Hart 2007) 287, 293; David A Fisher, "Insufficient Causes" (2005–2006) 94 Ky LJ 276, 290; for similar observations as far as continental Europe is concerned, see von Bar (n 10) 437–440.

[59] In this perspective, Richard W Wright has argued that many proximate cause cases can be solved with a refined understanding of (f)actual cause: see, eg, Richard W Wright, "Causation, Statistical Probability, and the Burden of the Proof" (2008) 41 Loy LA LR 1295; Richard W Wright, "Causation, Responsibility, Risk, Probability, Naked Statistics, and Proof: Pruning the Bramble Bush by Clarifying the Concepts" (1988) 73 Iowa LR 1001.

[60] See Simon Deakin & Zoe Adams, *Markesinis and Deakin's Tort Law* (8th edn, OUP 2019) 202–205.

[61] Goldberg, Kendrick, Sebok, & Zipursky (n 8) 273–274, 283, 352.

is that judges carefully select which causation issues to present to the jury, or even broaden the "law" category, so as to limit the scope of juries' role.[62]

In continental Europe (where there is no jury at all) and in England (where the right to jury trial, once omnipresent in tort law trials, is preserved only exceptionally[63]), it is for the judge to act as both fact-finder and law-giver. This by no means renders the distinction between factual and legal causation on the Eastern side of the Atlantic less relevant than on its Western one. As a first approximation, the rule in Europe is, like in the United States,[64] that only errors of law may be reviewed by upper courts.[65] This implies that in principle factual causation findings are unreviewable, while legal causation judgments can be reversed on appeal. The point is that everywhere upper courts show a great deal of flexibility in setting out the divide between facts and law, and are prone to describe factual causation issues as legal ones, and to review on appeal even decisions where the trial judge's factual views are supported by evidence.[66]

To sum up, the picture that emerges is one where both American and European judges—trial and upper courts—are well-accustomed to loose interpretations of the line between fact and law, according to what is suggested by the widely varying circumstances of each case. A similar flexibility is noticeable as far as the application of causation formulas is concerned. As we are going to see in the next sections, when confronted with real tort law cases, causation formulas seem unable to explain the whole range of solutions that should be grounded upon them. In innumerable combinations of circumstances any of the fixed, pre-constituted formulas fails to determine a conclusive or unique answer. We are about to show how but-for conditions,

[62] Goldberg, Kendrick, Sebok, & Zipursky (n 8) 273–274, 283, 352–353; Ann Scales, "'Nobody Broke It, It Just Broke'. Causation as an Instrument of Obfuscation and Oppression," in David Engel & Michael McCann (eds), *Fault Lines: Tort Law as a Cultural Practice* (Stanford University Press 2009) 268, 273.

[63] According to s 69 of the Supreme Court Act 1981, trial by jury can be held for hearing claims of fraud, malicious prosecution and false imprisonment. Trial by jury has been for a long time the rule in defamation cases, but s 11 of the Defamation Act of 2013 abolished the presumption in favor of the jury.

[64] Patrick J Kelley, "Restating Duty, Breach and Proximate Cause in Negligence Law Law: Descriptive Theory and the Rule of Law" (2001) 54 Vand LR 1039, 1054.

[65] Cf Markesinis, John Bell, André Janssen (n 6) 416; Christophe Quézel-Ambrunaz, "France, Case 4," in Infantino & Zervogianni (eds) (n 1) 242, 243; Jean-Sébastien Borghetti, "Litigation on Hepatits B Vaccination and Demyelinating Diseases in France," in Martín-Casals & Papayannis (n 21) 11, 18–19; Galand-Carval (n 17) 54; Yvonne Lambert-Faivre, "De la poursuite à la contribution: Quelques arcanes de la causalité" (1992) D 311. For the standards of review in common law jurisdictions, see, eg, William V Dorsaneo III, Judges, Juries, and Reviewing Courts (2000) 53 SMU LR 1497–1537 (on Texas's standards of review); Honoré (n 1) 20.

[66] See the authors cited above, n 65.

risk, adequacy, force majeure, multiple causes, may be used to justify seemingly irreconcilable results, and end up appearing as open notions, couched in language so vague as to permit courts to attach to them very different meanings.

3.1. The Limits of First-Stage Formulas

Let us start with considering the so-called first stage.

It is quite a common remark that the but-for/condicio sine qua non test, albeit universally considered as the factual basis of any causation theory, may produce outcomes that are regarded as unacceptable.[67]

First of all, the factual test displays a constant tendency to either exceedingly expand liability or miss the liability target. As some have stressed, the test, taken at its facial value, proves inapt to distinguish

> between causative and non-causative events: all events which cannot be "imagined away" without the removal of the subsequent "result" must be treated as being equally causative. In a world in which almost every event is linked with every other, every event must necessarily be viewed as the cause of every other.[68]

To be sure, the actual relevance of this critique may be countered by the observation that the overreaching tendency of the but-for test/condicio sine qua non is restrained by plaintiff's claims and allegations, which fix the boundaries of the judicial inquiry. What cannot be denied, however, is that the but-for/condicio sine qua non test, as already mentioned in section 2.1, fails to work in a number of critical circumstances and thus falls short of its pretended hegemony over the factual dimension of causation.

[67] Richard A Epstein, "Causation and Corrective Justice: A Reply to Two Critics" (1979) 8 J Leg Stud 477, 478 (1979); Spier & Haazen (n 10) 151; Hubert Groutel, "L'implication du véhicule dans la loi du 5 juillet 1985 (à propos des arrêts rendus par la 2° chambre civile, le 21 juillet 1986) » (1987) D 1, 2. By "unacceptable" we mean, as usual, the outcomes that are considered unfit to the values traditionally considered the yardsticks against which social facts are to be measured in a given community, at a given time.

[68] von Bar (n 10) 459. As Powells J put it in *Atlantic Coast Line Railway Company v Daniels* (8 Ga App 775, 778–779, 70 SE 203, 205 (Ga 1911)), to make such as a standard (that if the cause had not existed the effect would not have occurred) the basis of legal responsibility would soon prove unsatisfactory: for a reductio ad absurdum may be promptly established by calling to mind that if the injured person had never been born, the injury would not have happened.

The best example of the practical shortcomings of the test comes from the cases called of "duplicative causation,"[69] "overdetermined result,"[70] "combined forces,"[71] or (in the Restatement Third of Torts' language:) "multiple sufficient causes."[72] To illustrate: where A and B, using the same guns and the same kind of bullets, both shoot at C and hit him, causing him fatal injuries, the but-for/condicio sine qua non test would impose no liability on the hunters, notwithstanding that both of them hit C. The reason is that, had one of them not fired, C would have been killed anyway by the other's bullets. Yet, in these cases, many think that leaving the loss where it fell (upon an innocent victim) would be more unfair than making both the hunters pay. This explains why courts in most legal systems, when confronted with duplicative causation, get rid of the but-for/condicio sine qua non test, and hold all the defendants liable.[73]

A related and yet different situation which shows how the but-for/condicio sine qua non test might fail in practice comes from a variant of the hunting case described above. Take the same case of A and B who, using the same guns and the same kind of bullets, shoot at C and kill him, but imagine that C's death is actually caused by one bullet only, which might have been that of either A or B. If the origin of the bullet remains uncertain, the but-for/condicio sine qua non test simply cannot work. Nonetheless, with regard to these cases, many of the legal systems under review have struggled to develop rules for affirming both A's and B's liability—after all, once again, making the innocent defendant pay is less bad than let the innocent plaintiff pay the price of the evidence conundrum.

In some countries, civil codes provide a rule that can be stretched to this point. This is the case, for example, of § 830 I of the German Civil Code, which states:

> [i]f more than one person has caused damage by a jointly committed tort, then each of them is responsible for the damage. The same rule applies if it

[69] Richard W Wright, "Once More into the Bramble Bush: Duty, Causal Contribution, and the Extent of Legal Responsibility" (2001) 54 Vand LR 1071, 1098.

[70] *Boeing Co v Cascade Corp*, 207 F3d 1177, 1185 (9th Cir 2000).

[71] Wex S Malone, "Ruminations on Cause-in-Fact" (1956) 9 Stan LR 60, 88.

[72] Restatement Thirds of Torts—PEH, § 27, cmt a.

[73] As far as European countries (including England) are concerned, see Spier & Haazen (n 10) 128–130; von Bar (n 10) 440; Hart & Honoré (n 1) 239–240. In the United States, see *Anderson v Minneapolis, St P & S St Marie Railway*, 179 NW45 (Minn 1920), as well as § 432 (2) of the Restatement Second of Torts and § 27 of the Restatement Third of Torts—PEH, mentioned above, section 2.1.

cannot be established which of several persons involved caused the damage by his act."[74]

But also in jurisdictions where there is no provision that can be straightforwardly applied to the circumstances of the case, the defendants can be held jointly liable. In cases like the "two hunters" above, French courts have long imposed joint and several liability upon all the defendants who fired against the victim, no matter which one of them concretely fired the injurious pellet, by relying upon the assumption that they were participating in a dangerous activity. Such participation was either considered a proof of negligence per se,[75] or it allowed them to impose upon all of them strict liability for the use of the object which actually caused the damage.[76] The same reasoning was applied not only to hunting cases, but also to cases where some children took part in a dangerous game,[77] and where acts of violence are committed by a group of young people.[78]

The same arguments, and the same outcomes, found their way in the American case *Summers v. Tice*,[79] in which the plaintiff was shot by one bullet which was fired by one of two defendants, each of whom was found careless in aiming his gun in the plaintiff's direction. The court adopted the solution of reversing the burden of proof, so that each defendant had to show that he did not cause the injury. The *Summers v. Tice* then opened the way to further developments, such as the 1980 California Supreme Court's decision *Sindell v. Abbots Laboratories*,[80] which, in the quite unique circumstances of the DES litigation, held that plaintiffs unable to identify which manufacturer of a defective product caused their injury could recover on a proportional basis from each of the manufacturers that might have supplied the product.

Even in jurisdictions where there are no precedents of this kind[81] or where plaintiffs' claims of this sort have been rejected for lack of causation (such as in Italy[82]), chances are that plaintiffs could nonetheless receive compensation.

[74] See also, along similar lines, art 926 of the Greek Civil Code and arts 6:166 I and 6:99 of the Dutch *BW*.

[75] Cass civ 18 May 1955, D 1955, 520.

[76] CA Versailles, 20 January 1994, Rec D 1994, 104.

[77] Cass civ 16 January 1991, JCP 1991, IV, 97; Cass civ 9 February 1983, Gaz Pal 1983, II, 215 (playing with torches and candles); Cass civ 6 March 1968, D 1968, somm, 90 (throwing stones).

[78] Cass civ 2 April 1997, D 1997, IR, 105.

[79] 119 P2d 1 (Cal 1948).

[80] *Sindell v Abbott Laboratories*, 607 P2d 924 (Cal 1980). See also above, section 2.1, in this chapter.

[81] As to England, WV Horton Rogers, "Causation under English Law," in Spier (n 1) 39, 50.

[82] Constitutional Court 4 March 1992, no 79, Riv dir sport 1992, 73.

In England, although under a different set of circumstances of causal uncertainty, the House of Lords held that, in a case in which a worker contracted a mesothelioma because he was exposed to asbestos dust for long periods of time by three different employers, the latter were all jointly and severally liable for the worker's death, even if it could not be ascertained when exactly the worker inhaled the asbestos fiber that triggered the mesothelioma.[83] In Italy, when it became clear that courts were reluctant to refine the condicio sine qua non test, it was provided by statute that victims of hunting accidents, whose author remains unknown, have a right to an indemnity to be paid by a special compensation fund for hunting accidents financed by the insurance companies, thereby mandating compulsory hunting liability insurance.[84] The but-for test might be the queen of causation formulas, but tort law systems know how to dethrone it when it does not work properly.

3.2. The Sensitivity of Second-Stage Formulas

Second-stage doctrines do not survive their encounters with the real world any better. In spite of their aspiration to convey principles applicable to any tort law case, none of the formulas mentioned above, sections 2.1–2.2, seems able to explain the whole universe of causation judgments.[85] Some of them only fit specific circumstances; others cover a good deal of cases, but are of no use in the remaining ones; most of them break apart when facing intentional torts.[86] Most important of all, even within their own realms, causation formulas may be helpful to justify, against identical (or almost identical) factual patterns, diverging, if not opposite, conclusions. A couple of examples for each formula will suffice here to show us what these formulas actually do, and what they actually do not do.[87]

A caveat, before proceeding. Causation formulas satisfy judges' necessity to qualify their decisions so as to make the judgments acceptable by their

[83] *Fairchild v Glenhaven Funeral Services Ltd* [2003] 1 AC 32. See also *Fitzgerald v Lane* [1989] AC 328, where the English Court of Appeal gave support to the view that, in a car accident case, if both defendants cause an aggregate of different injuries and their individual contribution cannot be established, each defendant may be held liable for the whole.

[84] See art 25 of the Law no 157 of 1992, now replaced by arts 302–304 of the legislative decree no 205 of 2009. On these developments, see Busnelli & Comandé (n 16) 90.

[85] Magnus (n 6) 67–68; Trimarchi (n 46) 304; Stapleton (n 10) 966–967; Honoré (n 1) 66.

[86] Mauro Bussani, "Intention et lien de causalité dans le droit comparé de la responsabilité civile (la fable très peu convenue de la malice qui accroche)," in *De tous horizons* (n 10) 459.

[87] For further illustrations, see Infantino & Zervogianni (n 7) 601–609.

peers, the other legal actors of the system, as well as by the parties. But in common law countries, where judges are used to give open, often elaborate, accounts of the policy reasons which have dictated their conclusions, the flexible significance of causation formulas is more easily acknowledged than in civil law jurisdictions. In the latter, judges' legalistic, dry, and impersonal reliance on causation formulas enables them to signify (to peers, legal actors, parties) the existence of technical, insurmountable limits to their discretion. In this perspective, causation principles may become nothing more than a façade, a device that helps formulate judicial conclusions but does not actually fully explain them.

3.2.1. Civil Law

Let us review the tests most commonly employed in the civil law jurisdictions under analysis: foreseeability, direct/indirect consequences, adequacy, "scope of the rule," and "sphere of the risk."

Foreseeability. As to the civil law version of the foreseeability theory, useful illustrations of the malleability of the notion are offered by the so-called "ricochet" claims for economic loss (ricochet economic loss arises when physical damage is done to the property or the body of one person, and that loss in turn results in economic detriment for another person[88]).

For example, when a wife decides to retire from her job to look after her husband, who has been badly injured by a negligent driver, the Italian Supreme Court held that the the woman's choice to give up her own job "for family solidarity, to look after her husband" is nothing but the foreseeable outcome of the defendant's behavior, since "any reckless driver should expect that the victim will be a father or a mother, and that his wrong will therefore affect the lives of people other than his direct victim".[89]

In other cases, however, the suspect that the claimant is motivated more by the desire of making a profit out of the incident than by the true suffering of a loss, or the belief that she is trying to burden the defendant with costs that might have been easily avoided, may impact on the understanding of what is ordinarily foreseeable to negligent drivers. Ten years before the opinion just mentioned, the Italian Supreme Court denied compensation to a banker who

[88] Mauro Bussani & Vernon V Palmer, "The Notion of Pure Economic Loss and Its Setting," in Mauro Bussani & Vernon V Palmer (eds), *Pure Economic Loss in Europe* (CUP 2003) 10. See also Chapter VI, section 3.

[89] Cass 2 February 2001, no 1516, Giur it 2001, 2032; similarly, in France, see Cass civ 27 February 1991, JCP 1991, IV, 162.

left his job shortly after a car accident rendered his wife partially disabled and depressed, finding that the banker's decision was not a foreseeable consequence of the accident.[90] Similarly, in a French case, where a driver killed a young woman in a car accident, therefore forcing her husband to give up his well-paid expatriate position in order to take care of their child, the French Supreme Court concluded that the driver could not be held liable for the loss of the husband's employment. According to the Court, the husband's decision to abandon his work was an unforeseeable consequence of the driver's act, and, as such, it fell outside the scope of the latter's liability.[91]

Indirect/direct consequences. Equally ambiguous may be the meaning of the "direct"/"indirect" consequences rule. Suffice it to compare the following two opinions, one French and one German, on the recoverability of the economic losses caused by traffic jams.

In the French case, the City of Marseille claimed damages because its buses had been immobilized in a traffic jam caused by a car accident, and this diminished the revenues of the city's transportation company. The French Supreme Court considered the city's loss neither hypothetical nor indirect, and held the driver who caused the car accident liable.[92] What at Marseille seems close, however, may appear remote in Bremen, especially if the contribution of a number of unidentifiable persons intervenes between the defendant's act and the occurrence of the harm. In a well-known German case, a lorry of the NATO armed forces caused an accident on a street of Bremen, thereby blocking the way for other cars. To bypass the hindrance, several car drivers had to climb on a sidewalk, and the repeated action ended up substantially damaging the sidewalk itself, owned by the Bremen City. The latter sued the Federal Republic of Germany, which was obliged to assume liability, under the provisions of the NATO Armed Forces Statute, for damage done by NATO armed forces as if it had been done by German forces. No compensation was granted, though. According to the *Bundesgerichtshof*, the city's costs were a too remote consequence of the initial negligence to be recovered.[93]

Adequacy. As regards the adequacy theory, it is useful to compare two cases where the point at issue was whether who causes a traffic accident

[90] Cass 7 January 1991, no 60, Foro it 1991, I, 459.

[91] Cass civ 3 October 1990, Bull civ 1990.II, 184; along similar lines, Cass civ 14 June 1995, Bull civ 1995.II, 187.

[92] Cass civ 28 April 1965, D 1965, 777.

[93] BGH 16 February 1972, NJW 1972, 904.

should be held liable for the death of a person injured in the accident, when the death occurs because of an illness contracted by the victim at the facility where she was hospitalized after the accident itself.

The first case is from Germany. A pedestrian was shot at his arm by a policeman aiming at an escaping criminal. The victim was taken to the hospital, and there he contracted influenza (quite widespread in the region, at that time), and died from complications relating to it. The deceased's wife sued the state as the policeman's employer to obtain compensation for his husband's death, and the German Supreme Court upheld her claim. In the German Supreme Court's view, the sequence of the events was plain: the shooting was a but-for cause of the victim's hospitalization; in the hospital, the victim was exposed to an enhanced risk of infection, which actually occurred; the infection led him to death. Since the flu and the infection were all normal consequences of the initial injury, the shooting was therefore considered as the adequate cause of the victim's death.[94]

Our second case follows similar factual patterns, but leads to a different result. In a French case, a driver was moving at a normal speed in a city street. At some point, he was suddenly blinded by the sun, and was therefore unable to see, and to avoid the impact with a pedestrian who was lawfully crossing the street. Being this a French case, in principle the car driver's liability could not be questioned because of the no-fault liability regime applying to car accidents.[95] The point is that, as a result of the accident, the victim had to be taken in a hospital, where she became infected with an unspecified "*maladie nosocomiale*" that killed her. Against the circumstances of the case, the Court of cassation thought that the consequences of the accident were out of proportion with the driver's conduct, and held that there was no adequate causal link between the former and the latter. The victim's death was therefore considered to be an exceptional fallout of the original car accident, rather than its adequate consequence.[96]

Scope of the rule. Similar inconsistencies can be found also in the implementation of the so-called "scope of the rule" theory, as it is shown by Italian

[94] RG 13 October 1922, RGZ 105, 26.

[95] As is well known, traffic accidents liability in France is strict. Under the law n° 85–677 of 5 July 1985 (the so-called *loi Badinter*), the holder of a motor vehicle is liable for all damages caused by her vehicle. Neither force majeure nor the conduct of a third party can be invoked against the victim. The only defense available to the defendant is proving that the accident was exclusively caused by the inexcusable fault of the victim herself.

[96] Cass crim 5 October 2004, Bull crim 2004, no 230. For further examples of how differently "adequacy" might be interpreted with regard to subsequent accidents cases such as the ones described in the text, see national answers to Case 9 in Infantino & Zervogianni (eds) (n 1) 380–404.

and German judicial responses to cable cases (where the defendant negligently cuts off the cable providing energy to a business entity, interrupting the latter's work). Local ways of intending the requirements for negligence liability, and the opportunity to allow recovery in tort of pure economic losses, may have a direct impact on the range of accidents falling under the scope of the rules breached by the defendants.[97]

In Italy, where in principle pure economic losses are recoverable under the general clause of art 2043 of the Civil Code, the Supreme Court had no problem in straightforwardly connecting a building company's violation of basic rules of diligence and caution in carrying out excavation works near electricity cables to the loss of profits suffered by a nearby factory, which had to stop as a result of the power cut.[98]

Things go differently in Germany. As we know, while § 823 I BGB in principle does not allow compensation for pure economic losses, the ancillary rule enshrined by § 823 II BGB gives extracontractual relevance to the (purely economic) losses which may occur because of the breach of "a statute that is intended to protect another person." German regulations on excavation works requiring builders to take all the necessary precautions to protect public equipment (such as electric cables) would not help the plaintiff when a building company negligently damages an electricity wire running underneath the soil, and thus interrupts the current used in the plaintiff's manufacturing business.[99] In a legal environment hostile to tortious recovery of pure economic losses, the latter regulations are read as rules enacted to protect the public order, rather than "affording electricity users a claim to compensation not otherwise provided for, all the more since it would lead to a great and intolerable extension of liability."[100]

Sphere of the risk. Judicial variability in interpreting the "sphere of the risk" theory can be well exemplified by two German "pursuit" cases. In these decisions, the issue is whether the fugitive created a socially unacceptable risk for the plaintiff, placing the latter in a situation where she felt called upon to act in a way which turned out to be detrimental to her own interests. Obviously, it is up to the courts to determine which risks are below,

[97] On the Italian and German approach to the issue of recoverability of pure economic losses, see Chapter VI, sections 5.2 and 5.3.

[98] Cass (Plenary) 24 June 1972, no 2135, Foro it 1973, I, 99 (discussing also other causation theories, such as the directness theory and the adequate cause test).

[99] BGH 8 June 1976, BGHZ 66, 388.

[100] BGH 8 June 1976, BGHZ 66, 388 (available in English in Markesinis, John Bell, André Janssen (n 6) 365; the quotation is from 367).

and which risks are above the threshold of reasonableness. The result is that outcomes are often incompatible with one another, as shown by the following two decisions from the *Bundesgerichtshof*.

In the first case a minor was arrested with his friend on suspicion of car break-ins and house thefts, and was immediately brought before the juvenile magistrate. As soon as the judicial examination ended, the boy tried to escape through a window about four meters high above the ground. A police officer ran after him, and fractured both his legs in the jump. The police, subrogated into the policeman's rights, sued the defendant for the costs, it incurred for its employee's medical treatment and salary. The BGH embraced the view that the minor's flight provoked the police officer's pursuit, which exposed him to a substantial, and higher-than usual risk of personal injury, and therefore held the boy liable.[101]

Under similar circumstances, the same formula led the BGH to the opposite conclusion. The German Supreme Court was confronted with the following case. The defendant was a nineteen-year-old boy, who was sought at his home by a police officer for the serving of a weekend detention. The boy escaped through a toilet window situated at the height of 4.05 meters above the ground, and the police officer leapt after him, fracturing his heel bone on impact with the asphalt yard. In the lawsuit that followed, the BGH held that the causation requirement was not met. According to the judges, the risk involved in a police officer's employment commitment covered the "normal" risk of injury during a pursuit and nothing in the case suggested that the pursuit increased the ordinary risk of injury confronted by the policeman.[102]

3.2.2. Common Law

The unpredictability of the second-stage test in the civilian world is paralleled by the results of the common law courts as to the notion of foreseeability, the proximity requirement, the "scope of the risk" doctrine.

Foreseeability. A good illustration of the multiple purposes that might be served by the notion of foreseeability comes from the comparison between two renowned English rulings on causation: *In re Polemis*[103] and the *Wagon Mound (No 1)*[104] (the latter being seen by a majority of English lawyers as

[101] BGH 12 March 1996, BGHZ 132, 164.
[102] BGH 13 January 1976, NJW 1976, 568.
[103] *In re Polemis & Furness, Withy & Co* [1921] 3 KB 560.
[104] *Overseas Tankship (UK) Ltd v. Morts Dock & Eng'r Co* (*The Wagon Mound No 1*) [1961] 1 All ER 404 (PC).

overruling the former[105]). Both the decisions deal with fire damage in maritime settings. In *Polemis*, the employees of a ship charterer negligently allowed a heavy plank to fall into the hold of the plaintiff's ship, where, unknown to the servants, there was petrol vapor. The plank ignited a spark and set fire to the vapor; the ship caught fire and burned. The claim of the ship's owner against the charterer succeeded. According to the House of Lords, it was immaterial that defendants could not reasonably have foreseen the destruction of the ship at the time of the negligence act of their employees, since it was enough that they could and should have foreseen that some harm likely as a "direct consequence" of their action.[106]

Forty years later, the Privy Council was called to hear the *Wagon Mound (No 1)*,[107] a case very similar to *Polemis*.[108] Here the crew of the ship *Wagon Mound*, while it was moored in Sydney harbor, carelessly released a large slick of furnace oil into the harbor. Workers at a nearby dock, known as Morts Dock, were repairing another ship named *Corrimal*. Their repairs involved the use of acetylene torches for welding. Upon becoming aware of the oil spill, the supervisor who worked for Morts Dock ordered his workers to suspend their activities, and inquired with the owner of the wharf at which the *Wagon Mound* was moored whether the oil in the harbor might ignite. Based on that discussion, the supervisor concluded that there was no risk of ignition, and ordered his men back to work. The next day, sparks from the welding operations ignited some debris floating in the water, which in turn ignited the oil, resulting in a fire that destroyed Morts Dock and *Corrimal*. In the action for negligence brought by the owners of Morts Dock against the owners of the *Wagon Mound*, the Privy Council rejected the claim. Arguing that "it is the foresight of the reasonable man which alone can determine responsibility,"[109] the court, per J. Simonds, concluded that the defendant, though she might have actually expected that the oil spill produced some adverse effect on the dock, could not be held liable for something that no reasonable person would have foreseen.

105 Among the many, see Hart & Honoré (n 1) 174.

106 *Re Polemis & Furness, Withy & Co* [1921] 3 *KB* 560.

107 *Overseas Tankship (UK) Ltd v. Morts Dock & Eng'r Co (The Wagon Mound No 1)* [1961] 1 All ER 404 (PC).

108 Arthur L Goodhart, "The Imaginary Necktie and the Rule of Re Polemis" (1952) 68 LQR 514, 529. Moreover, one should consider that in *Polemis*, but not in *The Wagon Mound*, the defendant was bound by contract to take care of the burned ship: see ibid at 519.

109 *Overseas Tankship (UK) Ltd v Morts Dock & Eng'r Co (The Wagon Mound No 1)* [1961] 1 All ER 404 (PC) (Viscount Simonds at 414).

Proximity/remoteness. Like the notion of foreseeability, those of proximity and remoteness easily take a variety of shapes depending on an array of circumstances. Their flexibility has been substantiated since the very beginning of modern tort law. Good examples come, for instance, from U.S. cases on the railway companies' liability for the failure to stop at the correct station.

In a renowned Virginia case, a train driver failed to stop at the station where a young female passenger intended to get off, and then let her off approximately one-half mile farther down the line, in the evening, near a place called "Hoboes' Hollow." While walking home on the tracks, the woman was accosted and raped twice, first by a vagabond and then by a soldier. The court held that the choice of the conductor (to let the young woman wander in the dark and in an almost deserted land) were manifestly inconvenient to the passenger. According to the judges, while in general no responsibility for a wrong arises where a third person intervenes between the negligence complained of and the injury, the defendant's behavior remained the proximate cause of the harm because his very negligence consisted in having exposed the injured party to the act causing the injury.[110]

It is interesting to compare this decision with a case decided some years before in Georgia, in which, under largely similar circumstances, the notion of proximity took a different shape. There, the plaintiff's personal injury was deemed to be too remote a consequence of the defendant train company's negligence. Mrs. Price was a passenger on a train of the defendant company. Through the negligence of the conductor, she was not put off at her destination, but was carried on to a different place, where the conductor advised her to go to the hotel and spend the night, and promised to carry her back to her destination the next day. He accompanied her to a hotel, the conductor agreeing with the proprietor to pay her expenses. During the night, however, a kerosene lamp located in the room where she was sleeping exploded and set her bed on fire, causing her to burn her hands in the attempt to extinguish the flames. The plaintiff's claim against the railway, however, was rejected. According to the Court, "the injury was occasioned by the negligence of the proprietor of the hotel or his servants in giving her a defective lamp. The negligence of the company in passing her station was, therefore, not the natural and proximate cause of her injury."[111] The train conductor's helpfulness in remedying his error; the impossibility for him to foresee that a defective

[110] *Hines v Garrett*, 131 Va 125, 108 SE 690 (Va 1921).
[111] *Central of Georgia Ry v Price*, 106 Ga 176, 32 SE 77 (Ga 1898).

lamp in the hotel room could endanger the plaintiff's safety; the availability of a better candidate for the role of proximate cause (the hotel's negligence); the minor consequences suffered by the plaintiff: only and all these factors help understand the narrow interpretation that the court has given to the notion of proximity, and the consequent rejection of the lady's request.[112]

Scope of the risk. Unsurprisingly, the common law "scope of the risk" test also can lead to inconsistent outcomes. Railway cases again will help us to appreciate the inner possible contradictory uses of the formula.

In *Kuhn v Jewett*,[113] the defendant's negligence in detaching twenty-five cars loaded with petroleum from a locomotive caused them to collide with the locomotive itself. When the collision occurred, some oil tanks were thrown to the earth, and discharged their content. The oil was set on fire through contact with something on the ground, ignited, and ran down the embankment into a small brook. The brook carried it to a nearby river, and from there to the plaintiff's building, which was, in its turn, set on fire and destroyed it. As the Court noted, water, although generally considered as a means to extinguish fire, can also act as a vehicle for the transmission of burning oil, and for the spread of a fire. The spread of the fire was therefore within the scope of the foreseeable risk created by a railroad accident close to the river bank.[114]

By deciding so, the Court consciously departed from the rule set some years earlier by the Supreme Court of Pennsylvania in *Hoag v. Lake Shore and Michigan Southern Railroad Co.*[115] Here too, defendant's railroad ran along the bank of a creek. During a rainstorm, by reason of a landslide unnoticed by the locomotive driver, a train bearing crude petroleum went off the

[112] The presence of widely different views on remoteness is equally well known outside the personal injuries cases. For instance, still with regard to railroad's liability (here for fire damage to property), at the end of the nineteenth century, Kansas courts held that the liability extended at least for four miles (*Atchison, T & SFR Co v Stanford*, 12 Kan 354, 15 Am Rep 362 (Kan 1874)), while New York courts kept maintaining that it terminated after the first adjoining building (*Ryan v New York Cent RR Co*, 35 NY 210 (NY 1866)). As Prosser underlined, one cannot see the reasons of such diversity through the "remoteness" lens without considering that "Kansas has miles of uninsured wheat," while "New York is a state whose prosperity depends upon railroads," and whose courts "have in mind urban communities, in which most property of any values carry fire insurance" (William L Prosser, "Palsgraf Revisited" (1952) 52 Mich LR 1, 30).

[113] *Kuhn v Jewett*, 32 NJ Eq 647 (NJ Ch 1880).

[114] See also *In re Kinsman Transit Co*, 338 F 2d 708 (2d Cir 1964) for a classic example of a determination that a consequence unlikely in size or manner of occurrence was within the scope of the risk that made the defendant's conduct negligent.

[115] *Hoag v Lake Shore & MSR Co*, 85 Pa 293, 27 Am Rep 653 (Pa 1877) (arguing mainly in terms of proximate cause). The facts of Hoag resemble those of the *The Wagon Mound No 1* (on which see above, in this section), which was decided many decades later.

tracks. Oil tanks burst, its contents ignited, and flowed down the creek until it reached the plaintiff's premises more than a hundred yards away. The flames spread to the plaintiff's buildings and destroyed them. It was held that, even conceding the derailment of the train to have been due to the negligence of the locomotive driver in not seeing an obstruction—something that was far from being established—, the damage suffered by the plaintiff had to be considered too remote. The circumstances leading to the plaintiff's injury—the bursting of the oil tanks, the oil igniting, the burning oil flowing to and being carried down the stream, and the sudden rising of the waters of the stream, which made it possible for the burning oil to set the plaintiff's building on fire—went far beyond the scope of the risk for which the defendant could be held liable, and therefore had to be considered as exogenous factors, which superseded the defendant's but-for contribution to the accident.

4. Skepticisms, Caveats, and Lessons

The above divergences and contradictions do not stem from fanciful judicial applications. Rather, they illustrate the little guidance causation formulas offer, per se, in assessing and explaining decision over causation. This shortcoming has led some scholars to raise skepticism about the very possibility of framing general rules about causation. Such a skepticism has been advanced by a loud minority of voices almost everywhere, but it found its most vigorous advocates among the American realist movement of the 1930s, which denounced the futility of any attempt to make "word schemes" do in advance what can only be done by the exercise of judgment in particular cases.

The starting point of the realist position lies in a straightforward observation: most of the tort cases involve "simple" causal problems, which can be easily solved through common-sense principles of causation.[116] These cases explain why so often courts tackle causation issues with no difficulty, or make decisions about liability without even discussing the causation

[116] The loci classici are Leon Green, *Rationale of Proximate Cause* (Vernon Law Book 1927), especially at 132–133, and Henry W Edgerton, "Legal Cause" (1924) 73 U Pa LR 211, 343 (1924); but see also William L Prosser, *Handbook of the Law of Torts* (4th edn, West 1971) 237; in England, Peter Cane & James Goudkamp, *Atiyah's Accidents, Compensation and the Law* (9th edn, CUP 2018) 98; and Weir (n 11) 72; in Germany, Markesinis, Bell, & Janssen (n 6) 60–64; in Italy, one may see Marta Infantino, *La causalità nella responsabilità extracontrattuale: Studio di diritto comparato* (Stämpfli 2012) 70–74, 177–181. For an interesting effort, in the United States, to revive the realist project, albeit upon the basis of experimental data, see Joshua Knobe & Scott Shapiro, "Proximate Cause Explained: An Essay in Experimental Jurisprudence" (2021) 88 U Chi LR 165.

requirement.[117] Far less common are the so-called freak accidents, made up of "crazy concatenations of circumstances, no one of which ever has been duplicated or ever will occur in exactly the same way again. [...] Freak accidents, in the aggregate, follow no pattern at all; and even when some resemblance can be found, the details will vary so greatly and significantly from case to case that we may very well come to different conclusions."[118] Since the exceptionality of freak accidents prevents common-sense notions from determining a conclusive or unique answer, it is in these instances that causation becomes a hard issue, leading lawyers to extensive argumentation, obliging judges to provide carefully written explanations to justify their decisions, and inviting scholars to join the discussion by including these "hard cases" into academic essays and textbooks.[119]

Does all the above provide a solid ground to feed skepticism about the very utility of the notion of causation? The answer is neither affirmative nor negative. Tort law claims in the real world are neither simple nor freakish in themselves. What makes them fall under one of these categories is the clarity of the dispute's evidentiary and substantive background, the policy choices and reasons, and the level of detail available to lawyers and judges for examining the causal issues raised by that background.[120] It is these elements—rather than the alleged ordinary or freakish character of the events giving rise to the litigation—that matter. These elements make evaluations of causation an easy or a difficult task, and they are crucial in determining both the interpretation given by courts to common-sense knowledge, and the judicial selection of the policy considerations inspiring the attribution of liability.

Yet, to understand and explain causation outcomes one also needs keep in mind that, besides common sense and policy reasons, the notion and role of causation ends up affected by the notion and role attributed, in a given legal culture, to the other necessary elements of the cause of action.[121] This influence spreads itself over the causation issues through two different channels. The first path is related to the way in which national jurisdictions shape their own way of thinking tort law (section 4.1). The second path breaks its way across the relationship between courts and the circumstances of the cases they adjudicate (section 4.2).

[117] Green (n 116) 133–134; along the same lines, Prosser (n 116) 237.

[118] Prosser (n 112) 28.

[119] Prosser (n 116) 236–237, 239, 244–250.

[120] Guido Calabresi, "Concerning Cause and the Law of Torts: an Essay for Harry Kalven" (1975) 43 U Chi LR 69, 103–106 (1975).

[121] See also Chapter II, section 4.

4.1. The Geography of Causation

From a comparative law point of view, it is clear that causation theoretical and practical dimensions vary according to the specific technicalities of each tort law system, and the way in which these technicalities are "internalized" by domestic legal actors. In each jurisdiction, the framing of the inquiry on causation is bound to change, depending on the structure of tort law rules, the procedural mechanisms available to the claimants, the functions that these rules and mechanisms are expected to fulfill.

Let us consider, for instance, the effect that variations in the general rule and structure of negligence liability may have on the place assigned to causation in tort. Negligence liability rules such as the ones contained in § 823 BGB or in the Anglo-American tort of negligence, restrict recovery to damages which (have been caused by the defendant's fault, and) arise from the infringement of interests protected by the legislator (Germany), or fall within the scope of the duty breached by the tortfeasor (Anglo-American countries). As a consequence, ordinary scholarly and judicial accounts of negligence liability conceive causation as an inquiry one can engage in only after verifying that the injury allegedly suffered by the victim satisfies the statutory or common law requirements for recovery.[122] These approaches stand in contrast with the ones adopted in France and Italy, where codified clauses for fault liability (arts 1240–1241 of the French *Code civil*; art 2043 of the Italian *Codice civile*) require no a priori examination as to the plaintiff's infringed rights, or as to the duty breached by the defendant's behavior. Against these frameworks, causation analysis is said to perform its role on an equal footing with the other elements of the negligence tort claim (i.e., damage and fault).[123]

Presence or absence of preliminary conditions to the causal inquiry is key to understanding the varying emphasis placed on the causation element within the jurisdictions surveyed. Countries where the liability recipe calls for preliminary examination over the rights or duties infringed by the defendant, leave to causal considerations a space more limited than that assigned to causation by the systems whose tort law basic rules do not contain, or are interpreted as not containing any requirement other than damage, fault, and causation.[124] In the latter jurisdictions, rather than appealing to the

[122] As to Germany, Markesinis, Bell, & Janssen (n 6) 64; as per England and the United States, see respectively Weir (n 11) 33; Goldberg, Kendrick, Sebok, & Zipursky (n 8) 50.

[123] Quézel-Ambrunaz (n 4), esp 2–3, 10.

[124] Mauro Bussani & Vernon V Palmer, "The Liability Regimes of Europe—Their Façades and Interiors," in Bussani & Palmer (eds) (n 88) 120, 127–128; Marta Infantino, "El derecho comparado

preliminary right/duty issues mandating immunity from liability, courts are more likely to resort to technical observations about the lack or tenuousness of the connection between the injury and the allegedly wrongful behavior, the presence of superseding factors breaking the chain of causation, the evidentiary uncertainties surrounding the occurrence of the plaintiff's loss, and so on.[125]

Thus, the comparative picture confirms a familiar upshot: what, under some circumstances, is considered as an issue of causation may, on other occasions and/or under different skies, be scrutinized through the lenses of other elements of the cause of action—and vice versa.[126]

4.2. Interconnections

Comparative analysis also shows that it is only in the books, and under the previously discussed "modular approach,"[127] that causation assessments can be the same regardless of the parties to the conflict and whatever needs and interests are at play in the case at hand. In the real world, judgments on causation are always dependent upon the context, that is, by the circumstances of the case and the interplay between the elements of the cause of action triggered by those circumstances.[128] Depending on the peculiarities of each tort

de la causalidad aquiliana," in Mauro Bussani & Marta Infantino, *Responsabilidad Civil y Garantías Reales. Estudios de Derecho Comparado* (Ediciones Olejnik 2016) 30, 46–50; Michael S Moore, *Causation and Responsibility. An Essay in Law, Morals, and Metaphysics* (OUP 2009) 83.

[125] Marta Infantino & Eleni Zervogianni, "Unraveling Causation in European Tort Laws. Three Commonplaces through the Lens of Comparative Law" (2019) 83 RabelsZ 647; Infantino & Zervogianni (n 45) 661–662; Bussani & Palmer (n 124) 128.

[126] See esp Infantino (n 1) 267–269; Cees van Dam, *European Tort Law* (2nd edn, OUP 2013) 319–320. As to the United States, probably the best example of interchangeability between the elements of the cause of action comes from the renowned American ruling *Palsgraf v The Long Island RR*, 248 NY 339, 162 NE 99 (NY 1928), which denied recovery to a woman who had been injured by the explosion of some fireworks in a train station. The majority of the court, driven by Justice Benjamin Cardozo, stressed that the problem at stake was one about duty, rather that one of proximate cause (*Palsgraf* at 346, per Cardozo J: "the law of causation, remote or proximate, is thus foreign to the case before us"). The dissenting judge, Andrews J, maintained that the case should have been properly analyzed in terms of causation (see *Palsgraf*, per Andrews J, 347–356). But what is interesting to note is that both the opinions of Cardozo for majority and Andrews in dissent are imbued of the language and formulas of causation—from theories on foreseeability (*Palsgraf* at 351) and risk (*Palsgraf* at 342, 344, 345, 351, 353) to the ideas of proximate cause (*Palsgraf* at 346 f, 349 f) and of substantial factor of the harm (*Palgraf* at 354)—and that the judgment is traditionally discussed and reported in the textbooks under the chapter on causation: cf, for instance, Goldberg, Kendrick, Sebok, Zipursky (n 8) 309; Page (n 11) 382–395; Dan B Dobbs, *The Law of Torts* (West 2000) 445–457; Prosser (n 116) 265–267.

[127] See Chapter II, sections 4–5.

[128] See the authors quoted at n 126.

law case, factors driving the interpretation given to causation formulas, and impinging on decisions over causation issues, may vary.

Causal judgments may be affected by *(i)* the nature and the magnitude of the loss. The more important plaintiff's prerogatives are deemed to be (eg, life, health, personality), and the more serious the attack on them is, the larger is the causal range, and vice versa; the lower the rank enjoyed by the plaintiff's position and the lighter the offense, the more the causal range retracts.[129] Likewise, there is no doubt on that causal analysis is dependent

[129] In the comparative perspective, Infantino & Zervogianni (n 45) 662–663; Bussani & Palmer (n 88) 21. One of the best illustrations of the principle comes from the well-known eggshell rule, following which the defendant should take the plaintiff as she finds her: Galand-Carval (n 17) 58; Trimarchi (n 5) 90–92, 363–364; Magnus (n 6) 66–67, 71–72; Weir (n 11) 77; § 31, Restatement Third of Torts—PEH; Page (n 11) 83–85. This is the basic rule in the realm of personal injuries, not outside of it. Legal systems take a cautious approach toward psychological (as opposed to sheer physical) predispositions (see Chapter IV, section 6.1). Moreover, that tortfeasors take plaintiff's wallet or property as they find it is far from being an accepted principle.

When the economic loss suffered by the victim is more serious than it might be expected because of the plaintiff's difficult economic conditions, the harm is usually considered within the scope of the defendant's liability (Honoré (n 1) 75). Decisions such as *Liesbosch Dredger v Edison SS* [1933] AC 449 (where the defendant negligently caused the claimants' dredger to sink, and the claimants, being too poor to buy another dredger, were forced to hire a vessel at an inflated rate in order to fulfill contractual obligations; the House of Lords—prone to a debatable, to say the least, view of the world—held that the claimants could not recover for the additional expense which they had incurred under the hire contract, because that loss was the result of their own impecuniosity and was not foreseeable by the defendant) seem now overturned by a different line of reasoning, according to which, in *Liesbosch*-like cases, the defendant should pay the full costs supported by the plaintiff, even if these costs are higher than they could have been because of the latter's impecuniosity (see *Lagden v O'Connor* [2004] 1 AC 1067; *Alcoa Minerals of Jamaica Inc v Broderick* [2002] 1 AC 371; *Dodd Properties v Canterbury City Council* [1980] 1 All ER 928; in the contract law field, *Perry v Sidney Phillips* [1982] 3 All ER 705).

Much less certain is the conclusion when the harm done to the plaintiff's property is of a greater magnitude or different type that it might be expected because of a hidden characteristic of the property. The issue has been discussed before courts (especially with regard to harm done to animals) with conflicting results. In some cases, losses arising out of the animals' delicacy have been attributed to the defendant, because the latter engaged in his excavation works near a mink farm in the month of May, during which minks are particularly fragile (*Grandel v Mason* [1953] 1 SCR 459) or, more obviously, or because the defendant arranged for guns to be fired repeatedly near to the boundary with the plaintiff's silver fox farming with the sole purpose of preventing the successful breeding of the vixens (*Hollywood Silver Fox v Emmett* [1936] 2 KB 468). In the majority of cases, however, the consequences of the animals' susceptibility have not been shifted to the defendant. Thus, for instance, the defendant was exempted from liability when his blastings perturbated (in a different season from the facts in *Grandel*) the serenity of the plaintiff's minks (*Madsen v East Jordan Irrigation Co*, 101 Utah 552, 125 P2d 794 (Utah 1942); see also *Foster v Preston Mill Co*, 44 Wash2d 440, 268 P2d 645 (Wash 1954); *Gronn v Rogers Const, Inc*, 350 P2d 1086 (Or 1960)), or when the noise produced by defendant's airplanes caused minks to panic and to kill their youngs (*Nova Mink Ltd v TCA* [1951] 2 DLR 241; RG 4 July 1938, RGZ 158, 34). Similarly, the defendant was not held liable when he caused a car accident which provoked a lethal excitement in the nearby pig farm (BGH 2 July 1991, BGHZ 115, 84, available in English in van Gerven, Larouche, & Lever (n 41) 405–406), or when he made some mines explode to build an highway, so that the sound terrorized the pheasants of a nearby farm, which started crashing into the walls of their cages (*Heid v Red Malcuit, Inc*, 12 Ohio Misc 158; 231 NE2d 356 (Ohio 1967)).

upon *(ii)* the comparative value assigned to the parties' interests[130] and on their comparative blameworthiness.[131] The latter often matters in strict liability cases as well: as is well-known, framing a case under strict liability rules does not necessarily entail that judges screen out of the picture fault-based arguments that, though not fitting the theoretical shape of the cause of action, are conducive to what is deemed to be a fair solution of the dispute.[132] Yet, assessments of causation may also vary according to *(iii)* the parties' relative loss-bearing capacities, with regard to the resources that are available to them, or, as the case may be, to the presence of an insurance coverage.[133] But this is not all. The *(iv)* type of accident may matter, since special causation criteria may apply to particular sub-species of tort law actions—from medical malpractice claims to traffic accidents to work-related accidents—whose rules may be more or less deviant from the ordinary standard for liability. Further, the appreciation of the causal connection may be affected by—to mention but a few other factors: *(v)* the nature of the wrong (an act of commission or omission);[134] *(vi)* the number of victims and tortfeasors; *(vii)* the level of (un)certainty surrounding the evidence about the sequence of events, and *(viii)* the standard of certainty which is required in respect of such evidence.[135]

The list could be further enriched by including other contextual features, from outside the cause of action. The framing of the causation inquiry may be influenced, as we saw in the preceding section, by the general characteristics

130 André Tunc, "Les récents développements des droits anglais et américain sur la relation de causalité entre la faute et le dommage dont on doit réparation" (1953) RIDC 54; Paolo Cendon, *Il dolo nella responsabilità extracontrattuale* (Giappichelli 1976) 398; Trimarchi (n 5) 13, 47–49; Weir (n 18) 52, n 2; Williams (n 49) 81–82; Green (n 116) 37 ("this problem, however phrased, is one of weighing of interests"), 70, 77.

131 Viney, Jourdain, & Carval (n 4) 238–239, 247–248; Galand-Carval (n 17) 59; Bussani (n 86); Cendon (n 130), especially 368–370; Trimarchi (n 5) 107; Weir (n 11) 68–69; Green (n 116) 82.

132 See Chapter II, section 11.1. On the reverse scale, when defendant's blameworthiness is established, causation may be stretched as to capture the most remote consequences of a wrongful act, thus making the defendant liable even for harms that she could neither foresee nor prevent from occurring: see Franz Werro & Vernon V Palmer, "Strict Liability in European Tort Law: An Introduction," in Franz Werro & Vernon V Palmer (eds), *The Boundaries of Strict Liability in European Tort Law* (Carolina Academic Press 2004) 6–7.

133 Quézel-Ambrunaz (n 4) 568–570; Jörg Fedtke, "The Culture of German Tort Law" (2012) 3 JETL 183; Richard Lewis & Annette Morris, "Tort Law Cultures in the United Kingdom: Image and Reality in Personal Injury Compensation" 3 JETL 230; John G Fleming, *The American Tort Process* (Clarendon Press 1988) 13–14, 21–24. In a normative, rather than descriptive, perspective, see Jane Stapleton, "Tort, Insurance and Ideology" (1995) 58 Mod LR 820, 828–830; George L Priest, "The Current Insurance Crisis and Modern Tort Law" (1987) 96 Yale LJ 1521, 1535–1537; Geneviève Viney, *Le déclin de la responsabilité civile individuelle* (LGDJ 1965); Albert Jr Ehrenzweig, "Assurance Oblige—A Comparative Study" (1950) 15 L & Cont Probs 445.

134 Hodgson (n 18) 129. See also above, n 18.

135 See Infantino (n 1) 269–271.

of the tort law systems, which determine whether issues should be framed as pertaining to causation or as falling under the umbrella of some other element of the cause of action. Yet one should mention also the substantive and procedural technicalities of the tort law adjudication mechanisms, the United States' exceptionalism in assigning to juries the role of fact-finders, the importance attached to the presence of alternative private or public law remedies, the attention paid to (what are perceived as) the potential externalities of the decision, and the social cost entailed by either denying or imposing liability.

The above list is far from complete, but is sufficient to make clear that it is the interrelationship between factors such as the ones just mentioned that shapes (the role and scope of any element,[136] including) causation, and that the persistent reliance that lawyers, judges, and scholars make on the explanatory value of causation formulas is nothing but a sophisticated and useful role-game that supports and promotes the acceptability of the results.

[136] See also Chapter II, section 4.

VIII
Products Liability

1. Introduction

Products liability provides an excellent opportunity to look at the development of tort law comparatively for numerous reasons. First, the domain of law we now call "products liability" is a relatively new domain, in that lawyers, scholars, and courts did not use the term in English or its foreign language equivalents (*Produkthaftungsgesetz, responsabilité du fait des produits défectueux, responsabilità da prodotto*) until the 1960s. By this point in time a rich dialogue had developed among scholars and policymakers on both sides of the Atlantic about how to address injuries arising from mass-produced consumer and industrial goods. Second—and following on the first point—, the period of time in which products liability law developed paralleled the rise of (what is now called) the European Union (EU), and, more precisely, the rise of the use of the EU Directives as a mechanism for harmonization among the EU Member States' domestic private law. In 1985 the European Directive on products liability was adopted, and the drive toward its development required considerable comparative reflection by its drafters. Finally, during the same period, the American Law Institute in the United States developed two Restatements of products liability law, the first published in 1964 and the second in 1998. The Restatement process was accompanied by a

Common Law and Civil Law Perspectives on Tort Law. Mauro Bussani, Anthony J. Sebok, & Marta Infantino, Oxford University Press.
DOI: 10.1093/oso/9780195368383.003.0008

lively debate over the purpose and justification of products liability, a process which both influenced Europe and also, to a lesser extent, drew lessons from Europe's experience in adopting its own early versions of products liability.

In surveying the development of the products liability law in the United States and Europe, this chapter tells more than a simple binary story of comparison, although there are places where a binary contrast is appropriate and may provide useful lessons.[1] It tells the story of convergence from multiple starting points: from the tort/contract foundations of products liability law found in the United States and France; to the more unitary foundations found in England, Germany and Italy, where tort from early on provided the best (although not always adequate) avenue for redress. Even after the passage of the Directive, which should have had the effect of "resetting" the various national laws on products liability to the same starting point, the legacy of national laws and the choices made within national legal traditions have influenced the reception of the Directive in the various EU countries. The same dynamic, it could be argued, can be seen in the persistence of negligence concepts in American products liability law, where negligence came back into the Restatement Third after a brief exile imposed by many academics and some state courts.

2. American Law: From Nineteenth-Century Law to Cardozo's Revolution

American products liability law has its roots in the law of contracts and torts and their parallel treatment of injuries caused by consumer products to their users. In this respect, the law of torts in the nineteenth century followed the English precedent of *Winterbottom v. Wright*, which famously held that the tort duties of a builder of a coach were controlled by the rules of privity.[2] In other words, while the builder did have tort duties, those duties ran only to the direct purchaser of the coach, with whom, of course, the builder also had a contract. This rule had two important consequences. First, and of most importance to historians of tort law, the plaintiff in that case, a driver who had been employed by a third party to drive the coach, was owed no duty by the coach builder in tort. The second consequence, often ignored by those

[1] See, eg, Marshall S Shapo, "Comparing Products Liability: Concepts in European and American Law" (1993) 26 Cornell Int'l LJ 279–330.

[2] [1842] 152 Eng Rep 402.

who discuss the case, is that the tort duties the coach builder did have, which ran to the purchaser of the coach only, could be adjusted, altered, or waived by contract. A further point, also often ignored, is that the tort duties that ran between the coach builder and purchaser were not necessarily identical with the rights under the contract of sale; for example, the damages rule that would be available under a tort claim between the seller and purchaser would be broader than the damages rule later on established by *Hadley v. Baxendale*, which would apply to a contract claim.[3]

American lawyers and courts followed English law where they found it persuasive and *Winterbottom* was treated as binding precedent. It was, however, as in England, limited in its scope by subsequent decisions that took a broader approach to the duties of manufacturers and the sellers of services. The most important early challenge to *Winterbottom* was *Thomas v. Winchester*, where the seller of chemical extract used in the compounding of medicine by pharmacist mislabeled the extract at the point of production, so that the pharmacist who used it innocently conveyed it to the consumer, who was severely injured.[4] New York's highest court held that a duty ran between the seller of the extract and the consumer (no claim in negligence against the pharmacist being possible). The court discussed *Winterbottom* explicitly and distinguished its holding from the unique facts of the case before it. Where the manufacturer was in the business of making things that were "imminently dangerous," it said, its duty in negligence ran to all persons who could be foreseeably injured by the imminently dangerous thing, regardless of whether they were in privity with the manufacturer. The court compared the mislabeled extract to a unattended horse and carriage or loaded gun, which, due to the owner's carelessness, could harm anyone in the world who had the misfortune of encountering it. By investing the object itself with a potential for "mischief" in the world, the court was able to reclassify it within the older and more familiar tort doctrines of negligence based on foreseeable harm.[5]

The next step away from *Winterbottom* was *MacPherson v. Buick Motor Co.*, where Judge Cardozo famously rejected the privity rule.[6] MacPherson,

[3] [1854] 156 Eng Rep 145. "Although the principle [in contract law] is often characterized as a 'foreseeability doctrine,' the principle as traditionally formulated and applied cuts off most foreseeable damage." Melvin A Eisenberg, "The Principle of *Hadley v Baxendale*" (1992) 80 Cal LR 563, 566 (citation omitted).

[4] 6 NY 397 (NY 1852).

[5] See, eg, *Heaven v Pender* [1883] 11 QBD 503 (CA).

[6] 217 NY 382 (NY 1916).

who had purchased a Buick automobile from a dealer, was injured when one of the car's wheels broke while he was driving it. The consumer sued Buick on the grounds that the manufacturer failed to reasonably inspect the wheel before it assembled the finished product which it sold to the dealer who sold it to the consumer. Buick defended, in part, by arguing that the rule in *Winterbottom* applied to it; it was in the same position as the coach builder in that case. Cardozo refused to directly overturn the privity rule in *Winterbottom* but instead expanded the category of things "imminently dangerous" to include "things of danger"—anything which "it is reasonably certain to place life and limb in peril if negligently made."[7] Into this category Cardozo placed automobiles, which were designed, as he noted, to go up to fifty miles an hour and to be used not by the person who bought it from the manufacturer (the dealer) but by persons with whom the manufacturer was certain not to be in privity, such as the consumer and his passengers.

The holding in *MacPherson* worked a revolution in American tort law.[8] The privity rule soon disappeared completely, although, as will be seen in this chapter, questions remained concerning the tort obligation owed by a seller to a buyer. Cardozo's principle—that a manufacturer owed a duty to anyone who could be harmed by a "thing of danger" was soon expanded to bystanders, and not just consumers or their guests.[9]

2.1. The "Objectivization" of Liability: From the 1920s to the 1960s

The duty owed by a manufacturer to the consumer in *MacPherson* was in negligence, and, as such, permitted the manufacturer to avoid liability if the consumer could not prove that the defect which caused his injury was the result of the manufacturer's carelessness. While this was an improvement for injured consumers compared to the privity rule in *Winterbottom*, it did not help consumers who were injured by defects that were not the result of negligence or, if they were, the consumer could not prove that they were the result of negligence.

[7] 217 NY 382 at 389 (NY 1916).

[8] The "decision swept the country." William L Prosser, "The Assault on the Cathedral (Strict Liability to the Consumer)" (1960) 69 Yale LJ 1099, 1100.

[9] See, eg, *Flies v Fox Bros Buick Motor Co*, 218 NW 855 (Wis 1929).

Two doctrines developed in the early twentieth century which offered consumers a chance to recover from manufacturers even if they could not demonstrate fault. Both would fade away as modern products liability doctrine took effect in the 1960s but they are worth reviewing since they have paved the way to subsequent developments and still inform the American approach to the problems and issues at stake.

2.1.1. Implied Warranty Theory

By the early twentieth century many American states had adopted an implied warranty theory for food. Prosser counted twenty-two states that had adopted an implied warranty of fitness for food by either judicial decision or statute.[10] Under this theory, the seller of food—whether the retailer or the manufacturer—was to have warranted that the food was uncontaminated. This was a contract theory, and no proof of negligence was required for a finding of liability.[11] The rule of strict liability for contaminated food stood on a separate and independent ground than the rule articulated in *MacPherson*, and early on in its history there was some confusion as to whether it was a tort or contract rule. As one court in 1920 said in connection to a case of food poisoning caused by a contaminated can of beans:

> If we call it a duty to use care in the preparation and manufacture, then, in that sense, a breach of that duty would constitute negligence. Or it may be treated as a representation or a warranty that, because of the sacredness of human life, food products so put out are wholesome. In either event, a failure in this respect is a breach of duty and a breach of warranty, and the plaintiff suing may rely on either or both, and, when he makes a prima-facie case, he is entitled to go to the jury on the question as to whether defendant's evidence negatives plaintiff's prima-facie case.[12]

How exactly a consumer would carry his burden of proof of unreasonable care by the defendant in a case like this if he chose to go to the jury on a negligence theory is the subject of section 2.1.2, but for the moment let us remain on the option of implied warranty. It clearly had the advantage of requiring no proof of unreasonable care and in all other respects it served the same

[10] Prosser (n 8) at 1108.
[11] Prosser (n 8) at 1104.
[12] *Davis v Van Camp Packing Co*, 189 Iowa 775, 801 (Iowa 1920).

functions as tort law: the damages included personal injury and the obligation contained within the warranty extended not only to the consumers, but to others to whom the consumer might serve the food, such as his family and guests in his household.[13] As a model for products liability generally, it seemed to be an improvement, at least from the perspective of the injured consumer.[14]

But the limitations of the theory of implied warranty must also be noted. As a common law doctrine, it arguably was developed, or developed most completely, in the case of contaminated food. The theory was later extended more broadly under a variety of model laws, such as the Uniform Sales Act[15] and the UCC. Under UCC § 2-314 (2)(c), every sale of goods has, unless disclaimed, an implied warranty of that the product "is reasonably fit for the ordinary purposes for which such goods are used." As James Henderson and Aaron Twerski put it, "along with the 'good news'" of warranty law "the "bad news" was quite substantial."[16] UCC § 2-318 extended the warranty to include the consumer's household, but until *Henningson v Bloomfield Motors, Inc.*,[17] the implied warranty in UCC § 2-314 (2)(c), extended only to the party with whom the consumer had privity, which in most cases would be a store, not the manufacturer. This put the consumer in a worse position than he would have been in tort law if he could prove negligence.

The law of sales had other problems, including the requirement that prompt notice must be given by the purchaser to the seller and manufacturer in event of the breach of warranty (this becomes, for unsophisticated persons, a "trap for the unwary"), as well as the UCC's statute of limitations, which ran from the tender of delivery.[18] The problems were so great that Prosser concluded in 1960 that "the concept of warranty has involved so many major difficulties and disadvantages that it is very questionable whether it has not become rather a burden than a boon to the courts in what they are trying to accomplish."[19] As the Supreme Court of California concluded in 1963, "the remedies of injured consumers ought not to be made to

[13] See Mark A Geistfeld, *Principles of Products Liability* (Foundation Press 2006) 14.

[14] As Karl Llewellyn put it, "[t]his is not a question of food. This is a question of consumer [...] [the contaminated food cases] were typical of a general trend." Karl N Llewellyn, "On Warranty of Quality, and Society: II" (1937) 37 Colum LR 341, 404–405.

[15] 1 Uniform Laws Ann §§ 12–16 (1950).

[16] James A Henderson & Aaron D Twerski, *Products Liability: Problems and Process* (8th edn, Wolters Kluwer 2008) 15.

[17] *Henningson v Bloomfield Motors, Inc*, 32 NJ 358, 161 A2d 69 (NJ 1960).

[18] *Greenman v Yuba Power Prods, Inc*, 377 P2d 897, 900 (Cal 1963).

[19] Prosser (n 8) at 1127.

depend upon the intricacies of the law of sales," and it concluded, as has most American jurisdictions, that the sounder footing for strict products liability was the law of torts.[20]

2.1.2. Res Ipsa Loquitur

The doctrine of res ipsa loquitur ("the thing speaks for itself") is a common law doctrine that allows the fact-finder to infer that the defendant's conduct was negligent because of the occurrence of the accident. It is a doctrine that allows juries to decide cases that would otherwise be normally decided on behalf of the defendant on a motion for summary judgment[21] (for obvious reasons having to do with human psychology, the res ipsa loquitur is not typically employed when the fact-finder is the judge, but, in theory, it could be).

In a contaminated food case, like the one reviewed above, if the case went forward as a negligence case, it is likely that the plaintiff would invoke res ipsa loquitur to carry the burden of proof on negligence. This strategy clearly could be extended from contaminated food to the defective container in which the food was transported and sold to the consumer. One of the earliest cases in which the potential of res ipsa loquitur as a comprehensive option for products liability was *Escola v. Coca Cola Bottling Co.*[22] In this case the plaintiff was not a consumer but a waitress who was injured when a bottle of soda exploded, cutting her hand. She sued the company that filled the bottle with soda under the standard negligence principles established under *MacPherson*. The trial judge allowed the plaintiff's case to reach the jury despite the fact that she admitted that she had no evidence whatsoever about how the explosion occurred other than evidence that the bottle was not subjected to any unusual forces that could have caused the explosion after it was delivered to her place of employment by the defendant. She argued that, under the doctrine of res ipsa loquitur the jury could conclude that some unidentified unreasonable act on the part of the bottler caused the bottle to explode, since normally bottles that have been handled reasonably do not explode. An appeal was made by the defendant after the jury found for the

[20] *Greenman* (n 18) at 901 (quoting *Ketterer v Armour & Co*, 200 F 322 (DNY 1912)).

[21] In principle, trial by jury is the rule for both tort and contract cases, but in contractual litigation juries are often excluded by the (growing) practice of including a jury waiver in contracts. See Stephen J Ware, "Arbitration Clauses, Jury-Waiver Clauses and Other Contractual Waivers of Constitutional Rights" (2004) 67 L&Cont Probs 167–205.

[22] *Escola v. Coca Cola Bottling Co.*, 150 P2d 436 (Cal 1944).

plaintiff. The California Supreme Court upheld the trial judge's decision to apply the doctrine of res ipsa loquitur to the case.[23]

In a concurrence, Justice Traynor argued that the court had reached the correct result but for the wrong reason. He argued that the doctrine of res ipsa loquitur could not be applied in this case and, further, that the court's inclination to stretch the doctrine to allow plaintiffs to succeed in cases like *Escola* was unnecessary. His argument against the application of of res ipsa loquitur had technical, pragmatic, and theoretical dimensions. Technically, the doctrine can only be applied to cases where the accident attributed to the instrumentality in the defendant's control could not have occurred in the absence of negligence by the defendant, and testimony by various witnesses (including a witness from the company that made the bottles) clearly established that the bottle may have possessed a defect as a result of no one's fault.[24] As a tactical matter, Traynor argued, encouraging plaintiffs to seek redress through negligence and res ipsa loquitur was a losing game, since defendants could still win summary judgment in these cases where they can provide "clear, positive, uncontradicted" and credible evidence that they had in place adequate safety measures at the place of production, and the plaintiff will often not be able to challenge the defendant's rebuttal.[25] As a theoretical matter, Traynor argued, the liberal application of res ipsa loquitur should be seen for what it really was—a legal fiction, much like the idea of implied warranty, to smuggle strict products liability into the common law.[26]

As a matter of policy, the argument for strict liability in tort, unmediated by negligence or contract doctrine, was straightforward. First, by placing the cost of all accidents resulting from the activity on the manufacturer, the manufacturer will be incentivized to reduce the costs of accidents, even those accidents for which it could not be held liable under negligence. Second, assuming that perfect safety is unachievable and accidents will inevitably occur, the manufacturer is in a better position to pay for the cost of the accident in comparison with the consumer, and it is fairer to make the

[23] *Escola* (n 22) at 439.

[24] See Geistfeld (n 13) 23, according to whom in *Escola* the court misapplied the doctrine of res ipsa loquitur.

[25] *Escola* (n 22) at 461 (quoting *Blank v Coffin*, 126 P2d 868 (Cal 1942). The plaintiff's inability to rebut could be a matter of fact (in *Escola* there was evidence that it was commercially impracticable to inspect every bottle) or process (because the plaintiff could not afford to win a "battle of the experts").

[26] For example: "[i]t is needlessly circuitous to make negligence the basis of recovery and impose what is in reality liability without negligence" and "[i]n the food products cases the courts have resorted to various fictions to rationalize the extension of the manufacturer's warranty to the consumer." *Escola* (n 22) at 441–442.

manufacturer pay, since then the cost of the accident is spread out among all the users of the product (since "the risk of [accident] is a constant and a general one [...] [a]gainst such a risk there should be general and constant protection").[27]

2.2. The Rise of Strict Liability

By the 1960s three distinct theoretical arguments for strict liability for injuries caused by products had emerged: (a) deterrence, (b) cost spreading, (c) fairness. The normative valence of each of these theories will explain, to some extent, the development of products liability in the following decades.

(a) Deterrence. As Traynor noted in *Escola*, by forcing the costs of an accident on the producer, the producer "internalizes" the cost of the accident and is thereby left with a choice: either to absorb it or reduce it.[28] Accident cost reduction seemed to be within the capabilities of many large corporations; the only question was how to get them to achieve it. One approach available to society is regulation—to determine safe practices and then to order private firms to adopt them. But this kind of "command and control" approach was viewed with skepticism for numerous reasons, ranging from doubt over the efficacy of government actors to make the most efficient safety decisions to doubt that American political culture would accept regulation through government edict.[29] There was a great deal of optimism that private enterprises could achieve great safety gains if they put their efforts toward doing so.[30]

[27] *Escola* (n 22) at 441.

[28] This is the central insight of the theory of "enterprise liability." Enterprise liability was developed by many scholars associated with the legal realist movement such as Fleming James Jr, Leon Green, and Albert Ehrenzweig. See Anthony J Sebok, "The Fall and Rise of Blame in American Tort Law" (2003) 68 Brook LR 1031–1051 (2003). It is also, of course, an insight associated with Guido Calabresi, who explicitly accepted the premises of the earlier enterprise liability scholars. See, eg, Guido Calabresi, "Some Thoughts on Risk Distribution and the Law of Torts" (1961) 70 Yale LJ 499–553.

[29] See Jeffrey O'Connell, "Expanding No-Fault Beyond Auto Insurance: Some Proposals" (1973) 59 Va LR 749, 806–812.

[30] Large organizations could reduce overall costs if they could (1) remove consumers from a dangerous position; (2) train them to act safely despite their accident proneness; or (3) construct prophylactics so that when consumers act unsafely (an inevitable event), their injury is ameliorated. Of these three options, industrial America was especially keen on (2) and (3). See John Fabian Witt, "Speedy Taylor and the Ironies of Enterprise Liability" (2003) 103 Colum LR 1, 37 (describing the work of "safety engineers" on behalf of large corporations who wished to reduce their workman compensation costs after 1910).

There was, of course, also a political context to the belief that defendants could do more to reduce accidents than they were already doing. The consumer movement, which started with the publication of Sinclair Lewis's *The Jungle*[31] and reached its zenith with the publication of Ralph Nader's *Unsafe at Any Speed*,[32] fed a perception that private manufacturer's had no incentive to pursue safety and that both the government and consumer market behavior were too weak to drive them to invest in greater safety.

(b) Cost spreading. Again, as Traynor noted in *Escola*, even in an ideal world where manufacturers chose to invest in safety, accidents would still occur. This is for two reasons. First, perfect safety is simply impossible in this world, given the laws of statistics and the reality of human psychology.[33] Second, even where safety can be increased (and sometimes increased by a great deal), it is simply not rational to do so because over-investment in safety is inefficient from a standpoint of aggregate social welfare.[34] This conclusion—which comes from the so-called Hand Test for negligence—was taken by advocates of strict liability as an argument for spreading the costs of inevitable (or cost-justified) accidents on all the users of a product.[35] The cost-spreading argument was not motivated by a suspicion of the manufacturer, but rather the opposite: it saw the manufacturer as a trustworthy intermediary to transfer the cost of accidents among all the users of a product. As Jeffrey O'Connell (who could not be described as a friend of the plaintiffs' bar) saw it, the decision to permit a risky activity was a decision by society to allow a certain number of accidents.[36] Manufacturers were the most effective intermediaries to channel the true cost of those risky activities back to those members of society who were interested in engaging in those activities.[37] Without strict liability, people would engage "unwittingly [in] more of that activity [...] than people would choose if its full costs were known."[38]

[31] (Doubleday 1906).

[32] *Unsafe at Any Speed: The Designed-In Dangers of the American Automobile* (Grossman Pub 1965).

[33] James believed that most accidents were the inevitable consequence of certain persons being more "accident-prone" than others. Fleming James Jr & John J Dickinson, "Accident Proneness and Accident Law" (1950) 63 Harv LR 769–795.

[34] See Guido Calabresi, *The Cost of Accidents: A Legal and Economic Analysis* (Yale University Press 1970); and William M Landes & Richard A Posner, "A Positive Economic Analysis of Products Liability" (1985) 14 J Leg Stud 535.

[35] See George L Priest, "The Invention of Enterprise Liability: A Critical History of the Intellectual Foundation of Modern Tort Law" (1985) 14 J Leg Stud 461.

[36] Jeffrey O'Connell, *The Lawsuit Lottery: Only the Lawyers Win* (Free Press 1979) 183–184.

[37] O'Connell (n 29) at 781.

[38] O'Connell (n 36) at 184.

(c) Fairness. This approach views the political and social relations between consumers and producers very differently than the cost-spreading approach. Under this perspective, the act of selling a product in a market society is a private act that, while legal and perhaps desirable, is also an act of self-interest. The seller of a product gains from the imposition of risk of injury on the purchaser and the public in general. Even if the risk cannot be eliminated completely, or eliminated without making the cost unreasonably high, the fact remains that the seller is making a financial gain and the consumer or public suffer a risk of personal injury. Therefore, from the perspective of fairness (or corrective justice) the party who makes the gain in the transaction must repair the losses that flow from the transaction.[39] This approach is arguably an extension of the contract-based reasoning that motivated the effort to ground products liability on implied warranty theory.[40]

2.3. The Modern Doctrine. The Second Restatement

In 1964, the above rationales were summarized by the American Law Institute in § 402 A of the Restatement Second of Torts.[41] According to § 402 A (1), the seller of a product

> in a defective condition unreasonably dangerous to the user or consumer or to his property is subject to liability for physical harm thereby caused to the ultimate user or consumer, or to his property.

[39] See Virginia E Nolan & Edmund Ursin, "The Deacademification of Tort Theory" (1999) 48 Kan LR 59, 100–104.

[40] Dan B. Dobbs, *The Law of Torts* (West Group 2000) 976, according to whom the arguments put forward by Marshall Shapo (see Shapo (n 1)) in favor of strict liability are based on the latter's view that sellers are obliged to make good on the implicit promise of safety communicated by their act of entering the market.

[41] § 402 A of Restatement Second of Torts (1965):

> (1) One who sells any product in a defective condition unreasonably dangerous to the user or consumer or to his property is subject to liability for physical harm thereby caused to the ultimate user or consumer, or to his property, if (a) the seller is engaged in the business of selling such a product, and (b) it is expected to and does reach the user or consumer without substantial change in the condition in which it is sold.
> (2) The rule stated in Subsection (1) applies although (a) the seller has exercised all possible care in the preparation and sale of his product, and (b) the user or consumer has not bought the product from or entered into any contractual relation with the seller.

The term "Product" goes undefined in § 402 A.

The seller is liable even if he "has exercised all possible care in the preparation and sale of his product" and the user or consumer "has not bought the product from or entered into any contractual relation with the seller."[42] While the section leaves the notion of product undefined,[43] this has been always understood to cover personal property, including electricity but excluding vaccines and drugs, which were made subject by cmt k (devoted to "unavoidably unsafe products") to special rules.[44]

Section 402 A clearly reflects the influence of warranty. First of all, the rule imposes strict liability following from the *commercial* sale of a defective product. Section 402 A holds every commercial participant in the manufacturing and distribution process, including retailers, strictly liable for physical harm to consumers and users, so as to maximize latter's chances of getting recovery and to create incentives on downstream participants in the manufacturing and distribution chain to exert pressure on manufacturers to produce safer goods.[45] Second, the test for defectiveness is modeled upon the law of warranty, insofar as it is grounded on the reasonable expectations of ordinary consumers about product safety:

> the article sold must be dangerous to an extent beyond that which would be contemplated by the ordinary consumer who purchases it, with the ordinary knowledge common to the community as to its characteristics. Good whiskey is not unreasonably dangerous merely because it will make some people drunk, and is especially dangerous to alcoholics; but bad whiskey, containing a dangerous amount of fusel oil, is unreasonably dangerous.[46]

[42] See Restatement Second of Torts § 402 A (2), respectively (a) and (b).

[43] See Michael D Green & Jonathan Cardi, "Product Liability in United States of America," in Piotr Machnikowski (ed), *European Product Liability: An Analysis of the State of the Art in the Era of New Technologies* (Intersentia 2016) 575, 583.

[44] According to cmt k, [t]he seller of such products, again with the qualification that they are properly prepared and marketed, and proper warning is given, where the situation calls for it, is not to be held to strict liability for unfortunate consequences attending their use, merely because he has undertaken to supply the public with an apparently useful and desirable product, attended with a known but apparently reasonable risk.

[45] Mathias Reimann, "Liability for Defective Products at the Beginning of the Twenty-First Century: Emergence of a Worldwide Standard?" (2003) 51 AJCL 751, 764 (2003) (who also notes that many states limit retailers' liability by requiring fault).

[46] § 402 A, cmt i. On the warranty legacy of this version of the test, see W Page Keeton, "The Meaning of Defect in Products Liability Law—A Review of Basic Principles" (1973) 45 Mo LR 579, 589; Gary Schwartz, "Foreword: Understanding Strict Liability" (1979) 67 Cal LR 435, 438; John Wade, "Strict Products Liability" (1989) 19 The Brief 8, 57; Jane Stapleton, *Product Liability* (Butterworths 1994) 10–15.

By linking the idea of a defective product to consumer expectations rather than lack of care on the part of the seller, while at the same time eliminating the requirement of contractual privity, § 402 A brought together elements of negligence and warranty law to create a new form of tort liability.[47]

As is well known, the new tort proved to be extremely influential. In the 1960s and 1970s, as cases started to multiply, litigation moved from denouncing obvious manufacturing defects (such as those affecting exploding soda bottles and nonfunctional car brakes) to attacking products that should have been made safer than they were by adding safety features, modifying the design, or accompanying them with instructions or warnings. A tripartition between manufacturing, design, and warnings defects therefore started to emerge: manufacturing defects were defects arising accidentally during production; design defects concerned products that were (correctly made but) affected by flaws in their conception; and warning defects referred to cases in which the producer/seller failed to warn of reasonable dangers or to provide consumers with proper product use instructions.[48] Although the consumer expectation test posed the difficulty of determining who the "average" consumer was and whose expectations were to be taken into account,[49] manufacturing defects obviously fell beneath any average consumers' expectations. The test, however, proved much less satisfactory when applied to design and instruction/warning defects, with regard to which consumer expectations are often vague or nonexisting. The dissatisfaction with the indeterminacy of the consumer expectations test for these kinds of cases, as well as worries about the aggressiveness of the plaintiffs' bar, led since the mid-1970s many courts to differentiate more sharply among types of defects and to evaluate cases of design and warning defects through the lens of the so-called risk-utility test[50] and of negligence-based

[47] Green and Cardi (n 43) 582.

[48] Reimann (n 45) 769–770.

[49] James A Henderson & Aaron D Twerski, "What Europe, Japan and Other Countries Can Learn from the New American Restatement of Product Liability" (1999) 34 Tex Int'l LJ 1, 3. The problem is particularly hard in case of products injuring bystanders. In such cases, American courts tend to consider the expectation of purchasers of the product: see *Bellotte v Zayre Corp*, 352 A2d 723 (NH 1976) (a five-year-old child was burned when he was playing with matches and his cotton pajama top caught fire. The court held that the expectations as to the pajama safety were those of the parents who purchased the pajama for their kid).

[50] According to such a test, a product is defective only if the risk of danger created by the product outweighs its benefits. As to the development of such test, see the cases cited and arguments employed by John W Wade, "On the Nature of Strict Tort Liability for Products" (1973) 44 Miss LJ 825–851; Keeton (n 46) 592; John W Wade, "On Product Design Defects and Their Actionability" (1980) 33 Vand LR 551, 572–573; David G Owen, "Defectiveness Restated: Exploding the 'Strict' Products Liability Myth" (1996) U Ill LR 743, 754–755; David G Owen, "Toward a Proper Test for

doctrines.[51] From the 1980s, the judicial trend became consistently less plaintiff friendly[52] and, consequently, the frequency of product liability litigation began to decline.[53]

2.4. The Third Restatement

In 1998, skepticism of broad strict liability for defective consumer products was formally embodied in the American Law Institute's Restatement Third of Torts—Products Liability.

On the one hand, the Third Restatement maintains the focus on whoever is "engaged in the business of selling or otherwise distributing products" (§ 1), and on products as any "tangible personal property distributed commercially for use or consumption" (§ 1), including electricity[54] but excluding drugs and medical devices,[55] as well as blood.[56]

On the other hand, the new Restatement clearly embraces the tripartition of categories of defectiveness between defects in manufacturing, design, and instructions/warnings, and retains the consumer expectation test of

Design Defectiveness: Micro-Balancing Costs and Benefits" (1996–1997) 75 Tex LJ 1661, 1664. See also below, section 2.4.

[51] See for instance *Barker v Lull Engineering Co*, 573 P2d 443 (Cal 1978) (classifying product defects into the tripartition mentioned in the text).

[52] In the same period, courts started reducing punitive damages awards in products liability cases: see, for example, *Grimshaw v Ford Motor Company* (the so-called Pinto case), 119 Cal App3d. 757 (Cal 1981), in which the plaintiff, who suffered burns to 90% of his body because a design defect in his Pinto car, was awarded by the jury at the trial punitive damages in the sum of $125 million, but the sum was later reduced to $3.5 million on appeal. From the 1990s onward, the Supreme case law has imposed further restrictions on punitive damages awards: *BMW of North America, Inc v Gore*, 116 SCt 1589 (US 1996); *Philip Morris USA v Williams*, 549 US 346 (US 2007).

[53] Mathias Reimann, "Product Liability," in Mauro Bussani & Anthony J Sebok (eds), *Comparative Tort Law. Global Perspectives* (2nd edn, EE 2021)236, 238.

[54] Restatement Third of Torts—Product Liability § 19 (a).

[55] Restatement Third of Torts—Product Liability § 6 (b) (1). The manufacturer of a drug or medical device is liable only when the latter "is not reasonably safe due to inadequate instructions or warnings if reasonable instructions or warnings regarding foreseeable risks of harm are not provided" (§ 6 (d)). Thus, under the Restatement Third, the liability game in cases of drugs and medical devices is "with the warnings candle, not with design": Michael D Green, "Prescription Drugs, Alternative Designs, and the Restatement (Third): Preliminary Reflections" (1999) 30 Seton Hall LR 207, 209.

[56] Restatement Third of Torts—Product Liability § 19(c). With regard to defective blood, the majority of American States have "blood shield laws," that is, statutes immunizing blood providers from strict liability or breach of warranty actions for injuries caused by contaminated blood products: see Green & Cardi (n 43) 584 and, under the comparative perspective, see below, in this chapter, section 4; as well as Chapter III, sections 2.2 and 3.1.1. It should also be noted that the Third Restatement also provides for special liability rules in case of defective food and used products: see respectively §§ 7 and 8.

defectiveness and strict liability only for the former category. Thus, according to § 2 (a), anyone engaged in the business of selling or otherwise distributing products is liable for harm to persons or property caused by manufacturing defects, that is, "when the product departs from its intended design even though all possible care was exercised in the preparation and marketing of the product." By contrast, liability for products that are defectively designed arises under § 2 (b) only if

> the foreseeable risks of harm posed by the product could have been reduced or avoided by the adoption of a reasonable alternative design by the seller or other distributor, and the omission of the alternative design renders the product not reasonably safe.

In other words, § 2 (b) embraces the "risk-utility" test developed by many courts and scholars since the 1970s. As illustrated in the comments, the rationale of the rule is to create

> incentives for manufacturers to achieve optimal levels of safety in designing and marketing products. Society does not benefit from products that are excessively safe—for example, automobiles designed with maximum speeds of 20 miles per hour—any more than it benefits from products that are too risky. Society benefits most when the right, or optimal, amount of product safety is achieved. From a fairness perspective, requiring individual users and consumers to bear appropriate responsibility for proper product use prevents careless users and consumers from being subsidized by more careful users and consumers, when the former are paid damages out of funds to which the latter are forced to contribute through higher product prices."[57]

A similar rationale governs liability for defective instructions or warnings.[58]

[57] Restatement Third of Torts—Product Liability § 2, cmt a.

[58] Restatement Third of Torts—Product Liability § 2 (c). Under § 2 (c), anyone who sells a product with inadequate instructions or warnings is liable only if:

> the foreseeable risks of harm posed by the product could have been reduced or avoided by the provision of reasonable instructions or warnings by the seller or other distributor, or a predecessor in the commercial chain of distribution, and the omission of the instructions or warnings renders the product not reasonably safe.

As § 2 cmt a specifies, the balancing of risks and benefits in judging product design and marketing must be done "in light of the knowledge of risks and risk-avoidance techniques reasonably attainable at the time of distribution," that is, on the basis of what was reasonably foreseeable to manufacturers when they marketed the product (it is the so-called development risk defense).

The Restatement thus retains a strict liability rule only for manufacturing defects, while it makes design defects and inadequate instructions/warnings subject to what is essentially a negligence standard. Plaintiffs bear the burden of proof regarding all the elements of liability. The Restatement, however, eases that burden conceding that plaintiffs can establish the existence of a defect and causation by pointing to circumstantial evidence,[59] and admitting, in the case of liability for defective design or inadequate instructions or warnings, that the product's defectiveness might be proved by showing the product's "noncompliance with an applicable product safety statute or administrative regulation [...] with respect to the risks sought to be reduced by the statute or regulation" (§ 4 (a)).[60]

To escape liability, defendants might of course demonstrate that the elements of liability are absent or unproven; but they might also resort to defenses barring or reducing their liability. Besides the development risk defense for defects in design and instructions/warnings and cases of plaintiff's contributory or comparative fault (§ 17 (a)[61]), the doctrine of federal preemption, which blocks state products liability law when the defendant has complied with a federal statute that is thought to reflect, expressly or impliedly, the intent of Congress, provides a shield that is as good as a defense.[62]

[59] Restatement Third of Torts—Product Liability § 3:

> It may be inferred that the harm sustained by the plaintiff was caused by a product defect existing at the time of sale or distribution, without proof of a specific defect, when the incident that harmed the plaintiff: (a) was of a kind that ordinarily occurs as a result of product defect; and (b) was not, in the particular case, solely the result of causes other than product defect existing at the time of sale or distribution.

[60] It should further be stressed that, according to § 4 (b) of the Restatement Third, "compliance with an applicable product safety statute or administrative regulation [...] does not preclude as a matter of law a finding of product defect."

[61] According to the Restatement Third of Torts—Product Liability § 17 (a),

> [a] plaintiff's recovery of damages for harm caused by a product defect may be reduced if the conduct of the plaintiff combines with the product defect to cause the harm and the plaintiff's conduct fails to conform to generally applicable rules establishing appropriate standards of care.

[62] See Restatement Third of Torts—Product Liability § 2, cmt e. Federal preemption is a powerful defence whose contours are as vague as debated: Benjamin C Zipursky, "Federal Preemption and Products Liability" (March 11, 2014) Jotwell, at torts.jotwell.com/

The Restatement has no direct influence over statutes, so there remains untouched the several other statutory defenses to actions for product liability that might arise, for instance, from statutes of limitations or repose or statutory caps on damages.[63]

The adoption of the Restatement Third has created a great stir around the United States. Many jurisdictions have adopted at least parts of the Restatement Third either through legislation or judicially, while many others have not aligned with the standards and definitions it outlined, insofar as many provisions (in particular § 2 (b) and its negligence-based "alternative reasonable design" test) are thought not to reflect the law.[64] Yet it is fair to say that § 402 A of Restatement Second continues to wield considerable influence on state courts' case law on products liability.

The fragmented success of the Restatement Third, coupled with the variety of causes of actions, judicial doctrines, and statutory rules applicable to products liability claims across states, are among the factors that currently make the field "one of the most complicated areas of tort law."[65] Further complications are now posed by changes in supply management and development of new technologies. For instance, products liability litigation against e-commerce providers (such as Amazon) is now on the rise, although the majority of courts have so far refused to classify such providers as retailers and to hold them liable for damages caused by the defective goods sold through the platforms.[66] Defective software or AI have not so far been subject to product liability, but they might be as might "smart"

federal-preemption-and-torts-liability/; Catherine M Sharkey, "Products Liability Preemption: An Institutional Approach" (2008) 76 Geo Wash LR 449–521; as well as, and more in general, Mark A Geistfeld, "Tort Law in the Age of Statutes" (2014) 99 Iowa LR 957–1020.

[63] Green and Cardi (n 43) 603–605, 611–612.

[64] See Dominik Vetri, "Order Out of Chaos: Products Liability Design-Defect Law" (2009) 43 U Rich LR 1373, 1406–1408; James A Henderson & Aaron D Twerski, "The Products Liability Restatement in the Courts: An Initial Assessment" (2000) 27 Wm Mitchell LR 7.

[65] Green & Cardi (n 43) 616.

[66] *Fox v Amazon.com, Inc*, 930 F3d 415 (6th Cir 2019); *Eberhart v Amazon.com, Inc*, 325 F Supp 3d 393 (SDNY 2018); *Allstate NJ Ins Co v Amazon.com, Inc*, No 17–2738, 2018 WL 3546197 (DNJ 2018); see also *Loomis v Amazon.com, LLC*, 63 Cal App 5th 466 (Cal 2021) (classifying Amazon as a seller of a third-party defective hoverboard and therefore liable for the damage caused by the hoverboard when it got fire); *Bolger v Amazon.com, LLC*, No. D075738 August 13, 2020 (Cal 2020) (holding Amazon strictly liable for the injury caused by a defective battery offered on its website by a third-party seller). See Edward J Janger & Aaron D Twerski, "The Heavy Hand of Amazon: A Seller Not a Neutral Platform" (2020) 14 Brook J Corp Fin & Com L 259–273; Catherine M Sharkey, "Holding Amazon Liable As a Seller of Defective Goods: A Convergence of Cultural and Economic Perspectives" (2020) 115 Nw U LR 339–356.

products (eg, self-driving cars). The question, still hotly debated by scholars and largely unresolved, is who and under what conditions should be liable in such cases.[67]

3. Europe before the Directive

Even more fragmented are product liability developments in Western Europe.

Until the adoption of Directive 85/374/EEC, product liability developed on a national basis. English courts challenged the privity doctrine in the iconic 1932 case *Donoghue v. Stevenson*,[68] holding that manufacturers of defective products are liable in negligence to bystanders for the latter's personal injuries. Since the 1950s, French courts recognized that buyers of defective products have a direct contractual claim against the manufacturer for breach of warranty.[69] Italian courts definitely established that manufacturers were liable under a rule of presumed fault in 1964,[70] and Germany followed suit with the famous *Hühnerpest* case of 1968.[71] On paper, these divergences were superseded by the 1985 Directive, which required EEC (now EU) Member States to implement rules providing strict liability for manufacturers of defective products. Yet, as we will see, the Directive has given rise to scant litigation and limited harmonization, not the least because it only partially replaced national approaches to liability for defective products. We will first analyze the historical development of special product liability rules in England, France, Italy, and Germany, and then investigate the background, contents, and effects of adoption of Directive 85/374/EEC.

[67] Cf Steven Shavell, "On the Redesign of Accident Liability for the World of Autonomous Vehicles" (2020) 49 J Leg Stud 243–285; Alexander B Lemann, "Autonomous Vehicles, Technological Progress, and the Scope Problem in Products Liability" (2019) 12 J Tort L 157–212; Mark A Geistfeld, "A Roadmap for Autonomous Vehicles: State Tort Liability, Automobile Insurance, and Federal Safety Regulation" (2017) 105 Cal LR 1611–1694; Bryant W Smith, "Automated Driving and Product Liability" (2017) Mich St LR 1–74.

[68] [1932] AC 562. Strictly speaking, *Donoghue v Stevenson* is a Scottish case; yet English law and Scots law are identical on the subject.

[69] See the lower instance cases on damage caused by defective pharmaceuticals, household appliances, and body-care products cited by Jean-Sébastien Borghetti, "The Development of Product Liability in France," in Simon Whittaker (ed), *The Development of Product Liability* (OUP 2010) 87, 91, fn 12–14.

[70] Cass 25 May 1964, no 1270, Foro it 1965, I, 2098.

[71] BGH 26 November 1968, BGHZ 51, 91 (Chicken Pest).

3.1. England

In nineteenth-century England, harms caused by defective products were primarily regarded as a contract law issue, governed by the basic principle of the law of sales known as "caveat emptor."[72] Yet, since the middle of the century, courts started recognizing important exceptions to the principle by recourse to the technique of implication of terms. Through the notion of an "implied warranty" of merchantability—later codified by section 14 of the Sale of Goods Act of 1893—English judges imposed strict liability upon sellers for buyers' losses (including consequential damage, whether personal injuries or damage to property) arising from defective goods.[73] Outside the scope of implied warranties, by contrast, courts held to the non-liability rule of *Winterbottom v Wright*,[74] and kept affirming that, absent exceptional circumstances, manufacturers of dangerous products owed no duty of care to the final users of their products.[75] Liability was exceptionally imposed to suppliers only in cases of damage caused by chattels that were thought to be dangerous in themselves (such as guns) and by chattels that, though not dangerous in themselves, were known to be dangerous by their suppliers.[76] There were earlier attempts to overturn the rule, such as William Brett's obiter in *Heaven v. Pender*,[77] but they remained largely unsuccessful until 1932.

[72] Simon Whittaker, "The Development of Product Liability in England," in Simon Whittaker (ed) (n 69), 51, 61–62.

[73] While the doctrine of implied warranty was initially limited to recovery of economic losses, English judges rapidly extended it to property damage and personal injuries caused to the buyer by the defects: cf *Brown v Edgington* [1841] 2 Man & G 279; *Randall v Raper* [1858] EB & E 84; *Randall v Newson* [1877] 2 QBD 102 (CA). See also Whittaker (n 72) 61–69.

[74] *Winterbottom v Wright* [1842] 152 Eng Rep 402.

[75] Cf *Bostock &Co Ltd v Nicholson & Sons Ltd* [1904] 1 KB 725 and *Earl v Lubbock* [1905] 1 KB 253.

[76] See *Langridge v Levy* [1837] 2 M&W 519 (a seller of a gun that he knew to be unsafe was held liable for fraud to the buyer's son, who was injured by the gun being fired); *Clarke v Army and Navy Co-operative Society* [1903] 1 KB 155 (the seller of a tin of disinfectant powder was held liable to the buyer, as he knew it was likely to injure if special care was not taken and he gave no warning; since the seller had excluded warranties of quality, the buyer brought the claim in tort).

[77] In *Heaven v Pender* [1883] 11 QBD 503, a ship painter was injured at work due to the defectiveness of the ropes he was supplied with by the dock owner. He was allowed to recover against the dock owner on the basis of the latter's duty of care as occupier of land to invitees. In his opinion supporting liability, William Brett opined that the issue was whether the defendant owed a duty of care to the plaintiff. In a well-known passage (later cited by Lord Atkin in Donoghue), Brett argued that

> [w]henever one person is by circumstances placed in such a position with regard to another that anyone of ordinary sense who did think would at once recognize that, if he did not use ordinary care and skill in his own conduct with regard to those circumstances, he would cause danger of injury to the person or property of the other, a duty arises to use ordinary care and skill to avoid such danger (ibid at 509).

In 1932 a divided (3-2) House of Lords upheld the possibility of a claim for damages for personal injuries under the tort of negligence by a person injured by ingestion of a contaminated ginger beer against the beer's manufacturer, although the plaintiff was not party to the contract under which the beer was distributed. While the minority's position was to uphold the approach in *Winterbottom v. Wright*,[78] the majority treated *Winterbottom* as a contract case, which could not be considered an authority "for duties alleged to exist beyond or without contract."[79] Relying upon Brett's opinion and on American decisions that accepted manufacturers' liability,[80] the majority held that

> [a] manufacturer of products which he sells in such a form as to show that he intends them to reach the ultimate consumer in the form in which they left him with no reasonable possibility of intermediate examination, and with the knowledge that the absence of reasonable care in the preparation or putting up of the products will result in an injury to the consumer's life or property, owes a duty to the consumer to take reasonable care.[81]

As is well known, the decision and Lord Atkin's famous invention of the "neighbor principle" not only overturned the precedents barring damage recovery to plaintiffs because of the lack of privity and established the modern foundation of English product liability law, but also influenced the development of negligence theory (in the domain of physical injuries) wellvbeyond the field of liability for defective products.

Subsequent decisions extended the subjective scope of the *Donoghue v. Stevenson* rule, applying it in favor of causal bystanders[82] and against whoever was involved in the production process (including, for instance, assemblers).[83] The rule was applied to products other than food (such as

[78] [1932] AC 562 at 577, per Lord Buckmaster.

[79] Ibid at 593–594, per Lord Atkin.

[80] Ibid at 598–599 (Lord Atkin), 603 (Lord Thankerton), 617–618 (Lord MacMillan).

[81] Ibid at 599 (Lord Atkin).

[82] *Kubach v Hollands and Another (Federick Allen & Son (Poplar) Ltd, Third Party)* [1937] 3 All ER 803 (a supplier who sold a dangerous chemical to a school without warning was held liable to a student injured when the chemical exploded in a school experiment).

[83] *Malfroot v Noxal Ltd* [1935] 51 TLR 21 (an assembler was held liable because it negligently fitted a side-car to a motorcycle. The side-car came off and injured the passenger); *Howard v Furness Houlder Argentine Lines Ltd and A & R Brown Ltd* [1936] 2 All ER 781 (an assembler was held liable because it negligently re-assembled a valve chest with the bridge upside down for a steamship. An explosion occurred in the ship and injured an electric welder).

clothes[84] and chemicals[85]); occasionally, courts also held manufacturers liable in negligence for defective instructions and warnings and defective design of products.[86]

In appreciating the revolutionary reach of the *Donoghue* decision, one should however keep in mind at least two points. First, the *Donoghue* ruling did not prevent many courts from remaining loyal to displaced traditional doctrines of implied warranty and contractual privity, with the result that, even after *Donoghue*, many cases fell (and were rejected) under the traditional warranty-based remedial system.[87] Second, *Donoghue* established a principle of liability in negligence: in order to recover, plaintiffs had to show negligence of the manufacturer. Even though some rulings held that evidence of negligence could be inferred from the facts of the case,[88] a manufacturer could always escape liability by showing that he had taken all reasonable care in the circumstances to avoid the harmful attribute of the product in question.[89]

It was only in the course of the 1970s, after the outbreak of the Thalidomide scandal,[90] that public concern for the state of the law resulted in numerous calls for reform. In 1978, a Royal Commission on Civil Liability and Compensation

[84] *Grant v Australian Knitting Mills, Ltd* [1936] AC 85 (the plaintiff contracted dermatitis by a defective woolen underwear he bought from a retailer; both the retailer and the producer were held liable).

[85] *Vacwell Engineering Co Ltd v BDH Chemicals Ltd* [1971] 1 QB 88 (glass ampoules containing a chemical which combined explosively with water were unfit for their purpose when bearing a warning only of "harmful vapour").

[86] See *Vacwell v BDH Chemicals Ltd* [1971] 1 QB 88 and *IBA v EMI* [1981] 14 BLR 1 (IBA ordered a television mast from BICC; the mast was defectively designed by BICC and built by EMI; BICC was found liable in contract while EMI was liable for the negligent build).

[87] *Daniels and Daniels v R White &Sons Ltd and Tarbard* [1938] 4 All ER 258 (a man bought a bottle of lemonade—which, unknown to him, contained carbolic acid—and drank it with his wife; since the husband bought the bottle, his action for implied warranty was successful, while the absence of privity was fatal to his wife—on this case see also below, n 89). On the resistance of the pre-*Donoghue* perspective, see also Michael Lobban, "The Law of Obligations: The Anglo-American Perspective," in Heikki Pihlajamäki, Markus D Dubber & Mark Godfrey (eds), *The Oxford Handbook of European Legal History* (OUP 2018) 1037–1043; Ken Oliphant & Vanessa Wilcox, "Product Liability in England and Wales," in Machnikowski (ed) (n 43) 174, 175–176; Whittaker (n 72) 74–77.

[88] *Grant* (84) at 101. It is however debated whether the ruling accepted the application of res ipsa loquitur. See Whittaker (n 72) 74.

[89] *Daniels and Daniels* (n 87) (a man purchased a bottle containing carbolic acid; his claim in negligence against the manufacturer of the bottle failed, since the latter proved he adopted a fool-proof method of cleaning, washing, and filling bottles; however, the manufacturer was held liable under the doctrine of implied warranty).

[90] As is well known, Thalidomide was a medication for anxiety and morning sickness released in the early fifties by a German pharmaceutical company and marketed without having been tested on pregnant women. It later resulted that the use of thalidomide in pregnant women provoked miscarriages or severe deformities in the fetuses. On the scandal, see Richard Goldberg, *Medicinal Product Liability and Regulation* (Hart 2014) 1–17; Henning Sjöström & Robert Nilsson, *Thalidomide and the Power of the Drug Companies* (Penguin 1972).

for Personal Injury, established in 1982 under the chairmanship of Lord Pearson, recommended the introduction of strict liability for defective products.[91] The suggestion was not given effect by the Parliament, but the issue was overtaken seven years later by the developments at the European level, which resulted in the adoption of the (still-in-force) 1987 Consumer Protection Act.

3.2. France

On the other side of the Channel, France took since the mid of the twentieth century a different route, firmly grounded in contract law. Before 1950s, accidents that nowadays would be qualified as products liability injuries were either accepted as an unavoidable cost associated with the benefits of industrialization, or treated as cases of custodial liability of the owners of the products (most of the time: machines) which caused injuries.[92]

In the 1950s, with the gradual development of a mass consumer society that allowed wide access to consumer goods, (what nowadays would be called) product liability claims started to multiply.[93] Under the French principle of *non-cumul* (according to which victims of contractual harms cannot sue their counterpart under tort rules),[94] such claims were not framed in tort, though. Rather, they were largely based on the idea that the seller of a defective product is liable to direct and subsequent buyers for breach of warranty, and in particular of the warranty that the product did not have latent defects (*garantie des vices cachés*, provided by art 1641 and ff. of the French Civil Code).[95] The *garantie des vices cachés* was thought to be actionable by buyers not only against their direct seller, but also against any person higher up in the chain of sales, including manufacturers. This was made possible thanks to the judicially made principle of the *action directe*, according to which, in a chain of contracts transferring the property of a thing, the latest owner was

[91] Royal Commission on Civil Liability and Compensation for Personal Injury (1978), Cmnd 7054, Ch 22.

[92] Borghetti (n 69) 89–90. Reference to custodial liability was made possible by the liberal interpretation of (former) art 1384 of the Civil Code that the French Court of cassation established in 1896, with the seminal arrêt *Teffaine* (Cass civ 16 June 1896, DP 1897.1.433), making the keeper of a thing responsible for the damages caused to third parties by the thing, regardless of any fault on her part.

[93] It is not by chance that the first article formally devoted to products liability was published in 1955: Henri Mazeaud, "La responsabilité civile du vendeur-fabricant," RTD civ 1955, 611–621.

[94] See also Chapter 3, section 2.3.

[95] See the lower instance cases on damages caused by defective pharmaceuticals, household appliances, and body-care products cited by Borghetti (n 69) 87, 91, fns 12–14.

allowed to raise a claim in contract against any of the previous owners of that thing, despite lack of privity.[96] A further step forward was taken in the late 1960s, when the *Cour de cassation* applied to sales made by professional dealers an irrebuttable presumption that the seller was aware of the product defectiveness. In case a defect in the thing caused death, injuries or other damage to the (direct or indirect) buyer, the seller was bound to compensate the (direct or indirect) buyer, even if it was materially impossible for him to discover the defect.[97]

Alongside such developments, French courts developed a different rule for bystanders, that is to say, victims who could not qualify as subsequent buyers of the defective product. Given that the latter could not avail of the *action directe*, since the 1960s French case law has been allowing them to sue sellers and manufacturers of defective products in tort under (former) Article 1382 (now art 1240) of the *Code Civil*, on the ground that the sale of a defective product constitutes negligence toward the third parties damaged by the same products.[98] Although the action was based on fault, courts alleviated plaintiffs' burden of proof by holding that the manufacturing and sale of a defective good by a professional was a sort of negligence per se, so that plaintiffs only had to demonstrate (their damage, causation and) the defectiveness of the product in order to obtain compensation from either the seller or the manufacturer of the product.[99]

At the time in which the EEC Directive was adopted, French law was therefore subjecting manufacturers *and* sellers to strict or semi-strict liability for damages caused by defective goods produced or sold, either by virtue of contractual warranties or on the basis of the formally fault-based (but de facto semi-strict, especially for manufacturing defects) tort liability.[100] As we will

[96] The principle was developed as early as the 1820s: see Cass civ 25 January 1820, S 1.171, as well as Jean-Sébastien Borghetti, "Product Liability in France," in Machnikowski (ed) (n 43) 207; Borghetti (n 69) 93–94; Vernon V Palmer & Christel de Noblet, "Case 9—France," in Mauro Bussani & Vernon V Palmer (eds), *Pure Economic Loss in Europe* (CUP 2003) 306–308.

[97] Cass civ 24 November 1954, JCP 955.II.8565; Cass com 1 July 1969, Bull civ IV, no 243; Cass com 20 January 1970, JCP 1972, II, 17280; Cass com 27 April 1971, JCP 1972.II.17280; see also Borghetti (n 96) 206.

[98] This line of reasoning, already pioneered by a few decisions by the Court of cassation in the 1930s (Cass civ 22 July 1931, GazPal 1931, 2, 683; Cass req 8 March 1937, S 1937, 1, 241), was definitely established in the 1960s: see Cass com 20 March 1961, Bull civ III, no 148; Cass civ 11 December 1961, Bull civ I, no 595; Cass civ 16 March 1966, Bull civ I, no 189; Cass civ 5 December 1972, D 1973, 401.

[99] Borghetti (n 96) 207–208; Borghetti (n 69) 96–97.

[100] As Borghetti (n 69) 98, notes, liability for failure to warn was always considered as being grounded on fault, as was liability for defectively designed products, insofar as, in order to demonstrate the existence of a defect, the claimant in the latter cases had to demonstrate that the product had not been designed as it should have been, i.e., that the manufacturer had been negligent in designing the product.

see, the French regime was under many points of view broader and stricter than the European one, since it imposed strict (contractual or tortious) liability to sellers in addition to manufacturers and did not make available to them all the defenses contemplated by the Directive (most notably, the development risk defense). Such discrepancies may explain why it took France fifteen years to transpose the Directive into (former) arts 1386-1 to 1386-18 (now arts 1245-1 to 1245-18) of the Civil Code.[101]

3.3. Italy

Italian product liability law developed along different lines than the French ones.

The Italian 1865 Civil Code mandated sellers' warranty for the hidden defects of the goods sold, provided that the defects were known or should have known to them.[102] Yet, the majority of courts and scholars always applied provisions on warranty only between sellers and buyers, thus excluding the possibility of a buyer's direct action against previous sellers (including the manufacturer) in the contractual chain, and claims by bystanders who were not involved in the contract.[103]

Equally excluded, under the empire of the 1865 Civil Code (which, at its art 1151, contained a general clause of fault liability identical to art 1382 of the French Civil Code), was a tort action against sellers and manufacturers. Both courts and scholars displayed a considerable reluctance to apply tort law rules to award compensation for losses caused by defective goods. Such a position was based on technical and policy arguments: opening up to tort liability in these cases would have, on the one hand, emptied out the scope of rules on warranty; and, on the other hand, hindered economic and industrial development.[104]

Things changed with the enactment of the 1942 Civil Code. Since the entry into force of the Code, the Supreme Court interpreted the new tort law

[101] Borghetti (n 96) 209–211.

[102] See articles 1498, 1502, and 1503 of the 1865 Civil Code; the same provisions were maintained in the 1942 Civil Code, articles 1494–1495.

[103] Cf the literature and the case law quoted by Giovanni Comandé, "Product Liability in Italy," in Machnikowski (ed) (n 43) 275, 276–277; Nadia Coggiola, "The Development of Product Liability in Italy," in Whittaker (ed) (n 69) 192–205.

[104] See, eg, App 15 April 1932, Mon trib 1932, 510 (holding that the manufacturer of a soda bottle which exploded in a restaurant and injured a client could not be held liable for the victim's injuries since no fault of the manufacturers was proved), as well as the authors quoted by Coggiola (n 103) 196–197. One of the few scholars who opposed such position was Gino Gorla, *La compravendita e la permuta* (Utet 1937) 168–169, who supported sellers' liability in tort for injuries caused to third parties.

rules (which were not very far away from the old ones) by recognizing that bystanders damaged by manufactured goods had a tort law claim against the manufacturer. Since the end of 1940s, manufacturers have been held liable, for instance, when a defective hairdressing device caused harm to a friend of the original buyer,[105] a defective toy gun's blasting injured a child,[106] a gas cylinder exploded, killing the wife of cylinder's owner.[107] A further development occurred in 1964, in the *Saiwa* case, when the Supreme Court reversed the burden of proving both the defectiveness of the product and the manufacturer's negligence. The plaintiffs, a married couple, bought a box of Saiwa biscuits from a retailer shop, ate them, and then suffered severe food poisoning. The *Corte di cassazione* excluded the retailer's liability, since he was not at fault, but held Saiwa—the manufacturer—liable under the general clause for fault liability (art 2043 of the Civil Code), insofar as plaintiffs proved they suffered food poisoning after eating the biscuits and the defectiveness of the biscuits was the only possible reason for the injury.[108] Although framed in terms of fault liability, the Court herein applied a rule of liability for presumed fault once the defect is (somewhat) proven. Subsequent case law followed suit.[109] In the 1970s, the first scholarly books on the subject of product liability appeared, devoting substantial attention to foreign experiences, and largely supported the new judicial interpretation,[110] which remained the rule until the implementation of the EEC Directive with the Presidential Decree no. 224 of 24 May 1988 (later replaced by articles 114 to 127 of the Consumer Code of 2005).

3.4. Germany

Given the wide scope and usually broad interpretation of German contract law, one might expect Germany, prior to the enactment of the EEC Directive, to have resorted to contractual rules and remedies to establish manufacturers' and sellers' liability for defective products. This was largely not the case.

[105] See Cass 19 February 1947, Nuova riv dir comm 1948, II, 97.
[106] Cass 21 October 1957, no 4004, Foro it 1958, 45.
[107] Cass 2 April 1963, no 819, Foro it 1963, I, 2197.
[108] Cass 25 May 1964, no 1270, Foro it 1965, I, 2098.
[109] See the cases quoted by Coggiola (n 103) 209–212.
[110] Cf Ugo Carnevali, *Responsabilità del produttore* (Giuffrè 1974); Carlo Castronovo, *Problema e sistema nel danno da prodotti* (Giuffrè 1979); Guido Alpa & Mario Bessone (eds), *Danno da prodotti e responsabilità dell'impresa: Diritto italiano ed esperienze straniere* (Giuffrè 1980).

To be sure, German courts and scholars never put in doubt that sellers were answerable in damages for personal injury and property damage caused to buyers of defective products, provided that the former knew or could have known the defect.[111] Yet, sale contracts of defective products never qualified as contracts for the protection of third parties (*Verträgen mit Schutzwirkung zugunsten Dritter*), thus denying victims of defective products the right to lodge a contractual claim against the product's manufacturer or seller in cases in which a contractual relationship was absent.[112]

Rather, since the start of the twentieth century, the few cases of (what in retrospect might be defined as) product liability were brought and adjudicated as tort law cases, either under negligence and vicarious liability rules (§§ 823 I and 831 BGB)[113] or under the general clause against intentional torts in violation of good morals (§ 826 BGB).[114]

Such cases, however, generated little interest in legal scholarship until the 1960s, when the problem of product liability suddenly exploded. In the 1960s, after years of postwar reconstruction, the downsides of economic development started to surface to the attention of the general public, as illustrated by the tragic Thalidomide scandal[115] (which led in 1961 to the approval of the *Arzneimittelgesetz*, a law imposing strict liability for injuries caused by defective pharmaceutical drugs[116]). At the same time, the ever-increasing dialogue between German and American scholars (many of which were German émigrés) made the former interested in developments

[111] See RG 9 July 1907, RGZ 66, 289 (1907), as well as the authorities quoted by Gerhard Wagner, "The development of product liability in Germany," in Whittaker (ed) (n 69) 114, 115–116. The unanimity of this interpretation existed in spite of the silence on this point of the original version of the German Civil Code of 1900, whose gap on warranties was filled only in 2002, when the German sales law was reformed.

[112] Ulrich Magnus, "Product Liability in Germany," in Machnikowski (ed) (n 43) 239; Wagner (n 111) 116.

[113] RG 25 February 1915, RGZ 87, 1 (the buyer of bath salt was injured because the salt was contaminated with glass fibers; he brought an action against the bath salt manufacturer, who was held liable for the simple reason that the product was defective when it was put into the chain of distribution).

[114] RG 17 January 1940, RGZ 163, 21 at 25 (Ford was held liable under § 826 BGB for accidents occurred because of a defective brake system in the cars sold that was known to Ford—on the flexibility shown by German case law in applying § 826 BGB see also Chapter 6, section 5.3). Of course, actions could also be brought under § 823 II BGB, whenever the plaintiff was able to prove that the defendant violated a statutory provision (for instance, regarding product safety) which specifically aimed to protect interests such as those infringed in the case at hand: Magnus (n 112) 240 (also quoting case law from 1968 onward).

[115] See above, n 90.

[116] German Medicinal Products Act (*Arzneimittelgesetz*) of 16 May 1961 (as amended by Federal Law of 16 December 2005).

in the field in the United States and gave rise to numerous studies devoted to the subject.[117]

It is against this context that the German Federal Supreme Court openly confirmed the tort law approach to product liability in the *Hühnerpest* (chicken pest) case of 1968[118] (which is usually thought to be the first German case in which product liability was expressly discussed as such[119]). The case involved a chicken farmer who had his chickens vaccinated by a veterinarian against fowl pest. The veterinarian used a serum that the defendant company produced. A few days after the vaccination, the fowl pest broke out and more than 4,000 chickens died. It was later found that the vaccine contained the active virus of the deadly (to chickens) Newcastle Disease. In affirming defendant's liability, the BGH expressly rejected contractual theories and rather resorted to §§ 823 I and 831, adding that, once the plaintiff proves the presence of a product defect, it was upon the defendant manufacturer to establish that the defect was not caused by the negligence of his business organization. The following case law reaffirmed the principle, expanding it to cover cases in which the defect became apparent only after the product was put in the market, for the manufacturer failed to monitor the performance of the product.[120] When the EEC Directive was adopted, Germany therefore already had in place a statutory strict liability regime for drugs and a judicial-made rule of tort liability for presumed fault for all other defective products.[121] German implementation of the Directive into the *Gesetz über die Haftung für fehlerhafte Produkte* (*Produkthaftungsgesetz*) in 1989 was therefore a rather straightforward process.

[117] See, eg, Werner Lorenz, "Produkthaftung," in Paul Mikat (ed), *Festschrift der Rechts- und Staatswissenschaftlichen Fakultät der Julius-Maximilians-Universität Würzburg zum 75. Geburtstag von Hermann Nottarp* (Müller 1961) 59.

[118] BGH 26 November 1968, BGHZ 51, 91 (1968). For an English translation, see Basil S Markesinis, John Bell, & André Janssen, *Markesinis's German Law of Torts* (5th edn, Bloomsbury 2019) 439.

[119] Magnus (n 112) 239; Markesinis, Bell, & Janssen (n 118) 457; Konrad Zweigert & Hein Kötz, *An Introduction to Comparative Private Law* (Tony Weir transl, 3rd ed., Clarendon 1998) 666.

[120] Cf BGH 17 March 1981, BGHZ 80, 186 and BGHZ 80, 199 (two cases) (both cases concerned a fungicide that was sold for the protection of apples, but which failed because the organisms it was meant to kill had developed a resistance against the chemical used in the product; despite the fact that the failure of the product became apparent only after it had been put on the market, the BGH held that the manufacturer must monitor both the performance of the product and scientific progress in the field and is liable if he fails to do so).

[121] See, however, Wagner (n 111) 128, who stresses that the semi-strict nature of product liability fully applied to cases of manufacturing defects, but was less evident in cases of design and instructions defects, since in such cases plaintiffs, in order to prove the defect, were in fact requested to establish defendant's negligence.

4. The European Directive and Its Aftermath

In the mid-1970s, following mass tragedies such as the one caused by defective drug Thalidomide, and especially under German pressures, works for drafting a European directive on product liability commenced.[122] Officially, the initiative had the twofold aim of ensuring adequate levels of protection for consumers and of limiting legal divergences within the internal market, so as not to distort competition and affect the movement of goods.[123] As noted by commentators, however, the real driving force behind the Directive was to provide some states willing to enact reforms on the subject with "the confidence [...] to take the bold move of introducing strict product liability in the knowledge that they were not exposing themselves to a disadvantage

[122] A quick glance to the state of the art of product liability in other European countries before the enactment of the Directive (many of which, in 1985, were not part of the then EEC) confirms both an increasing trend toward the establishment of product liability, and the remarkable variety in time and space of the rules and doctrines applicable to such claims. Since the end of the 1930s Danish courts had established the principle that producers and suppliers were liable in negligence to buyers and bystanders for physical damage caused by dangerous/defective products (Marie-Louise Holle & Peter Møgelvang-Hansen, "Product Liability in Denmark," in Machnikowski (ed) (n 43) 155–156). Around the same period, Dutch case law too subjected manufacturers of defective products to fault liability in tort; a step further was taken in 1973 by the *Hoge Raad*, holding that, once the damage and defect were proven, fault was to be presumed (HR 2 February 1973, NJB 1973, 315; see also the case law collected by Ivo Giesen, "The Development of Product Liability in the Netherlands," in Whittaker (ed) (n 69) 152, 155–160). Since the 1960s, Austrian scholarship and courts by contrast preferred to resort to contract law, qualifying contracts between manufacturer and distributors as contracts with protective effect vis-à-vis third parties and thus entitling products' users to pursue contractual warranty and liability claims, even though they were not parties to the sale contract (cf Franz Bydlinski, "Vertragliche Sorgfaltspflichten zugunsten Dritter," JBl 1960, 359 and OGH 4 February 1976, 1 Ob 190/75, SZ 49/13; see also Bernhard A Koch, "Product Liability in Austria," in Machnikowski (ed) (n 43) 111, 113–114). In Eastern Europe, Polish and Hungarian case law established, respectively in the 1960s and in the 1970s, that sellers of defective products were not only contractually liable to buyers, but also liable under the general rules of fault liability in tort vis-à-vis third parties (see the cases quoted by Magdalena Tulibacka, *Product Liability Law in Transition: A Central European Perspective* (Ashgate 2009) 191–201; see also, as to Poland, Ewa Bagińska, "Product Liability in Poland," in Machnikowski (ed) (n 43) 377, 378–380. In Hungary, liability was based on the general fault rule, which put upon the defendant the burden of showing that he was not to blame: see art 339 of the Hungarian Civil Code of 1959. The same rule is now maintained under art 6:519 of the Civil Code of 2014. A similar reversal of the burden of proof, by contrast, was never included in the general provisions of Polish codifications: neither in articles 134 and 135 of the Polish Code of Obligations of 1933, nor in article 415 of the Polish Civil Code of 1964). By contrast, the gradual establishment in Sweden and Finland, from the 1970s onward, of public compensation schemes covering personal injuries—including, in the 1980s, schemes on injured caused by defective pharmaceuticals—rendered products liability claims in tort interstitial (Goldberg (n 90) 14–15). In Spain, only at the beginning of the 1980s the Tribunal Supremo admitted that producers could be liable in tort for negligence under Article 1902 of the Civil Code in case of damage suffered by persons who were not the direct buyers of the product (see the cases quoted by Miquel Martín-Casals & Josep Solé Feliu, "Product Liability in Spain," in Machnikowski (ed) (n 43) 407, 408–411; Miquel Martín-Casals & Josep Solé Feliu, "The Development of Product Liability in Spain," in Whittaker (ed) (n 69) 234, 237–248).

[123] This twofold aim will be later stated in recitals 2 and 1 of the final text of the Directive.

compared to other Member States."[124] Negotiations over the text lasted almost ten years because of political disagreement on many technical issues, such as the availability of a development risk defense and the provision about a ceiling on liability for death or personal injury.[125] The final text was approved on 25 July 1985 as "Council Directive 85/374/EEC on the approximation of the laws, regulations and administration provisions of the Member States concerning liability for defective products."

Under the partial influence of German law, as well as of American development at that time (as enshrined in the Second Restatement),[126] the Directive obliges Member States to implement a strict liability scheme under which "the producer shall be liable for damage caused by a defect in his product" (art 1), provided that plaintiffs "prove the damage, the defect and the causal relationship between defect and damage" (art 4). The ensuing provisions clarify that (i) "producer" only means the manufacturer of a product;[127] "damage" means death, personal injuriesm and damage to property exceeding 500 euros and affecting property other than the product itself;[128] "defect" means that a product does not provide the safety which a person is reasonably entitled to expect,[129] whereby "product" means any tangible and movable goods, including electricity[130] (but apparently excluding software and smart applications not included in physical products).[131] In other

[124] Duncan Fairgrieve, Geraint Howells, Peter Møgelvang-Hansen, Gert Staetmans, Dimitri Verhoeven, Piotr Machnikowski, André Janssen, & Reiner Schulze, "Product Liability Directive,",in Machnikowski (ed) (n 43) 17, 26; see also Piotr Machnikowski, "Conclusions," in Machnikowski (ed) (n 45) 670, 680–681.

[125] At the end, the state-of-the-art defense was included in art 7 (e) of the Directive, but states were allowed to exclude it under art 15 (1) (b). The Directive provides no cap on liability, but states may adopt a ceiling, provided that it is above 70 million Euro: art 16 (1).

[126] Ulrich Magnus, "Some Thoughts on Germany's Contribution to European and Comparative Law" (2006) 38 Bracton LJ 87, 93; Geraint Howells & Mark Mildred, "Is European Products Liability More Protective than the Restatement (Third) of Torts: Product Liability?" (1997–1998) 65 Tenn LR 985–1030.

[127] Art 3 of the Directive.

[128] Art 9 of the Directive. As the Court of Justice of the European Union (CJEU) later specified, the 500 euro sum is a threshold that, when reached, opens up the right to compensation for damage to property in its entirety: see ECJ 10 May 2001, C-203/99, *Veedfald v Århus Amtskommune* [2001] ECR I-3569.

[129] Art 6 of the Directive.

[130] Art 2 of the Directive. Included in the definition are to be considered also pharmaceuticals, medical devices, and vaccines (CJEU 21 June 2017, C-621/15, *NW et al v Sanofi Pasteur MSD*, ECLI:EU:C:2017:484; CJEU 5 March 2015, C-503/13 and C-504/13, *Boston Scientific Medizintechnik v AOK Sachsen-Anhalt*, ECLI:EU:C:2015:148), as well as blood and blood-derived products (cf *A v National Blood Authority* [2001] 3 All ER 289; Rb Amsterdam, 3 February 1999, NJB 1999, 621).

[131] Report from the Commission on the application of the Council Directive 85/374/EEC (COM(2018) 246 final), 7 May 2018, at eur-lex.europa.eu/legal-content/EN/TXT/HTML/?uri = CELEX:52018DC0246&from = EN, no 5.1. See also Fairgrieve, Howells, Møgelvang-Hansen, Staetmans, Verhoeven, Machnikowski, Janssen, & Schulze (n 124) 46–47. The Commission has

words, the Directive does not concern the liability of suppliers (who might be sued only if the producer remains unknown[132]), rejects the American distinction between manufacturing, design, and instruction/warning defects, and embraces the consumer expectation test as the only standard for evaluating any kind of defect—although national courts are free to take other circumstances into account.[133]

The Directive provides products' manufacturers with several ways to escape liability. Producers are exempted from liability if they prove one of the six circumstances mentioned by art 7 of the Directive, which includes compliance with mandatory regulations, the non-defectiveness of the product when it was put into circulation, and changes in the state of scientific and technical knowledge after the product was put into circulation.[134] In particular the last mentioned defense makes a producer's liability similar to that for negligence, insofar as it allows the producer to free himself from

already announced that the Directive will be revised to adjust it to new technologies: see Report from the Commission on the safety and liability implications of Artificial Intelligence, the Internet of Things and robotics (COM(2020) 64 final), February 19, 2020, at ec.europa.eu/info/publications/commission-report-safety-and-liability-implications-ai-internet-things-and-robotics_en.

[132] Art 3 (3) of the Directive. Yet, even in such a case, art 3 (1) allows the supplier to escape liability if he informs the victim within a reasonable time of the identity of the producer (or of the other supplier who supplied him with the product: ECJ 2 December 2009, C-358/08, *Aventis Pasteur SA v OB* [2009] ECR I-11305).

[133] Fairgrieve, Howells, Møgelvang-Hansen, Staetmans, Verhoeven, Machnikowski, Janssen, & Schulze (n 124) 56. Actually, the practice of European courts seem to be that the consumer expectation test is applied as a stand-alone test to manufacturing defects, while it is complemented with other tests when it comes to design and instruction defects: see Daily Wuyts, "The Product Liability Directive —More Than Two Decades of Defective Products in Europe" (2014) 5 JETL 1, 10–13; Cees van Dam, *European Tort Law* (2nd edn, OUP 2013) 428–429.

[134] According to art 7 of the Directive,

> The producer shall not be liable as a result of this Directive if he proves:
> (a) that he did not put the product into circulation; or
> (b) that, having regard to the circumstances, it is probable that the defect which caused the damage did not exist at the time when the product was put into circulation by him or that this defect came into being afterwards; or
> (c) that the product was neither manufactured by him for sale or any form of distribution for economic purpose nor manufactured or distributed by him in the course of his business; or
> (d) that the defect is due to compliance of the product with mandatory regulations issued by the public authorities; or
> (e) that the state of scientific and technical knowledge at the time when he put the product into circulation was not such as to enable the existence of the defect to be discovered; or
> (f) in the case of a manufacturer of a component, that the defect is attributable to the design of the product in which the component has been fitted or to the instructions given by the manufacturer of the product.

Contractual limitation of producer's liability, by contrast, are not admissible. See art 12 of the Directive.

liability by demonstrating that, while in possession of all knowledge objectively and subjectively available at a given moment, the defectiveness of the product could not be avoided (and conversely shifts the risk of injury caused by the marketization of a product whose externalities are unclear from the producer onto the injured person).[135] Liability is further disallowed or reduced if (the defendant proves that) the damage is totally or partially caused "by the fault of the injured person or any person for whom the injured person is responsible."[136] Producers may escape liability also if the plaintiff does not act within three years from the date on which the latter "became aware, or should reasonably have become aware, of the damage, the defect and the identity of the producer"[137] and anyway if the action is brought after ten years from the date on which the producer put into circulation the product.[138]

As clarified by subsequent interpretation by the Court of Justice of the European Union,[139] the directive aims at producing "maximal harmonization," that is, the text mandates enactment by Member States of national rules conforming to the Directive[140] and the repeal of any rules which, in the matters covered by the Directive's scope, provide for a different (whether lower or higher) level of protection than the Directive itself, except in cases where there is an express permission in the text to do so. While the Directive obliges Member States not to maintain any general system of product liability different from the one laid down in the Directive, it however does not preclude the application of rules based on other grounds and otherwise applicable to product liability cases. A rather ambiguous provision, art 13, provides that

[135] Fairgrieve, Howells, Møgelvang-Hansen, Staetmans, Verhoeven, Machnikowski, Janssen, & Schulze (n 124) 78; Simon Whittaker, "Introduction to Fault in Product Liability," in Whittaker (ed.) (n 69) 1, 35.

[136] Art 8(2) of the Directive.

[137] Art 10(1) of the Directive.

[138] Art 11 of the Directive.

[139] Cf ECJ 25 April 2002, C-52/00, *Commission v France* [2002] ECR I-3827; ECJ 25 April 2002, C-154/00, *Commission v Greece* [2002] ECR I-3879; ECJ 25 April 2002, C-183/00, *González Sanchez v Medicina Asturiana SA* [2002] ECR I-3901.

[140] Acts implementing the Directive took a variety of form. For instance, the United Kingdom and Germany transposed the Directive in ad hoc statutes (the Consumer Protection Act 1987 and the *Produkthaftungsgesetz* of 1989), France inserted the new rules in the Civil Code (former articles from 1386-1 to 1386-18 of the Civil Code, inserted in 1998, and nowadays renumbered as articles 1245-1 to 1245-18); Italy first adopted the Presidential Decree no 224/1988 and then transferred its content into articles 114–127 of the Italian Consumer Code of 2005.

this Directive shall not affect any rights which an injured person may have according to the rules of the law of contractual or non-contractual liability or a special liability system existing at the moment when this Directive is notified.

Article 13 is commonly interpreted as referring, for instance, to warranty for latent defects, fault liability under general tort law rules, and even special laws establishing deviating regimes for some products and injuries (such as the German and Scandinavian laws on pharmaceuticals[141]). This means that national rules providing remedies to victims of defective products might survive—which is exactly what happened. In the majority of European countries, the acts implementing the Directive were superimposed upon legal systems which, as we saw in sections 3.1-3.4, had already developed from general liability rules by their own responses to damages caused by defective products, giving rise to a dual track for compensation—one European-inspired and one grounded in national contract or tort law (or both).[142] Quite unsurprisingly, the coexistence of these two parallel regimes, if on the one hand smoothed down the process of reforming national laws, on the other hand allowed lawyers and judges to continue to rely upon the domestic and more familiar set of preexisting remedies.[143] It has been calculated that, between 2000 and 2016, only 798 cases under the EU-inspired regime were brought before European courts.[144]

The persistence of older regimes is only one of the factors explaining the limited harmonization reached by the Directive. Further reasons include the linguistic and technical divergences between national implementing acts and the number of issues which the Directive left to states' discretion or utterly unregulated (such as the requirement of causation and quantification of damages).[145] Therefore, anyone interested in knowing operative rules in

[141] See above, section 3.4 and n 122.

[142] Machnikowski (n 124) 673–687.

[143] Machnikowski (n 124) 673–687. See also the variety of national answers given to cases dealing with product liability in Miquel Martín-Casals, "Comparative Report," in Miquel Martín-Casals (ed), *The Borderlines of Tort Law: Interactions with Contract Law* (Intersentia 2019) 711, 815–820.

[144] Commission Staff Working Document, "Evaluation of Council Directive 85/374/EEC of 25 July 1985 accompanying the Report from the Commission on the application of the Council Directive 85/374/EEC" (COM(2018) 246 final) at eur-lex.europa.eu/legal-content/EN/TXT/PDF/?uri = CELEX:52018SC0157&from = EN, 10–14.

[145] For an evaluation of the limited harmonizing effect of the Directive, cf Machnikowski (n 124) 673–687; Simon Taylor, "Harmonisation or Divergence? A Comparison of French and English Product Liability Rules" (2007) 70 Mod LR 241, 242; Whittaker (n 135) 477–529; Mauro Bussani & Vernon V Palmer, "Comparative Comments to Case 9," in Bussani & Palmer (n 96) 325–326; Stapleton (n 46) 53–55.

Europe is still required to verify how, in each legal system, the Directive is implemented and interpreted vis-à-vis preexisting general contract and tort liability rules.

That being said, the Directive may be credited with having established the field as a subject in its own right[146] and as a burgeoning field for comparative studies.[147] Outside Europe, probably thanks to its easy-to-travel packaging, the Directive has provided the blueprint for special product liability rules in many countries in the Far East and in Latin America[148]—although the very low rates of litigation in all these countries call for further analysis on the effectiveness of the legal transplant.[149]

5. A Story of Convergence and Divergence

When looked at in the historical and comparative perspective, American and European development of product liability rules show remarkable lines of convergence. On both sides of the Atlantic, the need of special legal regimes for damages caused by defective goods arose from mass consumer societies and growing levels of consumers' awareness. The same pressures that, since the beginning of the twentieth century, led American courts to overturn English precedents and develop rules based on res ipsa loquitur first and strict liability then, drove a few years later European countries toward a similar direction, partly spontaneously, and partly under inspiration from the American experience. In both the United States and Europe, the new stricter-than-ordinary rules have been coexisting with a variety of other causes of

[146] Simon Whittaker, "Introduction to Fault in Product Liability," in Whittaker (ed) (n 69) 1, 3–9, 50.

[147] Cf the national reports collected in Whittaker (ed) (n 69); Martin Ebers, André Janssen, Olaf Meyer (eds), *European Perspectives on Producers' Liability: Direct Producers' Liability* (Sellier 2009); Whittaker (n 135); Duncan Fairgrieve (ed), *Product Liability in Comparative Perspective* (CUP 2005), as well as the forthcoming Monika Jozon & Markus Pilgerstorfer (eds), *Products Liability* (Intersentia 2020). See also, in a broader geographical perspective, Martín-Casals (ed) (n 143); Helmut Koziol, Michael D Green, Mark Lunney, Ken Oliphant, & Lixin Yang (eds), *Product Liability: Fundamental Questions in a Comparative Perspective* (de Gruyter 2017); Machnikowski (ed) (n 43); Christian Campbell (ed), *International Product Liability* (Yorkhill Law Publishing 2007); Reimann (n 45) 751–838; Geraint G. Howells, *Comparative Product Liability* (Dartmouth Pub 1993); Christopher J Miller (ed), *Comparative Product Liability* (BIICL 1986).

[148] This is, for instance, the case of Australia, China, Japan, as well as Brazil, Chile, and Peru: Mathias Reimann, "Product Liability in a Global Context: The Hollow Victory of the European Model" (2003) 11 ERPL 128, 136; Reimann (n 45) 761–762. The same holds true for Israel: Israel Gilead, "Product Liability in Israel," in Machnikowski (ed) (n 43) 523, 525.

[149] Reimann, "Product Liability in a Global Context" (n 148) 145–148.

actions and remedies, such as negligence and breach of warranty, and have been the object of struggles between domestic and supranational interpretations (led by the Restatements and federal rules in the United States and by the 1985 Directive and CJEU's case law in the EU). In the United States as in Europe, debates about product liability have given rise to intense public and scholarly discussions, often charged with ideological ammunition and more or less in touch with the real world, about the aims of tort law and the interests it should protect; the place and role for negligence and strict liability; the effects, risks, and fears that are associated to each regime; and so on and so forth.

Yet, as hinted at the beginning, the Euro-American history of product liability law is also a story of divergence. Many differences relate to technicalities of the United States and European models of product liability per se: retailers are generally liable under American law, while European law tends to focus on manufacturers; the American clear tripartition of manufacturing, design, and warnings/instructions defects, as well as the reliance upon the risk/utility test, are largely ignored in Europe. Other, perhaps deeper, reasons for divergence stem from differences in the wider legal, procedural, and institutional settings: from different understanding of notions of causation and recoverable damages, to the presence, in the United States, of juries, an entrepreneurial plaintiffs' bar (relying on contingent fee arrangements), and effective mechanisms of collective redress; from the extensive (in the United States) and limited (in Europe) focus on legal cases in the media, to the existence, in Europe, of solidarity schemes; social and public health insurances, which partially remove the space and the need for civil liability.[150] It is probably these differences that explain why litigation rates, to the extent that they are known,[151] have followed diverse patterns in the United States and in Europe. The alleged litigation explosion that has affected the United States after the approval of the Second Restatement has never produced anything comparable in Europe, neither before nor after the adoption of the EEC Directive.[152]

All the above makes it clear why product liability provides a privileged standpoint for observing the dynamics of contemporary tort law developments. The study of the history of products liability shows the relentless and nonlinear cycle between legal demands; hopes and fears; and legal

[150] Reimann (n 53) 244–246, 257–261; Reimann (n 45) 810–835; Stapleton (n 46) 70–75 and 82–84.

[151] The lack of reliable data (also) in the field of product liability law is sadly noticed, among others, by Mauro Bussani, *L'illecito civile* (ESI 2020) 120–122; Reimann (n 53) 257–258.

[152] Reimann (n 45) 803–809. See also Chapter 3, section 2.1.

answers, which in turn feed new demands, hopes, and fears. But the partial import of United States law into European national jurisdictions first and in the EU then, the forced transplantation of EU law into European laws and its spontaneous imitation outside Europe, also demonstrate how rules might experience a shift of meaning when they travel across borders, how they might end up being detached from their origins as well as from the context in which they live, and how they might nonetheless retain a symbolic value whose forms and functions might well deserve further study.[153]

[153] For similar conclusions, see Stapleton (n 46) 358–359; Mauro Bussani, "European Tort Law—A Way Forward," in Mauro Bussani (ed), *European Tort Law. Eastern and Western Perspectives* (Stämpfli 2007) 365–382.

Index

For the benefit of digital users, indexed terms that span two pages (e.g., 52–53) may, on occasion, appear on only one of those pages.

Printed in the USA
CPSIA information can be obtained
at www.ICGtesting.com
CBHW061919241123
2106CB00003B/6/J

9 780195 368383